Jefferson and the Presidency

Jefferson at the midpoint of his presidency. Portrait by Rembrandt Peale, 1805. Courtesy of the New-York Historical Society, New York City.

Jefferson and the Presidency

LEADERSHIP IN THE YOUNG REPUBLIC

❧

Robert M. Johnstone, Jr.

CORNELL UNIVERSITY PRESS

Ithaca and London

7 -11-78

$ /150⁰

Cornell University Press gratefully acknowledges a grant from the Andrew W. Mellon Foundation that aided in bringing this book to publication.

First published 1978 by Cornell University Press.
Published in the United Kingdom by Cornell University Press Ltd., 2–4 Brook Street, London W1Y 1AA.

International Standard Book Number 0–8014–1150–5
Library of Congress Catalog Card Number 77–17460
Printed in the United States of America
Librarians: Library of Congress cataloging information appears on the last page of the book.

To my parents,
Georgia B. Johnstone and
Robert M. Johnstone, Sr.

Contents

Acknowledgments

Though the responsibility for the work that follows is mine alone, I have had much assistance in its preparation. My thanks must first be expressed for the help of the late Clinton Rossiter of Cornell University, who shared with me his great understanding of the presidency and the American political tradition. It was he who guided the initial formulation of this study, although he well understood that my interpretation of Jefferson's presidency was not his own.

Andrew Hacker of Queens College supervised the original draft and offered other kindnesses of a professional and personal nature for which I shall be forever grateful. James Morton Smith of the Wisconsin State Historical Society and Andrew Milnor of Cornell University also read and criticized the earlier version. Louis Koenig of New York University, Dorothy Buckton James of the Virginia Polytechnic Institute and State University, and Lance Banning of the University of Kentucky read the revised manuscript, and their suggestions were of significant help in producing a better work.

I wish to thank James Twiggs and Kay Scheuer of Cornell University Press for their skillful editorial assistance; the staff of the Library of Congress for the use of the microfilm edition of the Jefferson Papers, which are the property of the Library's Manuscript Division; and the John L. Senior Fund of Cornell University and the Faculty Development Fund of Earlham College for financial support at various stages of writing.

Finally, I offer my deep appreciation to those I love most, for their encouragement in this as in so many other endeavors: my wife, Lynn;

my daughter, Gwyneth; and my parents, Georgia B. Johnstone and Robert M. Johnstone, Sr., to whom this book is dedicated.

ROBERT M. JOHNSTONE, JR.

Richmond, Indiana

Jefferson and the Presidency

CHAPTER 1

Introduction

In his influential book, *Presidential Power*, Richard Neustadt analyzes what he calls the "classic problem of the man on top in any political system: how to be on top in fact as well as in name."[1] Any political system, democratic or authoritarian, contains within it a web of personal, political, and institutional constraints—a product of culture, ideology, and historical experience—which serves to limit the flexibility and discretion of the leader. In a constitutional democracy these constraints are materially reinforced by the overarching controls of constitutionalism, that is, the commitment to limited government and the rule of law, and by the complex of restraints created by the requirements of popular representation.

In the American political system additional constraints are placed upon the power of the president by the peculiar pattern of institutions created by our written Constitution, most notably the separation of powers, or as Neustadt has felicitously revised the phrase, separated institutions sharing powers. Indeed, some scholars have seen as the central flaw in the American constitutional system the fact that while constitutionally the president is merely the second branch of a tripartite system of co-equal institutions, politically he must bridge, or try to bridge, the separation of powers in order to energize the motive power of government.

To carry out his constitutional and political responsibilities the modern president has a good deal of help. It has been a long time since the chief executive answered his own telephone, or ran his office with the aid of a single secretary whose salary was paid from his own

1. New York, 1964, p. vii. All references to this work are to the Signet edition.

pocket. Not only the size but the responsibilities of the office have expanded in this century as crises of war and economic depression have shifted the locus of power to the executive. It is at least arguable, however, that many of the problems of personal leadership confronted by modern presidents as they seek to exert influence have plagued presidents from the beginning of the Republic. It is probable that presidents in a different time and under vastly different conditions were nonetheless forced to operate within an established pattern of similar restraints, and therefore to develop techniques of personal leadership which permitted them to move beyond their constitutional and statutory authority to the imposition of their personal style and role concept upon their environment.

If this is indeed the case, then many of the theories of leadership developed by social scientists to order and explain modern leadership will be applicable as well to an earlier age. In this study of the presidential leadership of Thomas Jefferson, we shall explore in some detail the elements of his personal leadership in order to reveal the ways in which an early president operated within his social and political context to employ the resources of power available to him and to create new resources by which to effect his purposes. So doing will enable us to indicate the ways in which many of the problems of leadership which Jefferson faced and the techniques of leadership which he pioneered are, *mutatis mutandis*, being confronted and employed by presidents in our own time.

It is a central thesis of this book that Jefferson's presidency marked the pioneering effort in erecting a working model of presidential leadership characterized by persuasion and the cultivation of influence. Jefferson was the first president willing to implement the bargaining relationships that could enhance presidential influence, and he did so with great natural skill and patience. He was the first president to legitimize the utilization of a wide variety of extra-constitutional tools of persuasion with which the Constitution and political precedent had failed to provide him. Through his use of the most significant of these tools, the political party, Jefferson was able to span the chasm that separated the elected institutions of government from one another. By so doing he enlarged the horizons of acceptable political behavior and altered the climate of opinion.

In all these ways Jefferson may be said to have prefigured the modern presidency. Many of the resources he cultivated and the tools he employed had lain idle until he picked them up and put them to work. Some of them were to lie idle again after he left office. The limits of the presidency are elastic; they can be expanded by the force of a dynamic and skillful incumbent, just as they can be contracted when a less able man is at the helm. Each president who has exercised his powers energetically, however, has added an inalienable element to the shape and scope of the office his successors have inherited. The precedents of the strong presidents have served as the base upon which later presidents have built. Although the success Jefferson enjoyed in expanding the horizons of presidential influence was not shared by his immediate successors, the experience was not lost on future incumbents who possessed the personal skills and the political opportunity to resume the role that he had pioneered.

The Study of Individual Leadership

To study a president is not to study the whole of presidential government. It is rather to focus on the individual leader at the top whose influence over the corpus of executive functions can be most pervasive and whose style and intensity of performance can set the tone and the pace of executive government in its totality. Until recently, however, scholarship, particularly in the United States, has been reluctant to pursue the study of individual political leadership. This reluctance is in part attributable, perhaps, to the democratic "ethos" which, as Tocqueville observed, tends to produce in democratic historians a preference for the mass movement and the dominance of social forces. As Lewis Edinger has noted, American scholars especially have been likely to stress the social and political "context," thus "obscuring the individual personality in a vast panorama of 'man and his times'."[2]

2. "Political Science and Political Biography: Reflections on the Study of Leadership," in *Journal of Politics*, 26 (1964), 426. See also the illuminating discussion of the ongoing debate in individual leadership studies between the "mechanistic" view, which focuses upon the creative dominance of the leader, and the "organismic" interpretation, which places an emphasis upon the dominant effects of a given social system as a whole, in Donald D. Searing, "Models and Images of Man and Society in Leadership Theory," *Journal of Politics*, 31 (February, 1969), reprinted in Glenn D. Paige, ed., *Political Leadership: Readings for an Emerging Field* (New York, 1972), pp. 19–44. See also Lester G. Seligman, "The Study of Political Leadership," in *American Political Science Review*, 44 (December, 1950), and Dankwart A. Rustow, introduction to "Philosophers and Kings: Studies in Leadership," in *Daedalus*, 97 (Summer 1968).

Modern scholarship, particularly in the social sciences, has tended to study leadership in the plural, as "elites," rather than in the singular for a number of reasons: the group orientation of American politics and the concomitant pluralism of many of America's political scientists; the increase of bureaucracy, professionalism, and institutionalism in the political process, which has seemed to lessen the importance of any individual in the making of political decisions; the rise of behaviorism in the social sciences and the attempt by some of its proponents to obviate the need for a "psychology of human differences in which people are compared and described in terms of traits, capacities, and abilities."[3] Of equal importance in this emphasis on behavior in the mass is the fascination of the social scientist with "science" and with the corresponding search for methods of analysis productive of verifiable and replicable hypotheses, leading in turn to generalized theories of behavior. Thus far at least, the study of individual leadership has been maddeningly deficient in producing such results.

The study of individual leadership presents other problems, particularly when it focuses on political leaders of the past. There is the ever-present problem of the limited availability and reliability of data, especially data involving motivation. One of the thorniest but also one of the most important questions that the biographer seeks to answer is *why* a given political leader acted as he did. This question becomes exceedingly difficult when much of the evidence for a conclusion lies buried in the dim recesses of the past. There is often a paucity of written information concerning what occurred in the private corners of political life where so many important keys to motivation can be found.

Scholars who have attempted to study leadership in a systematic way are often struck by the "fuzziness" of the concept. Much of the earlier work by social psychologists and sociologists has focused on leadership as depending either upon (1) social structure, usually small groups, or (2) personality types or traits. Neither approach has proved wholly successful in unraveling the tangle of complexity that is political leadership.[4] The various studies indicate that the characteristics of

---

3. The phrase is B. F. Skinner's, in his *Beyond Freedom and Dignity* (New York, 1971), p. 9. He comes tantalizingly close to denying the existence of an autonomous "inner man," which he considers largely an "explanatory fiction" serving to "explain only the things we are not yet able to explain in other ways" (pp.14, 24).

4. See the summary of problems connected with the group approach in Seligman,

leadership vary widely. The nature of a particular type of leader is dependent in many ways on the social context in which he operates. Hence the importance in more recent analysis of situational variables in considering leadership. The emphasis on character traits or group process often leads the investigator to underestimate the influence of the immediate situation, the political and social environment, and political events, as well as to ignore the effect of purely institutional factors, such as incumbency.

In examining the performance of an individual leader, the scholar must not allow his inquiry to be too narrowly channeled by the blinders of a rigid formal model. He must bring to his work, in Edinger's words, "a conscious and disciplined imagination and even impressionistic speculation."[5] He must be reasonably eclectic, selecting and employing those theoretical "handles" that illuminate the subject matter of individual leadership without disguising its complexity. Slavish devotion to rigorous, systematic analysis may lead to an artificial, lifeless formalism. Rigid adherence to any conceptual model will almost inevitably distort the evidence and obscure an understanding of the complexity of individual human behavior, particularly if the tentative and heuristic nature of all useful models is forgotten.[6] Any useful model must allow for an emphasis upon the specific and unique aspects of leadership, especially the leader's attitudes toward power and his conception of his role in the political setting. It must also reflect the changing patterns and hence the uniqueness at any given time of the relationships between the leader and those he would lead. Only with a firm grasp of such essentials can one safely begin the task of abstracting from the particular experience to the development of some more general statements about leadership.

An Approach to the Study of Jeffersonian Leadership

With this caveat firmly in mind, I have found two conceptual ap-

pp. 907–908. For examples of trait analysis, see Ralph M. Stogdill, "Personal Factors Associated with Leadership: A Survey of the Literature," in *Journal of Psychology* 25 (1948) 66. See also Harold D. Lasswell, *Psychopathology and Politics* (Chicago, 1930), and *Power and Personality* (New York, 1948). For works by Lasswell's intellectual descendants, see Alexander and Juliette George, *Woodrow Wilson and Colonel House: A Personality Study* (New York, 1956); Lewis J. Edinger, *Kurt Schumacher: A Study in Personality and Political Behavior* (Stanford, 1965); and James D. Barber, *Presidential Character* (Englewood Cliffs, N.J., 1972).

5. "Political Science", p. 436.
6. See the useful discussion of this problem in Searing, pp. 22–23.

proaches particularly helpful in examining Jefferson's leadership: role analysis and a bargaining model best formulated by Richard Neustadt.

Role analysis allows the scholar to link an exploration of the situational and environmental variables that affect the political actor to an examination of the attitudes and assumptions the actor employs in a given set of relationships.[7] Role theory, therefore, provides a useful framework by which to integrate behavior with personality. By focusing on role, one may examine the leadership of a particular actor in terms of the expectations of other participants in the leader-led relationship as well as the expectations of the central actor himself. To discover the nature of Jefferson's leadership, for example, it is necessary both to examine his attitudes toward the political system and the nature of the power relationships within it and to gain some measure of the responsiveness of his environment to his leadership. Such an analysis is assisted by a role orientation.

While Jefferson had a general set of expectations concerning his role as president, his precise attitude toward his leadership role varied as the context of that leadership varied. His perception of his role vis-à-vis his colleagues in the executive branch differed significantly from his perception of his role with members of Congress or with the courts or with the party faithful in the states or with foreign representatives. The concept of "role-set" is thus useful in understanding the shifting nature of leadership in response to changes in the political environment.

To the role theorist a test of successful political leadership is the congruence between the leader's own perception of his role and the perceptions of other actors, or "counter-players," in the role-set. That is, his success often depends upon the similarity of his view of his function to the expectations of others who observe his conduct. One of Jefferson's great strengths as president, as we shall see, was the fact that he embraced in his own ideals and assumptions of political reality so many of the central values of the larger political community. He was sustained by the fact that the members of his cabinet, his party col-

7. The conceptual framework of role analysis which informs this study is developed by Edinger, "Political Science", pp. 650–655. See also "Role Theory," in Gardner Lindzey, ed., *Handbook of Social Psychology* (Cambridge, Mass., 1952), 1: 223–258; Neal Gross, Ward S. Mason, and Alexander McEachern, *Explorations in Role Analysis* (New York, 1958), and Andrew S. McFarland, "Role and Role Conflict," in Aaron Wildavsky, ed., *The Presidency* (Boston, 1969), pp. 3–17.

leagues in Congress, and increasingly a majority of the American people shared his political expectations and objectives. Role analysis is well suited as a glass by which to view the relationship between Jefferson's political personality and his behavior as a leader in a range of political settings. The following analysis will therefore rely, in part, upon the exploration of three key variables: role, style or political personality, and political setting.

As an additional framework for examining Jefferson's behavior as president the "bargaining" model of Richard Neustadt possesses utility. This conceptual framework embodies a set of hypotheses concerning the acquisition and use of political power which, when applied comparatively, enables us to see certain common threads of behavior and method linking modern presidents with their early predecessors. At the same time, however, the model allows for—indeed it stresses—the unique qualities of leadership each president brings to his office. A brief summary of Neustadt's ideas may be helpful for the reader who is unfamiliar with their major dimensions.

According to Neustadt, a president's leadership is measured not so much by his own actions as by his influence on the action of others; consequently, the central question to be asked is how he achieves and maintains that influence. In the modern presidency, the "powers" of the man in the White House are impressive, but formal powers are no guarantee of "power." Despite his formal authority and status a president rarely gains results merely by giving orders. Despite his preeminent position, "he does not get action without argument." To Neustadt, "presidential power is the power to persuade."[8]

A president's formal powers are useful in dealing with the men and women he must persuade. His status and authority give him leverage in the bargaining process. "From the veto to appointments, from publicity to budgeting, the White House now controls the most encompassing array of vantage points in the American political system."[9] Nevertheless, the president must have a capacity to combine these formal grants of authority with a talent for successful bargaining if he wishes to assert his influence in the policy process with any consistency.

In the American political system the context of leadership is to a

8. Neustadt, p. 22.
9. *Ibid.*, p. 43.

significant degree limited by institutional arrangements embodied in our written Constitution. "The separateness of institutions and the sharing of authority prescribe the terms on which a president persuades." The independent bases of power possessed by senior congressmen, the ability of entrenched bureaucratic power brokers to play off president and Congress, the conflicting demands upon the loyalty even of the members of the president's own cabinet—these underscore the difficulties of a president's persuasive task. According to Neustadt, the essence of that task "with congressmen and everybody else is to induce them to believe that what he wants of them is what their own appraisal of their own responsibilities requires them to do in their own interest, not his." This statement has been dismissed as merely belaboring the obvious, but its significance will become clearer as we observe Jefferson dealing ever so gingerly with his strong-willed and temperamental Republican allies in Congress, loyal to a point but fiercely jealous of their independence from the dictates of any man.[10]

Basic to Neustadt's model is the dictum that to be effective a president must seek to maximize his own personal power. "Modern understanding of presidential power demands respect for the view that a president's *desire* and capacity for leadership have much to do with the degree of influence which he is likely to achieve."[11] To be a successful bargainer a president must guard and judiciously exercise his generalized influence, his power prospects for the future. The process of bargaining requires that a president make choices, that is, decisions to act or not to act in a given situation. The general pattern of these choices over time, their general success or failure, will determine the measure of success he has in guarding these power prospects. To make the right choices the president must have access to the best available information and he must have the power of exercising decisions in his own hands. He must also possess the temperament and political experience to give him self-confidence and a sense of ultimate direction.

From a president's pattern of choices over time, the men and women a president must persuade will take their cues as to his skill and

10. *Ibid.*, pp. 43, 53. For criticism of this view, see Garry Wills, *Nixon Agonistes* (Boston, 1970), p. 221.

11. James Sterling Young, *The Washington Community* (New York, 1966), p. 191. The quote is Young's, but the idea is Neustadt's, as Young recognizes.

relative weight in the scales of power in Washington. This professional reputation, in turn, becomes a further source of power to the president who senses the need to preserve and enhance it. A president's influence also depends upon his popular prestige. The greater his standing with the public the more difficult it becomes for those Washingtonians who are themselves dependent on popular support to oppose him.[12] Personality and image are important here, but the primary determinant of a president's popular support is how well he is seen to be doing his job. He is judged by his ability to satisfy the needs and mitigate the frustrations of his people.

As a framework for the explanation of presidential leadership, the Neustadtian model has its limitations. In a thoughtful critique of *Presidential Power*, Peter Sperlich has concluded, for example, that Neustadt overrates bargaining and underrates command as mechanisms for the exercise of power. A command based on "mutual role expectations and shared norms and values" would not "cost" the president as much as one based merely on the president's legitimate right to issue a command. Related to this criticism is the observation that Neustadt's model relies perhaps too heavily upon instrumental rewards and punishments as incentives to bargaining. A president can gain effective influence even over those more distant from him than his immediate associates by stimulating feelings of subjective identification with him, by what Sperlich calls the exercise of "libidinal" power.[13] Efforts by a president to gain influence on the basis of appeals to pride, duty, or conscience, while often interladen with more instrumental appeals, may nonetheless be distinguished and do not involve the material trade-offs of the instrumental bargaining process, nor do they entail command. The extreme case of such symbolic

12. Neustadt, p. 68 and chap. 5. While certain forms of power, such as that of the prison guard over his prisoner, can occur without prestige, one can say in general that prestige is a crucial element in the exercise of political power. See E. A. Ross, *Social Control* (New York, 1916), p. 78.

13. "Bargaining and Overload: An Essay on Presidential Power," in Wildavsky, pp. 183–185. John R. P. French and Bertram Raven identify five bases of power that are of relevance here. *Reward* power and *coercive* power are analogous to Neustadt's instrumental "carrot and stick" bargaining power. *Expert* power has no direct analogy in Neustadt, but one can use it in the sense of the political expertise that contributes to a president's professional reputation. *Referent* power is analogous to Sperlich's "libidinal power." *Legitimate* power is equivalent to office, status, and authority. French and Raven, "The Bases of Social Power," in Dorwin Cartwright and Alvin Zander, eds., *Group Dynamics* (Evanston, Ill., 1960).

persuasion may be observed in the relationship of the charismatic leader to his followers. As we shall see, not a little of Jefferson's success as a political leader was derived from his symbolic reputation and the appeal to just such internalized values.

It is pertinent to observe about bargaining as a source of presidential influence that the effectiveness of such a technique varies with the nature of the participants. Bargaining works best in a situation where each side possesses incentives to bargain. The reciprocity essential to the bargaining process appears where a degree of mutual interdependence is required to achieve mutual goals. A president who possesses the most alluring charms and the most remarkable gifts for negotiation will nevertheless be unsuccessful in the bargaining process if the other side has nothing to gain from participating, has no need for the president's instrumental rewards and no fear of his punishments, or is constrained by other circumstances to refuse to bargain. It was precisely such a dilemma that frustrated Jefferson's struggles with the Federalist courts and doomed his hopes during the embargo of 1808–1809.

The Nature of the Early Presidency

Neustadt wrote of modern presidents—Franklin Roosevelt, Truman, and Eisenhower—presidents sitting at the apex of a many-tiered and ever-expanding labyrinth of aides, assistants, cabinet officers, agency heads, technicians, and civil servants who service and staff the executive establishment. His prescriptions for presidential leadership are designed to influence presidents of the future, political leaders who would be expected to function within the expanded environment and amid the inflated expectations of the modern presidency. How relevant is the Neustadtian power model to presidents of the past? Are its central concepts of use only for the age of the "imperial presidency," or can they be helpful, as well, in understanding the office and the men who held it in the nation's infancy?[14]

14. Most of the scanty literature dealing with presidential statecraft concerns the modern presidency. The most thoughtful exception is James S. Young's *The Washington Community*—as its name implies, a community study rather than an examination of individual leadership. One limitation of the work for explaining Jefferson is that by attempting to deal with "Jeffersonian" presidents as though they represented one "type," Young tends to underrate a number of significant distinctions between Jefferson and his less successful successors. If, as Young admits, differences in statecraft are largely personal, such an overview of Jeffersonian presidents grouped as one would

The contrasts in political values and institutions then and now are, of course, profound. Those who occupied the seats of political power as the government moved to Washington in 1800 sat at the "nerve center of a loose and fragile polity."[15] They shared with their constituents a fundamental suspicion of power which gave to the climate of opinion of the day one of its most salient characteristics. Despite the sense of obligation to public service that was a feature of eighteenth century Anglo-American political culture, the low opinion of politics generally held by public men and the public is remarkable and well documented. The possession of power was suspect, its use dangerous. The exercise of political power was a "splendid torment" to be borne only from a sense of duty. James Sterling Young writes of the "psychic stress of men who, even as they indulged the urge to power, could not easily turn aside their democratic conscience that instructed them of power's evil." There was, of course, an element of cant in the antipower posture of some of the public men of the day; often their attitude toward power depended upon who was exercising it. But the pervasive nature of the antipower bias colored the political life of the era. Any move to create a cohesive, well-disciplined political movement was suspect as an illegitimate use of coercive power. Young, writing of the capital city, observes, "in a social environment perceived as corrupting, a regime of assertive, inner-directed righteous individualism was called for."[16] To mold and lead a political movement under such conditions was a task summoning the highest political ability.

The universal validity of the Neustadtian maximization-of-power hypothesis, its applicability to presidents of the past, may depend on the nature and degree of the expectations of the presidential role possessed by the political cognoscenti of the day. It may be true that how a president conceives of power and the degree of his sensitivity to its uses will determine in large part the scope and intensity of his personal impact upon policy. In an age such as Jefferson's, however, when the very possession of power was suspect and its use limited in pervasive ways through the erection of elaborate "auxiliary precautions," efforts by a president to maximize his personal power could prove counter-

---

seem to place too much emphasis on structural and institutional factors and not enough on personal and situational variables.

15. The phrase is Young's, p. x.

16. *Ibid.*

productive. It has, after all, been a recurrent phenomenon of presidential history, extending well into our own century, that presidents who have attempted to exert their influence and extend their power have provoked a counterreaction by which the legislative branch has sought to restore the "balance," thereby severely restricting the room for maneuver of their unhappy successors.

The antipower bias of the age was institutionalized in the organic law of the new nation. The constitutional separation of powers fragmented the political process and insured that it would be characterized more by conflict than cooperation. As Young has brilliantly demonstrated, even the social and residential patterns of the early Washington community aggravated the cleavage between the constitutionally separated branches of government.[17]

The Framers of the Constitution further limited the possibility of effective management of the political process by their failure to provide a role for the chief executive in policy leadership. To be sure, the forces at the Convention advocating strength and energy in the national government had succeeded in creating an independent executive with some of the powers of the sovereigns of Europe. The president's authority in foreign relations; his powers as commander-in-chief; the power of a veto; the power to appoint federal officers—all were kingly powers of a sort. None of these powers was plenary, however; each was limited by the necessity to cooperate with Congress or the states. But the Framers had profited from the mistakes of the Confederation period and did create an executive who could stand on his own.

Nevertheless, beneath the panoply of kingly powers (effective more *in posse* than *in esse*) there was a fundamental weakness in the office that became all too apparent after 1801 to those who desired to use the federal machinery for political reform. Jefferson became president at the head of a political movement determined to reverse what it saw as the antidemocratic and reactionary trends of its predecessors and restore to the political system its democratic elements. To accomplish these intentions, Jefferson was determined to sweep away the last vestiges of Federalism. As president, however, he inherited an office that in terms of providing leadership of Congress was woefully weak. The Framers had taken special pains to prevent executive encroach-

17. *Ibid.*, pp. 77–81.

ment upon the legislative process. "Effective rulership tends to require what the Constitution clearly tends to discourage, namely, that a party or faction disperse its members or its influence across the branches of government."[18] Staggered elections from differing constituencies made this extremely difficult in the Congress, and the tenure system in the courts made it almost impossible in the judiciary. Furthermore, the legal authority for presidential policy leadership was minimal. Constitutionally, the president could give information to Congress on the state of the Union and could recommend measures for consideration. His power to veto legislation was not yet a weapon of policy, being strictly limited in its use by custom and precedent. The president had been granted few statutory powers with which to augment his meager constitutional access to the Hill. The budget was not in his hands. Machinery for assuring access was very scanty and suspect. Systematic congressional liaison was unknown and would have been resisted by the fiercely independent congressmen.

John Marshall's famous warning to the effect that Jefferson as president would weaken the office by embodying himself in the House of Representatives misses precisely this point: in terms of leading Congress, the presidency was weak to begin with.[19] Formal constitutional powers proved from the first to be inadequate in bridging the gulf between the executive and legislative branches and providing the stabilizing and mobilizing influences needed for effective government. The ideology of strict republicanism served to reinforce this separation, a fact that the more flexible Jefferson was obliged repeatedly to recognize. Marshall, like many of his contemporaries, failed to perceive and anticipate a need that was to become a permanent feature of American politics—the need for the president, through the use of his political and personal skills as opposed to his formal constitutional and prerogative powers, to provide unified and sustained policy leadership.

As much a requirement for presidential leadership as personal skills in the bargaining process is the availability of extra-constitutional power resources. By adding to his meager formal powers and his far-from-meager personal gifts a skillful use of the tools of persuasion available to him (patronage, appointments, party loyalty, a party press,

18. *Ibid.*, p. 81.
19. The charge is quoted in Albert Beveridge, *The Life of John Marshall* (Boston, 1919), 2:537.

legislative lieutenants on the floor of Congress), Jefferson could insure that his presidency would in fact be characterized more by leadership than clerkship.

This study of Thomas Jefferson's presidential leadership analyzes his ability to use the power resources available to him as president and his talent in creating new resources to facilitate the tasks he set himself. Part One is an examination of Jefferson's political personality and role concept, and begins with a consideration of his leadership style and the extent to which congruence existed between his style and role. His own conception of leadership is then examined, particularly his views on the proper role for presidential leadership in the federal system and the purposes for which that leadership should properly be exercised.

Part Two considers Jefferson's leadership as he acted amid the various elements of the political environment. The section begins with an examination of his relationship with the members of his own official family and the executive bureaucracy of the day, and his development of a policy of patronage and appointments, perhaps the most significant material resource for gaining influence within the executive branch.

The principal arena for the conduct of policy-making in Jefferson's day was Congress. Jefferson's relations with the legislative branch are considered with particular attention to the development and employment of his bargaining techniques, his use of the party in Congress, his cultivation of a corps of informal legislative lieutenants on the floor, and his influence over legislative output.

Of central importance to the achievement of the Jeffersonian program of reform was the curtailment of the power and pretensions of the federal courts, monopolized as they were by the partisans of the Federalist party. The president's role in the campaign to achieve this is examined primarily from the standpoint of the larger political struggles that underlay many of the narrowly constitutional arguments of the day. To Jefferson the significance of his battles with the courts lay in his struggle to maintain his power and the primacy of his purposes against what he deemed to be a final attempt by the discredited opposition to preserve their influence in the refuge of the federal judiciary.

The book then examines briefly the nature of Jefferson's relations with the state parties and their leaders, for it was these men who served as one of the major sources of strength to the Republican movement at the congressional level. We will focus upon the roles that the president saw himself performing amid the kaleidoscope which was the Republican party in the states of the Union. In this chapter particular emphasis is placed upon the extent to which Jefferson employed the resource of the party press in the communication of political intelligence and the mobilization of popular support.

Part Three is devoted to an analysis in some detail of the embargo of 1808–1809 as a case study in the limits of presidential leadership in the young republic. The failure of the embargo policy in the face of the most extensive employment of presidential power before Lincoln suggests the crucial importance of situation and circumstance, in this case the sheer intractability of events, in thwarting the best-intentioned of presidential policies. The embargo will also provide a key to understanding the decline of Jefferson's professional reputation in the closing days of his administration and the weakening of the resources of influence available to his chosen successor, Madison, a weakening that led directly to the shift in the locus of power from executive to legislature in the years after Jefferson's retirement.

The book concludes with some overall observations concerning Jefferson's presidential leadership and his contribution to the development of the office as well as some summary thoughts on the efficacy of the theoretical models employed in the study.

PART ONE

PRESIDENTIAL STYLE
AND ROLE

Political leadership can be understood as a phenomenon of interaction between the individual leader acting in response to the dictates of his political personality and style and his own conception of his role and purpose as a leader, and the political and social environment or setting against which, or at least in the context of which, he must move.[1] One must try, then, to understand *both* the leader himself, his political style and role expectations, and the surrounding environment that not only reacts to his leadership but to a large extent predetermines the contours or at least the outer dimensions of his leadership possibilities.

The relationship between leader and led is one of persistent though often unpredictable change. Not only is the setting, including the number and nature of the other actors, in more or less constant flux, but the role expectations and the behavioral responses of the leader himself change in response to what he perceives to be changes in his environment. Indeed, the degree to which a leader declines to modify his behavior in accordance with a changing external reality may be a measure of the degree of his failure as leader.

But while the role expectations of the leader must be responsive to alterations in those of others, his political personality and style are less subject to change. They are not wholly resistant to it, unless his inner emotional needs constitute so powerful a set of drives as to override all evidence of dysfunction between his personality and the demands of

1. See the useful conceptual framework of leadership contained in Paige, *Political Leadership*, particularly the introduction to Part II, pp. 69–81, which posits six concepts that may be analyzed in explaining leadership behavior: personality, role, organization, task, values, and setting.

his environment. Nevertheless, old habits die hard. Major personality characteristics and the political style which a leader has adopted and which has been successful in the past form a sort of inner reality that is resistant to, though not wholly defiant of, great modification.[2]

In general one can agree with the role theorists that the successful leader is one whose perception of his role is largely congruent with the expectations of those he would lead. Similarly a leader's political personality and style of operation, their impact on others, and the extent of their congruence with the requirements of the leader's own role are crucial to his success or failure. If there is not "fit" between the expectations of his environment and the personal needs or requirements of the leader, then his leadership will fail.[3]

In Chapter 2 we examine briefly some of the more salient dimensions of Jefferson's political personality and style with a view to discerning their "fit" with the role requirements of his office and the purposes of his leadership. No attempt is made at clinical analysis, a task that the author freely confesses himself incompetent to perform. Rather, data concerning the more evident characteristics of Jefferson's personality and style are presented, and an attempt is made to relate these dominant features to the demands of his role in such a way as to demonstrate the congruence that in the main existed between his personal style and his political purpose.

Heinz Eulau has written, "It may be argued that the best way to identify a man's role is to see how he actually behaves. A role, it would seem, is best constructed from performance. But this procedure . . . ignores meaning." One must examine the normative expectations of the actor himself so as to provide "meaningful criteria of evaluation," since a role is often defined "not only by other's expectations but also by an actor's own conception of his role."[4] This is particularly true of a newly created role or one in the process of being created—such as the presidency in 1800. Chapter 3 is devoted to a detailed exploration of Jefferson's own conception of his role and responsibilities as president. His view of the nature and scope of executive power is compared with

2. For a more detailed examination of presidential style, see Barber, *Presidential Character*.

3. Lewis Edinger argues that Kurt Schumacher's failure as leader of the postwar S.P.D. in Germany resulted largely from the irresolvable conflict between his role expectations and the inner needs of his own personality. Edinger, *Kurt Schumacher*.

4. *The Behavioral Persuasion in Politics* (New York, 1963), especially pp. 39–46, 100–107.

the views of his two predecessors in the office, and the elements of his alternative conception are outlined. Of significance are his attempts to popularize the presidency, to guard its independence, and to assert its authority in those areas where that authority was clear, while at the same time reducing the "monarchical" pretensions of the office to conform with the principles of republican responsibility and simplicity.

CHAPTER 2

❧

The Quality of Jeffersonian Leadership:
Style in the Service of Values

When one examines Jefferson's political leadership, one is struck
initially by apparent discrepancies between his personal style and the
expectations of a democratic polity. There is little doubt that Jefferson
ranks among the great political leaders of his age, yet it is equally
apparent that his leadership was achieved in the absence of many of
the qualities often associated with the effective democratic leader, qualities that were becoming a more essential part of the leader's repertoire
as the nation moved into the democratic age. For example, in an era
that prized the art of rhetoric above most other talents in its public
men, Jefferson was singularly lacking in forensic skills. He disliked
public speaking and displayed no talent for it. In a career spanning
over thirty-five years of almost continuous public service, he never
made a campaign speech, not even for others. As a legislator in the age
of Burke, Fox, Sheridan, and Patrick Henry, he entered debate only
rarely in the Virginia House of Burgesses and later in the Continental
and Confederation Congresses. As president his public utterances
were limited to two inaugural addresses (both delivered with such
diffidence as to be inaudible to most of his audience) and occasional
remarks before visiting delegations at the Executive Mansion or at
Monticello. He began the century-long practice of sending his State of
the Union messages to be read to Congress by the clerk of the House
rather than delivering them in person.[1] Jefferson's keen distaste for
crowds, his love of privacy, and his abhorrence of public ceremony
were notable even in an age of deference which normally frowned
upon the baser techniques of electioneering that were to characterize

1. His reasons for this practice extended beyond considerations of personal taste, as
we shall see below, Chapter 3.

political life in the coming democratic era. The immediate and calculated cultivation of popular approval would have to wait for a later time. Jefferson rarely appealed to the public directly.

The first decades of the young republic were characterized by the most intense and violent party wars ever carried on in the public press. Charges and countercharges echoed through the pages of the party newspapers with regularity, and the leading public men of the time participated, albeit with their identities veiled under the classical *noms de plume* that graced the political tracts of the period. Hamilton as "Pacificus," John Adams as "Clarendon," his son as "Publicola," Madison as "Helvidius"—these were but a few of the more prominent journalistic gladiators of the time. Yet Jefferson's name was not to be found among them. With one or two minor exceptions he never took part in these exchanges. This resistance to the temptation to sally forth in print stemmed from a mix of personal predilection and political calculation, but the fact remains that despite his acknowledged skill with the pen and his admitted contributions to American political letters, Jefferson rarely wrote for wide public consumption, under his own name or any other.

In personal appearance Jefferson seemed to lack some of the requisites of the successful democratic politician. As Malone observes, he did not strut a very imposing figure. In fact he did not strut at all; he slouched. Though tall like Washington, he lacked the majestic bearing of the general. He was red-haired and rawboned, with a face given to freckles under the sun. He was often careless in his dress, yet he was not consciously plebeian. No one ever assumed from the easy informality of his appearance a corresponding carelessness of breeding.[2]

He was an amiable man, friendly and open in private if somewhat reserved in public. He was fundamentally shy, though not introverted or taciturn. Margaret Bayard Smith, wife of the editor of Jefferson's administration organ, *The National Intelligencer*, and a woman devoted to Jefferson personally and politically, nevertheless described him critically as he appeared to many on first acquaintance: "To a disposition ardent, affectionate, and communicative, he joins manners timid, even to bashfulness, and reserved, even to coldness. If his life had not been proved to the contrary, I should have pronounced him rather a man of imagination and taste, than a man of judgment, a

2. Dumas Malone, *Thomas Jefferson as a Political Leader* (Berkeley, 1965), p. 5.

literary rather than a scientific man, and least of all a politician; a character for which nature never seemed to have intended him and for which the natural turn of mind, and his disposition, taste, and feeling equally unfit him."[3]

The fundamental characteristic of Jefferson's personality seems to have been an ardent desire for harmony, in both his public and his private life. His personality and character seem always to have favored conciliation rather than confrontation, the flanking movement rather than the frontal assault. He preferred to work his will by methods of persuasion rather than by force of command. His advice to others reflects a governing maxim of his own life: "to take things always by their smooth handle."[4] The written record of his public life is replete with evidence of his distaste for controversy. He had in common with many shy but ambitious men, furthermore, an extreme sensitivity to criticism. He had hesitated in accepting Washington's offer of the secretaryship of state because "to receive criticisms and censures of a public would be disagreeable to me." When he finally did accept the post, he said it was because by heeding his own preference to remain as minister to France he would have exposed himself "to the danger of giving disgust, and I value no office for that." Though Jefferson was driven by ambition and a need to be held in esteem by others, he did not hunger after office. The presidency he described characteristically as a "splendid misery," and there is no reason to assume the remark to be less than sincere. As president he sought actively to avoid disharmony even within his official family. When, rarely, his cabinet colleagues developed serious differences of opinion, the president would decide among them only with the greatest reluctance.[5]

3. Margaret Bayard Smith, *The First Forty Years of Washington Society* (New York, 1906), p. 80.

4. The phrase was a favorite of Jefferson's. He used it as a maxim of behavior for the grandson of a friend: Jefferson to Thomas Smith, February 21, 1825, in Paul Leicester Ford, ed., *The Writings of Thomas Jefferson* (New York, 1905), 12: 406 (hereafter referred to as Ford). He used it nearly forty years earlier in a letter to a friend in Paris: "The plan of my journey, as well as of my life, being to take things by the smooth handle, few occur which have not something tolerable to offer me" quoted in Merrill D. Peterson, *Thomas Jefferson and the New Nation* [New York, 1970], p. 350). At about this time, Jefferson was writing to his dear friend, Maria Cosway, "The art of life is the art of avoiding pain; and he is the best pilot who steers clearest of the rocks and shoals with which he is beset" (October 12, 1786, Ford, 5: 208).

5. Jefferson to Washington, December 14, 1789, and February 14, 1790, Ford, 5: 140–141, 148–149; to Albert Gallatin, June 9, 1804, in Henry Adams, ed., *The Writings of Albert Gallatin* (Philadelphia, 1879), 1: 196–197.

A letter of advice from Jefferson to his grandson deserves quoting at length because of the insights it allows into the moral and personal requisites for good conduct that governed his own attitude and behavior.

I have mentioned good humor as one of the preservatives of our peace and tranquillity. It is among the most effectual, and its effect is so well imitated and aided, artificially, by politeness, that this also becomes an acquisition of first rate value. . . . Politeness is the practice of sacrificing to those whom we meet in society all the little conveniences and preferences which will gratify them and deprive us of nothing worth a moment's consideration; it is the giving a pleasing and flattering turn to our expressions, which will conciliate others, and make them pleased with us as well as themselves. How cheap a price to pay for the good will of another! . . . Never enter into dispute or argument with another. I never saw an instance of one of two disputants convincing the other by argument. . . . It was one of the rules which, above all others, made Dr. Franklin the most amiable of men in society, "never to contradict anybody." If he was urged to announce an opinion, he did it rather by asking questions, as if for information, or by suggesting doubts.

Jefferson further cautioned his grandson about those who would argue passionately over politics: "Get by them . . . as you would an angry bull; it is not for a man of sense to dispute the road with such an animal." Good humor, politeness, deference to others, conciliation, the avoidance of disputatiousness—these mark the Jeffersonian ideals of proper conduct. In private as well as in public life, for Jefferson "the approving voice of our fellow citizens . . . is the greatest of all earthly rewards."[6]

This desire for harmony and conciliation at times seemed evidence to some of his critics that Jefferson lacked firmness and resolution in politics. William Plumer, then a political foe of some independence and later for a time an ally of like description, said of Jefferson that he was "too timid—too irresolute—too fickle—he wants nerve." The criticism was not uncommon among those who knew him only slightly or not at all and who were forced to view his conduct from afar. His preference for the persuasive approach also contributed to some of the charges of "deviousness" leveled against his political behavior. These elements in his personality, together somewhat ironically with his idealism, led him to veil his participation in the more

6. Jefferson to Thomas Jefferson Randolph, November 24, 1808, Ford, 11: 78–83; to the New London Methodists, February 4, 1809, in Lynton K. Caldwell, *The Administrative Theories of Hamilton and Jefferson* (Chicago, 1944), p. 108.

unsavory aspects of practical politics. They partially explain, as well, his penchant for covering his tracks in most political relationships and the care he took to maintain secrecy in his correspondence. He preferred to keep much of his political activity under wraps. His fear of spies reading his letters amounted, for a time, to an obsession. Though understandable in philosophical and psychological terms, this extreme caution and circumspection left Jefferson open to justifiable criticism. Care and prudence are, of course, laudable characteristics in a politician, but Jefferson's concern for concealing his activities helped at times to nurture the image of a backstairs intriguer maneuvering for improper ends, with one code of conduct for the public platform and another for the private chamber.[7] Such criticisms persisted and while there is little evidence that they hurt Jefferson politically, there is little doubt that they stung him personally.

The Advantages of the Jeffersonian Style

The cumulative consequences of such personal qualities as we have noted might have inhibited if not destroyed the prospects for an effective political career in democratic politics, and yet they seem to have had no such effect. It is clear on further examination that many of these same characteristics in fact contributed to his success.

"No one can know Mr. Jefferson and be his personal enemy." This categorical observation was offered not by a close friend or political ally but by a high member of the opposition, Supreme Court Justice William Paterson. "Few, if any, are more opposed to him as a politician than I am, and until recently I utterly disliked him as a man as well as a politician. And how was that dislike removed? By travelling together three days." This was the famous journey by coach during which the two men, neither of whom knew the other by sight, talked of many things including politics, each unaware of the other's identity. Said Paterson, "I was highly pleased with his remarks, for though we differed on many points, he displayed an impartiality and freedom from prejudice that at that period were unusual. There was a mildness

7. William Plumer, *Memorandum of Proceedings in the United States Senate, 1803–7*, E.S. Brown, ed. (New York, 1923), entry of March 16, 1806, p. 455. Even after he left the presidency, Jefferson continued to disguise his authorship of newspaper articles. See, for example, Jefferson to Thomas Ritchie of the *Richmond Enquirer*, August 28, 1817, in Frank Luther Mott, *Jefferson and the Press* (Baton Rouge, La., 1943), p. 26.

and amenity in his voice and manner that at once softened any of the asperities of *party* spirit that I felt, for, of course, we did not converse long without the mutual discovery that he was a *democrat* and I a federalist."[8]

Here is evidence of the effect of Jefferson's precepts of politeness and conciliation on those to whom they were directed. Not everyone was as receptive to his personal charms as was Paterson (and he probably would have been more resistant to them had he known in advance the identity of his seatmate). But the kindliness and grace of Jefferson's demeanor were remarked upon often enough, even by his political enemies, to constitute evidence of a sound political asset. To that he added a reputation for honesty and integrity that disarmed his critics as it bound his supporters to him with a loyalty born not only of a mutuality of political interest, but of deep respect and affection.

His demeanor served him well, furthermore, in the accumulation of that political capital vital to the bargaining process. His qualities of temperament happily coincided with the requirements of political persuasion as he cultivated the support he needed to further his goals. In his dealings with like-minded but independent congressmen of his own party, for example, the carrot was often more efficacious than the stick, the open hand more productive than the brandished fist. Indeed, too often there were few sticks to flourish even had the president been inclined to wield them. His personal charm and persuasive abilities, then, proved to be nicely attuned to the functional demands of his office.

Of equal importance in accounting for Jefferson's standing as a political leader were two other factors, considered separately for purposes of analysis, but in practice closely linked: his objective record of public service and his symbolic identity with the deeper principles and aspirations of the American people. In Neustadtian terms, Jefferson's public record is somewhat more important to an understanding of the nature of his professional reputation among the political elites of the day, while his symbolic identity is more directly relevant to an explanation of his towering public prestige.

James MacGregor Burns has observed that there are two (at least two) Jeffersons: Jefferson the Philosopher, the Whig theoretician, the champion of religious and political liberty, the spokesman for

8. This quotation and the authority for the entire story are found in Smith, *First Forty Years*, p. 406, emphasis in the original.

majoritarian values; and Jefferson the Politician, the statesman and man of affairs who spent some thirty-five years in almost continuous public service.[9] He began his public career in that crucible of parliamentary and revolutionary politics, the Virginia House of Burgesses. His service there as well as in the Virginia Constitutional Convention and the Continental Congress was characterized by a willingness to perform the grueling and often thankless tasks of committee work and an attention to the endless drudgery of legislative detail. His success in these endeavors earned him an early reputation among his colleagues as a man with a capacity for hard, sustained, and productive work. This reputation was of great significance in furthering his political prospects. The opportunity to author the Declaration of Independence, for example, came to him largely because of his already established renown as an excellent committeeman with a gift for the pen.

Jefferson's service as war governor of Virginia added greatly to his fund of administrative experience, while further service in the Confederation Congress, five years as minister to France, and the secretaryship of state in the first Washington administration not only added to his political knowledge and experience, but solidified his reputation as a very able man of affairs. His nomination for president and election as vice president in 1796 were a recognition by his colleagues and supporters of his preeminence as the leader of the new Democratic-Republican party. His success in furnishing a sense of confidence in the ultimate triumph of the movement, and his role as harmonizer of factional disputes within the party made him at the time of his election to the presidency its undisputed leader.

Jefferson's popular prestige was derived partially from his objective record of public service. It resulted as much, however, from the principles and aspirations that he embodied as from what he did, although his actions enhanced his symbolic prestige. Jefferson was one of the Founders. He had been prominent in the circle of those larger-than-life figures who declared independence and then won it, established state governments, created a national government seemingly out of whole cloth, and pioneered the political institutions of a new nation. As Dumas Malone put it, "He embodied the 'spirit of 1776' as fully as any civilian could."[10]

Jefferson was a leader in both the world of ideas and the world of

9. *The Deadlock of Democracy* (Englewood Cliffs, N.J., 1963), p. 25.
10. *Political Leader*, p. 33.

politics. He could combine the advantages of both worlds in that most important of political functions—the founding of a new state. As the author of its basic political testament he was instrumental in recasting the political institutions and behavior patterns of a people. His grasp of philosophy and his gift of phrase had enabled him to imprint with felicity the public values of his own mind upon the minds of his generation. In the first heady years of the new experiment in self-government Jefferson came to symbolize through his writings and his actions what Thomas Paine called the "birthday of a new world."

By the election of 1800, therefore, Jefferson's main strategy was "simply being Jefferson."[11] As the author of the Declaration, the early spokesman for revolution and for political and religious liberty, the people's advocate through trial after trial, Jefferson had a symbolic value to his party's cause that was of immense significance. His symbolic renown and his public service, furthermore, kept him in the public eye, serving further to enhance his reputation for wise, disinterested statesmanship.

There is another symbolic Jefferson, of course; that seen by his enemies. To the Federalists, particularly that band of brothers known to history as High Federalists, Jefferson was the archfiend, the Anti-Christ, the rabble-rousing demagogue whose purpose in life was to rip up the solid foundation stones of social stability and order and replace them with the shifting sands of mob rule. Timothy Pickering, for one, denounced the Virginian as a "cowardly wretch who . . . like a Parisian revolutionary monster, prating about humanity, would feel an infernal pleasure in the utter destruction of his opponents. . . . Virtue and worth are his enemies, and therefore he would overwhelm them." Ironically, however, the virulent attacks of the High Federalists served to solidify Jefferson's image in the public mind as the defender of popular rights. The series of newspaper assaults on Jefferson in the 1790's, particularly, is seen by some scholars as merely establishing him in the public consciousness as *the* leader of the antimonarchical forces.[12]

Without direct appeals to the people, with in fact little direct contact with the masses, Jefferson nonetheless possessed a formidable power

11. Burns, *Deadlock of Democracy*, p. 33.
12. Timothy Pickering to Rufus King, March 4, 1804, in Henry Adams, ed, *Documents Relating to New England Federalism* (Boston, 1877), p. 351; Malone, *Political Leader*, p. 34.

over the public imagination. This power was of incalculable benefit as the president sought to exert his influence over the activities of government. One can speak of him in a sense as having certain of the qualities of "charisma," if one interprets the term not in its religious or messianic meaning, but in a modified sense useful when applied to leaders in legal-rational polities.[13] Jefferson certainly possessed few of the personal traits commonly associated with the charismatic leader. The crucial test of charisma, however, is the response of the followers. An essential mark of the charismatic leader is that he be followed more out of a sense of love, devotion, enthusiasm, or any of a series of emotional reasons rather than primarily for more instrumental purposes. Charisma, furthermore, is usually associated with a process of summoning people to join in a movement for fundamental or at least major change.

Jefferson's leadership meets all of these criteria to a degree. To the rank-and-file his authority at the top was largely unquestioned and often based on an emotional as well as a more strictly instrumental base. To the party elite and particularly those closest to him his authority was accepted as a "given," even while particular tactics and strategies were debated and criticized. Jefferson's eloquent embodiment of the values of liberal republicanism called, furthermore, for new attitudes, new ways of life and thought, and evoked in many Americans a sense of a popular crusade, a second American revolution to rid the country of the evils of monarchism and privilege.

Too much should not be made of the charismatic element in Jefferson's leadership. Nonetheless, he expressed a confidence and enthusiasm in the people, in the rightness and inevitability of popular rule, which transmitted itself to the people in a manner that marked a unique relationship between leader and led—one that, like true charisma, could not be passed on to a successor.

The Functions of Leadership

We have examined certain of the characteristics of Jefferson's political personality and style, characteristics that enhanced his ability to perform his leadership function. What was the purpose or purposes for

13. For the modifications in the Weberian concept of charisma used here, I am indebted to the insights of Robert C. Tucker in "The Theory of Charismatic Leadership," in *Daedalus*, 97 (Summer, 1968), 731–756.

which he exercised leadership? What, in his view, was the function of leadership in effecting the political purposes he set for the nation?

From an examination of his writings as well as his behavior as a public servant, at least four basic assumptions about the purpose of leadership emerge, assumptions that governed Jefferson's conduct of the presidency. The first of these was that the leader in a republic must be attentive and responsive to the popular will. Such an assertion has a hackneyed quality to the modern reader, but in Jefferson's day the idea was hardly universally accepted, even in theory. The leader must be fully committed to the belief that public officials in a republic are the agents of the people and that their first allegiance is to the majority that elected them. The leader must never simply mirror the ever-shifting day-to-day expression of public opinion; he must not be a slave to popular pressures. But he must be constantly concerned to attend to the people's deeper desires and aspirations.

A second, related, assumption was his notion that the leader must be able and prepared to anticipate the popular will, to shape rather than be shaped by it, in order to educate the people to a recognition of their own best interests. He must have a vision that can transcend the mundane, routine, or transitory expression of popular sentiment in order to define and illuminate a more profound and permanent will. James MacGregor Burns has borrowed Isaiah Berlin's metaphor of the hedgehog and the fox to describe two ideal-types of political actor: the hedgehog who possesses a central vision, a unifying set of values that more or less coherently organizes "all that he says and is," and the fox who, without a coherent governing value system, pursues many ends, often unrelated and even at times contradictory, for more purely instrumental or short-term purposes. Jefferson clearly corresponds to the "hedgehog." His supreme faith in the people and their capacity for self-government was a value which gave to his leadership a sense of purpose and direction. Jefferson, says Burns, above all "believed in liberty and equality. Through all his twistings and windings . . . Jefferson was able in the end to stick to the central values of democracy—of government by and for and of the people—that can be captured now only in hackneyed words simply because they have become the central political values of the American people."[14]

The third assumption guiding Jefferson's view of political leader-

14. *Presidential Government* (Boston, 1966), pp. 18–27, 22.

ship was that leadership did not exist for itself, was not, in Stanley Hoffmann's phrase, "its own purpose."[15] Rather, the purpose of leadership was instrumental. The leader's function was to serve as the instrument for effecting the tasks of government in accordance with a sense of public purpose. It was his task to express and guide the creation of a program to make the institutions of government more responsive to the popular will. In conformity with sound republican doctrine, there was nothing "mystical" about Jefferson's view of the leader. His task was not seen primarily in terms of representing the "essence" of nationhood, in symbolizing national identity, in embodying the mystique or glory of the state. Nor was his purpose found in the exercise of power for power's sake, or the perpetuation of an elite or a class. The functions of leadership were seen in substantive, pragmatic, programmatic terms. This conception helps to explain Jefferson's indifference to the trappings of office or the quasi-royal panoply of power.

The fourth of the governing assumptions of Jefferson's leadership was that the leader must be able to change with circumstance, to grow in office, to be prepared to modify or reject outmoded views, to repudiate outworn dogmas. This capacity is not necessarily incompatible with the maintenance of a broad guiding vision, the hallmark of the "hedgehog." Certain students of Jefferson have attempted to divorce his idealism from his practical statecraft. The philosopher T. V. Smith, for example, argued that for Jefferson, "means existed not primarily as agencies to realize ideals, but as reproducers of themselves; that for him ideals existed not primarily as things to be realized through collective means but as ends of reflection to be enjoyed for their own sake."[16] Such a view of Jefferson serves to make his presidential career virtually unintelligible, save as an aberration. Political philosophy to Jefferson was rarely a pastime, a matter for idle speculation. His reflections on the philosophy of politics were far more often performed in the service of some practical purpose. It is by seeing Jefferson as one for whom political ideals are meaningless *unless* they can contribute to a proper ordering of political reality that one can begin to make sense of the course of his political life and to understand

15. Stanley and Inge Hoffmann, "De Gaulle as Political Artist," in *Daedalus*, 97 (Summer, 1968), 867.

16. "Thomas Jefferson and the Perfectability of Mankind," *Ethics*, 53 (July, 1943), 297.

the practical and philosophical tensions that he had, perforce, to reconcile in his presidency. If there is a unifying theme in Jefferson's public career, it is this effort to mold the nation's political institutions in such a way as to bring them into conformity with the ideals of the American experiment in self-government.

Jefferson can be better understood if he is viewed not primarily as a philosopher whose privilege it was to dabble in the practical world of affairs, but as a man of affairs whose conduct of public office was informed by a more or less coherent set of philosophical assumptions. Jefferson never produced a work of systematic philosophy. It is a mistake to see him as a visionary with his head in the clouds. He was a talented political animal with the skills of a seasoned politician, and he possessed a keen sense of the realities of power and the relationship between ideals and reality. He could write that "the ground of liberty is to be gained by inches . . . we must be contented to secure what we can get from time to time, and eternally press forward for what is yet to get. It takes time to persuade men to do what is for their own good."[17] There is no better statement in all of Jefferson's writings to illustrate his understanding of the nature of the political bargaining process.

Jefferson had a realistic sense of the limitations of power; he was alert to the restrictions imposed upon its exercise by the shifting forces of political life. He was, like most successful democratic politicians, acutely attuned to the art of the possible. "No more good must be attempted than the nation can bear."[18] He was conscious of the dissipating nature of political influence and realized the need to marshal and preserve his personal power and prestige. He would rarely risk the expenditure of his power on grand but futile gestures. He once declined to subscribe to an antislavery tract sent to him for endorsement by a friend on these grounds:

I have most carefully avoided every public act or manifestation on that subject. Should an occasion ever occur in which I can interpose with decisive effect, I shall certainly know and do my duty with promptitude and zeal. . . . The subscription to a book on this subject is one of those little irritating measures

17. Quoted in Peterson, *Thomas Jefferson*, p. 157. To Dupont de Nemours he observed, "What is practicable must often control what is pure theory; and the habits of the governed determine in a great degree what is practicable" (January 18, 1802).

18. Jefferson to Dr. Walter Jones, March 31, 1801, in Andrew A. Lipscomb and Albert E. Bergh, eds., *The Writings of Thomas Jefferson* (Washington, 1903), 10:256 (hereafter referred to as Lipscomb).

which, without advancing its end at all, would, by lessening the confidence and good will of a description of friends comprising a large body, only lessen my powers of doing them good in other great relations in which I stand to the publick.[19]

In this decision and others Jefferson displayed a sensitivity to the notion of power as a resource to be invested, not squandered, a sensitivity that, as Neustadt points out, is the *sine qua non* of the effective political leader.

The exigencies of holding power forced Jefferson the public servant to modify some of the principles of Jefferson the political thinker. There is no question but that political requirements at times necessitated actions that appeared to ignore or even to contradict certain of his stated views about the nature of government and the limits of power. Jefferson, like all effective public men, was accused of inconsistencies. But it is well to be reminded of what another great public man, Winston Churchill, wrote about consistency in politics:

A statesman in contact with the moving current of events and anxious to keep the ship on an even keel and steer a steady course may lean all his weight now on one side and now on the other. His arguments in each case when contrasted can be shown to be not only very different in character, but contradictory in spirit and opposite in direction; yet his object will throughout have remained the same. His resolves, his wishes, his outlook may have been unchanged; only his methods may be verbally irreconcilable. We cannot call this inconsistency. The only way a man can remain consistent amid changing circumstances is to change with them, while preserving the same dominating purpose.[20]

The Program for Leadership

Within the universe of these assumptions concerning the nature of leadership, what were the ends toward which Jefferson's presidency tended? He outlined the political principles that governed his rise to the office in a letter to Elbridge Gerry almost two years before his election. He would see effected

an inviolable preservation of our present Federal Constitution, according to the true sense in which it was adopted by the States. . . . I am opposed to the

19. Jefferson to Dr. George Logan, May 11, 1805, Ford, 10: 141. Malone cites the Yazoo controversy as another example of Jefferson's refusal to place his prestige on the line in a futile gesture ("Presidential Leadership and National Unity: The Jeffersonian Example," in *Journal of Southern History*, 35 [February, 1969]).

20. Quoted in Harry Jaffa, *The Crisis of the House Divided* (New York, 1959), p. 46.

monarchizing its features by the forms of its administration with a view to conciliate a first transition to a President and Senate for life, and from that to a hereditary tenure of these offices, and thus to worm out the elective principle. I am for preserving to the States the powers not yielded by them to the Union, and to the legislature of the Union its constitutional share in the division of powers; and I am not for transferring all the powers of the States to the general government, nor all those of that government to the Executive branch. I am for a government rigorously frugal and simple . . . and not for a multiplication of offices and salaries to make partisans, and for increasing, by every device, the public debt, on the principle of its being a public blessing. I am for relying, for internal defense on our militia solely, till actual invasion, and for such a naval force only as may protect our coasts and harbors.. . . . I am for free commerce with all nations; political connection with none; and little or no diplomatic establishment.[21]

This political testament, a compound of fears and aspirations, was written during the heat of controversy with the Adams administration and the Federalist courts over the Alien and Sedition Acts, and may fairly be said to embody most of what later came to be called the "principles of '98," that radical Republican catechism which, with the passage of years, was to become the platform of the "Old Republicans." The program thus outlined to Gerry was a summary of the issues the Republicans hoped to use in building their case against the Federalists: opposition to the Alien and Sedition Acts, the direct tax and the prospect of future taxes, a five-million-dollar deficit for building up the army and navy, the danger of a war with France. Eighteen months later, still in the grip of his battle with the administration, Jefferson repeated his desire to reduce the impact of government, lowering its presence "to a few plain duties to be performed by a few servants." As he put it in another context, the sum of good government is that it be "wise and frugal," that it "restrain men from injuring one another," and that it "leave them otherwise free to regulate their own interests."[22] With his belief in the natural benevolence of man and the corrupting influence of institutions, he spoke for a government whose arbitrary powers would be eliminated, whose lawful powers would be restricted by written rules, and whose scope would be narrowed within the limits imposed by necessity and a written constitution.

21. Jefferson to Elbridge Gerry, January 26, 1799, Ford, 9:17–19.
22. Jefferson to James Monroe, January 23, 1799, *ibid.*, p. 11; to Gideon Granger, August 13, 1800, *ibid.*, 10: 140; Peterson, *Thomas Jefferson*, p. 658.

But while Jefferson leaned heavily in one direction during the years of his rise to the presidency, he was not narrowly doctrinaire in his conception of the proper limits of power. His faith in the people gave to his views on power a flexibility that permitted the use of power in positive ways to emphasize the freedom to pursue happiness, not simply to insure freedom *from* government. Although he never lost his aversion to systems that relied on force and command, he was not reluctant to employ either when in his opinion the situation demanded it. He believed in a small central government limited primarily to external affairs and the regulation of relations between the states. He also believed that public affairs should be conducted at the lowest level of government possible to preserve a decentralization of administration and to promote responsibility of public officials to the people they served. Within the limits imposed by the Constitution on the general government, however, Jefferson would have the powers of government exercised with energy and efficiency.

This view placed him in a moderate position within the spectrum of opinion in his own party. His centrist posture was to prove, moreover, a significant source of strength to his leadership of that party, for he was in a position to bridge the gap that, despite outward unity during the years of struggle, had always existed between the radical Republicans who espoused the "principles of '98" and the moderates who more fully accepted the fundamental constitutional arrangements of 1787 and who were to embrace the nationalism of Madison. To both factions Jefferson was the champion. As the leader most immediately responsible for erecting and maintaining a united front against "monarchism" and its apologists, Jefferson leaned now one way (toward the principles of '98 when they constituted the most effective arguments against a state of affairs he wished to alter) and now the other (toward the moderate position when the overriding need appeared to be the conciliation of the opposition rank-and-file and the isolation of their defeated but irreconcilable leaders).

Jefferson's problem, then, as he took power in 1801 was to construct a program that would appeal to the broad spectrum of Republican opinion, radicals and moderates, while offering the open hand of friendship to those members of the wayward Federalist flock who would accept it. He was faced with the need to maintain sufficient militancy among the party faithful to prevent backsliding, while preparing the way to a full acceptance of the change of government and of

Republican policies and programs by the vast majority of Americans of all political persuasions.

Unfortunately the Republicans did not themselves agree upon a political program. To the radicals the fundamental institutional reforms implied in the principles of '98 were essential: legislative supremacy, decentralization of administration, radical reform of the federal judiciary, dismantling of the Hamiltonian fiscal system, encouragement of agriculture, and in foreign policy active support of the French. To the moderates, however, while the principles of '98 had provided a useful rhetoric and a convenient rallying cry in the war against Federalism, as a program of practical reform they were more often an embarrassment. The moderates preferred only to reduce the costs of government, pay off the national debt, reduce the influence of national financial institutions, and leave it to the good judgment of the new holders of power to place the ship of state back on its proper republican course. The Constitution and the basic political arrangements of the nation should be left largely intact.[23]

In devising his program Jefferson and his colleagues steered a course that, while accepting direction from both wings of the party, seemed more nearly to approximate the moderate program. The new president's inaugural address reflected this strategy, for it was a classic illustration of the attempt to mobilize support and neutralize dissent. He appealed to his opponents to abide by the rule of law and the voice of the electorate and "unite in the common good." He sought to minimize the differences between the parties. "We are all Republicans; we are all Federalists" meant that the admittedly bitter disagreements between the two factions nevertheless occurred within a fundamental consensus on essential values. It would be the purpose of the new administration to "retain the good opinion of those who have bestowed it in advance, [and] to conciliate that of others, by doing them all the good in my power."[24]

The policy of conciliation, the first policy decision taken by the new government, was greeted with skepticism in many Republican circles, with outright scorn in others; as harmony was an essential characteristic of Jefferson's own personality, however, so conciliation was an essential ingredient in his overall plan to eliminate the Federalist

23. For a discussion of this disagreement, see Richard E. Ellis, *The Jeffersonian Crisis: Courts and Politics in the Young Republic* (New York, 1971), p. 274.

24. First inaugural address, March 4, 1801, Ford, 9:199–200.

menace by undercutting its support in the country. The leader of the most powerful political organization then known, Jefferson nonetheless never fully approved of the concept of political parties. He never fully accepted, that is to say, the idea of a "loyal opposition." He sought, instead, the cultivation of a unity on fundamental principles which he always believed existed among his countrymen and which he felt would ultimately override the disaffections of the moment.[25]

The president defended conciliation in a letter to William Branch Giles, one of his principal legislative lieutenants: "It was a conviction that these people [the Federalist rank-and-file] did not differ from us in principle, which induced me to define the principles which I deemed orthodox, and to urge a reunion on those principles. . . . I do not speak of the desperadoes of the quondam faction in and out of Congress. These I consider as incurables, on whom all attentions would be lost, and therefore will not be wasted." His strategy was clear, even if there did exist a number of skeptics within his own party ranks: "If we can avoid shocking their [the rank-and-file's] feelings by unnecessary acts of severity against their late friends, they will in a little time cement and form one mass with us, and by these means harmony and union be restored to our country, which would be the greatest good we could effect."[26]

High Federalism was considered a disease, a variant strain of that malady which had supposedly been cured forever by revolution. Jefferson saw his role somewhat as that of a surgeon whose task it was to remove and isolate the infected tissue of Federalist leadership (the "incurables") from the basically healthy body of the larger citizenry. As we shall see, the implementation of this policy of conciliation was to give the administration many headaches, particularly in the early months when it affected appointments to office and other patronage considerations. Overall, however, the policy proved successful. The role Jefferson conceived for his administration seemed happily to coincide with the expectations of electoral majorities. Within two years, Federalism could command majorities in only four of sixteen states; within four years the shrinking rump could muster the electoral votes of only two states as their eminently respectable ticket of Charles

25. For an extended discussion of Jefferson's views on the nature of party and of a loyal opposition, see Richard Hofstadter, *The Idea of a Party System* (Berkeley, 1969).
26. Jefferson to Giles, March 23, 1801, Ford, 9:223–224.

Cotesworth Pinckney and Rufus King succumbed to the Jeffersonian juggernaut.

The Second American Revolution

Jefferson saw the victory of the Republican movement as constituting a "second American revolution," or at the very least the culmination and vindication of the first. March 4, 1801, represented in his eyes a revolution in American government fully as momentous as that of 1776. Not only did it witness a peaceful transfer of power from one political faction to another, an event of no little import in the history of free government. It represented as well a return to first principles after the long night of Federalist apostasy. The president breathed an almost audible sigh of relief as he observed to his friend, Joseph Priestley: "What an effort, my dear Sir, of bigotry in Politics and Religion have we gone through! The barbarians really flattered themselves they should be able to bring the time of Vandalism, when ignorance put everything into the hands of power and priestcraft."[27]

The Republican victory was reactionary only in the formal sense that it was a movement of restoration. To Jefferson and his supporters the Republican movement was progressive, not retrogressive. The principles it sought to restore to government were enlightened principles, principles of human liberation that had been distorted and nearly betrayed by the "temporary insanity" that had swept the country in the course of the Federalist sway. Federalism had imperiled the progressive experiment for which so many had struggled and died, and for this it could not be forgiven. Jefferson denounced as "Gothic" the notion that "we are to look backwards instead of forwards . . . to the annals of our ancestors for what is most perfect in government." He described his victory in 1800 as a "new establishment of republicanism." In an earlier letter to Priestley he reflected on the significance of recent events:

As the storm is now subsiding, and the horizon becoming serene, it is pleasant to consider the phenomenon with attention. We can no longer say there is nothing new under the sun. For this whole chapter in the history of man is new. The great extent of our Republic is new. Its sparse habitation is new. The mighty wave of public opinion which has rolled over it is new. But the most pleasing novelty is, its so quickly subsiding over such an extensive surface to

27. Jefferson to Dr. Joseph Priestley, March 21, 1801, *ibid.*, p. 217.

its true level again. The order and good sense displayed in this recovery from delusion . . . really bespeak a strength of character in our nation which augurs well for the duration of our Republic.[28]

Richard Ellis has observed that the years 1775–1815 constitute in many ways a unified whole, with the dates representing the beginning and the end of the American Revolution. The period marks an attempt to come to terms with the meaning of the Revolution and to make the society and its institutions reflect the democratic character of the revolutionary assumptions.[29] To Jefferson at the beginning of the century, the purpose of this "second revolution" was to democratize the country, to turn political control over to the people's representatives, and to make the national political institutions truly popular in character and responsive in behavior. This was his overriding goal, the core of his presidential purpose. He saw his election as the first step in a process that would sweep away the gilded encrustations of monarchy and privilege which befouled the administrations of his predecessors. He would restore a sense of responsibility and legitimacy to popular institutions and make them truly reflective of popular will.

A common thread running through the fabric of Jefferson's philosophy and, indeed, through the public philosophy of his day is the concept of mission. Dumas Malone has written: "Nothing was more characteristic of the Patriots at the birth of the Republic than the conviction that the American people were unique in their character, their opportunity, and their mission, and that their experiment in self-government was destined to set an example for the world. To that faith and vision Jefferson purposed that the country should return."[30] As we glance back from the world-weary perspective of a more complex age, we may well wonder at the naïveté of his faith in man's capacity for self-rule. We may shake our heads in bemusement at his conviction of the possibility of small government, of an agrarian economy, of the efficacy of education in improving the lot of mankind. Nevertheless, Jefferson articulated and symbolized a set of ideals that at the time seemed more possible of attainment than at any time before or since; a dream, in Lewis Mumford's words, of a "new world

28. Jefferson to Priestley, January 27, 1801, *ibid.*, p. 104; see also Jefferson to Elbridge Gerry, January 26, 1799, cited above; to R. R. Livingston, December 14, 1800, p. 153.

29. Ellis, p. 194.

30. *Jefferson the President: First Term, 1801–1805* (Boston, 1970), p. xvii.

utopia." Central to this dream was the belief that formal civilization had somehow gone astray, that its most successful institutions had somehow retarded rather than enhanced the full development of man. Mumford has described in modern language the core of assumptions that formed part of the climate of Jeffersonian opinion:

The State, the official religion, the bureaucracy, the army, these resurgent institutions of civilization were capable indeed of effecting great constructive transformations of the environment, but the human price of their success was heavy; the class structure, the lifetime fixation of function, the monopoly of land and economic and educational opportunity, the inequality of property and privilege, the chronic savagery of slavery and war. . . . Such constant miscarriages of power and organization offset the genuine claims that could be made for the system, and raised serious questions. . . . These doubts encouraged the notion that if only the past institutions and structures of civilization were destroyed, men would be happy, virtuous, and free.[31]

The colonization of the new world was in part based on such assumptions. The founding of a new nation on the North American continent took place within and as a response to a climate of opinion in which the concept of creating a wholly new human experience was controlling. Jefferson came to believe in and embody a return to first principles, to simpler ways of existence, to a more pristine environment, as liberating man from the prison of his own institutions. A whole complex of evils subsumed under the codeword "monarchy" had to be eradicated in order to realize the principles of the revolutionary struggle. In his own mind "monarchism" and "Federalism" became almost interchangeable terms to describe the problem to be resolved.[32] The definition of the problem and the marshaling of forces and designing of strategies to overcome it marked the dimensions of Jefferson's purpose as he assumed the office of president.

31. *The Pentagon of Power: The Myth of the Machine* (New York, 1970), pp. 22–23.
32. See, for example, the *Anas* of Jefferson, the pages of which are filled with criticisms, some of a most bitter kind, of the monarchical posturings of the Federalist leaders: Franklin B. Sawvel, ed., *The Anas of Thomas Jefferson* (New York, 1903), especially, pp. 35–37, 84, 110–111, 183, and 190–191.

CHAPTER 3

The Nature and Scope of the Executive Role

As Jefferson made clear in his inaugural address and from his early conduct as president, he intended no sweeping alterations in the existing constitutional arrangements, despite the hopes of radical members of his own party. He had pledged to preserve the general government "in its whole constitutional vigor, as the sheet anchor of our peace at home and safety abroad," and though a shift was to occur in the locus of power from the appointive to the elective agencies of government in accordance with the intent to popularize the system, there was to be no wholesale revamping of constitutional machinery.

In no institution of government was this decision for basic continuity more evident than in the presidency. While accepting and at times promoting the view that the legislature occupied a special place in the minds and hearts of all good republicans, Jefferson never accepted the more extreme belief in legislative *supremacy*. His conception was rather of a balanced federal system with an equilibrium of powers divided between the general government and the states and a similar adjustment of powers among the coordinate branches of the central government. His concern to preserve the separation of powers led him first as secretary of state and later as president to a firm defense of the independence and parity of the executive vis-à-vis the legislative and (especially) the judicial branches. It was his intention to remold the executive into a more popular instrument of government. No longer would the president yield by default to Congress the role of the people's advocate.

It is not going too far to assert, with Leonard White, that the Jeffersonians maintained the essence of the Federalist (although not the Hamiltonian) concept of executive power.[1] Hamilton, in fact, was among those who recognized that Jefferson was not opposed to the firm exercise of executive authority. In an oblique criticism of John Marshall's charge that Jefferson would weaken the office by a too slavish devotion to the House of Representatives, Jefferson's former cabinet colleague observed: "It is not true, as is alleged, that he [Jefferson] is for confounding all the powers in the House of Representatives. It is a fact which I have frequently mentioned, that while we were in the administration together, he was generally for a large construction of the Executive authority and not backward to act upon it in cases which coincided with his views. Let it be added that in his theoretic ideas he has considered as improper the participation of the Senate in the Executive Authority."[2] Hamilton's testimony is evidence against the charge that Jefferson's respect for a strong executive was newly discovered. His concern to assert executive independence and his concern about unbridled legislative supremacy were, in fact, both of long standing. His experience as war governor of Virginia when, with few powers and little independence of authority, he was responsible for defending his state against invasion caused him to have a dread of executive responsibility without power and of legislative omnipotence without responsibility. Later, as secretary of state, he was in a position to observe, welcome, and encourage the firm exercise of executive hegemony that President Washington exhibited in the conduct of foreign relations.[3]

But while it is true that Jefferson accepted the notion of a strong and independent executive, in its relationship to the people Jefferson's presidency nevertheless marked a significant departure in philosophy from those of his two predecessors. It remains one of Jefferson's principal contributions to the development of the office that he indicated

1. *The Jeffersonians* (New York, 1951), p. 30.
2. Hamilton to James A. Bayard, January 16, 1801, in Henry Cabot Lodge, ed., *The Works of Alexander Hamilton* (New York, 1904), 10:413. At the time of the Constitutional Convention Jefferson was uncertain as to the question of a plural or single executive. Discussions with Madison and others, however, coupled with the knowledge of the sad experiences of states which had experimented with plural executives soon convinced him that "for the prompt, clear and consistent action so necessary in an executive, unity of person is necessary with us" (Jefferson to John Adams, February 28, 1796, Ford, 8: 218).
3. For a detailed account of his trials as governor of Virginia, see Peterson, *Thomas Jefferson*, pp. 166–241.

its potentiality as an engine for constructive change should its authority ever be planted firmly upon a base of popular support. This
sense of the presidency as a popular office may be said to have emerged
from Jefferson's radical conception of American power and purpose.
The strength of the American government, he believed, grew not out
of the vigor of a centralized administration, nor from the martial might
of military force, nor from any aristocratic display of ministerial splen-
dor and authority. It emerged most directly out of the "affections of the
people," the true strength of democratic government resting in its
legitimacy in the eyes of its citizenry. While agreeing with Hamilton
that to be effective a government must have the capacity to be energetic, Jefferson denied that this energy was derived merely from the
perfection of its instruments of authority. As he wrote in March, 1801,
"a free government is of all others the most energetic . . . ; the inquiry
which has been excited among the masses of mankind by our revolution and its consequences" will provide the stimulation by pledging
the betterment of "the conditions of man over a great portion of the
globe."[4] Instruments of authority were necessary, to be sure, but the
true, the lasting strength of a government emerges by its capture and
cultivation of the active interest and lasting affections of the whole
people.

Such a role concept of the presidency marked an important departure from the immediate past. The first two occupants of the office,
while not *anti*republican, saw the presidency essentially as a *non*-
republican invention inserted into the Constitution to temper the effects and counter the excesses of republicanism. George Washington's
understanding of his office seems not unlike that contained in
Bolingbroke's famous notion of the "patriot-king," a view to which the
more erudite John Adams clearly subscribed.[5] Washington stressed
the necessity for the chief magistrate to occupy a position apart from
and above the people, not too remote nor too regal, but sufficiently
distant to preserve the dignity of the office. He was unfailingly aware
that his every act might well establish for all time a precedent to bind
future presidents. As his biographer James T. Flexner put it, Washington believed that "if he behaved like an ordinary citizen, he would
damage the prestige needed to carry out the presidential office." In

4. *Ibid.*, p. 657; Jefferson to John Dickinson, March 6, 1801, Ford, 9: 201.
5. See John Adams, "Discourses on Davila," in George A. Peek, Jr., ed., *The
Political Writings of John Adams* (New York, 1954), pp. 192–193.

addition, he strove to remain somewhat removed from active involvement in the murky waters of popular politics. He was enough the child of his colonial youth to reflect an image of the head of state as a figure above faction, a force for unity, a lofty arbiter much in the nature of a constitutional monarch whose function it was to reign as well as to rule. Washington never believed it to be a proper function of the president to influence legislative debates. His respect for the legislative branch as the "prime mover" was to his credit as a good republican, but nonetheless is noteworthy in light of the criticism some have leveled at Jefferson for his deference to Congress. As Flexner writes, "the separation of powers has never known a more devoted champion" than Washington. "The election of the different branches of Congress by the freemen, either directly or indirectly," wrote the first president, "is the pivot on which turns the first wheel of government, a wheel which communicates motion to all the rest."[6] The presidency, despite the obligation to recommend measures and the right to veto, was not seen as an integral part of the legislative process, nor was Washington prepared to argue that the executive possessed, or could possess, any relationship to the people more special or more direct than that which was enjoyed by the members of Congress.

To Washington's idea of the president as a republican "patriot-king" his secretary of the Treasury gave a ready assent. While Washington lent to the presidential office the strength of his great prestige and character, Alexander Hamilton contributed to the executive branch his own sizable talents for administrative innovation. Hamilton was fond of the British system of ministerial government (as he but imperfectly understood it) and conceived of himself as an unofficial "first minister." Deriving his legitimacy indirectly from his appointment as Treasury secretary by the president, he quickly exploited his position to initiate legislation and shepherd it safely through Congress. Like Jefferson but unlike Washington, Hamilton perceived that Congress could not provide its own motive power; to be effective in any sustained and purposeful way it would have to be led from without. Hamilton assumed the role of administration spokesman to Congress, and for a time his leadership of the legislature was remarkably successful. Indeed, Hamiltonian initiatives in fiscal policy seemed to many to pose a threat to the traditional legislative prerogative over the purse.

6. James Thomas Flexner, *George Washington and the New Nation* (Boston, 1970), pp. 221, 168.

This scheme for executive (but not presidential) government by department heads was, for Hamilton, less consciously the result of a theory of executive power than it was a practical solution for gaining the policies he favored. As a long-term answer to the problem of bridging the separation of powers, moreover, the Hamiltonian design possessed a major flaw, one that Jefferson as president sensed and sought to correct. The limiting factor in Hamilton's ministerial concept was its lack of a popular base of legitimacy. It was not grounded in that support which comes in a republican form of government from direct responsibility to the people.

Jefferson realized that the separation of powers demanded executive leadership. He believed, however, that the more effective and responsible way to mobilize the government was through the employment of mechanisms rooted in a popular base. His own solution was at once more realistic and ultimately more effective than Hamilton's: use the president's leadership of the political party as a device to bridge the separation of powers, a means more consonant with a government of divided powers resting in a democratic polity than was Hamilton's concept of ministerial discretion. Jefferson recognized that an appointive first minister, lacking the electoral or parliamentary base that even then undergirded ministerial authority in Britain could never replace the president himself in the exercise of leadership. Furthermore, for a president to delegate the responsibility for ongoing policy leadership to another ignored a fact of political life which Jefferson sensed and which has been effectively expressed more recently by Richard Neustadt: that the president occupies a unique position of authority precisely because no other man, not even a trusted "first" minister, sits where he sits; no other man in government possesses quite as comprehensive a sense of the totality of events, combined with the unavoidable responsibility for action. Jefferson made the point well in his first inaugural address: "I shall often go wrong through defect of judgment; where right, I shall often be thought wrong by those whose positions will not command a view of the whole ground. I ask your . . . support against the errors of others who may condemn what they would not if seen in all its parts."

By replacing ministerial direction with presidential direction, and by preferring party leadership to purely administrative leadership, Jefferson's role concept combined the constitutional powers of the presidency with a "political" power grounded on popular support.[7] He sensed, as Washington and Hamilton did not, the tremendous sources of legitimate strength upon which a president could draw when he rested his authority more directly upon a popular mandate. "In a government like ours, it is the duty of the Chief Magistrate, in order to enable himself to do all the good which his station requires, to unite *in himself* the confidence of the whole people. This alone, in any case where the energy of the nation is required, can produce a union of the powers of the whole, and point them in a single direction, as if all constituted but one body and one mind."[8]

Jefferson's republicanism and his Whig heritage made him ever an advocate of limited government, but he also realized the importance of a source within that government for strength and unity "in any case where the energy of the nation is required." For a president to mobilize popular support through the party in Congress and in the states was, he believed, a more suitably democratic, and ultimately more effective, technique than a reliance on narrowly administrative methods. Jefferson's creation of the presidential role of party leader served as a way station on the road to the president's full assumption of his role as popular leader. It remained for Jackson, Lincoln, Wilson, and the two Roosevelts to develop more fully the image of the president as the "tribune" or "steward" of the people. Nevertheless, sensing the resources for leadership available to a president whose authority rested on popular support, Jefferson moved within the limits of his own political experience and the climate of opinion of his time to create a new role for the chief executive and by so doing to develop a new relationship between president and people.

The Cultivation of a Republican Image

Murray Edelman has written, "A leader who is regarded as the epitome of his times is necessarily an artful exponent of the quality of his setting."[9] Jefferson attempted to expand the horizon of presidential influence by dramatizing the linkages between the office and popular

7. See Caldwell, *Administrative Theories*, p. 210.
8. Jefferson to Garland Jefferson, January 25, 1810, Ford 11: 133, emphasis added.
9. *The Symbolic Uses of Politics* (Urbana, Ill., 1964), p. 105.

opinion and by cultivating his own image as a man of the people. In numerous ways he worked to strip the office of many of its "monarchical" trappings, feeling as he did that the return to republican values should begin in the Executive Mansion. He did not emulate Washington by employing a coach and four with liveried outriders in the capital city, but chose to ride astride with only a lone servant in attendance. (The quality of the roads in the raw young capital on the Potomac may have had something to do with this decision.) His personal appearance reflected a conscious attempt to stress republican simplicity; in fact he carried simplicity of dress to the point of offending some who felt his appearance unsuitable for a head of state. "The President was in an undress-Blue coat, red vest . . . white hose, ragged slippers, with his toes out, clean linnen [sic], but hair disheveled," observed William Plumer. Even at his best the president simply could not measure up to the senator's standards: "I found the President dressed better than I ever saw him at any time when I called on a morning visit. Though his coat was old and threadbare, his scarlet vest, his corduroy small clothes, and his white hose were new and clean—but his linnen was much soiled and his slippers old." His critics sensed what he was attempting in affecting such a mode of dress, however, for Plumer grumbled that it would probably be considered as suitable "court dress" for the "democratic" administration.[10]

Indeed, others more favorably disposed toward the president, found his style of attire and manner of behavior perfectly suitable for the first magistrate of a republic. To Margaret Bayard Smith, his dress, "if plain, unstudied, and sometimes old-fashioned in its form, was always of the finest materials; in his personal habits he was always fastidiously neat." Mrs. Smith found his simplicity never to "degenerate into vulgarity, nor his affability into familiarity."[11]

In other ways the president sought to remove the "monocratic" features from the executive. His decision to submit his first annual message to Congress in writing rather than deliver it in person was a

10. *Memorandum*, November 29, 1805, p. 296; November 10, 1804, p. 193.
11. *First Forty Years*, p. 386. Of course, Jefferson the Virginia aristocrat could be the soul of grace when the occasion demanded it. In the opinion of the rather foppish comedic actor, John Bernard, Jefferson had few equals in social discourse. In relating a story at dinner, "Jefferson displayed the grace and brilliance of a courtier." And with the ladies, said Bernard, the president's refinement "had the veritable odor of Versailles" (*Retrospectives of America, 1797–1811* [New York, 1887], pp. 241–242).

calculated political act designed to underline the return to sound republican simplicity. The decision came after extensive discussions
with Republican leaders and seems to have been reached as early as
seven months before the delivery of the address, precisely to reduce
the "relics" left by the Federalists.[12]

Some of his efforts to develop a pattern of republican simplicity ran
afoul of deep-seated and politically sensitive patterns of traditional
behavior, and none had more political repercussions in official Washington than the president's decision to simplify diplomatic protocol
and official etiquette. The furor that surrounded these innovations
centered around the experiences of the British envoy, Anthony Merry,
and his wife. That unfortunate man suffered the first of a series of
indignities shortly after his arrival at the capital when he appeared at
the Executive Mansion in full court dress to present his credentials to
the President of the United States. He was received by Jefferson
dressed in his "usual morning attire," which to an impressionable
young diplomat accustomed to the ceremony of a European court
could only be interpreted as a calculated insult. Other affronts occurred in rapid succession, from the "impossible" requirement that
foreign envoys make the first visit to heads of departments to the
"shocking" omission of all distinctions of rank at the president's dinners. The minor tempest tossed by the minister and his imperious wife
provided Washington gossips with hours of delightful scandal and
caused the president much annoyance. The incidents did serve, however, to impress upon foreign diplomats and, more important, the
American people the egalitarian nature of the new administration. As
a former envoy himself, Jefferson was hardly ignorant of protocol
practices in Europe. His decision to abolish them at home, though it
disrupted the capital city's social harmony for a time, was a calculated

12. Nathaniel Macon wrote to Jefferson in April that "the people expect . . . that
the communication to the next Congress will be by letter, not a speech" (April 20,
1801, *The Papers of Thomas Jefferson* [Microfilm edition, Library of Congress], No.
19198, hereafter referred to as LC). Jefferson replied a month later assuring Macon
that such would be the case (May 14, 1801, Ford, 8:52). Jefferson wished to avoid as
well the time-consuming and politically sensitive practice of previous administrations
whereby the president delivered an address, Congress in turn prepared, debated,
voted, and delivered a reply to the address, and the president, in his turn, delivered a
formal reply to the reply! See Jefferson to Dr. Benjamin Rush, December 20, 1802,
ibid., 9:343–346.

and effective political ploy carried out in furtherance of his effort to chart a new role for the chief executive of a democratic republic.[13]

The Chief Executive in the Federal System

As a believer in a simple government of limited powers, Jefferson was a consistent advocate of decentralization and a firm defender of the federal arrangement. Of decentralization he had written, "It is by this partition of cares descending in gradation from general to particular, that the mass of human affairs may be best managed for the good and prosperity of all."[14] In his mind there was a neat division of public concerns between domestic and "foreign" matters (under which latter classification he included interstate relations), and this division seemed to correspond nicely to the subdivisions within the federal system. Jefferson hoped to preserve a balanced distribution of powers between the national and state governments, realizing that the only way to prevent a slow drift of authority to the central government was to insure the full and effective employment of their powers by the states. To this end he sought as president a cordial and close relationship with the state governors. In the course of developing his concept of the presidency, he searched for ways to improve the working relations between the governors and the national executive, even to the consideration of an annual message to the governors, patterned on the annual State of the Union message to Congress, to advise the states of needed measures that their legislatures alone could enact. This idea was abandoned chiefly because of continuing Federalist control in several states, but Jefferson's concern to include the state governments in the planning and execution of public policy was one he never abandoned.[15]

In his personal dealings with the governors, as with foreign envoys, Jefferson sought to promote the facilitation of business at the expense of formality. As he told James Monroe (then governor of Virginia), he preferred to adopt the practice of President Washington as to the mode of correspondence between the two executives. The president might

13. Minister James Monroe in London had to suffer through the chill of a London social season "in Coventry" while the British government retaliated for the treatment of Merry. See Harry Ammon, *James Monroe: The Quest for National Identity* (New York, 1971), pp. 228–229.

14. Ford, 1:123.

15. Jefferson to Gov. James Sullivan, June 19, 1807, *ibid.*, 10:420–421.

write directly to the governors if business dictated it, otherwise governors could correspond with department heads. Were there to arise a need for stricter adherence to form in a case involving rights "transferred by the Constitution to the general government, the general executive is certainly preordinate—e.g., in a question concerning the militia, and others easily to be recollected." In such a case, "the governor must be subject to receive orders from the War Department, as any other subordinate officer would." In cases where foreign or interstate matters were at issue, Jefferson took for granted that the national government was supreme; where the "independent or reserved" rights of the state were involved, the two executives were seen as "each the supreme head of an independent government."[16] This overly neat picture was soon to be obscured by political realities. Nevertheless, Jefferson's conscientious effort to preserve a constitutional balance in federal-state relations and his concern to underscore the importance and cultivate the *amour propre* of the governors was to redound to his credit in the years to come, particularly as the success of his party was to place in most of these positions men who owed him thus a double allegiance.

The Defense of Executive Independence

While Jefferson was concerned to preserve a balance where balance was called for, in those areas where the authority of the national government was clear he would grant powers as broad as the national interest required, particularly in areas where his own presidential powers were dominant. He never doubted that to be effective the president must possess the power to act promptly and with vigor when occasion demanded it. He had favored the Constitution of 1787 because it had provided for a government with powers more commensurate with its responsibilities than had prevailed under the Confederation.

As Hamilton had pointed out, Jefferson as secretary of state was zealously protective of the independence of the executive from encroachments by the other branches of government. In the 1790's he had upheld the authority of the president to make appointments to office with as little interference from the upper house of Congress as possible, advising President Washington that, in his opinion, "The

16. Jefferson to Monroe, May 29, 1801, *ibid.*, 9:260–262.

Senate is not supposed by the Constitution to be acquainted with the concerns of the Executive Department. It was not intended that these should be communicated, nor can they therefore be qualified to judge of the necessity which calls for a mission to any particular place, or of the particular grade. . . . All this is left to the President. They are only to see that no unfit person be employed."[17]

As president, Jefferson reaffirmed his earlier position. Writing to Gallatin in 1803, he confessed:

I have always considered the control of the Senate as meant to prevent any bias or favoritism in the President toward his own relations, his own religion, toward particular states, etc., and perhaps to keep very obnoxious persons out of offices of the first grade. But in all subordinate cases I have ever thought that the selection made by the President ought to inspire a general confidence that it has been made on due inquiry and investigation of character, and that the Senate should impose its negative only in those particular cases where something happens within their knowledge, against the character of the person and unfitting him for the appointment. To Mr. Tracy [a Federalist Senator] at any rate, no exhibition or information of recommendation ought to be communicated. To exhibit recommendations would be to turn the Senate into a court of honor, or a court of slander, and to subject the character of every man nominated to an ordeal without his own consent.[18]

This strong view did not prevent Jefferson from violating his own rule concerning the availability of letters of recommendation for congressional scrutiny if it suited his purposes. For example, he sent a packet of confidential papers to Senator Giles on the nomination of William Pinkney as minister to Britain, cautioning the senator to make discreet use of them without revealing their source, "knowing as you do the invidious sensations produced in others by any *known* discrimination of confidants." But it remained the president's right to control outside access to "privileged" information. He consistently acted on the belief that while Congress might legitimately call for papers, the executive should refuse to submit those "the disclosure of which would injure the public." The judgment of public injury, furthermore, lay with the president exclusively.[19]

17. Jefferson to Washington, April 24, 1790, Lipscomb, 3:17.
18. Jefferson to Gallatin, February 10, 1803, Ford, 9:443–444; see also Jefferson to Uriah Tracy, January, 1806, 10: 218–219.
19. Jefferson to Giles, February 20, 1808, LC No. 27473, emphasis in the original. See also Jefferson to Samuel Kercheval, July 12, 1816, Lipscomb, 15:37, for evidence that Jefferson continued to hold that nomination to office "is an executive function."

Presidential independence from Congress could not be maintained unless the president preserved his authority within his own branch. Jefferson objected to the heads of departments receiving orders or requests from Congress directly. He denied that a congressional committee or indeed the House itself "had a right to call on the Head of a department who or whose papers were under the President alone, but that the committee should instruct their chairman to move the House to address the President."[20]

Jefferson also asserted executive independence from the dictates of the judiciary by his strong claims of executive privilege for himself and his closest advisers. In Chapter 6 we will examine his famous refusal to be subpoenaed by the Court in the Aaron Burr conspiracy trial. A year before the Burr case, the president ordered his cabinet officers to invoke a form of executive privilege after three of their number had been subpoenaed to give testimony in the New York trial of two men charged with illegal filibustering activities in Venezuela. The defendants had claimed that tacit sanction for the expedition had been given in discussions with the three cabinet officers. In a joint letter to the Court, the three declined to attend on the grounds that the president had forbidden it, lest the orderly process of government be disrupted by prolonged absence of nearly the entire cabinet from the seat of government (this despite the fact that the trial would have taken place in July and August when nearly everyone in official Washington fled the capital and its unhealthy climate). The Court prudently avoided the issue by ruling the secretaries' testimony irrelevant to the case.[21]

The Presidential Role in Foreign Relations

Jefferson's determination to use the powers that were clearly his was never more evident than in his attitude toward the conduct of foreign relations. Henry Adams, whose famous *History* of the Jefferson administration was to set the early pattern of interpretation of his presidency, characterized Jefferson's ideas of presidential authority in foreign affairs as "little short of royal." We need not accept Adams's conclusion as to Jefferson's motives, that "he loved the sense of power and the

---

20. *Anas*, March 12, 1792, p. 70; April 2, 1792, p. 71. This excluded the secretary of the Treasury, whose statutory relationship to Congress differed from that of the other department heads.

21. Irving Brant, *Madison: Secretary of State, 1801–1809* (Indianapolis, 1953), pp. 335–337.

freedom from oversight which diplomacy gave," to agree that the Republican president's view of executive authority in this area was unequivocal.

"Foreign affairs are executive altogether," he had written as secretary of state. The statement echoes the description of executive powers found in Locke's *Second Treatise on Government*, where it is made clear that in the conduct of foreign affairs the executive is not simply putting into effect the laws passed by the legislative, but is rather exercising a wholly separate function. To Locke, the purely executive nature of the "power of war and peace, Leagues and Alliances, and all the transactions, with all Persons and Communities without the Commonwealth" was not in doubt.[22]

Jefferson agreed with this interpretation wholeheartedly, with the exception of the "war" power, which was constitutionally to be shared with Congress. He accepted as unequivocal grants of power the constitutional provisions relative to the president's power to conduct the foreign relations of the United States. He recognized, of course, the constitutional right of the Senate with regard to treaties and appointments, and he was careful to attend to senatorial sensibilities in these as in other areas. There was never any doubt in his mind or in the minds of those with whom he dealt, however, that the preponderance of authority and responsibility lay with the president alone. Jefferson's correspondence reveals numerous illustrations of his guardianship of presidential prerogatives. Shortly after assuming office he issued an executive order restoring to France certain prizes taken at sea by American warships after the ratification of the French treaty. In soliciting Madison's opinion of the action, taken without consulting Congress, the president declared that "the executive, charged with our exterior relations, seems bound, is satisfied of the fact, to do right to the foreign nations, and take on itself the risque [sic] of justification." Less than a year later in referring to a similar action, Jefferson informed Congress that the decision whether and in what manner to deliver a ship under the treaty with a foreign government "was of

22. Henry Adams, *The History of the United States during the Administration of Thomas Jefferson* (New York, 1930), 1:245; John Locke, *Second Treatise on Government* (New York, 1965), Book XII, para. 146, p. 411. Locke, of course, drew an analytical distinction between the executive power proper and the *federative* power of war and peace, but as the same individual was to exercise both powers, the distinction is lost in practice. For a discussion of this point see M. J. C. Vile, *Constitutionalism and the Separation of Powers* (New York, 1967), pp. 60–62.

executive cognizance entirely and without appeal." Congress had no right, the president warned, even to ask for the reasons for the decision and should they persist "our duty will be to resist it."[23]

With regard to the related but constitutionally distinct question of the "war" powers, Jefferson's views of executive prerogative were tempered by the reality of congressional powers. Aware that only Congress could declare war and sensible as well of congressional authority over the "purse strings" in raising and equipping military forces, he took care that his conduct in defending American interests when and where they were attacked would be such as would indicate a respect for the ultimate responsibility of the legislative branch. He never doubted that the power of the executive extended to repelling a sudden attack by an enemy. Whether that power went further, however, and included the duty to "go beyond the line of defense" and take counteroffensive action against an aggressor was a question much debated in the executive council. Early in his first term following an attack against an American warship by Barbary corsairs, Jefferson asked Congress to authorize "measures of offense" so as to "place our force on an equal footing with that of its adversaries." Perhaps the most pacific of his cabinet advisors, Albert Gallatin, argued for a more aggressive response: "The Executive cannot declare war, but if war is made, whether declared by Congress or by the enemy, the conduct must be the same, to protect our vessels, and to fight, take, and destroy the armed vessels of the enemy." In the secretary's view, the limit of response in each case should not be determined by constitutional scruples, but by "the power we have at our disposal" in the theater of operations.[24]

While American foreign policy in the Jefferson years was decidedly presidential, that policy was based on a conviction that the nation would prosper best under a posture of isolation and neutrality. Jefferson stated his hopes for his country in the world with a decidedly non-Napoleonic beatitude: " . . . more blest is that nation whose silent

23. Jefferson to Madison, July 15, 1801, Ford, 9:278; to Giles, April 6, 1802, pp. 361–362.
24. Gallatin to Jefferson, August 16, 1802, Gallatin, *Writings*, 1:89. See also Gallatin's notes on the president's second annual message to Congress where he opposes as unnecessary the attempt to obtain legislative sanction to act offensively in the case of war waged by the Barbary pirates (p. 105). Jefferson's request of Congress is found in J. D. Richardson, ed., *The Messages and Papers of the Presidents* (New York, 1917), 1:315.

course of happiness furnishes nothing for history to say." In the optimism of his first days in office, the president outlined the principles of his foreign policy to Dr. George Logan: "It ought to be the very first object of our pursuits to have nothing to do with European interests and politics. Let them be free or slaves at will, navigators or agricultural, swallowed into one government or divided into a thousand, we have nothing to fear from them in any form." He followed this assertion with an expression of that grand delusion which was to form the basis of the embargo policy in the last years of office: "Our commerce is so valuable to them that they will be glad to purchase it when the only price we ask is to do us justice. I believe we have in our own hands the means of peaceable coercion."[25]

The purpose of such a foreign policy, seen by Jefferson as representing in effect a return to the neutrality pursued by the Washington administration, was to provide a breathing spell for the fledgling nation, to give it time to grow and prosper and to consolidate its successes in self-government. To accomplish this task it was necessary, as Jefferson told Thomas Paine, to "avoid if possible wasting the energies of our people in war and destruction."[26] The foundation of his thinking was the conviction, again, that a new world and a new way of life which he saw dawning in the Western Hemisphere could be preserved only if the nation could sit out the costly dance of power politics that exercised the Powers of Europe. Rejecting the Hamiltonian concept of national greatness based on traditional measures of military and economic might, Jefferson dismissed the view that the best interests of the United States could be attained by placing its slight weight on the scales of the international balance of power.

It was doubly unfortunate, given such aims, that save for a few brief months of uneasy peace, nearly the whole of Jefferson's presidency was to be spent under the threat of war. The military conflict between France and Britain, their allies and satellites, and the implications of that conflict for American commerce and national security required the president to lay aside his calculated indifference to the affairs of Europe. Never surrendering his hopes for preserving peace through neutrality, Jefferson felt nevertheless compelled to defend the vital

---

25. Jefferson to Comte Diodate, March 29, 1807, Lipscomb, 11:181–182; to Logan, March 21, 1801, Ford, 9:219–220.

26. Jefferson to Thomas Paine, March 18, 1801, *ibid.*, pp. 212–214.

interests of his country whenever they were directly threatened by Great Power activities.

The Case of Louisiana

When one searches the landscape of events for examples of presidential protection of these vital interests, one's eye comes naturally to rest on the high ground of the Louisiana Purchase. No other measure of Jefferson's administration so captured the public imagination, and no other policy initiative so significantly affected the character of the nation as did the acquisition of this vast land. The prospect of gaining territory that more than doubled the size of the country at first dazzled, then delighted the American people. The fact that such an empire had been gained peacefully served to vindicate the faith of the Founders, Jefferson preeminent among them, that "truth and reason have been more powerful than the sword."[27]

It will not be our purpose to describe in detail the chain of events that culminated in the Purchase. An examination of certain of its salient aspects, however, will serve to illustrate some of the assumptions that governed Jefferson's understanding of his executive responsibilities, and will thus shed some light upon the quality of his presidential leadership.

As president and as leader of his party Jefferson sought to dispel the sectionalist image of his political movement implied by the opposition's pejorative label, "the Virginia Party." He appointed only one Virginian to his cabinet, filling it instead with New England and Middle Atlantic men; much of his time in the first year of his presidency was devoted to staffing the federal posts in the New England states so as to broaden the base of his party. Nevertheless, the election of the Jeffersonians clearly represented the "arrival" of the emerging agrarian and frontier interests of the South and West to parity with the older commercial and financial interests of the East that had hitherto controlled national politics. Jefferson knew that the men of the South and West formed the backbone of his support, and he was determined to secure the economic prosperity and security of the frontier regions.

Of vital importance to the protection of those interests was an assured access to the port of entry at New Orleans for western goods transported down the Mississippi River. The protection of the right of

27. *National Intelligencer* of Washington, July 8, 1803.

deposit became, therefore, a key provision of Jefferson's foreign policy. Although the ideal solution to the problem was American possession of the port of New Orleans, the administration felt that as long as the port remained in the weak hands of Spain American interests could be safeguarded. Should the river mouth ever become the property of a more "energetic" foreign power, however, the prospects for future strife would be greatly increased.]

It was with alarm, therefore, that Jefferson and Madison learned in the spring of 1802 of the retrocession of Louisiana from Spain to France. It had been the president's task to steer a safe course between the treacherous reefs of British and French power, and in 1801–1802 the greatest danger by far seemed to arise from Napoleon. French interference with American trade in the West Indies, particularly in Santo Domingo, as well as private American aid to the rebels on that island, had increased the tensions between the two former allies. The new administration was under increasing pressure from New England merchants to demand a normalization of trade with the French possessions, and Jefferson, seeking as always to cultivate his political strength in this Federalist stronghold, had managed to placate the merchants while keeping a French army tied down on Santo Domingo fighting the American-assisted rebellion. With the retrocession of Louisiana it became imperative to prevent that French army from proceeding to take possession of New Orleans.

The administration took pains to apprise the French Government of the ominous nature of its activities in the Gulf. Secretary of State Madison cautioned that Louisiana in French hands would "cause daily collisions." Jefferson was even more blunt, warning that Napoleon's possession of Louisiana would drive the United States into the arms of England. The president brashly asserted that the French would remain in New Orleans "no longer than it pleases the United States."[28]

In April, 1802, Jefferson informed the American minister in Paris, Robert Livingston, of administration thinking in the matter. "There is on the globe one single spot, the possessor of which is our natural and habitual enemy. It is New Orleans." In the hands of France, with the "impetuousity of her temper, the energy and restlessness of her character," the area poses a serious threat. "The day that France takes posses-

28. Brant, pp. 66, 73. For the diplomatic considerations, see pp. 93ff. The *Aurora* reported an offhand remark by the president to the same effect at one of his dinners.

sion of New Orleans . . . seals the union of two nations who in conjunction can maintain exclusive possession of the ocean. From that moment we must marry ourselves to the British fleet and nation." Dreading the consequences of such a development for American independence and long-term security, however, Jefferson spoke of the still strong sympathies of the American people for the French, stemming from their common struggle in the War of Independence. Livingston was instructed to inform the French government that it was in their power to remove "the causes of jarring and irritation" by ceding New Orleans and the Floridas to the United States, or at the very least giving ironclad assurances that the right of deposit for American goods at New Orleans would not be disturbed.[29]

In the autumn, spurred by Spanish suspension of this precious right, Jefferson dispatched James Monroe to Paris with full powers to negotiate the purchase of New Orleans and the Floridas. The story of the negotiations in Paris is well known and need not be repeated here. From the beginning of talks with the French, the administration was prepared to purchase the port of New Orleans and the Floridas. The constitutional question of the right of the United States to acquire new territory had been discussed in cabinet and settled to Jefferson's satisfaction, at least for a time, well before Monroe sailed for Europe. Attorney General Levi Lincoln, a New Englander, had perhaps reflected his region's reluctance to see new territorial acquisitions in the West when he urged a narrow construction of the power to acquire territory. Gallatin spoke for most of his colleagues, however, in rejecting this crabbed interpretation of American sovereignty. In the Treasury secretary's view, the United States "as a nation have an inherent right to acquire territory." Furthermore, "whenever that acquisition is by treaty, the same constituted authorities in whom the treaty-making power is vested have a constitutional right to sanction the acquisition . . . the power of acquiring territory is delegated to the United States by the several provisions which authorize the several branches of the government to make war, to make treaties, and to govern the territory of the Union." Jefferson agreed that there seemed no constitutional difficulty in acquiring the territory. "Whether, when acquired, it may be taken into the Union by the Constitution as it now stands, will

29. Jefferson to Livingston, April 18, 1802, Ford, 9:365.

become a matter of *expediency.* I think it will be safer not to permit the
enlargement of the Union but by amendment of the Constitution."[30]

The president was plainly eager to settle the question of trade access
to the Gulf ports once and for all and wished no constitutional questions to interfere with this object. He was prepared to take sterner
measures, in fact, should the Paris negotiations fail. By the late spring
of 1803, the cabinet had agreed not to accept a mere assurance by the
French of the right of deposit "or any improvement of it short of the
sovereignty of the island of New Orleans." The direct seizure of New
Orleans was contemplated should negotiations break down.[31]

The atmosphere of *realpolitik* evidenced in this contingency session
should give pause to those who would see Jefferson simply as a pacifist
whose conduct of foreign relations was governed almost exclusively by
a passionate search for any alternative to war. He did have a keen
desire for peace as the central condition for the success of all his plans.
He always considered himself, furthermore, an antiimperialist, and his
sense of the American "mission" called not for physical expansion but
a moral hegemony through force of example. Nevertheless, a clear
understanding of his conduct as president must give full attention to
the Jefferson who could demand New Orleans as a matter of right,
cheerfully accept all of Louisiana in language which presaged the
years of "manifest destiny," and intrigue for the acquisition of Florida
by peaceful means or otherwise.[32]

When word reached Washington on July 3, 1803, of the acquisition
not of New Orleans but of all Louisiana, Jefferson was delighted. He
quickly adjusted to the scope of the windfall and assured his two
envoys in Paris that they were fully justified in exceeding the letter of
their instructions. He rejoiced in the new territory, as he wrote John
Dickinson, because by giving the United States "sole dominion of the
Mississippi, it excludes those bickerings with foreign powers, which

30. Gallatin to Jefferson, January 13, 1803, Gallatin, *Writings*, 1:111–114; Jefferson to Gallatin, January, 1803, *ibid.*, p. 115, emphasis added.

31. *Anas*, May 7, 1803, p. 220.

32. For an example of the pacifist view, see Louis Sears, *Jefferson and the Embargo*
(Durham, N.C., 1927). For a description of Jefferson as among the first to articulate
the myth of the purity of America's international intentions, see Reinhold Niebuhr,
"The Social Myths of the Cold War," in his *Faith and Politics* (New York, 1968), p.
231. Jefferson called Louisiana an "Empire for Liberty" (Jefferson to Madison, April
22, 1809, quoted in Ammon, *Monroe*, p. 214).

we know of a certainty would have put us at war with France immediately; and it secures to us the course of a peaceable nation."[33]

Popular reaction to the purchase of Louisiana was overwhelmingly favorable. Celebrations and feasts were held throughout the country to toast the nation's good fortune and (not incidentally) to sing the praises of the leader responsible for this great achievement. Jefferson received the public credit for the activities of his envoys, and the months following the news of the Purchase marked the high-water mark of his presidency.[34]

Opposition to the treaty came almost exclusively from Federalists who questioned the French title to the land, pointed to the vaguely defined limits and extent of the cession, and argued the doubtful amenability of the inhabitants of the region to republican government. Underlying these arguments was the fear that this vast extension of uncultivated land would depress land values in the East and draw settlers away from the older parts of the country. Interestingly enough, few Federalists chose to emphasize the question of the constitutionality of the Purchase.[35]

There were in fact two aspects of the issue of constitutionality. We have noted the first, the constitutionality of acquiring territory by treaty, which had been answered earlier to Jefferson's satisfaction. The second aspect, the constitutionality of allowing citizenship for the new inhabitants and ultimate statehood for the newly acquired territory, was more difficult. In a provision of the Louisiana Treaty, the United States was pledged to incorporate the people of the area into the Union. This question had been left in abeyance by the administration, which did not wish to disturb congressional waters with such a question before the Paris negotiations had borne fruit. By late summer, 1803, doubts, perhaps prompted by the sheer magnitude of the contemplated action, had reappeared in Jefferson's mind even about the constitutionality of acquisition. In writing of this problem the president seemed to evoke as justification for his actions the argument contained in Chapter 14 of Locke's *Second Treatise*, "On Prerogative," with a pointed reference to the duty of the executive to transcend the

33. Jefferson to Dickinson, August 9, 1803, Ford, 10:28–29.

34. One such celebration held in the capital is described by Plumer, *Memorandum*, January 27, 1804, p. 123.

35. *Ibid.*, pp. 2, 6. For an excellent short discussion of the constitutional question, see Malone, *First Term*, chap. 7.

law if need be to further the public interest, throwing himself on the good judgment of the people to justify and legitimate his act.

The Executive in seizing the fugitive occurrence which so much advances the good of the country, have done an act beyond the Constitution. The Legislature in casting behind them metaphysical subtleties, and risking themselves like faithful servants, must ratify and pay for it, and throw themselves on their country for doing for them unauthorized what we know they would have done for themselves had they been in a situation to do it. It is the case of a guardian, investing the money of his ward in purchasing an important adjacent territory; and saying to him when of age, I did this for your own good; I pretend no right to bind you; you may disavow me, and I must get out of the scrape as I can; I thought it my duty to risk myself for you. But we shall not be disavowed by the nation, and their act of indemnity will confirm and not weaken the Constitution, by more strongly marking its lines.[36]

It seems that at this stage Jefferson was contemplating that the "act of indemnity" mentioned above should take the form of amendment. On the other hand, letters such as the one quoted may have been, as Malone suggests, designed to disarm in advance those colleagues and supporters whom he expected to harbor such constitutional scruples, for in neither of the two drafts of an amendment he actually drew up did he include a specific grant of power to the national government to acquire territory.[37] Accepting the interpretation that this power was indeed a prerogative of sovereignty, he focused rather on the question of citizenship and statehood.

His desire for constitutional purity was never so firmly maintained as to endanger the successful ratification of the treaty. Louisiana was more important to him than the "metaphysical subtleties" of constitutional exegesis.[38] Congress was called into session three weeks early, and Jefferson's ardor for an amendment quickly cooled. To Madison he wrote: "I infer that the less we say about constitutional difficulties respecting Louisiana the better, and that what is necessary for surmounting them must be done *sub silentio*." And to Gallatin: "Would it not be well that you should have a bill ready drawn to be offered on the first or second day of the session? It may be well to say as little as

36. Jefferson to John C. Breckenridge, August 12, 1803, Ford, 8:244n.
37. Malone, *First Term*, p. 314.
38. Speed was essential, particularly after an alarming letter was received in August from Minister Livingston warning that Napoleon was having second thoughts about the wisdom of the sale and that should the United States fail to ratify the treaty within the stipulated six months the agreement would be allowed to lapse (Livingston to Jefferson, June 2, 1803, LC No. 22793).

possible on the constitutional difficulty, and that Congress should act on it without talking."[39]

The extent of Jefferson's control over Congress at that time is unmistakably evident in this passage, and his determination not to lose the Purchase by an absorption in constitutional niceties is clear. The president had not given up entirely the idea of an amendment, but his concern in the matter was echoed by none of his colleagues. While continuing to voice his scruples privately, putting himself on record, as Malone observes, "as recognizing dangers of construction against which (in the future) they must ever be on guard," Jefferson was prepared, "if our friends think differently," to "acquiesce with satisfaction, confident that the good sense of our country will correct the evil of construction when it shall produce ill effects."[40]

Of most immediate impact on the president's thinking was the overwhelmingly favorable reaction in the country and in Congress to the Purchase. Letters to the President, from the South and West in particular, attest to the public's approbation, as do the evidences of celebration to be found in the provincial press. Congress reflected the public's enthusiasm. The Senate approved the treaty in only four days, and a bill authorizing the president to take possession of the Louisiana Territory passed both houses with equal ease and dispatch.

The speed with which the entire matter was concluded, the near unanimity of public approval, and the absence of serious opposition in Congress served to confirm in Jefferson's mind the wisdom of his course in pressing on without an amendment. His conception of his role as a popular leader, his faith in the good sense of the people, and his conviction that the highest calling of the public servant is to risk himself in the popular interest triumphed over his fears of turning the Constitution into a blank paper by extension. In foreign affairs, and not only there, Jefferson extended the scope of the enumerated powers of the executive in order to accept "great charges." In the late 1790's at a time when opposition to the discretion of public officials seemed to him justified by Federalist abuses of the public confidence, he had

39. Jefferson to Madison, August 18, 1803, *ibid.*, No. 23173; Jefferson to Gallatin, August 23, 1803, Gallatin, *Writings*, 1:146.

40. Jefferson to W. C. Nicholas, September 7, 1803, LC No. 23273–4; such a strict constructionist as Senator Nicholas advised against raising the specter of possible unconstitutionality lest the Senate reject the treaty (Nicholas to Jefferson, September 3, 1803, in Malone, *First Term*, pp. 318–319).

written, "In questions of power . . . let no more be heard of confidence in man, but bind him down from mischief by the chains of the Constitution."[41] Yet as president he was to stress the need for the responsible officials in high places to risk exceeding the constitutional limits placed upon him if the public good demanded it. The contradiction between these two positions is more apparent than real, however. Jefferson summed up his own attitude shortly after his retirement to Monticello in this anticipation of Abraham Lincoln:

A strict observance of the written laws is doubtless *one* of the highest duties of a good citizen, but it is not *the highest*. The laws of necessity, of self-preservation, of saving the country when in danger are of higher obligation. To lose our country by a scrupulous adherence to written laws, would be to lose the law itself . . . thus absurdly sacrificing the end to the means. . . . It is incumbent on those only who accept great charges, to risk themselves on great occasions, when the safety of the nation, or some of its very high interests are at stake. An officer is bound to obey orders; yet he would be a bad one who should do it in cases for which they were not intended, and which involve the most important consequences. The line of discrimination between cases may be difficult; but the good officer is bound to draw it at his peril; and throw himself on the justice of his own country, and the rectitude of his own motives.[42]

In the normal course of events the public official must act within the restraints placed upon him by law. It is only in those rare instances when great issues are at stake, issues that affect the integrity or "the very high interests" of the nation, that those in the highest positions of authority must be willing to hazard their reputations and risk great actions, prepared the while to accept the consequences of their acts at the bar of public accountability. Some would argue that it is at these times, times of great issue, when the rule of law is most crucial. As a firm believer in the rightness of popular rule and as an experienced political realist, Jefferson seldom doubted his capacity to discern the public good and never shrank from the obligation to try. It is, of course, not easy to perceive accurately the difference between acts in furtherance of and acts detrimental to the public good, especially when the political actor is judge in his own cause. "The line of discrimination between cases may be difficult." This is not to deny, however, that

41. Quoted in Saul K. Padover, ed., *The Complete Jefferson*, (New York, 1943), p. 133.
42. Jefferson to John Colvin, September 20, 1810, Ford, 11:146.

the difference exists and that it is incumbent upon the responsible public servant to attempt the judgment.

Neustadt had observed that the pattern of decisions, their success or failure over time, contributes to the president's professional reputation and popular prestige and thereby serves to determine his generalized influence. Louisiana contributed to an already substantial political reputation the stimulus of immediate gratification of popular demand. In addition, the success of the Purchase made easier the task of redefining the role of the president as the spokesman and agent for the people's own best interests. Jefferson's confidence in the congruence of his own understanding of his role and the expectations of the people never left him, and if the political transformation that his tenure as president witnessed is any measure, his assumption to speak for them more often than not was fully justified.

PART TWO

THE CONTEXT OF
PRESIDENTIAL LEADERSHIP

The political role a leader adopts reflects his own judgment of the purposes of his office, his estimate of the quality of resources available to pursue such purposes, and his evaluation of his own talents and capacities for accomplishing those purposes. In addition, however, his role selection reflects his sense of the acceptability of his chosen role configuration to those he would lead. In this way the context shapes the nature and quality of leadership.

The leader's environment produces a general set of expectations that may be said to constitute the outer boundaries of acceptable behavior. Both leaders and followers exist within what Carl Becker called a "climate of opinion," a set of overarching assumptions or values that color the behavior patterns of a people in fundamental, although often unconscious ways. A central value within the climate of opinion in Jefferson's day, for example, was a pervasive suspicion of power, and particularly governmental power, as the handmaiden of tyranny. This antipower bias was a "given," a fundamental normative assumption which was basic to the political outlook of nearly everyone and the effects of which no political leader could escape. In the process of exercising power the effective leader, therefore, had to appear to reject it. Those leaders, and Jefferson was one, who desired to effect political change and who realized that change even in the direction of *limiting* power required its exercise, had imposed upon them by the climate of opinion a pattern of constraints that channeled their political styles and behavior into culturally acceptable paths.

As well as being shaped by climate of opinion, the style and behavior of Jeffersonian leaders was directly affected by the value system imposed and expressed through the dominant political ideology. The imperatives of republican orthodoxy imposed very real limits upon the development of leadership roles. In studying Jefferson's leadership one sees at every hand the evidence of the effects of the republican faith. His relations with Congress, his conduct of foreign policy, his attitude toward war and the management of crisis, his battles with the courts, his program of financial reform—each shows evidence of the pervasive impact of republican values.

Beneath the general climate of opinion and the value system of a dominant ideology, the context of leadership is not monolithic but segmented. A political leader performs in a variety of relationships, or role-sets, simultaneously. Each of these role-sets calls forth a separate configuration of responses from the leader, prompted by differences in purpose, in priority, in expectations, in organization, in resources, in access. The pattern of behavior adopted by the president in dealing with his inner circle of advisers and department heads, for example, is affected by the existence of a relative unity of purpose, a hierarchy of administrative and political authority, and the consequent ease of access by the president. When presidential leadership of Congress is considered, however, the role concept is necessarily altered to reflect the character of the relationship prompted by the constitutional separateness of the institutions involved and by the presence of an organized opposition.

These dissimilar conditions, moreover, require somewhat different resources with which to effect the leader's purposes. In some role-sets certain resources of presidential leadership might be readily available for use, while in others they might be weak or absent entirely. For one example, the nature of Jefferson's role vis-à-vis the Republican majority in Congress gave to the president a bargaining leverage there, but such leverage was minimal when he was dealing with the Federalist-dominated Supreme Court and virtually nonexistent when he was conducting relations with certain foreign governments. As another example, the use of the resource of appointment to office, effective in building a loyal executive bureaucracy, proved remarkably ineffective in producing a loyal federal judiciary.

In Chapter 4 we consider Jefferson's leadership of the executive branch, his relations with his cabinet colleagues and their departments, and the nature of his authority over the internal executive machinery. Of particular importance is his development of a policy of patronage and appointments as the principal resource of leadership in this role-set.

Chapter 5 explores Jefferson's relations with Congress, the fundamental relationship in the policy-making process and the one where the constitutional guideposts were of least benefit and the informal bargaining relationships of primary importance. The emphasis is upon the development of the resource of the political party as a device for the extension of presidential influence into the legislative branch.

The study of Jefferson's battles with the third branch of government occupies Chapter 6, as we examine his attempts to reduce the importance of the appointive judiciary and curtail the independence of judges from the influence of majority opinion as reflected in the elective branches. The absence of meaningful bargaining resources in this context caused Jefferson to lay aside his preference for negotiation and persuasion and adopt a more direct posture of confrontation, with results that were mixed and therefore highly instructive in leading to an understanding of the limits of leadership.

In Chapter 7 the horizon of the environment is expanded to explore the methods by which Jefferson sought to cultivate political support and disseminate his political message to the nation at large. This is accomplished through an examination of his relations with the party faithful in several of the states and his use of the party press, a device the Jeffersonians developed to a heretofore unattained significance.

CHAPTER 4

❧

The President as Chief Executive: Patriarch of the Official Family

Of central importance to Jefferson's conception of democratic government was the belief that the legitimacy of office was not a product of title, pomp, or prerogative, but rather was bestowed by the confidence of the people and maintained by the faithful representation of their essential will. His belief in the capacity of ordinary men and women to decide their own affairs, and of their right to do so, is fundamental to an understanding of his administrative theory and practice. From this belief stemmed the importance to him of political responsibility as well as the desire for simplicity and decentralization of administration.

His leadership was not primarily administrative in character. Complex administration and a concern for form and organization had served too often in the past as a cover for duplicity, intrigue, and privilege. Jefferson, as Merrill Peterson has observed, "was more concerned with the control rather than the organization of power, with responsibility than with energy, with administration as a simple tool rather than an awesome machine."[1] He was not notably interested in day-to-day administration (although he was not indifferent to it), nor did he concern himself with the derivation of a theory of administration. Fortunately he was blessed on the whole with subordinates of sound administrative ability, most notably at the Treasury where such competence was essential and where Gallatin demonstrated abilities to rival even Hamilton. Furthermore, despite his distaste for the details of administration, Jefferson brought to the presidency an informed skill in using administrative means to further normative ends.[2] For Jeffer-

1. *Thomas Jefferson*, p. 663.
2. See White, *Jeffersonians*, pp. 4–6.

son there was little sense in Pope's celebrated maxim, "Whate'er is best administered is best;" to him administration was and had to remain a tool for the pursuit of larger political ends.

Although Jefferson never articulated a theory of administration, students of the subject have isolated a number of principles that governed his approach to the problem.[3] Perhaps the most important of these was his belief in the necessity for administrative responsibility. In political terms this was reflected in his reliance upon popular control over public officials and the obligation on the part of those officials faithfully to represent the public interest. In administrative terms this responsibility was expressed as an opposition to broad discretionary powers and a demand for strict accountability in administrative actions. Despite his clearly expressed concept of emergency executive powers, Jefferson considered such powers suitable only in situations of genuine crisis. In the ordinary course of events the behavior of officialdom must be strictly controlled by law and rules of procedure. We have noted his doubts concerning the expediency of adding to the Union without constitutional amendment. On several occasions his constitutional scruples prevented him from pursuing courses of action he would normally have desired. He declined a request from the town fathers of Wilmington, Delaware, for construction of piers in the Delaware River on the grounds that his power to do so would be valid only under the "Commander-in-Chief" clause of the Constitution, not the "Commerce" clause as they had pleaded. His views of the feasibility of federal measures for internal improvements were to undergo subsequent modification, but his conviction of their unconstitutionality never changed.[4]

In the interpretation of statute law, as well, Jefferson generally favored a narrow construction. He would not take advantage of a laxly worded appropriation for road construction lest he violate the "intent" of Congress. He agreed with Gallatin that many of the excesses of Hamilton's tenure at the Treasury could have been avoided by stricter

3. For the following, I am indebted to Caldwell, *Administrative Theories*, especially pp. 130–141, although the order of priorities has been altered to reflect my own preferences. See also White, *Jeffersonians*, pp. 1–15, 29–76, 162–182, 412–422, and 546–560.

4. Jefferson to Gallatin, October 13, 1802, Gallatin, *Writings*, 1: 96. In his second inaugural address, the president advocated a constitutional amendment authorizing the application of surplus revenues during peacetime to internal improvements (Ford, 10:130).

congressional control over expenditure, and he advocated the practice of specific appropriations for specific purposes. They both felt that the general "relaxation" of administrative bookkeeping under President Adams's reign of "energy" was the result of excessive discretion and too little reliance on the principle of public accountability.[5]

A second principle marking Jefferson's administrative practice was his concern to promote governmental simplicity. "We are endeavoring . . . to reduce the government to the practice of a rigorous economy, to avoid burthening the people, and arming the magistrate with a patronage of money, which might be used to corrupt."[6] His goal was a frugal administration attentive to the public welfare rather than to the aggrandizement of wealth and power among the privileged classes. He believed that the overblown administrative apparatus thrown up by the Federalists had not been required by the complexity of administrative responsibilities, but had been designed merely to serve as the means for creating an "interested" class of bureaucrats. We may note in Jefferson the radical Whig antipathy to the creation of a "court" party with its legions of parasitical courtiers feeding off the corrupt patronage of a powerful executive. The experience of the past had convinced him that "the natural progress of things is for liberty to yield and government to gain ground." Every effort must be made, therefore, to keep the reins of government under tight control. "Let us deserve well of our country by making their interests the end of all our plans, and not our own pomp, patronage, and irresponsibility." One of the first goals of his administration was to reduce the size of the bureaucracy to the bare essentials needed for the efficient transaction of public business. Jefferson worked closely with Gallatin to cut back the personnel of the Treasury Department. It was their further purpose to simplify the financial system which, in their view, had been unnecessarily complicated by Hamilton in order that by confusing the people and their representatives, "he might have the entire government of his machine." Jefferson saw no reason why the general government's finances should not be "as clear and intelligible as a merchant's books."[7]

---

5. Jefferson to Robert Brent, March 10, 1807, Ford, 10:371–372; first annual message, December 8, 1801, 9:336.

6. Jefferson to M. Pictet, February 5, 1803, *ibid.*, 10:310.

7. Jefferson to E. Carrington, May 27, 1788, *ibid.*, 5: 5:402; to Gallatin, April 1, 1802, 9:360–361.

To the modern mind the quest for such simplicity may seem quaint and naive. In our own day of massive bureaucracy it is well to recall, however, that in Jefferson's time the press of public business was on such a reduced scale that Congress sat for only three months out of the year, the business of whole departments was often administered by the department head and a few (albeit overworked) clerks only, and presidents and cabinet officers could afford to leave the capital city for the summer months without seriously disrupting the conduct of affairs. Given the conditions of the day, Jefferson's hope for simplifying governmental administration was not only in keeping with sound republican doctrine but was within the realm of possibility.

It must be observed, however, that Jefferson's confident assurances of the feasibility of simplification could on occasion inhibit the effective prosecution of government business. His wholesale reductions in the size of American diplomatic representation abroad did not contribute to the facilitation of negotiations during his presidency. Domestically, as well, the administrative task could sometimes prove unduly onerous, even the president himself at times bending under its weight. In common with other chief executives of the last century, Jefferson was burdened with a load of petty administrative details which, by statute, none but he could attend to. The swarm of detail that he and Gallatin handled as they administered the far-flung (for that day) financial activities of the United States must certainly have reinforced the president's determination to seek a simpler administration. In any case, to make the bureaucracy a tool and not the master of his political purpose was an abiding characteristic of his presidency.

Equally central to his administrative practice was the principle of decentralization. Republican orthodoxy tended to equate consolidation with tyranny. Only through decentralization of function could the danger of despotism be averted. More important to Jefferson than the threat of despotism was his belief that the affairs of the people could be handled most efficiently and effectively at the local level by officials aware of local problems and local sensibilities. It was in this manner, Jefferson believed, that a decentralized administration aided in cultivating the affections of the people. "I believe that government to be the strongest of which every man feels himself a part."[8] By expanding the scope of popular control, the people would come to have a stake in

---

8. Jefferson to Gov. H. D. Tiffin, February 2, 1807, quoted in Caldwell, p. 136.

society and a feeling that their destinies were in their own hands. To this end Jefferson sought to reduce both the size and the reach of the central government in Washington, to distribute other functions to federal officers in the field, or to eliminate them altogether from federal cognizance. Ironically, the greatest threat to decentralized administration in the first seventy years of the republic was to occur in the closing months of Jefferson's presidency as he sought to extend federal control over embargo enforcement through an expansion of the administrative authority of the Treasury.

A further feature of Jeffersonian administration was his desire for harmony. Jefferson's personal desire for peaceable social relations and his pronounced sensitivity to hostility and criticism were carried over into his public concern for harmony within the executive. A basic mutuality of interest, achieved by the force of a common ideology, was abetted by the impact of the president's prestige and personal authority as well as his great talent in the arts of bargaining. If presidential power is largely the power of persuasion, then Jefferson's achievement of an overall unity of purpose and coordination of effort within the executive branch is one of the clues to his success in promoting his programs in Congress and the country. The cultivation of this harmony will be explored in some detail below.

An important factor in the success of his administration and one that indeed could be elevated to the level of an additional principle of administration is the concept of adaptability. There was a strong current of pragmatism in Jefferson's conduct of government. Combined with a commitment to progressive change and an indifference to precedent and tradition, this provided a necessary leavening influence upon the mix of principles inherited from his republican ideology. He was prepared to impose a rigorous centralized control over the peoples of the newly acquired Louisiana Territory, for example. Despite his commitment to decentralization and to government by consent, he chose to recognize the political realities of an uneducated, undisciplined population, largely unacquainted with the English language and unaccustomed to the requirements of democratic government. His willingness to strengthen and employ the central governmental machinery in pursuance of the embargo policy is another example—perhaps a less fortunate one—of his adaptability to what he saw as the exigencies of an overriding political priority. There is little doubt that the application of the other administrative principles of the Jeffersonians would have foundered quickly on the rocks of rigidity and dogmatism were it not for the existence of such a principled adaptability.

The Choice of a Cabinet

The application of these principles of administration is evident as one examines Jefferson's working relationships with his cabinet and with the individual members of his official family. From service within as secretary of state and from critical observations from without as vice-president, Jefferson brought to the presidency a well-defined view of the relationship which should prevail between the chief executive and the heads of the executive departments. The Constitution vested the executive power in the president, and to Jefferson the president *was* the executive. Heads of departments and other officers of the executive branch were considered as "auxiliaries" associated with the president in the "executive functions" of government.[9] The authority of department heads was derivative, stemming from the constitutional authority of the president. Final responsibility for the execution of the laws rested, therefore, with the elected chief executive. Jefferson was determined never to allow this authority to slip away through a repetition of developments that occurred in the last years of the Washington administration when Hamilton came to dominate the conduct of affairs, or in the course of the Adams presidency when the president's own authority was jeopardized by the independence and disloyalty of nearly his entire executive council.

Jefferson preferred rather to look to the *first* Washington administration for his model of president-cabinet relations. Central to the effectiveness of this model was the unifying authority of the president. As Jefferson had cause to remember from his days in the Washington cabinet, days marked almost from the beginning by deep divisions of principle among the members, the president alone provided a "regulating power which would keep the machine in steady movement." His early doubts of the wisdom of a single executive were forever dispelled by his experience in these often stormy councils where, but for the firm and final authority of the president, stalemate and crisis would have been their daily lot. To Jefferson, the American solution to

9. The phrases are contained in Jefferson's second inaugural address, Ford, 10:136.

the problem of organizing the executive combined the advantages of presidential unity with the advantages of collective consultation. "Aided by the counsels of a cabinet of heads of departments . . . with whom the President consults, either singly or altogether, he has the benefit of their wisdom and information, brings their views to one centre, and produces an unity of action and direction in all of the branches of government." He relied upon his department heads for counsel, but he dominated their collective proceedings and insured his final authority so that there was never any doubt "in Cabinet, in Congress, in the public mind who was master."[10]

It was Charles G. Dawes who observed that the members of the cabinet are a president's natural enemies. If not, their position and responsibilities at least place them in the position of his natural rivals. This was just as much the case in the early years of the nation when the members of the cabinet were nearly always selected because of their political eminence as well as, or even despite, their administrative abilities. From his own experience in political administration, Jefferson was well aware of the deep centrifugal forces that could tear an administration apart unless subdued by a superior hand, and he was willing to provide one. Writing in 1811 of his years in the White House, he remarked that they

presented an example of harmony in a cabinet of six persons, to which perhaps history has furnished no parallel. There never arose, during the whole time, an instance of an unpleasant thought or word between the members. We sometimes met under differences of opinion, but scarcely ever failed, by conversing and reasoning, so to modify each other's ideas, as to produce an unanimous result. Yet, able and amicable as these members were, I am not certain this would have been the case, had each possessed equal and independent powers. Ill-defined limits of their respective departments, jealousies, trifling at first, but nourished and strengthened by repetition of occasions, intrigues without doors of designing persons to build an importance to themselves in the divisions of others, might, from small beginnings, have produced persevering oppositions. But the power of decision in the President left no object for internal dissension, and external intrigue was stifled in embryo by the knowledge which incendiaries possessed, that no division they could foment would change the course of the executive power.[11]

Despite the outward harmony fondly remembered in the foregoing

10. Jefferson to Destutt de Tracy, January 26, 1811, *ibid.*, 11:184; Peterson, *Thomas Jefferson*, p. 662.

11. Jefferson to Destutt de Tracy, cited above, pp. 185–186.

passage, it is clear that jealousies, rivalries, and tactical differences did occur among his cabinet colleagues from time to time, although none of a fundamentally divisive nature. Equally clear, however, is the assurance that the unified responsibility of the president and his willingness to exercise it prevented these differences from erupting into major disputes.

Jefferson's concern to insure his authority reflected, in Neustadtian terms, a keen awareness of the need to guard his power prospects. This sensitivity governed even in the process of selecting the members of his cabinet. For the most important positions he chose men upon whose personal loyalty he could rely. Madison and Gallatin were his closest political allies, and in Madison he appointed his closest personal friend. Loyalty, congeniality, and the ability to cooperate were not the only criteria that had to be considered in selecting a cabinet, of course, not even by Jefferson. In addition to administrative ability and political acumen, geographical distribution and factional representation were important considerations. Jefferson's personal prestige and political authority in leading his party to victory and his preeminence as a symbol of party unity meant, however, that he was not forced to operate under the constraints that often limited less politically secure presidents in selecting cabinets.

By broadening the geographical representation of his cabinet, Jefferson sought to extend the influence of his party into heretofore "unregenerate" climes, and to point the way for moderate Federalists who might wish to join the Republican ranks. The appointment of Madison as secretary of state was a foregone conclusion, but his fellow Virginian was the only representative of the South in the cabinet. The selection of Gallatin for the Treasury portfolio was also an obvious choice, although the Pennsylvanian was not universally popular even within his own party. But the appointments of Henry Dearborn and Levi Lincoln, both from Massachusetts, as secretary of war and attorney general respectively, were more clearly political in character. Both choices served to stimulate the growth of the Jeffersonian movement in "enemy" country, for, as Gallatin noted, "both appointees were sound and decided Republicans" and both, "but Mr. Lincoln principally, have a great weight of character to the Eastward with both parties." [12] By filling his major posts with men who were bound to

12. Gallatin to Maria Nicholson, March 12, 1801, in Malone, *First Term*, p. 58. Jefferson said of Lincoln: "He will be a host in himself, being undoubtedly the ablest

him by personal friendship, political necessity, or both, Jefferson preserved the power options in his own hands from the outset and safeguarded his authority in the new administration.[13]

The Official Family

To understand more fully Jefferson's conduct of executive business we must examine more closely the individuals who comprised his inner council. The nature of his relationship depended upon the intimacy of their personal and political ties or the priority assigned by the president to the business of their departments.

His most frequent contact was with Albert Gallatin. No other executive department required such a continuous collaboration on the details of administration as did the Treasury. Financial reform was high on the Republican agenda during Jefferson's first term, and the necessity for regulating and enforcing the embargo required even more frequent contact with Gallatin during the second. Gallatin, as Leonard White has observed, was "the fiscal and administrative architect of Jefferson's administration." The Treasury was easily the largest executive department, numbering nearly 1300 persons and carrying the widest responsibilities for the formulation and execution of domestic policy. Gallatin administered the regular Treasury functions of revenue collection, customs, debt payment, and the sale of public lands. In addition he planned, with Jefferson, the estimates for other departments, a practice carried over for a time from Hamilton's tenure. Under the Treasury Acts of 1789 and 1800 the secretary was given the duty to lay before Congress the estimates of executive receipts and expenditures. While Gallatin never attempted to issue instructions to other departments limiting their expenditures (as Hamilton had done), he did exercise considerable influence for economies. The beginnings of budgetary coordination through central control by the president and the Treasury was one important way in which Jefferson sought to insure that he would remain in control of his

and most respected man of the eastern states" (Jefferson to Madison, September 17, 1800, *ibid.*).

13. The postmaster general was not a member of the president's cabinet. The sole exception to this cabinet of "Jefferson" men was perhaps Robert Smith, the secretary of the navy, who, while loyal enough to Jefferson, was a potential source of factionalism within the cabinet as the brother of the powerful Maryland senator, Samuel Smith.

administration. The practice, however, informal as it was, was not further developed by later presidents. By abandoning such attempts, President Madison was to lose an important resource of power over a cabinet that was largely not of his own choosing.[14]

Gallatin was a skillful financial planner with a gift for simplifying the complexities of fiscal procedure. Together he and Jefferson were determined to rationalize the administration of the nation's finances by simplifying bookkeeping and dispersement procedures and reducing the number of intermediate office holders between the secretary and the customs collectors in the field. In terms of financial policy Gallatin and the president were as one in their desire to pay the interest and principle of the public debt, cut back the expenses of government, repeal the internal taxes, and limit the discretionary expenditure of appropriated funds.[15] Both men were aware of the need for close collaboration and full exchange of information in financial matters. Gallatin submitted all Treasury reports to the president for his information before dispatching them on to Congress, and he submitted all important Treasury appointments to Jefferson for final decision.[16]

When they differed on matters of policy, Gallatin's greater financial experience often served as a corrective to presidential thinking. Jefferson, for example, was eager to use the resources of his administration to bring the Bank of the United States to heel. The president inquired of the secretary whether "we could not make a beginning towards an independent use of our own money, towards holding our own bank?" Gallatin, however, was more aware of the utility of the Bank in providing a safe and efficient engine for monetary transactions throughout the country and in facilitating the collection of the revenues. He advised the president that the bankers were more dependent on the government than Jefferson realized. Anticipating General Jackson,

14. White, *Jeffersonians*, p. 135. Gallatin's efforts to economize at the expense of the navy brought on the only potentially divisive quarrel within the cabinet as Secretary of the Navy Smith waged a futile battle to preserve his estimates (*ibid.*, pp. 140–142).

15. See Gallatin to Jefferson, April 1, 1801, Gallatin, *Writings*, 1:28; Jefferson to Gallatin, same date, Ford, 9:358–359. In 1803 Jefferson is supposed to have impounded money appropriated by Congress for the construction of gunboats. In fact he merely deferred expenditure of the funds for a few months. The story is told in Arthur M. Schlesinger, Jr., *The Imperial Presidency* (Boston, 1973), pp. 235–236.

16. See, for example, Gallatin to Jefferson, July 25, 1801, Gallatin, *Writings* 1:28; August 10, p. 33; August 17, pp. 38–39; also Gallatin to Jefferson, (received) November 15, 1801, p. 61.

the secretary wrote, "Whenever they shall appear to be really dangerous, they are completely in our power and may be crushed."[17] Jefferson accepted his colleague's more informed opinion in the matter.

In addition to his authority in matters of finance, Gallatin served the
president in other ways. Within the executive branch he made policy
recommendations on a variety of issues outside his immediate concern.
He worked closely with Jefferson in the preparation of presidential
messages to Congress. He advised on foreign policy, although he was
careful not to overstep the bounds of Madison's authority. He also
advised the president on judicial and territorial appointments and was
an influential political counselor on matters of patronage, particularly
in Pennsylvania and New York.[18]

Lastly, Gallatin served to great effect as Jefferson's principal political
lobbyist with Congress. As the chief Republican spokesman in the
House during the Adams administration, Gallatin had gained a high
reputation with his congressional colleagues, many of whom continued to serve in Congress throughout the Jefferson presidency. He
began almost immediately to provide Congress with advice on financial policy and procedure and on other matters of presidential policy.
He had no hesitation in recommending measures to Congress as the
president's agent and in his name, and would draft bills at Jefferson's
request for submission to appropriate legislative lieutenants.[19] In the
discussion on Congress in Chapter 5 we will examine this side of
Gallatin's performance in more detail. Suffice it to say at this point that
his influence with Congress, particularly his ability to reach the radical
faction around John Randolph, was to prove of great utility to the
president as he sought to work his will upon that body.

The third member of the close policy-making triumvirate was
James Madison, the secretary of state. While Gallatin played a domi-

17. Jefferson to Gallatin, December 13, 1803, Ford, 10:57–58; Gallatin to Jefferson, same date, Gallatin, *Writings*, 1:171–172.

18. See the series of letters contained in Gallatin, *Writings*, 1:61–74; Ford,
9:321–331, and 10:211–216; for examples of his patronage advice, see Gallatin to
Jefferson, August 17, 1801, Gallatin, *Writings*, 1:38–39 and September 12, pp.
44–45.

19. See, for example, his agenda for congressional inquiries, sent to Joseph H.
Nicholson, January 19, 1802, Gallatin, *Writings*, 1:74–76; also Jefferson to Gallatin,
August 3, 1802, p. 81: "What are the subjects on which the next session of Congress
is to be employed? . . . I know but two: 1. The militia law. 2. The reformation of the
civil list recommended to them at the last meeting, but not taken up through want of
time and preparation; that preparation must be made by us."

nant role as the chief lieutenant in domestic affairs and congressional liaison, Madison was clearly the principal adviser in matters of foreign policy. Jefferson took a keener professional interest in foreign affairs than he did in financial policy, rightly feeling himself to be an expert in the field. He did not attempt to be his own secretary of state, however, and left most of the administration of the department to Madison.

Madison had been one of the major legislative architects of the Republican party in the 1790's. As secretary of state, however, he tended to remove himself from party politics and in so doing lost touch with Congress, a development that hurt him later when he became president. Coupled with this self-imposed distance was a personality which, though possessed of wit and good humor in private, appeared to the public to be characterized by a reserved and diffident austerity, prompting Washington Irving's famous disparagement of Madison as a "wizened little apple-john."

Within the administration, however, and particularly in terms of the creation of foreign policy, his collaboration with Jefferson was close and marked by great mutual affection and respect. They thought as one on basic policy, and Madison's more cautious, practical, and analytical mind provided an appropriate counterpoise to Jefferson's more impulsive and imaginative spirit. Together they made an excellent political team, each balancing the other's deficiencies while pursuing a common approach to policy.[20]

Communication between them was of necessity frequent. When both men were in Virginia in August and September of each year, the thirty miles that separated their residences were covered by a special mail route, and a three-way courier service was established for special dispatches between Monticello, Montpelier, and Washington, where Gallatin alone remained.

In addition to providing advice on policy, Madison fulfilled his administrative responsibilities with efficiency, although his task was somewhat less onerous than that of his Treasury colleague. The State Department staff in 1801 numbered one chief clerk, seven clerks, and a messenger. Twenty years later it was little changed. This tiny staff, moreover, served not only as the nation's Foreign Office but as a sort of Home Office as well. It was charged with the responsibility for the

20. Brant, *Madison*, p. 303. For a brilliant analysis of their intellectual relationship, particularly in the early years, see Adrienne Koch, *Jefferson and Madison: The Great Collaboration* (New York, 1964).

census, the patent office, claims, pardons, the regulation of weights and measures, and the library, as well as the publication of the laws. This last responsibility gave to the secretary what little patronage he possessed, as it was his task to distribute the contracts for the public printing. This privilege was a plum eagerly sought by Republican editors, but it proved more often a pain for Madison, who felt compelled to placate those who were not so favored.[21]

The other members of Jefferson's cabinet, while enjoying his confidence and contributing to more general policy-making through their comments in cabinet meetings, were usually concerned with the narrower affairs of their particular departments. What influence these men possessed beyond the scope of their portfolios was gained largely through the assertion of political influence in the party, particularly within their home states or regions.

General Henry Dearborn, a physician by training and a soldier by circumstance, had achieved a sound reputation during the Revolution. More to the point of his appeal for Jefferson was his well-known opposition to an extravagant military establishment. As a citizen-soldier Dearborn was known to rely primarily upon the volunteer militia for defense, fearing as did Jefferson the consequences to liberty of a standing army. In addition, Dearborn was from the District of Maine and was expected to cultivate Republican interests in that frontier region of Massachusetts.

Throughout the Jefferson years, the regular army was tiny and for the most part dispersed in distant garrisons. During Dearborn's tenure there was no central procurement machinery in the War Department and no system of unified command. Indeed the secretary of war had no military advisers in Washington to help manage the army until the War of 1812. There was no staff corps, and each garrison operated virtually as an independent entity.[22] Given the prevalent fundamental suspicion of a military establishment, Dearborn performed his duties well. He sought to strengthen the fortifications guarding the frontier, particularly along the borders of Spanish America, and he supported Jefferson's unsuccessful attempt to standardize the organization and classification of the militia. There can be little disagreement with Leonard White's conclusion, however, that

21. White, *Jeffersonians*, pp. 187–188.
22. *Ibid.*, p. 213. The Army Act of 1802 authorized an army of two regiments of infantry, one of artillery, totalling 3350 officers and men.

the Republican ideology interfered with a satisfactory defense establishment.[23]

If the army suffered, the navy was reduced to skeletal proportions under the force of the same ideology. Being far more expensive to operate than the army, the navy bore the brunt of Republican drives for economy. When Jefferson took office he caused all six frigates to be laid up in harbor, had work halted on the construction of shore facilities, and cut the number of naval employees. Aside from the fear in some quarters of war provocations that a strong naval establishment might create, the major reason for such retrenchment was economy. Gallatin lobbied against a large navy as useless, expensive, and provocative. His attempts to cut the naval estimates to the bone, in fact, provoked a cabinet row with the navy secretary. To Gallatin the naval estimates represented the largest potential source of savings in government expenditures.[24]

Jefferson, too, disliked a large navy. He was never sea-minded and had little appreciation of the effective uses of sea power. This was starkly revealed in his championing of the idea of replacing ocean-going warships with a fleet of small, inexpensive, shallow-draft gunboats. Congress responded to his requests by authorizing the construction of many of these coastal vessels over several years.[25] The president's critics were at first amused and then appalled by the gunboat panacea. Plumer denounced "this whimsical phylosophic [sic] president" for building boats "that are incapable of sailing on the rough sea or of being of use to us, instead of building ships of the line and frigates to defend our national honor and the commerce of our country." The criticism was to the point. Jefferson's innocence in naval matters continued, as is evident from his later defense of the same discredited gunboats during the War of 1812, even as the success of the larger warships was being demonstrated.[26]

The man selected to preside over this backwater department was

23. Malone, *First Term*, p. 272; Jefferson to Madison, May 5, 1804, Ford, 10:392–393; White, *Jeffersonians*, pp. 213–214.

24. White, *Jeffersonians*, p. 267. For examples of his views, see Gallatin to Jefferson, May 30, 1805, Gallatin, *Writings*, 1:234, and August 16, 1802, p. 84.

25. The boats as Jefferson proposed them were fifty feet long, of shallow draft, low freeboard, propelled by oar and sail, and mounting one or two medium cannon. See White, *Jeffersonians*, pp. 267–268.

26. Plumer, *Memorandum*, November 8, 1804, p. 192. See Jefferson to Madison, May 21, 1813, Ford, 11:288–289; to Gallatin, June 15, 1806, 10:269–270.

not the president's first choice. He had offered the secretaryship of the navy to several men, including Robert Livingston, who preferred the attractions of a Paris diplomatic post. Finally he chose Robert Smith, a maritime attorney from Baltimore, whose older brother Samuel was a political power in Maryland and a force to be cultivated in the United States Senate. Smith's performance as navy secretary was not highly successful, even after the unattractiveness of the post is considered. He was no match for Gallatin in cabinet and was not an efficient administrator. With three clerks he presided over a department that had little direct control over naval personnel or materiel; each ship operated largely on its own. Smith, like Dearborn, did not have the benefit of a professional service adviser in Washington. He seemed, as well, to be insensitive at times to the policy preferences of the president. While accepting the gunboat scheme, for example, his urging of preparations for offensive warfare was so stridently performed as to doom any chance of its being accepted by the president.[27]

The attorney general, while he attended cabinet meetings had no department to administer and was not even required to live in the capital. His role was simply to advise the president personally on legal and constitutional questions presented to him. A measure of his unimportance may be gleaned from Gallatin's remark to Jefferson when the post fell vacant in 1804: "That appointment, however, does not press; but unless there shall be a district attorney at New Orleans, not a single prosecution can take place in the name of the United States."[28] Jefferson's choice of Levi Lincoln for the position reveals the importance attached to political considerations in forming his official family. Lincoln was a Massachusetts Republican of high reputation who, in addition to his legal advice, provided the president with detailed information on political developments in New England.

The most narrowly political appointment in the president's keeping was the patronage-rich postmaster generalship. The post was not considered part of the cabinet, but since the postmaster general appointed the postmasters, supervised the mails, and designated the post roads, he was with the Treasury head the major dispenser of administration favors. The Post Office was an important device for Republicans in opening up the burgeoning new regions of the West and

27. Robert Smith to Jefferson, September 16, 1805, in "Some Papers of Robert Smith," *Maryland Historical Magazine*, 15 (1925), 143.
28. Gallatin to Jefferson, September 18, 1804, Gallatin, *Writings*, 1:208–209.

extending the flow of political communication throughout the nation. As White notes, the congressional Republicans opened the public coffers for the development of post roads more frequently than for any other domestic purpose. Each new post office, regardless of size or volume of business, required a postmaster, and these patronage positions proved useful in cementing the loyalties of important worthies in towns and villages across the country; they were avidly sought, and there are examples of men resigning even from the United States Senate to take a lucrative postmastership.[29]

In appointing Gideon Granger of Connecticut, Jefferson left no doubt that his purpose was to weld the "talents and virtues of our country" into a Republican phalanx by filling the lesser offices with loyal men. The appointments were apparently made without presidential consultation, but Granger appointed only tried and true Republicans. He was careful, in addition, to cultivate the good will of members of Congress by consulting them as well as local party men before making the appointments.[30]

Jefferson's Cabinet Authority

What were the sources of Jefferson's influence over these men whom he chose to help him? Status and authority add something to persuasiveness; as Neustadt put it, they reinforce a president's logic and charm. Jefferson's formal authority over his executive heads of departments made it more difficult for them to oppose him, particularly after he had made clear the limits and dimensions of that authority. In the case of cabinet officers, furthermore, each was aware far more than the congressmen on the Hill that, to quote Neustadt, "the doing of *their* jobs, the furthering of *their* ambitions, may depend upon the President of the United States."[31]

To make assurance doubly sure, Jefferson took care to select a cabinet of men who were known to be loyal to his own general conception of values. In appointments to the cabinet and in other major posts in his administration, the moderate Republicans were clearly in the ascendancy: Madison; Robert Smith; Federalists Charles Pinck-

29. Jefferson to Gideon Granger, October 31, 1801, LC No. 20210; White, *Jeffersonians*, p. 300, 322.

30. White, *Jeffersonians*, p. 323. Plumer observed of Granger that he will "renew his labors to disseminate democracy through the medium of his office" (*Memorandum*, December 29, 1803, p. 97).

31. *Presidential Power*, p. 43.

ney and Rufus King as ministers to Spain and England; Robert Livingston to France; the New Englanders Dearborn, Lincoln, and Granger. Only Gallatin was close in political principles to the radical Republicans, and he quickly allied with Jefferson and the moderates. (In addition Jefferson chose Samuel Harrison Smith, a moderate, over the radical William Duane, to edit the party newspaper.) He did not include in his cabinet any Federalists, despite his stated aim at conciliation of the moderate opposition. His cabinet appointments illustrate the importance to Jefferson's future power prospects of his ability to select his closest advisers on the basis of his own needs rather than the needs of powerful factions with a veto over policy.

Formal authority and statutory powers, however, cannot account for Jefferson's hold over the loyalties and service of his cabinet colleagues. Presidents before and after him possessed similar authority and status, but were continually beset by the frustrations of an uncontrollable cabinet. It is not terribly helpful to indicate the lines of hierarchical authority that exist on paper, for while the cabinet officer does not possess the immunity from presidential direction enjoyed by a "safe-seat" congressman with his independent power base, the conflicting demands of loyalty upon a cabinet officer from his own bureaucracy, from his clientele interests, and from Congress, and the consideration of his own political needs give him a leverage with the president that is different only in degree, perhaps, from that of a powerful congressional committee chairman.

In Jefferson's day, of course, the resources upon which the cabinet officer could draw were far fewer and less intense than they later became. The bureaucracy was tiny and its internal interests less institutionalized; interest group pressure was far less important, in some cases nonexistent; congressional pressure was more episodic, in part because of the minimal organizational development of Congress as well as the executive departments; even the political considerations were somewhat less demanding because of the rudimentary party organization and the undeveloped state of the organs of constituency pressure. The same situation existed for the president as well, however. The resources available to him were also on a reduced scale, so that the balance of resources between president and cabinet officers was perhaps not so different from today. Had Jefferson not begun by being mindful of his colleagues' own status and authority as department heads as well as presidential advisers and spokesmen for their own political factions and geographical areas, it is likely that sooner or later he would have been made mindful of them. In any case he was far too sensitive not to realize the dangers involved in taking their loyalty for granted, and he made a conscious effort to reinforce that allegiance.

The key to Jefferson's success in maintaining cabinet harmony must be discovered elsewhere than in the Constitution and statute books. A good part of the answer may be indicated when we again reflect upon the political bargaining leverage he acquired through his towering public prestige and impressive professional reputation. Jefferson took office as the undisputed head of an ascendant political movement. The venom with which he was attacked by his political enemies only served to increase the scope and intensity of his followers' support. Jefferson was already a symbol of American public ideals and his popularity in the nation was to wax, not wane, in the years to follow as the "Jefferson" party expanded its influence into every corner of the Union.[32] His reputation as president, beginning with his sweeping electoral victory and extending to his success in leading Congress, was almost a self-perpetuating phenomenon. As his reputation for invincibility grew, it itself became a resource of power, thereby increasing his chances for future success by making it more difficult to resist such a force. In terms of our bargaining model, Jefferson's ability to make the right "choices" strengthened his position and enhanced his ability to make his choices binding in the future.

Jefferson's personal qualities of leadership, expressed through his political style, enhanced his authority in cabinet. His benevolent and conciliatory manner was combined with a pragmatic intelligence and soundness of political judgment to add an almost irresistible quality to his persuasive talents. These personal qualities indicate an additional source of Jefferson's authority, a source that cannot be discovered simply by the application of an instrumental bargaining model. To be sure, his cabinet officers benefited from the prestige, power, status, and influence that service in the highest councils of government can bestow. There is no question but that they sensed the material benefits which would accrue from embracing the Jeffersonian cause. It is misleading, however, to assume that Madison and Gallatin, or even Dearborn, Lincoln, and Granger served Jefferson merely out of such considerations. A leader often acquires influence over his most im-

32. For a discussion of the Jeffersonian symbolism, see Merrill D. Peterson, *The Jeffersonian Image in the American Mind* (New York, 1962).

mediate associates by means other than (or at least in addition to) the promise of reward or the threat of punishment. Some supporters are bound as well by a subjective identification with him, through personal affection and respect, or through an ideological union with his aims, or more often a combination of both. They *want* to support him; they do not need to be persuaded constantly.

Madison was a colleague, an intellectual companion and political counselor of many years, and a close friend. His loyalty was the result of a complex of political, intellectual, ideological, and emotional considerations. While Gallatin could not equal Madison in the length and depth of his personal relationship with Jefferson, he too acquired a subjective identification with the president, first as an invaluable colleague throughout the political wars of the 1790's and then as Treasury chief through a close, almost daily, collaboration in the work of eight years. The political futures of the others were more clearly dependent on the president's good will and their personal intimacy was less pronounced. They too, however, were bound to Jefferson by strong ideological ties, and during their tenure in the cabinet they developed a personal respect and affection for the president that further insured their support.

It would appear, then, that Jefferson was able to develop and maintain the loyalty and cooperation of his executive colleagues by his ability to combine (1) the formal authority and status of his office, (2) the political power of his position as party leader and symbol of national public ideals, (3) the force of a personal style supremely gifted in the arts of persuasion, and (4) an uncommon capacity to engender personal loyalty, compounded of ideological, intellectual, and emotional identification with him and with his purposes. The combination of these factors, the weight of each varying with the man and the circumstances, insured Jefferson's authority in the executive establishment and gave him the unity of executive will that proved so important as he sought to bridge the separation of powers and influence Congress.

The Conduct of Cabinet Operations

Jefferson worked to promote his authority through his conduct of public business. His refusal to hold regular weekly cabinet meetings underscored his understanding of the executive council as an advisory body and an instrument of *his* leadership, to be employed as he saw fit.

His immediate reason for avoiding frequent cabinet meetings was the argument that they were too time-consuming and that private contact with individual department heads would better expedite the public business in most cases. He may have sensed, however, that frequent meetings on a regular basis might serve to routinize and legitimate "cabinet government," and in so doing weaken presidential authority.[33]

A letter to Gallatin written near the close of his first term reveals the manner by which Jefferson sought to keep the reins of power in his own hands. The question under discussion involved the removal of a subordinate officer from the Treasury. Gallatin had proposed to inform the individual that " . . . I had for some time determined to remove you from office, although a successor has not yet been appointed by the president." Jefferson suggested that Gallatin include in his letter the reasons for the removal. In suggesting a substitute draft, however, the president subtly altered the wording: "I think it due to candor at the same time to inform you that *the President*, considering that the patronage of public office should no longer be confided to one who uses it for active opposition to the national will, had for some time determined to place your office in other hands."[34] In this way Jefferson affirmed, delicately but unmistakably, the power of the president, and not a cabinet officer, to remove executive officials.

Jefferson enhanced his reputation for running things in his administration by the way he took advice. In the preparation of public messages the president normally worked in close collaboration with his department heads, notably Madison and Gallatin, readily accepting their counsel whenever it coincided with his general views. He had no fierce pride of authorship, and the public record is replete with the often detailed comments of his advisers on public messages submitted in response to drafts circulated to them by the president. It is clear from an examination of this correspondence, however, that it is the message of the *president* which is under preparation, and that while

33. Gallatin had recommended conferences once a week with additional private conferences between the president and each of his secretaries once or twice a week to discuss public business (Gallatin to Jefferson, November 9, 1801, Gallatin, *Writings*, 1:58; Jefferson to Gallatin, July 10, 1807, Ford, 10:452–453). Malone finds that cabinet meetings in Jefferson's two terms averaged less than one a month. Meetings became even less frequent in his second term as foreign political troubles caused tension within his official family (Malone, *First Term*, p. 61).

34. Jefferson to Gallatin, May 30, 1804, Ford, 10:81–82, emphasis added.

decisions would be made as often as possible after full consultation with his advisers the decisions would finally be the president's own.[35] This practice of consultation was not only a useful way to insure that all viewpoints were considered, but also served to provide collective support for the president's program. The message was the president's, but it could hardly hurt to have it known that the entire cabinet had participated in its preparation and approved its contents. In this way Jefferson used the cabinet to good effect in strengthening and legitimating presidential decisions.

Though the president quickly established a firm control over his executive subordinates, his rule was more benevolent than despotic. He was careful to conciliate his colleagues at every opportunity. Indeed his sensitivity to these considerations was remarkable and was a significant asset in promoting internal harmony and enhancing his bargaining position.[36] When differences did arise between two or more colleagues, Jefferson sought to have them reconciled at the lowest level with the least possible friction. If he was forced to intervene, his decision was never appealed to Congress or the public—mute evidence of his unquestioned authority within the executive.

Such domination did not go entirely uncriticized by his cabinet officers, and it could be serviceable as an alibi when a department head wanted to explain his inability to satisfy a constituent's request or a congressman's pet project. Always the most removed from the inner circle of the president's advisers, partly because of the low priority his department enjoyed in presidential eyes, Secretary of the Navy Robert Smith once bemoaned his inability to gain approval for a particular measure: "Nay I, even I, did not dare to bring forward the measure until I had first obtained his approbation. Never was there a time when executive influence so completely governed the nation."[37] There are surprisingly few such complaints in the written correspondence of his cabinet officers, however, (although many in the

35. See, for example, the correspondence concerning the preparation of the annual message to Congress in November, 1805, contained in Brant, p. 302.

36. For example, when in consultation with Madison at Monticello Jefferson made certain appointments of lesser personnel, he hastened to inform Gallatin of the action and to assure him that they had waited until the last moment and then had made the fewest possible changes from what had been provisionally approved by the department heads in cabinet (Brant, p. 208).

37. Robert Smith to W. C. Nicholas, January 9, 1807, in White, *Jeffersonians*, p. 75.

correspondence of his enemies), and for the most part it appears that the unity displayed in Jefferson's cabinet room was as genuine as it appeared to the world outside.

The president specified his method of operation in a "Circular to the Heads of Departments" issued in late 1801. Citing the procedure employed during the first Washington administration as a suitable model, he proposed that all letters of business addressed to department heads be submitted to him, either for information if no answer was required or for approval if one were, in which case the proposed answer should accompany the original letter. Jefferson assured his colleagues of his "unlimited, unqualified, and unabated" confidence in their abilities, noting that in adopting the procedure outlined, President Washington had generally sent the documents back after having read them, "which signified his approbation. Sometimes he returned them with an informal note, suggesting an alteration or a query." Only if a doubt of importance arose would a conference with the secretary be necessary. Jefferson left no doubt of his purpose in suggesting such a procedure. By this means, he wrote, General Washington "was always in accurate possession of all facts and proceedings in every part of the Union, and to whatsoever department they related; he formed a central point for the different branches; preserved an unity of object and action among them; exercised that participation in the suggestion of affairs which his office made incumbent upon him; and met himself the due responsibility for whatever was done." Jefferson thus stressed his obligation "to meet personally the duties to which they [the public] have appointed me."[38]

Much of the public business was conducted individually with the cabinet officer concerned in a particular question. Cabinet meetings were reserved for large matters of policy, questions with major political or constitutional significance, key appointments, party matters, and issues of foreign policy. Jefferson kept only sketchy accounts of these meetings, but the agenda of one, in 1801, will indicate the type of questions discussed:

1. appointments and removals.
2. shall squadron be ordered to Mediterranean?
   shall captains be allowed to search and destroy enemy vessels?
3. treaties with Indians.

38. Circular to the Heads of Departments, November 6, 1801, Ford, 9:310–312.

4. shall we proclaim the French treaty?
5. negotiations with Britain.[39]

The President's conduct of these meetings was informal. His purpose in calling them was to receive opinions on matters upon which he needed advice. Occasionally he would call a meeting to solicit support for a decision already determined but which would be strengthened by a demonstration of cabinet assent. In grave matters he would call his department heads together, and proceed by "discussing the subject maturely and finally taking the vote, on which the President counts himself but one. So that in all important cases the Executive is in fact a directory, which certainly the President might control; but of this there was never an example either in the first or the present administration."[40] He was not simply *primus inter pares*, however, as this overly modest and somewhat misleading account might imply. He called the meetings and established the agenda to be discussed. Furthermore, a "directory" that one member might easily control is hardly a directory. There is no record of Jefferson's ever being overruled on an important matter by a vote of his cabinet, nor even a record of the results of any vote taken as such. He was willing to accept advice and he trusted the judgment of his principal advisers, but he was not to be denied in any policy matter on which his mind was formed.

The Resource of Patronage

Disraeli once remarked that "patronage is the outward and visible sign of an inward and spiritual grace, and that is power." Jefferson would have shrunk from so cynical an observation; yet it is evident that as president and leader of his party he was keenly aware that his prospects for political success depended in no small part upon the creation of a partisan administration. Successful leadership not only required the effective management of his immediate cabinet colleagues but demanded as well that the subordinate bureaucracy be staffed by

39. *Anas*, November, 1801.
40. Jefferson to William Short, June 12, 1807, Ford, 10:414–415. Jefferson poked gentle fun at his predecessor who "sometimes decided things against his counsel by dashing and trampling his wig on the floor. This only proves what you and I know, that he had a better heart than head." Had Jefferson known the full import of these stormy sessions of Adams's cabinet, he might have had more sympathy for his old friend.

persons willing to accept his leadership and direction. This exploration of Jefferson and the executive branch should therefore conclude with an examination of the major resource for insuring that leadership, patronage.

The party battles of the 1790's had disenchanted Jefferson with the practice of public officers using their positions for direct partisan advantage; or, more accurately, this experience served to reinforce his philosophical opposition to a swollen civil list as the mark of good government.[41] No doubt much of his opposition to patronage was at that time the result of Federalist monopolization of its sources. It is nonetheless true that Jefferson embraced an eighteenth-century Whig conception of public office as in the nature of a public trust, a view that gave to his later employment of patronage its tentative and equivocal nature.

Central to this view was a distinction between higher and lower offices. In common with much of his generation, Jefferson looked upon higher (that is, nonbureaucratic policy-making) office as an honorable, though burdensome, duty to be performed by a disinterested public-spirited class that spurned the baser motives of material gain. Lower offices, however, were looked upon as necessary evils, to be held under strict supervision for the livelihoods they provided. The careerism and job-seeking that marked the lower bureaucracy merely betrayed the weakened characters of those pursuing places. This class of lower office-holders was dangerous if enlarged and should be kept as small as possible. To Pennsylvania Governor Thomas McKean (himself a spoilsman of the first order), Jefferson deplored the fact that "office began to be looked to as a resource for every man whose affairs were getting into derangement, or who was too indolent to pursue his profession. . . . In short it was poisoning the very source of industry by presenting an easier source for a livelihood, and was corrupting the principles of the great mass of those who passed a wistful eye on office."[42]

This view was echoed by many influential spokesmen for republi-

41. Jefferson to Edmund Pendleton, April 22, 1799, *ibid.*, 9:65. Not only on appointments was Jefferson opposed to a large patronage. See his letter to Madison opposing federal construction of post roads as a "source of boundless patronage to the executive . . . and a bottomless abyss of public money" (March 6, 1796, 8:226–227). He was later to profit from the patronage of post roads and postmasterships during his own presidency.

42. Jefferson to Thomas McKean, February 19, 1803, *ibid.*, 9:450–451.

can principles, among them the aged Edmund Pendleton, whose pamphlet, "The Danger Not Over," expressed an abhorrence of the practice of appointing men to office with a view to enhancing the executive's reelection prospects.[43] Gallatin, even as he sat astride the patronage machinery of the Treasury, never fully accepted the use of appointments to office as a means of building partisan power. To him the party should aim to "asperse Administration"; they should not worry about a "few paltry offices ... mere inferior administrative offices of profit." He and Jefferson deplored the growing audacity of urban political machines that attempted to influence political appointments, and decried the practice of organized pressure groups, "unknown to the Constitution," in submitting formal addresses to the president on matters of appointment. Only the opinions of individuals could be legitimately received by public officials as expressions of opinion sanctioned by the Constitution.[44]

Jefferson clearly had serious reservations about the wisdom and propriety of patronage, doubts that never left him and were to give to his performance in such matters a decidedly ambiguous cast. The fact remains, however, that in matters of appointments, if not so much in other aspects of patronage, the president behaved in a partisan manner. While he continued to oppose an inflated governmental establishment, he was convinced that the existing vacancies should be filled with Jeffersonians.

There is some controversy among students of the subject as to whether Jefferson "founded" the spoils system. Writers of an anti-Jeffersonian perspective generally claim that he did, while others place responsibility for it at the feet of Washington and Adams. Edward Channing quoted Washington to the effect that to appoint to office men whose political tenets were adverse to the measures of government would be a "sort of political suicide."[45] Jefferson did begin the practice of partisan *removals*, but this was necessitated by his predecessors' practice of appointing only Federalists to office. The impetus toward partisanship in appointments was further supplied,

43. Cited in David John Mays, *Edmund Pendleton* (Cambridge, Mass., 1952), pp. 334–335.

44. Gallatin to Jefferson, August 11, 1803, Gallatin, *Writings*, 1:141; June 21, 1803, p. 129; See also a draft of a letter of Jefferson to William Duane, July 24, 1803, pp. 123–125. Gallatin persuaded the president not to send it.

45. See, for example, Henry Cabot Lodge, *Studies in History* (Boston, 1892), p. 288; Edward Channing, *The Jeffersonian System* (New York, 1906), p. 14.

however, by the responsibilities Jefferson felt as party leader. Basic to such a role was the necessity to fill as many places in as many areas of the government as possible with partisans in order to provide at least the minimum basis for coordination of policies and programs. He sensed what Neustadt has observed, that to make the right decisions the president must insure that the power of effective choice be in his own hands, and that it not be subject to sabotage at the hands of unsympathetic subordinates. "I had foreseen years ago," Jefferson reminded a colleague in 1801, "that the first republican president who should come into office after all the places in government had become exclusively occupied by federalists, would have a dreadful operation to perform. . . . On him—was to devolve the office of an executioner, that of lopping off."[46]

The initial purpose of Jefferson's appointments policy was to further the strategy of conciliation and unification outlined in his first inaugural address and elaborated in his private correspondence. He wished to eliminate the Federalist faction as a serious political alternative by embracing those members who were "detachable" while freezing out their leaders from a share in the government.[47] To accomplish this delicate purpose it became necessary to steer a middle course between partisanship and conciliation. As is common in such situations, the "temporizer" ran the risk of pleasing neither side.

When Jefferson took office, his appointments policy had not fully matured; it developed under the force of circumstances and was modified as the result of the clash of competing interests. To the radical Republicans the election of 1800 presaged a total transformation of the federal government, in policy and personnel. The sufferings and humiliations inflicted upon them by the hated Federalist regime had to be avenged by the wholesale removal of all Federalists and their sympathizers. Even before Jefferson took the oath of office, he was besieged by letters from Republican stalwarts of high and low station demanding their pound of flesh. Some were more impatient than others. John Beckley, the archetypal political manager who had contributed greatly to the organization of the recent victory, spoke for the more partisan Republicans, reminding the President that while Republicans made up five-eighths of the voters of the country, the

46. Jefferson to Levi Lincoln, August 26, 1801, Ford, 9:289.
47. "I shall hope to be able to obliterate, or rather to unite the names of federalists and republicans" (Jefferson to Horatio Gates, March 8, 1801, *ibid.*, p. 205).

Federalists monopolized all the offices under the general government. From his wide contacts with party leaders, Beckley believed "there is but one opinion, and that is a change, thorough and complete, but gradual, should be made." Beckley feared that a temporizing approach would weaken the emerging unity of the party, while a firm policy would "speedily put an end . . . even to the very name of a federal party." He also perceived the threat apparent vacillation might bring to the president's own power prospects, fearing that it would "essentially injure your reputation and the success of your administration" by cultivating a reputation for a "want of political firmness."[48]

Similar sentiments were expressed by key legislative supporters of the president. William Branch Giles warned Jefferson that "many of your best and firmest friends already suggest apprehensions that the principle of moderation . . . may by too much indulgence degenerate into feebleness and inefficiency." He advised Jefferson that a "pretty general expurgation of office has been one of the benefits expected by the friends of the new order of things." To many Republicans, smarting under the late sting of Federalist arrogance, it made no sense to placate the vanquished at the expense of the victor.

There was no unified position within Republican ranks on this question, however. Such sentiments did not reflect the views of the moderate wing of the party, and it is important to recall that the moderate viewpoint prevailed in the president's cabinet and inner circle of advisers. Madison had always favored a conciliatory policy of appointments and removals. The influence of Gallatin, whose credentials among the radicals were genuine, was undoubtedly significant in reinforcing Jefferson's own inclination toward moderation. The secretary had cautioned that Republican principles of limited government and public economy "should rest on a broad basis of the people, and not on a fluctuating party majority" which a spoils system would create. He complained of wholesale removals in New York, decrying a general "spirit of persecution which, in that state particularly, disgraces our cause and sinks us on a level with our predecessors." Supporting this view, at least in part, were such congressional leaders as Nathaniel Macon (whose monopoly of patronage in North Carolina perhaps provided him the luxury of a gradualist policy) and such state leaders as Alexander James Dallas in Pennsylvania.[49]

48. John Beckley to Jefferson, February 27, 1801, LC No. 18801.
49. Gallatin to Jefferson, August 10, 1801, Gallatin, *Writings*, 1:33; also Septem-

Jefferson began his presidency, then, with only a general commitment to adopt the strategy that would best serve the interests of his conciliation policy. Clearly he was determined at least to avoid a policy of wholesale removals. Of one thing he was convinced, however: the necessity to remove the "midnight appointments" made by John Adams after the results of the presidential election were known. "All appointments to *civil* offices *during pleasure* made after the event of the election was certainly known to Mr. A, are considered as nullities. I do not view the persons appointed as even candidates for the office, but make others without noticing or notifying them."[50]

In one other respect the president was of a firm mind: "Good men, to whom there is no objection but a difference of political principle practiced on only as far as the right of a private citizen will justify, are not proper subjects of removal, except in the cases of attorneys and marshals. The courts being so decidedly federal and irremovable, it is believed that republican attorneys and marshals . . . are indispensably necessary." He informed Monroe as well that he would not give office to Federalist leaders, but by the same token would not deprive men of office on the basis solely of political principle. "Perhaps," he wrote, "we shall proceed *a talons*, balancing our measures according to the impressions we perceive them to make."[51]

Unfortunately for moderation, the impression he perceived from the Federalist organs of opinion and from the more partisan Republicans as well caused him to modify his policy almost immediately in a more partisan direction. Federalist editors and office holders failed to recognize in his policy any spirit of moderation, preferring to view the removal of even a handful of Federalists as a threat to the very integrity of the Union. Oliver Wolcott, former secretary of the Treasury in the

ber, 1801, p. 41; Macon to Jefferson, May 24, 1801, in Elizabeth Gregory McPherson, "Unpublished Letters from North Carolinians to Jefferson," in *North Carolina Historical Review*, 12 (1935), 271–272.

50. Jefferson to Giles, March 23, 1801, Ford, 9:222–223, emphasis in the original. Jefferson was deeply offended by this attempt on the part of Adams to inflict upon the new administration a civil list of Federalist diehards. It still rankled after three years, as he wrote to Abigail Adams (a letter that for a time reopened the breach between the two old friends): "I can say with truth that one act of Mr. Adams' life, and one only, ever gave me a moment's personal displeasure. . . . It seemed but common justice to leave a successor free to act by instruments of his own choice" (June 13, 1804, 10:84–86).

51. Jefferson to Giles, cited above; Jefferson to Monroe, March 7, 1801, Ford, 9:202–203.

Adams administration, warned that the president by his conduct in making new appointments "has incited a spirit of rivalship, passion, and resentment which is utterly uncontrollable." Unable or unwilling to admit that by filling virtually the entire federal establishment with their supporters during the earlier administrations they had in fact begun the partisan policy, the erstwhile majority denounced Jefferson for considering "himself as the head of a party, more than of a nation." The Federalists continued also to fill vacancies in those states where they retained power with "federal men only," thus providing the president with additional justification for his own removals.[52]

Such intransigence on the part of the opposition was accompanied by increasing unease and discontent among office-hungry Republicans. Jefferson realized that the success of his program rested on the strength and unity of his party, and while he still hoped to attract the loyalty of the partyless ex-Federalists, he was not prepared to risk a party split to do it, especially as Federalism in 1801–1802 showed little sign of lying down in meek submission. His policy began to conform, therefore, to a more partisan mold. In the more unregenerate Federalist strongholds he soon decided that conciliation was impossible. "In Connecticut alone," he wrote, "a general sweep seems to be called for on principles of justice and policy. . . . There then we will retaliate."[53]

By midsummer, 1801, he had determined upon an appointments policy that he was prepared to announce. Seizing upon the occasion of a remonstrance received from a number of disgruntled merchants in New Haven complaining of the appointment of a Republican to the lucrative collectorship of the port, Jefferson laid down guidelines for a modified policy to shape the future conduct of his administration. Assuring his critics that the appointment in question was based on a sound and careful evaluation of the fitness of the candidate, he cautioned them that they should not infer from his expressed desire for political tolerance any willingness to leave the "tenure of offices" undisturbed.

When it is considered that during the late Administration, those who were not

---

52. Oliver Wolcott to John Steele, March 12, 1802, in H. M. Wigstaff, ed., *The Papers of John Steele* (Raleigh, N.C., 1924), 2:260; Plumer, *Memorandum,* July 25, 1801; (New Hampshire) *Columbian Sentinel,* June 13, 1801, cited in Carl Russell Fish, *The Civil Service and the Patronage* (New York, 1905), p. 39.

53. Jefferson to W. C. Nicholas, June 11, 1801, Ford, 9:266.

of a particular sect of politics were excluded from all offices; when by a steady pursuit of this measure, nearly the whole offices of the United States were monopolized by that sect; when the public sentiment at length declared itself, and burst open the doors of honor and confidence to those whose opinions they more approved, was it to be imagined that this monopoly of offices was still to be continued in the hands of the minority? . . . Is it political tolerance to claim a proportionate share in the direction of public affairs? . . . If a due participation of office is a matter of right, how are vacancies to be obtained? Those by death are few; by resignation none.

Regretting that Federalist precedent had made such a policy of reprisals necessary, Jefferson assured his critics that when the balance of office had been corrected to reflect the strength of republican sentiment in the country, he as president would gladly return to "that state of things" where honesty, capability, and loyalty to the Constitution were the only criteria for office.[54]

This policy was reflected almost immediately in Jefferson's administrative conduct. In replying to a note from Gallatin enclosing a directive to customs collectors to "divide your offices equally between federalists and republicans, talent and integrity to be the only qualification for office," the president demurred, saying that such a policy should be effected only after half the appointees were of the Republican faith. Enlarging upon his rapidly developing policy a few weeks later, he cautioned that "while we push the patience of our friends to the utmost it will bear, in order that we may gather into the same fold all the republican Federalists possible, we must not even for this object, absolutely revolt our friends. It would be a poor maneuver to exchange them for new converts."[55]

Jefferson's view of the proper proportion of offices between the two parties was to change over the years. In favor of one-half for the Republicans in 1801, he was finding by the summer of 1803 that from two-thirds to three-quarters was a more accurate representation of the party's actual strength in the country. The few "Federalists" permitted to remain in office, furthermore, failed to include any of the quondam leadership of that faction. In one of his very few excursions into the

---

54. Jefferson to Elias Shipman and others, a Committee of the Merchants of New Haven, July 12, 1801, *ibid.*, pp. 270–274.

55. Gallatin to Jefferson, July 25, 1801, Gallatin, *Writings*, 1:28; Jefferson to Gallatin, July 26, 1801, p. 29, and August 14, 1801, pp. 32–34. See also Jefferson to Robert Smith, August 28, 1804, Ford, 10:97–98, where the president cautions that "we must be neutral between the discordant Republicans, but not between them and their common enemies."

newspaper wars, Jefferson "lobbied" himself and his own appointments policy in an article prepared for the *Massachusetts Chronicle*
under the *nom de plume*, "Fair Play." His purpose as he stated it in a
covering letter to Levi Lincoln was to "reconcile the parties among the
Republicans by attacking a common enemy, the federalists." Drawing
his familiar distinction between the "great mass of well-meaning followers and the heretical sect of monarchists . . . those pitiable ma-
niacs" (Jefferson's polemical talents were allowed full sway in this
piece), "Fair Play" denounced the latter in forceful terms: "Afraid to
wear their own name they creep under the mantle of federalism, and
the federalists, like sheep, permit the fox to take shelter among them,
when pursued by the dogs. These men have no right to offices. . . . I
should hold the President highly criminal if he permitted such to
remain. To appoint a monarchist to conduct the affairs of a republic is
like appointing an atheist to the priesthood, but as to the real
federalists, I take them to my bosom as brothers." [56] There seems little
doubt that to Jefferson the only "real federalists" were those who had
turned Republican.

As his first criteria for removing Federalists, Jefferson had settled on
the elimination of Adams's "midnight appointments" and the removal
of federal marshals and attorneys. In addition, although he continued
to feel that removals for political opinion only were improper, he felt
no hesitation about removing any public officials who attempted
through an "open and industrious opposition to the principles of the
present administration" to influence elections. He urged Lincoln to
seek out such persons, to "mark them," and "to leave the rest to me." [57]

The president adopted four basic criteria for appointments to those
offices that fell vacant. [58] Sound republicans, particularly in the lower
posts, were the only individuals considered. Second, he favored men
with military experience, particularly service in the Revolution. A
particularly good military record could sometimes sway Jefferson into

56. Jefferson to Levi Lincoln, June 1, 1803 (with enclosed article), Ford, 9:
469–474.
57. See, for example, Jefferson to Gov. Thomas McKean, February 2, 1801, *ibid.*,
p. 175; to Lincoln, October 25, 1802, p. 401; also to Gallatin, September 8, 1804,
10:101, where Jefferson suggests the propriety of a circular letter admonishing officials, friend and foe alike, to refrain from any "interference" with public elections.
58. These criteria are in basic agreement with White, *Jeffersonians*, p. 356, Fish,
pp. 45–52, and Sidney H. Aronson, *Status and Kinship in the Higher Civil Service*
(Cambridge, Mass., 1964).

retaining a man in office despite other disqualifications. Third, the president was concerned to have a proper geographical apportionment in the distribution of offices. He was sensitive that Virginia, particularly, tended to be overrepresented, and for a time it was very difficult for his fellow citizens of the Old Dominion to gain any appointments to federal posts except within their own state.[59]

A fourth criterion for appointment was that the nominee have respectability and standing in his community. Jefferson as a child of his time felt the importance of social status, general respectability, good family, and all that proper breeding implied in the way of education, culture, and social grace. Thus kinship with respected families continued under Jefferson, as under his predecessors, to be a sign of availability for high office. Sidney Aronson has indicated, however, that Jefferson did begin a trend toward a more representative elite in public office. While there was no marked change in the socioeconomic status of public appointees from Adams to Jefferson, the high correlation between social-class origins and social-class membership began to decline under Jefferson. To be a Republican in 1801 was in many places to be antiestablishment in outlook and background. Jefferson's appointees were new men, in many cases men who were challenging the established leadership in their communities. In Massachusetts and Connecticut, particularly, the Jeffersonians were expanding the old power structure, opening it up to new blood. While Adams's elite was dominated by financial, commercial, and trading interests, Jefferson's appointees more often reflected less established economic interests. There were fewer kinship relations in Jefferson's elite, more "self-made" men. In summarizing the distribution of social status characteristics in the Adams, Jefferson, and later the Jackson Administrations, Aronson found that of thirteen indicators, the Jeffersonians were nearer the Jacksonians than the Federalists in ten.[60]

Two *dis*qualifications for office should be mentioned. Jefferson never yielded to nepotism. Whenever relatives applied to him, as often happened, he would gracefully but firmly refuse. In addition, as he dryly observed to Gallatin, "the appointment of a woman to office is an innovation for which the public is not prepared, nor am I."[61]

59. Jefferson to John Page, July 17, 1807, Ford, 10:468, and February 20, 1802, 9:350–351.
60. Aronson, pp. 13–14, 157–158, 192–193, 195.
61. See, for example, Jefferson to George Jefferson, March 27, 1801, Ford,

While Jefferson was determined to reach a proportion in office between Republicans and Federalists that more accurately reflected political reality, the axe of the spoilsman fell more rarely than the opposition believed (or the writings of some future historians would seem to indicate). Carl Russell Fish calculated that in eight years in office Jefferson removed 109 of 433 officers subject to his direct appointment. In addition, of course, Granger removed some postmasters. Aronson calculates that Jefferson appointed 92 "elites" (defined as full-time, nontenured civil positions, filled by presidential appointment and affecting national policy). Of these 92, 72 were new appointments and 13 were retained from the Adams administration, the highest of the latter being Rufus King, the minister to England. Jefferson himself in the summer of 1803 prepared a table from which he figured that of 316 offices subject to presidential appointment, 130 were still in Federalist hands.[62]

The clamor of office seekers seemed continuous and unrelenting. Letters from those soliciting office may be found scattered liberally through the collections of his correspondence. A few represent the better sort who petitioned the president with some hope of gratification. But Jefferson and his cabinet officers were more often plagued by incompetent petitioners who alternately begged, flattered, cajoled, or threatened their way into favor. There was the obsequious fawner:

My very soul exalts in the pleasing prospect of Republican Government, once languishing under the pangs of desolation. . . . The Blinded Multitude appear to have discovered a ray of light to direct their wandering steps from the Gloomy regions of aristocracy to the bright sunshine of Republican Government. . . . Permit me to mention the application of Mr. Lawrence Dorsey for the appointment of Marshall of this state. . . .

And the ghoulish opportunist:

Mr. Vandervall the present postmaster at Richmond has been in a declining state of health for 12 months past and I have been lately informed is now confined to his bed and cannot live but a little time. By his death that office will become vacant and having no acquaintance with Mr. Granger have to solicit the favour of your friendly aid in obtaining that berth for me.[63]

9:238–239, and a reiteration of his position, Jefferson to J. Garland Jefferson, January 25, 1810, 11:133–134. For the comment on women, see Jefferson to Gallatin, January 13, 1807, 10:339–340.

62. Fish, pp. 42–43; White, *Jeffersonians,* pp. 150–151; Aronson, p. 32 (Table 1 and Appendix 3); Jefferson memorandum, July 24, 1803, Ford, 10:26.

63. Timothy Bloodworth to Jefferson, December 14, 1802, in McPherson, pp. 277–278; Letter to Jefferson, June 1, 1807, in White, *Jeffersonians,* p. 366.

And there was the threatening scandalmonger, such as the notorious James Thompson Callender, who in appealing to Madison for the postmastership of Richmond, cautioned that if the job were not forthcoming he would be compelled to "deliver a small piece of history" concerning Jefferson into Federalist hands. Few petitioners can have been quite so desperate, however, as the poor soul who, after camping on Madison's doorstep seeking unsuccessfully to be named to a territorial governorship, a collectorship, or a postmastership, finally asked the secretary if he had any old clothes to spare![64]

To Jefferson the problem of appointments and removals constituted the most abiding headache of his presidency. He personally gave his attention to every one of the appointments directly at his disposal. A person of his sensitivity would always be reluctant to incur the anger and cause the disappointment that accompanied such business, and he was all too aware that the benefits patronage brought were sometimes outweighed by the problems it presented. "Every office becoming vacant, every appointment made *me donne un ingrat, et cent ennemies*."[65] Yet it was largely through his appointive power that the new president was able to recast the political complexion of the executive, bringing it into line with the dominant philosophy of his party. Through his middle course in patronage he succeeded in staffing the government, at least the more politically sensitive parts of it, with his own people. In so doing he broadened the social, geographical, and political base of the civil service and provided his party with the machinery by which he hoped to return the country to republican paths. Jefferson lived in an age which did not fully appreciate or exploit the possibilities opened to government through an active use of patronage, and which denied its legitimacy when so used. As president, therefore, his record in the use of this resource is mixed. He was not to exploit its effectiveness to the same extent as future strong presidents. But he clearly understood the importance of a partisan appointments policy in extending his personal influence. Through his development of such a policy he enhanced his ability to exercise power over a broad range of policy areas, and laid the groundwork for a fuller mobilization of personal and political power, which later presidents were to employ.

64. J. T. Callender to Madison, May 7, 1801, in Brant, pp. 50–51; William Nisbet Chambers, *Political Parties in the New Nation* (New York, 1963), p. 180.

65. Jefferson to George Clinton, May 17, 1801, Ford, 9:254–255; to John Dickinson, January 13, 1807, 10:340–342. See also Jefferson to Benjamin Rush, March 24, 1801, 9:230–232.

CHAPTER 5

Jefferson and Congress:
A Government by Chance or Design?

Unlike his more ideological republican colleagues, Jefferson was not a legislative supremacist. In this, as in certain other features of his public philosophy, he was not, strictly speaking, a "Jeffersonian." He preferred a balanced constitutional arrangement with each branch of government possessing an integrity and independence of its own, an independence that extended (as we shall see in Chapter 6) to the equal right of each branch to decide for itself the constitutionality of its own actions. Formal separation of institutions is still a central reality governing the conduct of relations between president and Congress. The relationship has been likened to "sustained diplomatic negotiations between two sovereign powers . . . motivated by different sets of conventions."[1] But this description is more directly applicable to the realities of the Jeffersonian era than our own, when the sovereignty of the "separated powers" seems more often to have been replaced by a suzerainty of the executive over Congress.

Jefferson's long experience with legislatures had enabled him to view them with a certain realistic detachment. His approbation of popular government and the elective principle had not blinded him to the deficiencies of elected assemblies, nor to the potential for an arrogation of undue power by the legislative as well as the executive machinery of government. In one of the most famous and oft-quoted passages from his writings, he criticized the Virginia Constitution of 1776 for uniting all the powers of government in the legislative:

The concentrating these in the same hands is precisely the definition of des-

1. Charles E. Jacob, "Limits of Presidential Leadership," in *South Atlantic Quarterly*, 62 (Autumn, 1963).

potic government. It will be no alleviation that these powers will be exercised by a plurality of hands, and not by a single one. One hundred and seventy three despots would surely be as oppressive as one. . . . As little will it avail us that they are chosen by ourselves. An elective despotism was not the government we fought for, but one . . . in which the powers of government should be so divided and balanced among several bodies of magistracy, so that no one could transcend their legal limits, without being effectually checked and restrained by the others.

His views on the importance of balance in constitutional arrangements were reiterated in his correspondence with Madison at the time of the Constitutional Convention of 1787.[2]

Jefferson could also be critical of the quality of legislators, as in his denunciation of the majority in the Second Congress as consisting of "1, bank directors; 2, holders of bank stock; 3, stock jobbers; 4, blind devotees; 5, ignorant persons; . . . 6, lazy and good-humored persons who . . . were too lazy to examine or unwilling to pronounce censure." As a man of wide executive experience, Jefferson was aware as well of the obstructionism and delay endemic to legislatures. After six years in the presidency, he stoically observed to Joel Barlow: "There is a snail-paced gate for the advance of new ideas on the general mind, under which we must acquiesce. A 40-years' experience of popular assemblies has taught me, that you must give them time for every step you take. If too hard-pushed, they baulk, and the machine retrogrades."[3]

The Nature of the Congressional Party

Before we examine Jefferson's methods in dealing with Congress, it is necessary that we look rather closely at the chosen instrument for his exercise of leadership, the Republican party in Congress. How effective was the party as an instrument for policy-making? How organized was it for the prosecution of party business and how disciplined and unified were the congressional Republicans for the tasks of political reform?

As Jefferson assumed the presidency he knew that the newly victorious Republicans, in order to effect their program of reform, would have to unite their energies and pool their resources in a common

2. Quotation is from the *Notes on Virginia*, in Padover, *The Complete Jefferson*, p. 648; Jefferson to Madison, June 20, 1787, Ford, 5:284.

3. *Anas*, March 2, 1793, p. 114; Jefferson to Joel Barlow, December 10, 1807, Ford, 10:529–530.

effort cutting across the boundaries of constitutional structure. During the struggle in the Seventh Congress to repeal the Judiciary Act of 1801, a strategy of leadership began to crystallize as Jefferson came increasingly to assume the role of party leader in Congress. As Alexander B. Lacy notes, "Jefferson's role as organizer and leader of the members of his party in Congress was the vital factor in the strategy of political reform which constituted the Republican program."[4] If the party was to be a programmatic as well as an electoral force there could be no substitute for such leadership from the executive, which alone possessed the unity, the energy, and the direction to establish clear priorities and to mobilize the resources of the party for effective action.

But if the effectiveness of the Republican party depended largely on the prestige and leadership of Jefferson, it was nevertheless imperative that he step warily as he sought to exercise his leadership. He possessed decided advantages in asserting party leadership, but he was constrained to exercise it within a particular circumstantial, institutional, and ideological context, the dominant feature of which was the suspicion of power, particularly executive power, which had for so long been an integral part of the republican creed.

It is significant that the Republican party had begun in Congress. Formed in the 1790's under the leadership of Madison and Gallatin, the party had embraced as one of its cardinal tenets a resistance to executive authority.[5] The Republicans had started political life by attacking Hamilton's influence over Congress as a threat "to swallow up the legislative branch." They objected most strenuously to ministerial participation in the legislative process, notably in the drafting of bills. The Republican leadership recognized the president's right to recommend measures, and they perceived the usefulness of executive expertise in advising on legislation. They would, however, have sharply circumscribed it. In their view, the president should confine himself to the broad identification of problems and the recommendation of general subjects for consideration. Republican doctrine required an independent examination and evaluation of presidential recommendations by a Congress unfettered by executive control. When the Republicans gained control of the House of Representatives

4. "Jefferson and Congress," unpublished Ph.D. dissertation, University of Virginia (1964), p. 25.

5. In this regard, see Burns, *Deadlock of Democracy*, pp. 30–32.

in the Third Congress, they sought to institutionalize their views by replacing the expertise of department heads with standing committees of Congress. "If department heads continued to provide advice and plans in major areas of business, the introduction of committees as middlemen provided a counterweight to executive influence."[6]

Executive control of the legislature actually declined before Jefferson took office. By 1797 when the Federalists regained control of Congress, they had accepted the committee system begun by their opponents, and the Adams administration was unable to regain the initiative formerly enjoyed by Hamilton. To be sure, the years following 1801 witnessed changes in Republican attitudes toward executive participation in the legislative process. The attitude of the party leaders (many of whom, of course, were now in the executive branch), became less negative, less adamant, more receptive to executive influence and direction.[7] Nonetheless, the kind of legislative management open to Republican executives was limited by the party's ideology. Control had to be maintained informally and with circumspection. Jefferson chose to operate within the limits of existing constitutional arrangements and the power of the developing congressional committee system in order to avoid the impression of undue pressure on Congress.

The president knew that he was leading a collection of like-minded individuals rather than a solid phalanx of party operatives. These individuals, furthermore, had been conditioned through long years in the political wilderness to habits of behavior more conducive to obstruction and factionalism than to constructive cooperation under a central leadership. This legislative "type" was particularly common in the southern delegations, where a fierce and touchy individualism combined with an often cantankerous combativeness to produce the sort of legislator colorfully described by John Quincy Adams:

6. Joseph Cooper, "Jeffersonian Attitudes toward Executive Leadership and Committee Development in the House of Representatives, 1789–1829," in *Western Political Quarterly*, 18 (March, 1965), 47–62.

7. The shift in attitude can be represented by Madison, who in 1795 was adamantly opposed to the practice of a president pressing his views and advice on Congress, but by 1811 was chiding a critic of such practices that "where the intention was honest, and the object useful, the conveniency of facilitating business in that way was so obvious that it had been practiced under every past administration, and would be so under every future one; that Executive experience would frequently furnish hints and lights for the legislature" Madison to Robert Smith, in Gaillard Hunt, ed., *The Writings of James Madison* [New York, 1900–1910], 8:143–144).

full of Virginian principles and prejudices, a mixture of wisdom and Quixotism. . . . His delight was the consciousness of his own independence, and he thought it heroic virtue to ask no favors. He therefore never associated with any members of the Executive and would have shuddered at the thought of going to the drawing room. Jealousy of State rights and jealousy of the Executive were the two pillars of Burwell's political fabric. . . . Such men occasionally render service to the nation by preventing harm; but they are quite as apt to prevent good, and they never do any.[8]

Such men were not easily adapted to the lash of party discipline and strong leadership, particularly that imposed by an external force such as the president, and it became a test of great importance whether they could be gently but firmly molded into a force for political action.

Jefferson wrote often of the difficulty of working with such uncongenial material. He complained that "our leading friends are not sufficiently aware of the necessity of accommodation and mutual sacrifice of opinion for conducting a numerous assembly."[9] The fissiparous tendencies that lay only partially submerged within the body of Republicanism were to prove an abiding source of irritation to Jefferson, and were to emerge with great force after he left the White House. Through the years of his presidency, however, his own unifying presence and the talents he demonstrated in the subtle arts of persuasion and bargaining served to mobilize the Republican majority behind his leadership to a remarkable degree.

The conventional wisdom concerning the Jeffersonian party in Congress was expounded by a number of early students of party development, among them Ralph V. Harlow, M. I. Ostrogorski, and later Leonard White.[10] These scholars and others pictured the Republican party during Jefferson's administration as an organized, tightly disciplined body of men united on principle and determined to employ the force of their cohesive majority in order to effect great changes. Each scholar emphasized what he saw as a highly centralized system

8. Diary entry of February 16, 1821, in Charles Francis Adams, ed., *Memoirs of John Quincy Adams* (Philadelphia, 1874), 5:281–282. Adams was describing William A. Burwell, a Virginia congressman and a former private secretary to Jefferson.

9. Jefferson to Clinton, December 2, 1803, Ford, 10:55.

10. See particularly Harlow, *A History of Legislative Methods Before 1825* (New Haven, 1917); Ostrogorski, *Democracy and the Organization of Political Parties* (New York, 1902), and his "The Rise and Fall of the Nominating Caucus, Legislative and Congressional," in *American Historical Review*, 5 (December, 1899); also White, *Jeffersonians*, especially pp. 45–59.

of party control. To Harlow the dominant impression of the party in the years 1801–1809, was of "drilled platoons" marching into the legislative chamber to vote the party line. Ostrogorski, more appalled than impressed by what he saw, wrote of a party that "compelled obedience to the word of command from whatever quarter it proceeded." Writing half a century later, White concluded that "the floor leader, the party caucus, the intimate personal relations between members of the two branches, the willingness of the House to accept drafts of important bills" from the executive, constituted sound evidence of a tightly centralized system of party organization.[11]

More recent studies of party politics and congressional organization call into question many of the assumptions of the established interpretation, however. Alexander Lacy in his study of Jefferson and his Congresses describes the Republican majority as a "conglomerate of individuals who were more at home as an opposition than as a majority." At the outset of the new administration, the congressional Republicans were poorly organized as a legislative machine and jealous of their independence from any leadership. Indeed, it was difficult to get an accurate *count* of the Republicans in Congress. Party identification was not kept as part of the voting records in either house. Furthermore, the leadership cadres of the Republicans were weak as the Jefferson administration began.[12]

James Sterling Young, in his *The Washington Community, 1800–1828*, has taken the "revisionist" approach to Jeffersonian party politics even further. In attempting to enumerate the values and structures that reinforced political independence and weakened party cohesion during the Jeffersonian period to 1828, Young comes close to denying the very existence of a Republican "party" in Congress as the term "party" is understood by modern scholarship. Legislative politics of the period were characterized by weak party organization, a high rate of turnover, divergent constituency obligations, an eighteenth-century ethos of independence from party control, rules of procedure that encouraged dissent, and "patterned social avoidance" among men of different regions. Young stresses the low opinion of politics held by its

11. Ostrogorski, "Nominating Caucus," pp. 263–264; White, *Jeffersonians*, p. 46.
12. Lacy, pp. 24–25. Various estimates put the breakdown of House membership at 67–68 Republicans and 37–38 Federalists. See Jefferson to T. M. Randolph, January 1, 1802, for his own estimate, and Jefferson to John Wayles Eppes, January 1, 1802, in Lacy, p. 25.

practitioners of the period. Power was suspect, its exercise immoral, said the prevailing climate of opinion. He ascribes the high rate of Senate turnover, particularly by resignation, in part to the antipower feeling that the politicians shared with their lay countrymen.[13] A corollary to this antipower bias was that many members of Congress distrusted the very objective of party solidarity as tending to undermine the integrity of the individual members.

To Young the strength of these values was underscored by the absence of any firm party organization in Congress. Far from seeing parties as the well-drilled phalanxes of the traditional interpretation, Young finds them "largely unorganized groups . . . without openly recorded membership, much less with differentiated leadership roles," and unsustained by regular social interaction. He discerns no formal structures of organization in the congressional party, save for a "campaign committee." "Party members elected no leaders, designated no functionaries to speak on their behalf or to carry out any legislative task assignments. The party had no whips, no seniority leaders. There were no Committees on Committees, no Steering Committee, no Policy Committees; none of the organizational apparatus that marks the twentieth-century parties as going enterprises." Finding no twentieth-century party organization, Young comes perilously close to denying the existence of any effective congressional party. Borrowing a less than felicitous term of David Truman's, he describes the Jeffersonian Republicans as more nearly approximating a "potential group," without intensity of feeling or regularity of interaction. "It would seem," he writes, "that no more influence upon policy should be attributed to the congressional party than is attributed to the unorganized in politics generally."[14] No stronger denial of "party" significance could be made.

Such an interpretation serves a useful purpose in deflating the myth of the party "leviathan" promoted by earlier scholars. Resting his denial of party status on the absence of firm organizational structure, however, Young obscures certain other factors that serve to qualify the Republicans as a functioning "party" group. It is not necessary, in stressing the rudimentary nature of party organization, to deny the

13. *Washington Community*, p. 146. Between 1787 and 1829, more senators resigned than were defeated for reelection; 17.9 percent of the Senate resigned every two years, nearly six times the modern rate (*ibid.*, p. 57).

14. *Ibid.*, p. 147, 126–127.

party an existence. Not only has the emperor no clothes, there is no emperor!

Perhaps the flaw in Young's argument lies in his assumption that a group can be nothing more than "potential" unless it possesses a formal organization. A more functional and less structural definition of "group" might have served to reveal the weakness in such an assumption. Muzafer Sherif has defined a group as a social unit which (1) consists of "individuals who are more or less interdependent with one another and which (2) explicitly or implicitly possesses a set of values or norms of its own regulating behavior of individual members at least in matters of consequence to the group."[15] The definition serves with reasonable accuracy to describe the congressional Republicans, who were formed as a group around a common set of ideological assumptions and a common political allegiance, which with the passage of time evolved into a significant group consciousness. An organizational flow chart is not necessary for a collection of individuals to be considered a viable and cohesive group. Consciously shared values and aspirations and, in Sherif's phrase, "ideal modes of behavior, defining for members the limits or latitude of acceptable behavior" can be sufficient to bind a group of individuals together. As the group stays together over time, as awareness of shared values increases among the members, as the group's functions expand and diversify, a rudimentary organization will develop and a division of labor, formalized by titles and status levels, will emerge.

A group can have a definite organization with differentiated status levels without the existence of formal positions, titles, and job descriptions. Status level can be determined by observing the "frequency of suggestions concerning group activities addressed or relayed" to the individual, or by observing the extent to which he asserts his authority in leading group activities or in furthering group goals. The example of Jefferson's legislative lieutenants will serve to illustrate the point. While none of them ever carried the title majority leader, it is not difficult for students of the period to determine who they were at any given period. The fact that more than one served at most times does not indicate the absence of organization, merely its flexibility and lack of specificity, a not unexpected phenomenon in a day when organized life was far more uncommon than it is today. Jeffersonian America was

15. Sherif, ed., *Intergroup Relations and Leadership* (New York, 1962), pp. 4–5.

a "casually patterned" society.[16] The Republican party, furthermore, functioned in an environment, Congress, which itself had developed little organizational specificity in its early years. The committee system was rudimentary, and rules of procedure were loose and constantly under revision. It is not difficult to see why the subsystem of party failed to develop an elaborate organization when the parent system itself remained so undeveloped.

To reinforce his thesis concerning the weakness of the Jeffersonian party, Young indicates that, contrary to the traditional view, the party caucus was not used by the Republican party except to nominate a president. He rests his conclusion on the apparently plausible assertion that the only evidence of Republican use of the caucus to plan party strategy comes from their Federalist opponents. He takes Harlow to task in particular for his use of "flimsy" evidence based on exclusively Federalist suspicions. Young finds it highly unlikely that regular or even frequent caucuses would have gone unrecorded in the many informal chronicles of the period.[17]

On closer scrutiny it may be unwise to dismiss the evidence of a party caucus on such grounds, however, and not simply on the assumption that "where there is smoke there is fire." Harry Ammon, in discussing the activities of the secret but nonetheless very real Richmond Junto, cautions that the existence of an oligarchy or a powerfully organized bloc ran counter to the principles of republican ideology.[18] Secrecy was an essential requirement for the effectiveness of such an organization. Similarly, it is not surprising that few loyal Republicans would readily acknowledge the regular activities of a party caucus which, while often necessary for the efficient operation of the party in Congress, still lacked the legitimacy that would have permitted its frequent overt usage.

But one does not have to rely on such speculation only. An examination of the evidence reinforces the need for caution in dismissing the notion that the party caucus was frequently employed. There is, for one thing, direct evidence of *Federalist* use of the party caucus to plan strategy, decide the order of speakers in debate, and so on. Lacy cites, for example, a letter from Manasseh Cutler to his son in which he

16. The phrase is Robert Lynd's, quoted in *ibid.*, p. 18.
17. *Washington Community*, p. 126.
18. "The Richmond Junto: 1800–1828," in *Virginia Magazine of History and Biography*, 61 (1953).

writes, "Our arrangements are made the evening before, but the speakers on our side are *always* conditional, and depend on who may arise on the opposite."[19] The word "always" would seem to indicate that such a strategy session was not a one-time occurrence, and the tone of the letter indicates that the writer did not expect his revelations to surprise his reader. Referring to the same debate, Lacy remarks that while it is impossible to estimate how frequently the Republicans met, the "exceedingly well-managed" nature of the long debate seems to indicate that they, too must have held strategy sessions "out of doors."

The record of the period does contain, furthermore, a few references by Republicans to party caucuses. For example, in a letter to the *Richmond Enquirer*, Giles refers to a caucus of all the Republicans in Congress held in February, 1809, to determine upon a repeal of the embargo. Though much of the evidence of caucuses would perhaps be considered as hearsay in a court of law, there is little reason to ignore it simply because it comes from the pens of Federalists. Much of the evidence from "Federalist" sources is gleaned, moreover, from the writings of two men, John Quincy Adams and William Plumer, whose loyalty to the Federalist party was suffering severe strains during this period and whose reputation for independence of thought and deed was high; this period marks, indeed, the transformation of Adams from maverick Federalist to independent Republican. Two instances from the Adams *Memoirs* will serve to indicate the unremarkable nature of the use of party caucuses. During a Senate debate in February, 1805, Adams confided to his diary: "an incident not very singular in those times soon occurred," a procedural maneuver by the leadership which, to Adams, was "so evidently the result of consultation out-of-doors." During the debate Adams hinted at the out-of-doors consultation, but was called to order by a Republican senator. The Chair ruled, however, that Adams's remark was *in* order, an indication of Aaron Burr's growing alienation from his party. On a later occasion when Adams was being wooed by the Republican leadership, he was informed by Giles, the Senate leader, that "the details of a bill have been settled out of doors."[20]

Plumer, too, seems to serve as a reasonably accurate source of evi-

19. Lacy, p. 57.
20. *Richmond Enquirer*, October 25, 1828, reprinted in Henry Adams, *Documents*, p. 39; J. Q. Adams, *Memoirs*, February 5, 1805, 1:346–347; March 2, 1805, 1:465.

dence for the use of a caucus. He reports a caucus of "democratic" senators on the night of February 7, 1804, to settle the principles of the Louisiana government bill. Again, on December 11, 1804, he writes of a private caucus of Republicans to agree on the appointment of a governor of the Louisiana Territory. During this period Plumer had the confidence of certain Republican colleagues. He reports the gist of a long conversation with Senator Stephen Bradley, in which the Vermont Republican speaks of a recent Senate caucus of which he was the chairman. His remarks are of interest in what they reveal of caucus purpose and procedure. The subject was the removal of the secretary of the Senate, a move Bradley opposed. According to Plumer, the senator remarked that

He had long been acquainted with caucuses—That the great object was to settle principles—not the election or removal of men to or from office—That the only exception to this rule arises from its vast importance, the election of President and Vice President of the U.S. . . . That it is derogatory to the dignity of a senatorial caucus to take a vote for the removal of Otis—And that at all events he would not suffer a vote to be taken. [De Witt] Clinton then said they would appoint another chairman. Bradley told them, even caucuses were bound by rules—and before another chairman could be chosen, this caucus must be dissolved and another called—And then a new chairman might be elected.[21]

Such evidence, while not conclusive, would seem to show that caucuses were held with some regularity, enough so as to warrant some rudimentary organization and rules of procedure, and that their usual purpose was to decide principle and agree on policy.

It seems reasonable to agree with William Nisbet Chambers that "the Republican congressional caucus was employed from 1801 on. Differences were ironed out, the party position on specific measures was shaped in detail, discipline was established—generally at the behest of or in accord with the party's executive leadership."[22] While one may accept Young's persuasive evidence that the organizational cohesiveness and effectiveness of Jefferson's party was not as all-pervasive as Harlow and others had assumed, it is nonetheless true that this era

21. Plumer, *Memorandum*, pp. 141, 220, 597.

22. Chambers, *Political Parties*, p. 171. Voting blocks of substantial persistence and stability, if not parties in the modern sense, had emerged as well by the time of Jefferson's presidency. See Mary P. Ryan, "Party Formation in the U.S. Congress, 1789–1796: A Quantitative Analysis," in *William and Mary Quarterly*, 28 (October, 1971).

marked the first effective beginnings of party government in the United States and that, to the men of the time, the performance of the party under Jefferson was more often impressive than not.

It is clear that to speak of the "parties" of the Jeffersonian period as though they were parties in the modern sense, with a central organization of professionals, an elaborate structure of machinery in Congress, and a fully developed consciousness in the electorate, is to distort the facts. Even to speak in terms of a "party system" at this time might serve to obscure rather than to clarify an accurate conception of political reality. Perhaps what is needed is a new term by which to identify the phase in party development that occupied these years of transition from a pre-party pattern characterized by elite groupings of political notables in a "deferential" political culture to the stage of full party development in the "participant" culture after 1840. Ronald Formisano has suggested the term "interests" rather than party to describe the Republican and Federalist groupings, which in the Jeffersonian period "remained much closer to 'relatively stable coalitions' than to durable cadre parties of regular internal organization and fairly stable, self-conscious followings."[23] Such a description would permit us to recognize the tentative nature of party formation in these years without causing us to deny the very real and compelling evidence that despite the absence of formal organization and structural sophistication the Jeffersonian "party" or "interest" was a functioning reality. Its activities were praised by its friends, damned by its enemies. Its members worked and voted together far more often than not—which is all that anyone can ever expect from an American political party in Congress. The members were motivated by considerations of party, and its presence as a compelling factor in political behavior was felt as no such political force had been felt before. The effective use of this rudimentary machinery of party as an instrument of presidential power was one of Jefferson's most important contributions to the presidency.

One further point should be made concerning the nature of the Republicans in Congress before we proceed to examine Jefferson's methods in leading it. Young has emphasized the low saliency of Washington and of national politics, and the general indifference of the American public to both. Jeffersonian government, he writes, "was

23. "Deferential-Participant Politics: The Early Republic's Political Culture, 1789–1840," in *American Political Science Review*, 68 (June, 1974), 473–487.

not one of the important institutions in American society—important as a social presence or important in its impact upon the everyday lives of the citizens." It was too new, too small, promising too little reward and too little challenge. Most of the positions of power had less attraction than did similar posts in the state governments. Most people felt a primary attachment to their states rather than to the central government. "How attenuated were its functions as an instrument of social control is indicated by the fact that there were more people making the law than enforcing it." Quoting Hamilton, Young describes the government of the period as government "at a distance and out of sight."[24]

Much in this analysis is well taken. Certainly the day-to-day impact of government activities on the lives of the citizenry was much less important than it was to become as the nation grew and the conception of government's role in society changed. Equally true, many of the essential governmental services—education, law enforcement, poor relief—were performed by state and local authorities, not by the national government. It is correct to note that the raw new capital at Washington was geographically isolated from the population centers and economic centers of the country.

It does not follow, however, as Young asserts, that "the rulers had become pariahs, quarantined in the countryside," and permitted to proceed as they pleased, unnoticed and unremarked upon by the people whom they represented. To assume "the low temperature of national politics and its relative decorum before the Jacksonian era" is misleading. Nor is it accurate to say that "isolated circumstances of the early governing group must have afforded a freedom of choice as nearly uninhibited as any representative government could have."[25]

Ample evidence exists to show that not only did congressmen feel severe constraints imposed upon their behavior by their own ideologies and by constituent demands and attitudes, but that in fact the electorate demanded a fairly strict accounting from their representatives of their performance at the distant seat of government. Certain decisions of Congress provoked sharp retaliation by the voters. One of the greatest turnovers in congressional history followed the decision of Congress to vote itself a pay raise in 1810. Every congressman in the

24. *Washington Community*, pp. 27, 30.
25. *Ibid.*, pp. 35–36.

North Carolina delegation who voted against repeal of the Judiciary Act of 1801 was defeated for reelection. Elected representatives have always looked over their shoulders at their constituents, but perhaps even more so in the early years of the republic when both issues and alternatives were fewer, and when the political landscape was less cluttered by cross-cutting and conflicting demands and opinions, the myriad of countervailing pressures behind which the modern congressman can seek refuge from the glare of constituent criticism.

Young seems to have overemphasized the importance of the geographical isolation of the Washington community. Since Congress met only three or four months a year, members were at home in their districts a good deal of the time, feeling the public pulse, receiving and dispensing political intelligence, and sensing the ebb and flow of political currents through direct contact with them. In addition, the identification of popular opinion was made easier by the homogeneity of most congressional districts in terms of socioeconomic interests and regional affections. Writing of the relationship between the capital and the provinces in the early years of the century, Margaret Coit has captured the point:

> Though Washington was three weeks hard travel from Abbeville [South Carolina], actually the little country village in the foothills and the overgrown village on the Potomac were closer to each other than automobiles and railroads would make them a century later. The government in Washington was no abstract mechanism, where responsibility to the people was lost in a tangled mesh of weavings and interweavings. It was a vital living organism, dreamed and shaped by men still alive, who had given their *personal* consent to its formation and who could, at will, withdraw it.[26]

Thus it is misleading to assume from geographical isolation an isolation of the members of the Washington community from the political attentions of their constituents. The interest was there, and all in Washington were alert to its political implications. Not a little of Jefferson's success with Congress can be attributed to the relationship between the esteem of the Republican rank-and-file for their president and his policies and the sensitivities of the congressional Republicans to that popular prestige. To be "constituency-oriented," as Young admits the congressional community was, was to perceive the strength of that relationship and to reflect it by loyalty to the president and his program within the halls of Congress.

26. Margaret Coit, *John C. Calhoun* (Boston, 1950), p. 46.

Congress and the Jeffersonian Style

We have observed that Jefferson chose to base his presidential leaderhip on the extraconstitutional and political influence of his party leadership rather than to place primary reliance upon his formal status and authority as president. He did not propose to ignore the importance of prerogative as a resource of power, but his influence rested in the main on the mechanism of party and his role as its leader. If his purpose then was to assert his authority as party leader and to enlist his colleagues under the party banner, it was essential that he cultivate Congress, earn and maintain the approbation of the leading men in each house, and avoid any impressions of domination, the evidence of which so quickly triggered the tender sensibilities and destructive jealousies of that co-equal branch. He was obliged to employ the subtler and more indirect weapons in the arsenal of his political talents. He had to conquer, if indeed "conquer" is the word, by seduction rather than coercion. Such methods, so in harmony with his deeper instincts, reflect the same conclusions based upon the same set of conditions which, *mutatis mutandis*, are illuminated in the modern presidency by the Neustadtian bargaining model. Fortunately the character of his political style was congruent with the nature of his political task as he conceived it.

It was first of all essential, in his view, to maintain a public attitude of deference toward Congress as the embodiment of the popular will. This was demanded not only by the general climate of opinion and republican ideology, but by the realities of opinion among congressional leaders. In his state papers and other public pronouncements Jefferson carefully cultivated congressional sensibilities. In his formal Reply to the notification of his election, he pledged that, "Guided by the wisdom and patriotism of those to whom it belongs to express the legislative will of the nation, I will give to that will a faithful execution." His remarks to the Senate at his leave-taking as presiding officer in February, 1801, were designed, as well, to disarm senatorial critics and conciliate opposition to the new administration in a body that was still Federalist in character.[27]

As they worked on presidential messages to Congress, Jefferson

---

27. February 20, 1801, in Padover, pp. 382–383; February 28, 1801, Ford, 9:189–190. Jefferson owed his election in real measure to the House, which chose him over Burr.

and his cabinet colleagues were careful to couch their language in terms that stressed legislative hegemony in policy-making, even as that hegemony was being circumscribed by executive action. In October, 1802, for example, following the resumption of war in Europe, Gallatin urged the president to note in his annual message to Congress the happy circumstance of American neutrality; this should be done, however, "without expressing anything like executive self-applause, but referring everything to the moderate and wise policy adopted by the last Congress under great provocations." Jefferson took the advice: "let us bow with gratitude to that kind Providence which, inspiring with wisdom and moderation our late legislative councils while placed under the urgency of the greatest wrongs, guarded us from hastily entering the sanguinary contest, and left us only to to look and to pity its ravages."[28]

Jefferson showed his alertness to congressional sensibilities through his actions as well as his rhetoric. He saw no need to ruffle congressional feathers when it could be avoided. Whenever he received petitions or letters from citizens asking his intercession in a legislative matter he would forward the request to the man's congressional delegation, noting carefully as he did so his refusal to "place myself between the legislative Houses and those who have a constitutional right to address them directly."[29] Such touches of consideration, insignificant as they might appear, contributed to ease his relations with Congress.

The reward structure available to presidents in the early republic was woefully inadequate to insure congressional cooperation. Members of Congress, as Young as observed, were "denied the opportunity to perform a wide range of citizen services . . . were denied the rationale of contributing significantly to the public weal." The president, too, was often denied such opportunities. In the absence of the host of services and benefits at the disposal of the modern president to withhold or disperse in accordance with services rendered, the patronage of appointments and removals from office was the major weapon available to President Jefferson. We have observed his ambivalence toward such a device for promoting executive influence with Con-

28. Gallatin to Jefferson, October, 1803, Gallatin, *Writings*, 1:158–159; third annual message to Congress, October 17, 1803, Ford, 10:41.
29. Jefferson to Andrew Gregg, Michael Leib, and John Smilie of Pennsylvania, March 2, 1809, LC No. 33162.

gress. There is no evidence that Jefferson ever used his power of appointment as a carrot or a stick to secure a *vote* from a legislator. He consulted congressmen primarily for the information they possessed, not for indirect political reasons. Nevertheless he did use patronage as a means of cultivating general influence and rewarding political allies. In a few instances he gave almost the entire power of recommending appointments in a state to a leading member of Congress. His powerful congressional ally, Nathaniel Macon, benefited from such a relationship as Jefferson's patronage chief in North Carolina.[30] The practice of consulting a state's congressional delegation before making appointments within that state and the corollary practice of senatorial courtesy were not yet firmly established customs under Jefferson. While the Republicans in the Senate were developing the habit of hearing from the Senator in whose state an appointment was proposed (much to the annoyance of the Federalist remnant),[31] Jefferson's practice seemed to be to consult the party leaders in a state whether or not they were in Congress. Factionalism within several state parties made it dangerous for him to rely on only one source in the state for advice on patronage. Thus while he would rely on Macon in North Carolina, Giles in Virginia, and to a lesser extent Smith in Maryland, he turned to state officials and local leaders in New York, Pennsylvania, and Massachusetts. In the main Jefferson's influence with senators was sufficient to override objections based upon senatorial courtesy.

Jefferson's Legislative Lieutenants

To provide a focus of leadership and to facilitate the consideration and passage of administration measures, it was necessary for the president to have spokesmen within the halls of Congress. The fractious and at times contrary majority party in each house needed a floor leader to establish priorities, set agendas, and shepherd the flow of legislative business. Jefferson wanted floor leaders, furthermore, who

30. Jefferson to Macon, May 14, 1801, Ford, 9: pp. 253–254: "And in all cases when an office becomes vacant in your state . . . I should be much obliged to you to recommend the best characters." See also Gallatin to John Steele, undated, but summer, 1801, in Wigstaff, *Papers of John Steele*, 1:238: "If agreeable, will suspend appointment of collector of Wilmington till meeting of Congress, as requested by Mr. Macon."

31. See John Quincy Adams to John Adams, December 11, 1804, in Worthington C. Ford, ed., *The Writings of John Quincy Adams* (New York, 1914), 3:83–84; also Lacy, pp. 104–105.

could combine standing in their house with loyalty to the president, for ideally they should serve as administrative spokesmen to Congress *and* as congressional spokesmen to the executive branch. Jefferson conceived of these legislative lieutenants as the most legitimate instruments with which to bridge the gap between the branches. They would constitute a two-way transmission network, mobilizing and maintaining congressional majorities for presidential programs while keeping the president informed of the state of congressional opinion. The floor leaders planned the schedules of the two houses, directed referrals of matters to committees (in conjunction with the Speaker in the House) and controlled those committees, mobilized members' support behind administration bills, defended the administration on the floor, and served as the principal communications link across the separation of powers.[32]

Jefferson's conception of the ideal floor leader was well developed by the time he outlined it to one whom he was grooming for such a post, Barnabas Bidwell, in the summer of 1806. In Congress there was a constant need for one member "to take the lead in the House of Representatives, to consider the business of the nation as his own business, to take it up as if he were singly charged with it, and carry it through. I do not mean that any gentleman, relinquishing his own judgment, should implicitly support all of the measures of the administration; but that, where he does not disapprove of them, he should not suffer them to go off to sleep, but bring them to the attention of the House and give them a fair chance." The President realized the difficult position in which his legislative lieutenants were placed by their double loyalties to president and Congress, and the damage to their effectiveness should they appear too slavishly devoted to the fulfillment of any and all presidential wishes. Party leaders, then as now, were confronted with the need to oppose the president upon occasion, if only to assert and demonstrate their continued independence from outside control and to reestablish their oneness with their congressional colleagues. But although he conceded the delicacy of the relationship, Jefferson was quick to defend his use of floor leaders to help pass his program. In the same letter to Bidwell he observed; "if the members are to know nothing but what is important enough to be made known to all the world; if the Executive is to keep all other

32. Lacy, p. 121.

information to himself, and the House to plunge on in the dark, it becomes a government of chance and not of design."[33] Jefferson was a keen enough student of legislative behavior to know that if left to chance, the result would be waywardness, indecision, and drift, and the hopes of achieving a successful program of political reform would fade quickly away. The engine of state could run well only if it were kept well tuned and its moving parts well oiled by the lubrication of executive leadership.

Harlow is inexact in saying that the floor leaders were "appointed and dismissed" by the president. There was, of course, no formal process of appointment, as indeed there was no official post of majority leader. Furthermore, Jefferson was limited in his ability to select his lieutenants by the "material" at hand, although, as we shall see, he tried to create new material by recruiting particular men to assume leadership positions in Congress. In the main, he accepted the man who, "for a complex set of reasons, was already generally accepted as the leader of the party in the House."[34]

For the early years of the administration, Young's implication that the floor leaders were the president's men only, with little standing in the congressional wing of the party is inaccurate.[35] William Branch Giles, John Randolph, Nathaniel Macon, Stevens T. Mason, and Joseph H. Nicholson were highly respected in Congress and were looked to as leaders by their colleagues even before assuming the tasks of presidential spokesmen. It is true, however, that as time passed and for a variety of reasons (death, resignation, or schism) new leaders were needed, they tended to be the personal representatives of the president, possessing influence and power solely because they were identified as his voice in the halls of Congress. Men such as Joseph B. Varnum, George Washington Campbell, Caesar Rodney, and Barnabas Bidwell, while politicians of ability, lacked the independence and authority of earlier floor leaders. They had not won their spurs through congressional service or parliamentary brilliance, but rather owed their prestige to the fact of having the president's ear.

The absence of specialized leadership roles in the party structure in Congress meant that at times there was more than one floor leader in

33. Jefferson to Barnabas Bidwell, July 5, 1806, Lipscomb, 11:115–117.
34. Harlow, p. 177; Lacy, p. 122.
35. *Washington Community*, pp. 129–130. For an equally erroneous view, see Claude G. Bowers, Jr., *Jefferson in Power* (Boston, 1936), pp. 223–225, 338ff.

each House. In the first Congress under Jefferson, the party leadership in the House of Representatives, for example, was exercised by Speaker Nathaniel Macon and William B. Giles. Following Giles's resignation because of illness after the first session, leadership devolved upon a triumvirate of Macon, John Randolph, and J. H. Nicholson. At least twenty men were referred to as "leaders" by various shades of party (and opposition) opinion during the eight years of Jefferson's presidency, but of these only nine seem to have exercised significant authority as the president's spokesmen: Macon, Giles, Randolph, Rodney, Bidwell, and Campbell in the House, and Mason, John C. Breckinridge, Wilson Cary Nicholas, and again Giles in the Senate.[36]

Jefferson was fortunate during the first two years of his administration to have William Branch Giles as his chief spokesman and floor leader in the House. When he assumed these responsibilities in 1801, Giles had the experience of eleven years in legislative service. He was already the acknowledged leader of the Virginia delegation, a tried and true Republican stalwart who was eager to apply the "principles of '98" in the attainment of fundamental reform. Giles had a reputation for a certain hotheadedness, but he was enough the prudent politician to realize the need to trim his sails when practical affairs demanded it. His partisanship may have exceeded Jefferson's own, but his skill as a party leader made him invaluable to the president and played a significant role in the legislative success of Jefferson's first Congress. His leadership of the Republican majority emerged quickly during the first weeks of the session and by February, 1802, he had earned the title bestowed upon him by a Federalist member as the "premier or prime minister of the day." He was an effective legislator, prudent, conciliatory, yet firm when he needed to be and capable of arousing the fighting spirit of his party colleagues. Partisan as he was, however, he could at times apply a not inconsiderable charm and tact to the conciliation of moderate Federalists.[37]

Giles's position as the president's spokesman was never in doubt. Unfortunately his health was none too robust and he was forced to

36. Others mentioned included Joseph B. Varnum, Samuel Smith, De Witt Clinton, Jacob Crowninshield, Joseph H. Nicholson, Stephen Bradley, Joseph Anderson, and Jefferson's two sons-in-law, Thomas Mann Randolph and John Wayles Eppes.

37. Lacy, p. 126. The best biography of Giles, though out of date, is Dice R. Anderson, *William Branch Giles* (Menasha, Wis., 1914).

leave Congress after the 1801–1802 session. He recovered sufficiently to return to the Senate in 1804, whereupon he quickly assumed control of the leadership in that body, remaining as Jefferson's chief lieutenant for the remainder of the administration. Because of his continuing ill health he missed a good deal of the debates, and in his absence the Republicans appeared at times confused and rudderless. Nevertheless, the administration lost no major bills in the Senate for lack of leadership. It was with understandable hyperbole that John Quincy Adams, that most independent of men, referred to Giles as "our present sovereign . . . who rules without control as Lord of the Ascendant. . . . His power is such that if he should move my expulsion from the Senate because he does not like my looks, he would stand a very fair chance of success." Adams, however, recognized Giles's great talents for leadership, his tact, and his good humor. "He has nothing insolent in his manner, which cannot be said of all his associates."[38]

With Giles's departure from the House in 1802 the floor leadership of the majority fell largely upon the narrow shoulders of the beardless, brilliant little eccentric from the Virginia southwest, John Randolph of Roanoke. Jefferson's relations with this "pale, meagre, ghostly man" were friendly without being intimate, and Randolph's assertion of leadership owed less to the presidential imprimatur than to the congressman's own talents and connections in the House. He was an intimate friend of Speaker Macon and profited greatly from his appointment by the latter to the chairmanship of the Committee on Ways and Means.[39]

Randolph reached the pinnacle of his performance as floor leader during the session of 1803–1804, when he skillfully piloted the Louisiana Purchase bill and the most controversial Louisiana government bill through the House. His greatest talent as leader was his forensic eloquence. His rhetoric, filled with classical allusions (some of dubious relevance) and laced with a devastating capacity for invective, thrust him into a position of prominence in a body where a premium was placed upon such talents. His sharp tongue and wit of biting

38. John Quincy Adams to John Adams, December 24, 1804, in J. Q. Adams, *Writings*, 3:102–103. The younger Adams felt that even Vice President Burr was subservient to Giles. See also John Quincy Adams to John Adams, January 5, 1805, p. 104.

39. The description is Plumer's from a letter to Nicholas Emory, January, 1803, cited in Malone, *First Term*, p. 444. The standard biography of Randolph, in many ways inadequate, is William C. Bruce, *John Randolph of Roanoke* (New York, 1922).

sarcasm, however, made him few friends on either side of the aisle. Members could never be sure when the sting of his venom would be directed against them. He did not suffer fools lightly, and at one time or another most of his associates seemed to qualify as such. Randolph earned the cordial hatred of the Federalists, and while for a time he possessed the respect of his Republican colleagues, he never won their affection.[40]

While Randolph assumed responsibility for floor leadership, he was very jealous of his own independence from executive direction. In the beginning he got along well enough with Jefferson. Even during his battle against the administration's Yazoo settlement in 1804 he referred to the president as "the great and good man who . . . I hope and trust will long fill the Executive chair."[41] He had cordial relations with Gallatin, who acted as the principal executive liaison with Randolph. He disliked Madison, although this feeling did not erupt into hatred until the Yazoo controversy.

From the beginning of their relationship, however, Jefferson had to handle Randolph gingerly. The eccentric congressman could and did irritate the president with his waywardness and prickly personality. Jefferson needed him, however. No other strong leader had appeared in the House as an available alternative, and to have in opposition a man of Randolph's proven talents for obstruction was a fate no one in the party leadership relished. The president sought to avoid pricking the sensitivity of his legislative prima donna by always treating him with an elaborate courtesy and by keeping him informed of executive plans and activities. In late 1804, for example, when Jefferson followed up his message to Congress concerning "insults to our harbors" by the British navy with a bill, drawn up by the executive and transmitted to a member of the special congressional committee convened to deal with the subject, he was careful to inform his floor leader of the bill's contents and to assure Randolph that "the communication of them in form of a bill is merely as a canvass or *premiere ebauche* for Congress to work on, and to make of it whatever they please. They cannot be the worse for knowing the result of our information and

40. For evidence of his decisiveness and authority during the Louisiana debates, see *Annals of Congress*, 8:1, pp. 387–389, 406–410, 434–440. For a critical description of his style of leadership, see Plumer, *Memorandum*, October 25, 1803, pp. 24–25.

41. *Annals of Congress*, 8:2, p. 1025.

reflection on the subject which has been privately communicated as more respectful than to have recommended these measures in the message in detail as the Constitution permits."[42] Jefferson asserted his constitutional right to behave the way he did, while heading off any objections from Randolph about presumed slights to congressional dignity and independence.

Randolph, however, did not possess the conciliatory skills necessary in a parliamentary majority leader. He was born to oppose, not to propose. He did not work well harnessed to the reins of the executive, or indeed of anyone else. For a time, as Jefferson put it later after Randolph's break with the party, "the principles of duty and patriotism induced many [Republicans] to swallow the humiliations he subjected them to, and to vote as was right, as long as he kept the path of right himself."[43] But as his differences with administration policies grew and his chafing under the imperatives of party unity increased, Randolph's effectiveness as party leader in the House waned. His first major embarrassment occurred with the failure of the impeachment trial of Justice Samuel Chase, at which Randolph was the chief manager for the House. His wild speeches against the Yazoo settlement in late 1804, exceeding in ferocity the bounds of political prudence as well as taste, further alienated him from the administration and its principal allies in Congress. We will later examine in more detail the Randolph schism and its threat to Jefferson's party leadership. Here it is sufficient to note that by the session of 1805–1806 Randolph's effectiveness as floor leader was ended.

Even before Randolph's differences with the administration became apparent, Jefferson had tried to enlist the aid of others to serve as his congressional lieutenants. To Caesar Rodney he complained of the lack of "men of business' in Congress. "I really wish you were here," he wrote in December 1802. "I am convinced it is in the power of any man who understands business, and who will undertake to keep a file of the business before Congress and press it as he would his own docket in a court, to shorten the sessions a month one year with another." Rodney had taken the hint and won a seat in Congress in 1802, but he failed to provide the sort of leadership Jefferson desired. Still, the president deplored Rodney's decision to retire in 1804. "I had looked to you as one of those calculated to give cohesion to our

42. Jefferson to Randolph, November 19, 1804, Ford, 10:118–122.
43. Jefferson to Monroe, May 4, 1806, *ibid.*, p. 260.

rope of sand," he wrote, again stressing the need for "system" and "plan" in leading Congress. Rodney entered Jefferson's cabinet in 1805 as attorney general, and the search for effective congressional assistance went on.[44]

The two men who served as the recognized floor leaders in the House following Randolph were Barnabas Bidwell of Massachusetts and George Washington Campbell of Tennessee. A jurist, legal scholar, and protege of Levi Lincoln, Bidwell was a man of great intelligence and sober judgment, but was unskilled in the political or parliamentary arts, dull in debate, and not given to the behind-the-scenes work expected of a first-class party leader. Nevertheless, within a month of arrival in Congress in December, 1805, he was being described by Federalists as "the sworn interpreter of executive messages."[45] Jefferson expected great things from Bidwell, which the latter felt were "more than it will be in my power to perform." In a thoughtful letter to Jefferson from Massachusetts during the summer recess of 1806, Bidwell sought to apprise the president of certain facts of life, facts of which Jefferson was no doubt aware, but for which the modern scholar must be grateful, as they illuminate the nature of congressional power relationships at this period. "For me," Bidwell wrote,

the charge of backstairs influence has no terrors, but there are obstacles in my way. In every legislature, the introduction, progress, and conclusion of business depend much upon committees; and in the House of Representatives of the United States more than in any other legislative body within my knowledge the business referred to committees and reported on by them is by usage and common consent, controlled by their chairmen. As the Speaker, according to the standing rules of the House, has the appointment of committees, he has it in his power to place whom he pleases in the foreground, and whom he pleases in the background, and thus, in some measure, affect their agency in the transactions of the House. From the connections and attachments of the present Speaker [Macon], I have, alas, no reason to expect to be very favorably considered in his distribution of committee business. This circumstance, with others of more importance, which I forbear to mention, but of which I am deeply sensible, will prevent my acting a very conspicuous part. So far, how-

44. Jefferson to Caesar Rodney, December 31, 1802, *ibid.*, 9:415–416, February 24, 1804, 10:72–73. For examples of his appeals for assistance, see Jefferson to W. C. Nicholas, February 28, 1807, 10:370–371, and to William Wirt, January 10, 1808, in John P. Kennedy, *Memoirs of the Life of William Wirt* (Philadelphia, 1849), p. 208.

45. Samuel Taggart to Rev. John Taylor, January 12, 1806, in "Letters, 1803–1814," in American Antiquarian Society *Proceedings*, new series, 33 (1923), 173: "His talents are considerable and in smoothness and hypocrisy he is not lacking."

ever, as industry and moderate abilities may be relied on, I shall feel it a duty to be attentive to the business of the House, and it will be my happiness to give [the executive] the feeble aid . . . of my support, both in and out of the House.[46]

George W. Campbell proved a more capable floor leader than Bidwell, but like his Massachusetts colleague, he held little independent strength in the House, being seen simply as the president's man. Campbell was an efficient manager of House business. He possessed an amiability combined with a firmness of manner that enabled him to smooth over Republican differences, particularly over the president's emergency defense measures of 1807–1808, so that the party continued to present a unified front to the weakened but vocal Federalist opposition. Campbell's dependence on Jefferson, however, meant that if the president's leadership faltered, Campbell's own effectiveness would diminish by a like amount. This occurred in late 1808 when Jefferson's failure to take the policy initiative after Madison's election as president and the relative loss of presidential influence occasioned by the unsuccessful embargo stripped Campbell of much of his base of support. The unity of the party, in fact, underwent considerable strains as the administration came to a close, and Campbell was unable to exert much independent authority over his restless colleagues.[47]

Things went more smoothly on the Senate side of the Capitol. The recognized leader of the Republicans at the time of Jefferson's inauguration was Stevens T. Mason of Virginia, a man of sound Republican principles, moderate debating abilities, and a personality which, if a bit pompous, was sufficiently amiable to ingratiate him with his colleagues. Even the critical eye of Plumer could find little to criticize, falling back upon the usual opposition "old saw" that "his *moral* qualities were never *burthensome* to him."[48] Unfortunately for Jefferson, Mason's steadying hand was not destined long to remain on the tiller. His health was failing and, while he was persuaded by the president to remain in the Senate another term, he died shortly before the second session of the Seventh Congress.

His place as floor leader was shared in an informal arrangement by

46. Barnabas Bidwell to Jefferson, July 28, 1806, LC No. 28111. Macon at this time was sympathetic to the schismatic John Randolph, a flirtation for which Macon himself was to suffer the losing the Speakership in the session of 1807–1808.

47. Lacy, p. 195, See Chapter 8 below for an account of these strains.

48. Plumer, *Memorandum*, October 31, 1803, p. 30, emphasis in the original. Plumer's remarks were made on the occasion of Mason's death.

John C. Breckinridge of Kentucky and Wilson Cary Nicholas of Virginia. Breckinridge had been close to Jefferson since he had guided the Kentucky Resolutions through that state's legislature. It was Breckinridge who was given the task of leading the drive to repeal the Judiciary Act of 1801, and it was he who skillfully guided through an initially hostile Senate Jefferson's plan for the government of Louisiana. The vicissitudes of politics forced Jefferson, as Peterson puts it, to "rob the Senate of one of his most reliable lieutenants" when he named Breckinridge attorney general in 1805; unfortunately he died before he could assume his new duties.[49]

Nicholas, a scion of an old Albermarle family and a member of Jefferson's "inner circle" in the late 1790's, had worked with Jefferson on the Kentucky and Virginia Resolutions and was a devoted political friend of the president. He seems, however, to have lacked that spark of ambition that often distinguishes the great political leader from the merely competent. His attitude toward public service as a duty was typical of many of his social class and position. He held high office almost as a matter of right, ending his career as governor of Virginia, but his public record, while distinguished, was never brilliant. As Jefferson's close friend, he necessarily occupied a position of influence in the Senate and during the hiatus caused by the death of Mason he assumed even greater burdens of responsibility for the president's program. He was willing, however, to yield pride of place to an abler man whenever one should appear. That man was Giles, who came to the Senate in 1804 and immediately assumed the mantle of party leadership. Despite his illnesses he controlled affairs in the upper House with effectiveness throughout Jefferson's second term.

Executive Liaison With Congress

The operation of party government demanded the creation of effective liaison between Congress, the president, and the executive departments to supply information and policy guidance and to insure a two-way flow of political intelligence on a regular basis. Channels had to be available for the transmission of congressional requests for services, mainly jobs, which kept the party faithful happy. In addition, the more subtle needs of legislators could be attended to by meeting

49. See Peterson, *Thomas Jefferson*, pp. 780–789, 805; also Jefferson to John C. Breckinridge, November 24, 1803, Ford, 10:51–52, in which the president transmits his proposed organic law for Louisiana.

the members of Congress socially, showing them little kindnesses, entertaining them, and smoothing the paths of official relations by cultivating personal contacts.

Jefferson had no scruples against "preparing" material for congressional attention. He did not hesitate to have not only information on pending legislation forwarded to the Hill but actual bills drafted by the executive departments concerned. Despite its objection to executive interference during the years of Federalist control, the Republican Congress continued to rely on executive departments for assistance and, if it were done subtly and with proper deference, the drafting of a few bills by the executive "for guidance only" was acceptable to most. Jefferson justified the practice as the most efficient means of providing Congress with the benefits of executive "information and reflection" on matters of common concern. Among the major legislation written in whole or in part by the executive departments we may include the 1803 organic law for Louisiana, the 1804 bill on foreign armed vessels in U.S. harbors, the 1805 militia reorganization bill, and the 1807–1808 non-importation and embargo legislation, but these by no means exhaust the list.

In addition to the formal preparation of bills and the transmission of information to Congress, the executive provided a number of services to the party majority. Department heads not only testified before congressional committees, but were willing to stay behind to assist in executive session while the bills were drafted. Administration officials, particularly Gallatin, attended party caucuses to plan legislative strategy. This use of department heads, in addition, permitted the president himself to preserve at least the appearance of a proper detachment and distance from Congress.

Gallatin served as the principal legislative liaison for the president. Having been a leader in Congress during the formative years of the party, he not only respected Congress as an institution but possessed a keen knowledge of its customs and methods of operation. He understood the proprieties to be observed in dealing with the members from a position outside the congressional halls. His political influence as a party leader was enhanced by his position as head of the Treasury, which post had a unique relationship with Congress stemming not only from its special statutory authority but also from Hamilton's precedents. Gallatin worked with Congress as closely as Hamilton had done, but he did not make the mistakes of the New Yorker in assuming a sort of prime ministerial posture with the legislators. Gallatin left no doubt that he was acting solely as the president's agent, and he was a vital factor in creating the success Jefferson enjoyed with Congress.

It was in the Treasury that most of the bills originated by the executive were drafted. Most fiscal measures were prepared by the secretary and his aides because of their complexity and because of the access to statistical information possessed by Treasury officials. The secretary's expertise in these matters was respected, at least by the Republicans. He freely consulted with legislators, collectively and singly, concerning pending measures and was a frequent visitor to the financial committees of Congress.[50]

Gallatin operated as the president's congressional "eyes and ears" in subjects outside his departmental ken as well. His cordial relations with many congressmen and the fact that he was the only member of the executive branch to live on Capitol Hill made his home a natural place for Republicans to congregate, either in formal caucus or simply dropping by for refreshments after a long day's session. (Unfortunately, as Henry Adams pointed out in his biography of Gallatin, "the communication was almost entirely oral" in these meetings, "and hardly a trace of it has been preserved either in the writings of Mr. Gallatin or in those of his contemporaries.") Gallatin's house became the recognized headquarters of the Republican caucus and much "of the confidential communication between Mr. Jefferson and his party in the legislature passed through this channel." It was relatively simple for Gallatin to pick up valuable information and to sample political opinion through this relaxed means.[51]

While Gallatin was clearly Jefferson's major lobbyist, other department heads contributed their talents, though less frequently, to the task of congressional liaison. Madison dealt with legislators on questions of foreign policy and was concerned to be informed of actions

50. "Mr. Wright was against every amendment that could possibly be proposed to the bill [to create stock to purchase Louisiana] because it was drawn up by the Secretary of the Treasury, who could better legislate for us on this subject than we could do congressionally" (J. Q. Adams, *Memoirs*, November 1, 1803, 1:270). Adams revealed numerous instances of such consultations with committees. See entries for November 7, 1803, p. 272, and January 27, 1807, p. 447.

51. White, *Jeffersonians*, p. 50. Lacy cites evidence that Macon, Randolph, and Nicholson visited Gallatin's "nearly every afternoon" after Congress recessed for the day. Macon to Nicholson, cited in Lacy, p. 102. For evidence of Gallatin's political usage of such gatherings, see Gallatin to Jefferson, October 28, 1803, Gallatin, *Writings*, 1:162–163.

contemplated by Congress in this area. He did his share of entertaining, although he preferred formal gatherings whereas Gallatin's open houses and Jefferson's famous dinners were more informal. Madison was not above talking shop at these affairs, as Adams reports more than once. Particularly as Jefferson's second term drew to a close, Madison's soirees increasingly took on the character of campaign meetings as the secretary of state cultivated the members of the Republican congressional nominating caucus.[52]

Secretary of the Navy Smith and Secretary of War Dearborn proposed legislation to Congress and lobbied for their bills from time to time. Smith wrote a draft of the president's pet gunboat legislation. In addition, he entertained at formal balls. Plumer reports an evening visit from Smith, which evolved quickly into a two-hour chat "with the gentlemen who board at Coyle's." The secretary was "very desirous of knowing our opinions of the President's message and of the State of the Union." Plumer for one had no doubt but that Smith was there at the president's behest.[53]

The importance of these social and political activities, formal and informal, to the members of Congress is indicated by the regret expressed at the decline in their frequency. In the later years of the administration, Plumer complained that

> the Heads of Department visit few members of either House. Mr. Madison for this 2 or 3 years past has entirely omitted even the ceremony of leaving cards at their lodgings. He invites very few to dine with him. Mr. Gallatin leaves no cards, makes no visits—scarce ever invites a member to dine—or even has tea parties—Genl Dearborn leaves cards for all the members—invites few to dine—some to tea parties. He has taken care to avoid company by living in a remote part of George Town. Robert Smith leaves cards with all the members—invites few to tea and scarse [sic] any to dine—These gentlemen do not live in a style suited to the dignity of their offices.[54]

Plumer, of course, was not a member of the majority party and had always deplored the loss of "tone" that had accompanied the shift of the government to the "democrats." He was clearly not aware of the extensive activities Gallatin performed with the majority. But there is

---

52. J. Q. Adams, *Memoirs*, October 28, 1803, 1:268. Adams has recorded as well a consultation Madison had with Senator Nicholas at this time with regard to a pending resolution on the treaty with England, p. 273; November 13, 1807, p. 475; February 13, 1806, p. 408; November 19, 1807, p. 478, 281–282.

53. Plumer, *Memorandum*, December 7, 1805, p. 343.

54. *Ibid.*, March 1, 1807, p. 634.

evidence that as the foreign situation heated up and the focus of attention shifted to larger questions of foreign policy, the little attentions that the executive officials had paid to individual legislators declined. Is it a coincidence that congressional dissension on smaller matters was on the rise during these months?

The President as Chief Legislator

The greatest asset the administration possessed in terms of providing leadership of Congress was the president himself. Jefferson was not content to act the role of a "patriot-king" aloof from the political struggle. He preferred to take an active hand in the legislative process, realizing that if it was to be *his* administration in anything but name, he must lend to the enterprise not only his prestige but his talents for persuasion.

In addition to directing the liaison activities of his department heads, the president did not hesitate to make his views known in personal interviews with congressmen. He was aware, however, of the need for circumspection in this undertaking to avoid offending the sensibilities of his highly independent-minded friends. "With other members," he wrote to his then floor leader, John Randolph, "I have believed that more unreserved communication would be advantageous to the public. This has been, perhaps, prevented by mutual delicacy. I have been afraid to express opinions unasked, lest I should be suspected of wishing to direct the legislative action of members. They have avoided asking communications from me, probably, lest they should be suspected of wishing to fish out executive secrets."[55]

Despite his politic disclaimer, Jefferson did manage to express his opinions to members, although rarely in a blunt fashion, preferring if possible to inject his views "by asking questions, as if for information, or by suggesting doubts" in the manner of his old friend, Dr. Franklin. Most of these personal conversations with legislators are lost to history. They were necessarily private, and Jefferson kept no personal record of such meetings. There are glimmers of such encounters in the papers of some of his contemporaries, though they are of tantalizing infrequency. Adams and Plumer, whose diaries are the two most valuable records kept by members of Congress in these years, were not of the president's party, although fortunately for the historian both men

---

55. Jefferson to Randolph, December 1, 1803, Ford, 10:53–54.

were of sufficient political independence to be courted by the president or his colleagues from time to time. Adams reports being approached by a number of Republicans, including Jefferson, in an effort to discount charges of pro-French bias in the administration. Plumer reports a conversation with the president during which Jefferson actually solicited the senator's vote for an "absolutely essential" bill to people the New Orleans Territory with men of "militia" age.[56] Certain of Jefferson's efforts to mobilize support are revealed in his private correspondence with legislative lieutenants, material much of which has been preserved.

Perhaps the most consistently useful and certainly the most renowned of Jefferson's informal tools of persuasion were his famous dinners. As a method of cultivating the acquaintance of legislators without violating the norms of distance and decorum expected between the two elective branches of government, these dinners were both functional and unique. Their uniqueness flowed from the skill with which Jefferson pursued his political purposes while outwardly avoiding the merest breath of politics. The dinners gave every appearance of being purely social occasions, and Jefferson's charm, hospitality, and his excellent taste in food and wine as well as in the selection of his guests managed to veil from all but the most detached of witnesses the full extent of political advantage that these evenings afforded their host!

Jefferson selected his guests for each occasion with great care. For the most part while Congress was in session the company was legislative in character, although one or two cabinet officers might be invited with their wives, an occasional foreign emissary would attend, and table conversation would be enlivened whenever possible by the presence of a luminary of the literary or scientific world who might be passing through the capital. When Congress was not in session, according to Mrs. Smith, "the respectable citizens of Alexandria, George Town, and Washington were frequently invited to his table."[57]

While Congress was sitting, Jefferson purposefully used his dinners to promote a sense of party feeling among the congressional Republicans. Young has suggested that not only did he preserve a party

56. J. Q. Adams to John Adams, February 11, 1806, J. Q. Adams, *Writings*, 3:134; Plumer, *Memorandum*, April 3, 1806, pp. 474–475.
57. Smith, *First Forty Years*, p. 389.

atmosphere by not mixing Republicans with Federalists, but he seems to have brought Republicans from different boardinghouses together at table, thus affording them an opportunity for social intercourse not normally available to them. Federalists, on the other hand, were invited strictly by boardinghouse bloc. The opposition was put off balance by the president's dinners. Federalist legislators were not fools; if they but dimly perceived the full extent to which these social gatherings cemented Republican allegiances, they were quite aware of the insidious effect which such fraternization with the "enemy" had upon the militancy of their own criticism of administration measures.[58]

The Federalists soon knew, if only because dissident Republicans so often grumbled about it in their presence, of the influence the president was having on his legislative colleagues through his informal dealings with them, and none appeared more effective in this regard than his dinners. Plumer reports one gathering around the fire in the Senate chamber at the close of the day where Vice President Burr and Senator Bradley, both at least nominal administration supporters, complained that the president's dinners had silenced Senate criticism of him and "Senators are becoming more servile." Yet such knowledge did not stay many legislators, Republicans or Federalists, from accepting an invitation to dine at the president's. Like it or not, he *was* the president. Furthermore, such meetings could afford an opportunity of gaining a greater knowledge of the chief executive's character and views and those of his party as well. As Plumer observed, "he is naturally communicative."[59] Thus the seductive power of these "social" affairs continued to work its magic.

Politics aside, invitations to the president's dinners were highly prized by the officialdom of the frontier village that was Washington. Boardinghouse food, though ample, was never fancy, and as yet the capital was not graced with either public restaurants of quality or private homes of sophistication. At the president's house, one could always be assured of tasteful courses prepared in the French manner and the finest of wines. Jefferson's *maître d'hôtel* had served the finest families of Europe, and the meals were prepared by a French chef and a staff of fourteen. Jefferson spent over twelve thousand dollars his first

58. Young, *Washington Community*, p. 169; see Plumer's criticisms, *Memorandum*, December 3, 1804, p. 212.

59. Plumer, *Memorandum*, December 12, 1804, pp. 220–221; November 10, 1804, p. 193.

year in office on food, wine, and servants, more than his total yearly salary as president. He kept an extensive recipe book of French and Italian dishes, including ice cream, and he introduced several foods from Europe to America, among them waffles, macaroni, and vanilla. He kept charts listing the seasons when fresh vegetables could be bought in Washington. It is little wonder that his guests were impressed, many of them being exposed to such finery for the first time. Even that crabbed old Federalist parson, Samuel Taggart, was driven to admit to the high quality of the president's table wine. And for once he found the president "dressed like a gentleman."[60]

Jefferson, by all accounts, presided at table with a courtesy, tact, and enlivening social charm "so true and discriminating that he seldom missed his aim, which was to draw forth the talents and information of each and all of his guests and to place everyone in an advantageous light." The dinners were kept small, never more than fourteen people, and the table was circular, to preserve informality, avoid precedence in seating, and improve conversation. One of Jefferson's inventions, a dumb waiter, dispensed with the need for servants in the dining room. The president, who served the dishes himself, could truthfully say "our walls have no ears."[61] The secrecy this device afforded seems not to have implied the exchange of political confidences, however. Shop talk was scrupulously avoided. Yet somehow the president's opinions were communicated. An idea of the flavor and tone of these dinners, as well as the ways in which by insinuation and indirection the President's political views were revealed, may be glimpsed in the following excerpts from Adams's diary, Adams being one of the few legislators who was invited to both Republican and Federalist gatherings at the Executive Mansion.

Dined with the President.... Mrs. Adams did not go. The company were Mr. R. Smith, the Secretary of the Navy, and his lady, Mr. and Mrs. Harrison, Miss Jennifer and Miss Bouchette, Mr. Brent, and the President's two sons-in-law, with Mr. Burwell, his private secretary. I had a good deal of conversation with the President. The French Minister just arrived had been this day first presented to him, and appears to have displeased him by the profusion of gold lace on his clothes. He says they must get him down to a plain frock coat, or the boys in the streets will run after him as a sight.... He also mentioned to me the extreme difficulty he had in finding fit characters for appointments in

60. Smith, *First Forty Years*, pp. 42–43; Samuel Taggart to Rev. John Taylor, December 3, 1804, A.A.S. *Proceedings*, p. 140.

61. Smith, *First Forty Years*, pp. 389, 188.

Louisiana and said he'd give the *creation* for a young lawyer of good abilities, and who could speak the French language to go to New Orleans as one of the Judges of the Superior Courts in the Territory.[62]

Jefferson seems to have been hinting for a suggestion from Adams, but the senator, whose talents for insinuation were negligible, refused to accept the bait. Adams seems to have been a frequent guest at these affairs. Again, during the same session of Congress, he reported:

Dined at President's—Vice President Burr was there. The President appeared to have his mind absorbed by some other object, for he was less attentive to his company than usual. His itch for telling prodigies, however, is unabated. Speaking of the cold, he said he had seen Fahrenheit's thermometer in Paris at 20 degrees below zero, and that, not for a single day, but that for 6 weeks together it stood thereabouts. . . . He knows better than all this; but he loves to excite wonder. Fahrenheit's thermometer never since Mr. Jefferson existed was at 20 degrees below zero in Paris.

Adams enjoyed the breadth and color of the president's table talk, describing the conversation of another memorable evening as ranging over the subjects of wines, Epicurean philosophy, the inventions of Robert Fulton, the geography of Humboldt, and agriculture. On still another occasion, Adams reported that the dinner guests, all Republicans except himself, were joined after dinner by "Mr. Macon, the Speaker of the House, Mr. John Randolph, and Mr. Venable [senator from Virginia]. We came home at about six."[63] Clearly, Adams did not stay for what may well have been a strategy session with the congressional party leadership.

These remarks by one who was not, at least at this time, a political ally of Jefferson's reveal somewhat the nature of the president's success in extending his influence upon legislators through these dinners. Few men could attend these gatherings so fully shielded by their own political animosity as to withstand entirely the seductive force of the president's personality. Whether such evenings substantially altered the behavior of individual legislators we can merely surmise. Perhaps not. It is not unreasonable to assume from the evidence that does exist, however, that whether or not votes were changed the presidential dinners did serve to strengthen the bonds of loyalty that already existed in the Republican ranks, and perhaps managed to soften

---

62. J. Q. Adams, *Memoirs*, November 23, 1804, 1:316, emphasis in the original.
63. *Ibid.*, January 11, 1805, 1: 330–331; November 3, 1807, pp. 472–473; November 7, 1803, p. 272.

somewhat the personal if not the political opposition felt toward the president by the other side. Certainly Jefferson on these occasions displayed a zest for the task of influence and great skill in the use of the "smooth handle." As Young so aptly put it, in politics Jefferson was "Bre'er Rabbit in the briar patch."[64]

Jefferson's hold over his party colleagues in Congress was exaggerated for obvious reasons by the opposition. The Federalists sought to tarnish the popular image of Republicanism with the brush of "dictatorship." In the very first days of the new administration, they charged that Jefferson sought to make the legislature the "instrument of his ambition," an allegation that was disregarded by Republicans as nothing more than evidence of Federalist envy of the successes of the new majority. Federalist writings of the period are certainly filled with references to the president's power over the wills of Republican congressmen. To Robert Troup, Jefferson was the "idol to whom all devotion is paid." Plumer criticized his Senate colleagues for a slavish devotion to "their file leader." Connecticut Senator James Hillhouse grumbled, "Never was a set of men more blindly devoted to the will of a prime minister than these Republicans to that of the President."[65]

Adams articulated his misgivings about the effect of unquestioned party loyalty upon the due deliberation on men and measures expected of a legislative body. "The cooperation of the Senate in all appointments," he wrote in December, 1804, "is at present a mere formality, and a very disgusting formality." The *forms* of deliberation "are however tenaciously adhered to, and with some degree of affection. Nomination lists are postponed from time to time, without any other reason for postponement, and when acted upon the candidates regularly received from the Senators of their state a panegyric usually very highly charged . . . nobody can be appointed without a puff, just fit for a newspaper obituary." To Adams, Jefferson's system of administration was founded on the strength of his "personal or official influence," "influence" being the operative word: "There is a certain proportion of the members in both Houses who on every occasion of emergency have no other enquiry but what is the President's wish. . . . Another

64. *Washington Community*, p. 170.
65. Robert Troup to Rufus King, April 9, 1802, in Charles R. King, ed., *Life and Correspondence of Rufus King* (New York, 1896–1897), 4:103; Plumer, *Memorandum*, March 12, 1806, p. 449; J. Q. Adams, *Memoirs*, April 8, 1806, 1:331; Brant, *Madison*, p. 84.

part adhere to him in their votes, though strongly disapproving the measures for which they vote."[66] To a man of Adams's independence of mind, seemingly suspended in an alien environment "totally given up to the spirit of party," such blind allegiance to the dictates of a central authority was difficult to accept or condone.

As Jefferson's second term progressed, Republican leaders in Congress became more sensitive to attacks of this sort from the opposition. During the debate on the fortifications and gunboats bill in 1807, Federalists and Republican "Quids" alike attacked the provisions of the bill as "an unaccountable passion or whim of the Executive." A New England Federalist complained of the prevailing political dogma that seemed to say "he who doubteth is damned; that he who does not believe in the absolute perfection of the present Administration is guilty of the worst of all political heresies." Rather than simply permit such attacks to pass unnoticed, Jefferson's new floor leader, G. W. Campbell, rose to a defense of the president, likening the effect of his critics to "the feeble gleam of the glowworm before the splendid glory of the noon-day sun." Seizing upon the metaphor, however, John Randolph, now in violent but isolated schism, likened the president to a "sun around which the officers of government, and others, revolve as satellites." And Samuel Taggart moaned that "a great majority receive all their impressions from the Executive with the same facility that the wax receives from the seal."[67]

Jefferson's handling of his chief legislative lieutenants demonstrated his great skill in dealing amicably and fruitfully with a wide range of personalities to effect his policies. His personal relations were good with all his floor leaders, including Randolph. He never dictated policy positions to them; he only suggested. He never seemed to inflict his opinions upon them; he only insinuated them. His moral authority and prestige were such that often a mere suggestion of opinion was sufficient to mobilize the desired result. Explicit demands were never employed where implicit methods could suffice. Again and again, reference is made to the undoubted influence of the president's persuasive talents. We have noted that the president and his department heads would occasionally draft important bills. In matters of foreign

66. John Quincy Adams to John Adams, December 11, 1804, J. Q. Adams, *Writings*, 3:82–83; *Memoirs*, 1:403–404.

67. *Annals of Congress*, 10:1, pp. 1119–1120; Samuel Taggart to Rev. John Taylor, March 21, 1808, cited in Lacy, pp. 193–194.

policy, Jefferson and Madison often collaborated on the resolutions that Congress would be requested to pass.[68] The president preferred, however, to use more informal methods of effecting his will through private conversations with key members and the reliance on the skill of his floor leaders in mobilizing the majority behind his measures. Rarely did he suggest specifics when recommending legislation, preferring to leave room for compromise with congressional interests.

One should not underestimate the self-perpetuating nature of party success. Having demonstrated through their support for the president the success that unity could bring, many Republican congressmen developed a vested interest in continued unity. They were reluctant to tarnish the image of their party's invincibility by permitting the president to be defeated on a significant bill. Plumer reported one Republican senator telling him, after the Senate had approved the two-million dollar appropriation to purchase Florida, that his colleagues "are heartily sorry the bill was ever bro't into the Senate—But since it was they must pass it—or publish to the world that the President has not a majority of the Senate in his favor."[69] Not for the last time would a president find appeals to party solidarity to be an effective device in the struggle for his legislative program.

The Louisiana Government Bill

The Senate debate in late 1803 on the bill establishing a government for the Louisiana Territory will serve to illustrate some of the methods Jefferson and his colleagues could employ in influencing the course of legislation. The bill itself struck many sound Republicans as a measure that violated fundamental republican principles, for it gave the people of the newly acquired territory little or no voice in their government. Jefferson had received detailed information on Louisiana and its inhabitants from a number of sources, and the sum of this intelligence led him to conclude that the peoples of the area were presently unfit to govern themselves. The population was a polyglot assortment of Creoles, Frenchmen, Spaniards, Indians, Negroes, and a scattering of American adventurers. Ignorance abounded, few people

68. For example, the Spanish Resolutions of December 4, 1805, Ford, 10:200–201, and the Resolution of December 19, 1806, authorizing the president to employ naval forces for restraining the "irregularities and oppressions of our commerce," LC No. 28711.

69. Plumer, *Memorandum*, February 7, 1806, p. 425. Adams, too, found the president's friends reluctant to pass the appropriation, but persuaded by "his private wishes signified to them" (J. Q. Adams, *Memoirs*, February 6, 1806. 1:403).

spoke or wrote English, religious liberty was unknown. The previous government had been despotic, offices were bought and sold, and the tradition of venality was firmly rooted. Taxation was low, land titles were obscure, the law was Roman and unfairly administered. In the face of this situation, the practical side of Jefferson's nature won out over the idealist. Ignorant as they were of American law and custom and of the tradition of political liberty, the inhabitants of Louisiana would have to be educated through an apprenticeship into the ways of republican self-government.[70]

Jefferson's plan of government, which he drafted himself, gave the president the power to appoint a governor, a secretary, and the judges. Instead of a popularly elected legislature, his plan called for an "assembly of notables" appointed annually by the governor. The plan was certainly inconsistent with strict republican dogma, but Jefferson, who had witnessed what theory untempered by experience could do to effective government, preferred a solution that dealt with Louisiana on its own terms. Therefore he was prepared to "suspend" principle in order to provide the most effective interim government under existing conditions.

In late November, 1803, Jefferson sent his draft to Breckinridge in the utmost secrecy lest the president's hand in it be revealed. "You know with what bloody teeth and fangs the federalists will attack any sentiment or principle known to come from me." Eleven days later Breckinridge moved the creation of a Senate committee to deal with the government of Louisiana. In chairing the group he was able to introduce Jefferson's draft as the working paper for the committee, although its authorship remained a secret. Even before a bill closely resembling his draft was reported to the floor, Jefferson had talked privately with enough members to get a view of the strength and nature of possible objections. Opposition to the bill as a subversion of republican principles developed quickly after it reached the floor on December 30. Adams, indeed, had fought it in committee on just such grounds. Not only Federalists found the bill difficult to accept. Senator Joseph Anderson of Tennessee could find "no single feature of our government in it—it is a system of tyranny, destructive of elective rights," and a military despotism.[71]

---

70. For a discussion of this subject, see Peterson, *Thomas Jefferson*, pp. 777–785.

71. Jefferson to Breckinridge, November 24, 1803, Ford, 10:51–52. See also Jefferson to De Witt Clinton, December 3, 1803, p. 55; Plumer, *Memorandum*, January 24, 1804, p. 132.

Despite the opposition, principled and partisan, which developed, Jefferson and his legislative supporters did their work well. Breckinridge worked behind the scenes to line up speakers for the bill, and the arguments they presented closely mirrored Jefferson's own. James Jackson of Georgia spoke of the necessity for the people of Louisiana to undergo a "state of probation." Samuel Smith of Maryland stressed their present incapacity for self-government, and Nicholas echoed those sentiments in cautioning delay in giving them political liberty. The president entered the fray at crucial moments, first communicating a private letter from Governor Claiborne of Louisiana that deplored on the spot the ignorance and incapacity of its citizens for "receiving the blessings of free government," and second making a tactical concession to western senators concerned with removing the Indian threat by inducing the tribes to move west of the Mississippi.[72] In private conversations Jefferson furthered his objective through a combination of concessions on minor points and firmness on essentials. There is some evidence that he tried to ease the fears of republican purists at the undemocratic nature of the plan by presenting that staunch Republican James Monroe as the likely first governor of the territory.[73]

The bill that finally emerged in March, 1804, was largely Jefferson's, although there were minor alterations and the measure was limited to one year. That it was replaced at Jefferson's instigation within a year by a liberalized plan does not detract from the impressive victory he achieved with his original scheme. It demonstrated the strength of his hold on his party in Congress and the skill with which he participated in the legislative process.

The president was not always successful, of course, although he suffered no major defeat until 1809. The bonds of party loyalty could chafe upon occasion, and when the friction became particularly acute Congress would restore its faith in its independence from executive authority by individual acts of defiance. Most often this took the form of defeats of presidential appointments to office.[74] He was rebuffed occasionally on minor pet projects of his own. He was turned down

72. Plumer, *Memorandum*, pp. 133, 138–139.
73. See Jefferson to Monroe, January 8, 1804, Ford, 10:62–63.
74. According to Lacy (pp. 109–115), a total of 15 nominees was rejected by the Senate in eight years, most in the last years of the second term. Jefferson's nominee as consul in Santo Domingo was turned down after Senator Smith of Maryland revealed the man to be a British subject (Plumer, *Memorandum*, January 29, 1805, p. 254).

twice on his plan "to plant 30,000 well-chosen volunteers" on government-donated land west of the Mississippi to be used as militia for the defense of New Orleans. Congress, it seems, was not ready to provide for a large military force under any circumstances. Occasionally the administration would drop its guard and suffer embarrassment in losing a bill it favored. Plumer reports such a result on a measure to cut back the size of the Marine Corps. Passed easily by the House, the bill failed to pass a second reading in the Senate through the negligence of the leadership.[75] A more serious defeat for Jefferson personally and one that he could never reverse was Congress's rejection of his plan to organize and classify the militia under a uniform national system. The principle behind the bill was sound from a military and administrative point of view, but it came up against congressional preference for local regulation of militia and its reluctance to institutionalize any organization that might smack of a standing army. Jefferson tried session after session to get his proposals adopted, showing great willingness to compromise on details if only Congress would accept the principle. His attempts were to no avail.[76]

Party Schism as a Threat to Jeffersonian Leadership

These legislative setbacks, however, were mere puffs of wind rippling the normally glassy waters of party government in these years. In the session of 1805–1806 a squall of potentially sizable proportions threatened to disturb the relative tranquillity of Jefferson's relations with Congress. It came in the form of a danger Jefferson had anticipated almost from the moment he took office: that of internal party schism.

Serving as the undisputed leader of an ascendant political movement of national proportions, Jefferson nonetheless had to face the fact that the Republican party, its congressional origins notwithstanding, was a collection of state groups each with its own political needs and aspirations and its own internal power relationships, and each jealous of its own importance within the broader electoral coalition that had put Jefferson in the Executive Mansion. Jefferson realized the impor-

75. Jefferson to Chandler Price, February 28, 1807, Lipscomb, 11:159–160; to John Armstrong, May 2, 1808, Ford, 11:30–31.

76. See Jefferson's annual message to Congress, December 2, 1806, Ford, 10:302–320; also Jefferson to Henry Dearborn, December 31, 1805, LC No. 27091, and to William Burwell, January 15, 1806, No. 27248.

tance to party effectiveness of preserving his position as the unifying force in this rather disparate congeries of interests (see Chapter 7 below). He maintained a careful neutrality in most factional disputes within the state parties except, as in the case of New York and Aaron Burr, when it became imperative to eliminate a factional leader whose power posed a threat to his own.

In addition to factional squabbles within the states, there was a fundamental sectional cleavage within the Republican party which, while largely submerged during the early years, was to emerge with increasing significance as the Jefferson administration progressed. This sectionalism has most often been symbolized in the rivalry between Virginia and New York. The "Virginia Dynasty" had cemented an electoral alliance of great importance with the Clinton-Livingston-Burr Republicans in New York. The coalition had formed the basis of a national rather than a purely sectional party. But there were major differences between the southern Republicans and their northern brethren, differences of an ethnic and cultural as well as an economic and political nature, which served to strain the alliance of convenience then existing. In Congress, the arena in which these political rivalries were played out, the disenchantment of northern Republicans with the "Virginia Dynasty" was evident in the political controversies over the Yazoo settlement and the embargo. The Virginians could on occasion display a rather proprietary air over their party, and it was not unusual for the "democratic" representatives from the North to feel the "encroachments of Virginia."[77]

Such internal tensions within the fabric of Republicanism were largely concealed in the early years by the overriding pressure for unity in the battles with the Federalists. . By the standards of the day, party cohesion and party spirit were high during the first Congress of the Jefferson administration. The victory over the hated foe was fresh in Republican minds, and the need for political reform served to bind the elements of the party together. The strength and durability of this unity was threatened, however, by the very broad extent of the party's triumphs. It is almost an axiom of party politics that internal dissension increases as external opposition declines. The near cataclysmic collapse of the Federalists at the national level and the resultant decline of the external threat to the new majority worked to undermine the

77. Samuel Taggart to Rev. John Taylor, November 17, 1804, A.A.S. *Proceedings*, pp. 132–133.

party solidarity that had flourished under the attack of a viable opposition.

No one perceived the nature of this menace more clearly than the party's leader. As early as May, 1802, Jefferson was warning of the likelihood of schism as the Federalist opposition waned.

Our majority in the House of Representatives has been about two to one—in the Senate eighteen to fourteen. After another election it will be two to one in the Senate, and it would not be for the public good to have it greater, a respectable minority is useful as censors. . . . We shall now be so strong that we shall certainly split again; for freemen thinking differently and speaking and acting as they think will form into classes of sentiment, but it must be under another name, that of federalism is to become so scouted that no party can rise under it. . . . As yet no symptoms show themselves, nor will till after election.[78]

His prediction of the future course of party development was prescient, but it was clearly his duty to postpone or mitigate the predicted schism for as long as possible. The success of his program depended on it.

If the collapse of an effective opposition served to fertilize the dormant seeds of Republican factionalism, the first shoots began to sprout during the session of 1804–1805 in the controversy surrounding the settlement of the Yazoo land claims. The details of the dispute need not be examined here.[79] Essentially, the Yazoo claims involved some 35,000,000 acres of land in Alabama and Mississippi (then part of Georgia) which had been fraudulently deeded to land speculators by the Georgia legislature in 1795, nearly all of the legislators having profited from the corruption. The legislature rescinded its action amid the storm of protest that followed, but by then the speculators had sold much of the land to third parties, many of whom were innocent of the fraud involved in the original sales. In 1802 Georgia ceded its western lands, including the Yazoo claims, to the United States. A commission appointed by the president, consisting of Madison, Gallatin, and Levi Lincoln, negotiated the cession, agreeing to set aside 5,000,000 acres to settle any claims which might arise.

Early in 1803 the commission sent its report on the disputed claims to Congress. It did not recognize the validity of the claims made under the act of 1795. To make honest men of the Georgia legislators and

78. Jefferson to Joel Barlow, May 3, 1802, Ford, 9:370–371.
79. The best account of the Yazoo question is C. Peter Magrath, *Yazoo: Law and Politics in the New Republic* (Providence, R.I., 1966).

the speculators was beyond even "Jeffersonian omnipotence."[80] But the innocent involvement of other claimants and the difficulty of resolving the intricate question to everyone's satisfaction made a reasonable compromise necessary. The administration and its moderate supporters reasoned, however, without a contingent of southern agrarian Republicans who, under the leadership of John Randolph, determined to defeat such a compromise with cupidity.

The problem for Jefferson was to settle the issue in a way that would cause the least damage to party unity. The only way to preserve that unity was to reduce the impact of divisive economic and sectional issues. Jefferson, furthermore, sought to maintain his own reputation with all sides by staying out of the forefront of the battle. Madison and Lincoln and to a lesser extent Gallatin took the heat from critics of the compromise, while the president remained publicly silent. The essential requirement was to avoid alienating large numbers of anti-Yazoo southerners who, after all, formed the backbone of the party.

Randolph's bitter opposition threatened to upset administration calculations. The Yazoo controversy served as the opening gun in the Quiddist revolt from the Jeffersonian Republicans, which was to erupt fully in the next session. Randolph, as we have noted, was never an easy man to get along with. His character was ill suited to the subtleties and compromises of majority leadership, and it must have seemed to Jefferson and his colleagues in retrospect inevitable that the fiery Virginian would sooner or later demonstrate his proclivities for opposition. Randolph's distaste for the fraudulent Yazoo land claims was understandable, but the bitterness of his attacks on the compromise, which erupted in January, 1805, was not. At the same time, administration confidence in Randolph was shaken by his woeful conduct of the prosecution in the impeachment trial of Justice Samuel Chase. Some of the more moderate Republicans were dubious about Randolph's capacity to handle the complexities of the trial with fairness and skill, but it took the course of the trial itself to reveal his inadequacies fully. Randolph in effect lost his own case by his poorly drawn charges, his ill-prepared defense of them, and his intemperate and vindictive conduct in prosecuting the case before the Senate.

Randolph's diatribes against Yazoo, coming as they did together with his bungling of the Chase trial, did much to destroy the con-

80. Samuel Taggart to Rev. John Taylor, January 13, 1804, A.A.S. *Proceedings*, p.126.

fidence of moderate Republicans in their floor leader, and in the long run contributed to his final failure to attract large numbers of supporters when he broke with the administration a year later. At any event, by the close of the session of 1805–1806, the evidence of his disaffection was mounting and his usefulness to the administration was severely compromised. The major break with the president, however, occurred in the session of the following winter when Randolph launched a sustained personal attack against the secret request by Jefferson for two million dollars to purchase Florida. During the same session he widened the breach with a denunciation of the president's non-importation bill against Britain and a personal attack on Madison which Plumer called "the most bitter, severe, and eloquent phillippic I ever heard. . . . Mr. R. has crossed the Rubicon, neither the President or the Secretary of State can after this be on terms with him." The erstwhile administration floor leader also denounced in private and in print the "backstairs influence" of the executive in Congress. To Jefferson this was the unkindest cut of all. "He speaks of secret communication between the executive and members, of backstairs influence, etc.," he wrote to Burwell. "But he never spoke of this while he and Mr. Nicholson enjoyed it almost solely. But when he differed from the executive in a leading measure, and the executive not submitting to him, expressed its sentiments to others . . . then he roars out upon backstairs influence."[81]

Had Randolph's break with the administration been only an isolated incident, it would have posed little trouble for Jefferson. Randolph was not alone, however, and for a while it appeared to many that his "schismatic" measures were becoming popular with the people in the South and West, the heart of Jeffersonian strength.[82] Some feared for the future of the party, since one or two of the most influential Republicans flirted with the Virginian's dissident cause. As early as the winter of 1803, Speaker Macon had been influenced by Randolph toward a suspicion of Madison's Republican orthodoxy. Macon be-

81. Plumer, *Memorandum*, March, 5, 6, 1806, pp. 443–444. Randolph is remembered to have remarked, "Why, Sir, this is nothing; it is done every day, and every hour of the day. It is there at the firesides—and not on the floor that the affairs of the country are discussed—" (William E. Dodd, *The Life of Nathaniel Macon* [Raleigh, N.C., 1903], pp. 205–206). Jefferson to William A. Burwell, September 17, 1806, Ford, 10:289.

82. Plumer, *Memorandum*, April 8, 1806, pp. 478–479. Plumer is quoting Kentucky Senator John Adair, a Burrite.

came seriously disaffected over the Florida appropriation, and he had supported Randolph in the Yazoo struggle. Subsequently, Randolph had been cultivating the allegiance of James Monroe in Europe and grooming him to challenge Madison for the Jeffersonian succession. The strength of the Quids (as Randolph and his little band came to be called) was at one point such that in coalition with the Federalists they could have controlled the House. Jefferson's legislative program was in large measure frustrated in this session by the factional dispute, particularly his bills to provide for the defense of New Orleans and to reclassify the militia. The president lamented that a phalanx of seven Federalists, joined by "some discontented Republicans, some oblique ones, some capricious, have so often made a majority as to produce very serious embarrassment to the public operations."[83]

The Jeffersonian forces were thrown into temporary disarray by the schism, not only in Congress but outside as well. The president was besieged with letters from political advisers asking for information on the extent of the revolt and seeking guidance from the party leader in dealing with it.[84] It was essential to avoid additional rumblings among the party faithful, and Jefferson moved quickly to close the breach and restore the morale of his shaken followers. To Speaker Macon he warned that "some enemy, whom we know not, is sowing tares among us. Between you and myself nothing but opportunities of explanation can be necessary to defeat those endeavors." He called a conference and assured the speaker of his "unqualified" confidence. The president also moved to prevent Monroe from allying with the Randolph forces and thereby constituting an additional rallying point for disaffection. "The great body of your friends," Jefferson pointedly advised his young friend, "are among the firm adherents to the Administration."[85] Monroe seems to have heeded the warning implicit in the president's remarks, for after a brief flirtation he returned to the fold.

The revolt in Congress, potentially so threatening, had run its course by the spring of 1806. In mid-March Jefferson could report the overwhelming passage of "Mr. Nicholson's Resolutions" (actually the

83. Dodd, pp. 197, 206–207; Plumer, *Memorandum*, April 4, 1806, p. 475; Jefferson to W. C. Nicholas, April 13, 1806, Lipscomb, 11:98–100.

84. See, for example, William Duane to Jefferson, March 12, 1806, in Worthington C. Ford, ed., "Letters of William Duane," in Massachusetts Historical Society *Proceedings*, 20, 3d series (1906–1907), 281–284.

85. Jefferson to Macon, March 26, 1806, Ford, 11:248–249; to Monroe, May 4, 1806, pp. 261–262.

Florida resolutions suggested by the president) with only 9 of 96 Republicans in dissent. A short time later he could write with evident relief: "The House of Representatives is as well disposed as I ever saw one. The defection of so prominent a leader threw them into dismay and confusion for a moment, but they soon rallied to their own principles and let him go off with 5 or 6 followers only. . . . The alarm the House has had from this schism has produced a rallying together and harmony which carelessness and security had begun to endanger."[86] Jefferson felt that Randolph's declaration of "perpetual opposition" to the administration had sobered several members who for a time had been drawn into his orbit, and caused them to rejoin the majority.

The consolidation of the moderates followed apace. Macon, who lost his Speakership, saw the handwriting on the wall and rejoined the administration forces, although he maintained his personal friendship with Randolph. Several Quids lost their bids for reelection. The voice of the radicals in the party was for a time stilled. The Republican press by and large stayed with the administration. By December, 1806, Jefferson was sufficiently confident of his restored authority to dismiss Randolph and his followers casually as "our little band."[87]

Nevertheless, the Randolph schism represented a watershed in the president's control of Congress. It disrupted the pattern of success that Jefferson had enjoyed with his party in Congress for five years. Seen in the short term of a year's time, the schism may well have seemed of little importance, but viewed from a greater perspective it appears as the portent of things to come. The president's hold over Congress weakened for the first time in the session of 1805–1806. Randolph's opposition over the Florida appropriation and the non-importation bills, while only temporarily providing a rallying point for dissident members, still served to shake the confidence of congressional Republicans, not so much in their leader as in the general strength of the diverse party itself.

Lacy has seen in the party's quick closing of ranks after the schism

86. Jefferson to Nicholas, April 13, 1806, Lipscomb, 11:98–100; See also Jefferson to Caesar Rodney, March 24, 1806, Ford, 10:245–246, and to John Tyler, April 26, 1806, pp. 251–252.

87. Dodd, p. 214; also Noble S. Cunningham, *The Jeffersonian Republicans in Power: Party Operations, 1801–1809* (Chapel Hill, N.C., 1963); and Norman K. Risjord, *The Old Republicans: Southern Conservatives in the Age of Jefferson* (New York, 1965), pp. 22–80; Jefferson to Thomas Leiper, December 22, 1806, LC No. 28615.

evidence of its "maturity." "When the experience was completed, the party was healthier than it had been before."[88] When one compares the almost unbroken record of success that the president enjoyed before the schism with the record of the closing years of his second term, however, not to mention the difficulties faced by the next administration, this conclusion must be questioned. True, the party managed to rally behind the president, shake off its irreconcilables, and demonstrate its capacity to modify its outworn principles in the face of altered circumstances. Its ability to bounce back from its factional squabbles stimulated it to a new confidence. As the presidential election of 1808 approached and the rush of ambitions for the succession grew, however, the old divisions once again threatened party unity. Gallatin sensed the problem with his usual political acumen. In assuring the president of *his* continued loyalty in the face of efforts by enemies to "sow tares" within the official family, the Treasury secretary warned: "I am, however, a secondary object, and you are not less aware than myself that the next Presidential election lurks at the bottom of the congressional dissensions. . . . They afford abundant matter of triumph to our opponents; they discredit at all events, and may ultimately ruin the cause itself."[89]

Gallatin feared the conflicting passions and jarring interests that increasingly surfaced around the administration as factions jockeyed for position at the electoral starting gate. It is impossible to measure the effect of Jefferson's announcement to his friends in mid-1805 of his intention to retire from office at the conclusion of his second term, but there is no doubt that it damaged his capacity to lead his party in the final months. The evidence is clear that the central factor in the party's remarkable unity amid diversity had been Jefferson's presence at the helm. As the one figure to whom all could willingly pledge allegiance, Jefferson had succeeded in welding the elements of his party into an effective tool for political action. Wtih the sure and certain knowledge of his imminent departure, however, the centrifugal force of factionalism once again exerted its inexorable pressure.

Jefferson's hold over his party, his capacity to command its allegiance, was by no means ended in 1805–1806. The majority con-

---

88. Lacy, p. 312.
89. Gallatin to Jefferson, October 13, 1806, Gallatin, *Writings*, 1:310–311. Unable to resist the lure of the presidential race himself, Gallatin, in a draft of this letter not sent, supported Madison to succeed Jefferson.

tinued to support its leader on the major points at issue over the next two years, most notably during the months of the embargo. As Peterson writes, however, the party after 1806 would prove uncontrollable on lesser issues, and "the loyalty of many would be given less in trust than in fear of injuring the party that revolved on the prestige of the President."[90] The seeds of internal disorder were still there, ready to blossom when the force of Jefferson's leadership was removed. What Randolph did was to show that opposition was possible. The twin factors of the succession and the embargo were to provide the fuel to feed the flames of faction. The failure of the embargo and the factional leadership of the next president, Madison, were to remove from party government the one element that made it workable within the American constitutional framework—a president with sufficient standing and skill as party leader to bridge the separation of powers and energize the motive force of government. The record of these years underscores the crucial effects of personal qualities of leadership, qualities that, as Neustadt has shown, even in the presence of the more material reward structures and substantial institutional mechanisms of our own day, are essential for the effective employment of presidential power.

90. *Thomas Jefferson*, p. 840.

CHAPTER 6

꧁

The Struggle with the Judiciary: The Elected or the Anointed?

Political actors and institutions not only perform objective instrumental functions; they serve as symbolic representatives of political ideals and passions. To friend and foe alike in the Jeffersonian period, the federal judiciary represented a set of political values that, if legitimated, would determine the future power relationships within the American political system. The question of what to do about the judiciary became the overriding issue of Jefferson's first term, the issue "around which the meaning of the 'Revolution of 1800' was to be defined."[1]

Edelman has observed that "For the spectators of the political scene every act contributes to a pattern of ongoing events that spells threat or reassurance. This is the basic dichotomy for the mass public."[2] To the Jeffersonians the judiciary constituted the final barrier to be assaulted in the advance of popular government and political liberty. To the Federalists the courts represented the last bastion of moderation and sanity arresting the progress of mob rule and anarchy. Without underestimating the significance of the constitutional and philosophical issues involved, we can fairly say that to the protagonists of the day the question of the judiciary was at bottom a matter of power and power relationships. For both sides the courts assumed great symbolic significance as the principal battleground in the struggle for the control of America's political destiny.

Before the turn of the nineteenth century, the problem of the proper place for the federal courts in the republic had occupied the attention of men only fitfully. At the Constitutional Convention of 1787 the

---

1. Ellis, *Jeffersonian Crisis*, p. 16.
2. *Symbolic Uses of Politics*, p. 13.

delegates largely avoided the thorny constitutional questions concerning the judiciary. Controversy among scholars still exists as to the precise attitudes of the Framers toward the concept of judicial review.[3] During the ratification struggles of 1787–1788, the antifederalists objected principally to the provisions of Article III, Section 1, giving Congress wide latitude in creating a lower federal court system, and to Section 2, giving the Supreme Court jurisdiction over cases arising between citizens of different states. The critics of the Constitution seemed little exercised over a possible judicial tyranny arising from the power to nullify acts of the legislative branch. Hamilton, it seemed, had spoken for moderate opinion when he summed up the case for judicial review in Federalist Number 78:

The interpretation of the laws is the proper and peculiar function of the courts. A constitution is in fact, and must be regarded by the judges as, a fundamental law. It therefore belongs to them to ascertain its meaning as well as the meaning of any particular act proceeding from the legislative body. If there should happen to be an irreconcilable variance between the two, that which has the superior obligation and validity ought, of course, to be preferred; or, in other words, the constitution ought to be preferred to the statute, the intention of the people to the intention of their agents.[4]

Two alternative positions on this issue had developed in the 1780's. One position placed final power over constitutional questions in an independent judicial branch, the other in the popular branches of government, particularly the legislature. To antifederalists the question was simple: if the judiciary had sole power to check the legislature by nullifying its acts, then who would check the judiciary from its assumption of minority rule? To advocates of judicial review the question was rather how to avoid a tyranny of the majority over the minority. The issue was not joined, however, until the late 1790's when the constitutional question of judicial power was swept up into the larger issue of the political control of the government.

There is evidence to indicate that during Washington's presidency the federal courts, to use a modern barbarism, maintained a "low profile," avoiding political controversy in an attempt to gain legitimacy in the eyes of moderate antifederalists.[5] This attempt foundered

3. See, for example, Charles A. Beard, *The Supreme Court and the Constitution* (New York, 1962), especially the Introduction by Alan Westin.

4. In Clinton Rossiter, ed., *The Federalist Papers* (New York, 1961), p. 467.

5. See Ellis, pp. 12–13.

upon an increased polarization of opinion with the rise of political parties in the late 1790's. Washington and Adams refused to appoint Republicans to the courts. In the face of this growing homogeneity of judicial opinion, the earlier antifederalist enemies of an independent judiciary joined in opposition with newer partisan Republicans who were seeking to sever the links between Federalists in the elective branches of government and their brethren on the bench.

After 1796 a series of court decisions served to reinforce the growing conviction among the Republicans that the judiciary had become little more than a partisan servant of the Federalist party. Anti-British feeling among Republicans was rekindled by a decision striking down a Virginia law that had confiscated prerevolutionary British war debts.[6] Republican hostility to the courts reached a fever pitch two years later when the judges lent their ready assistance to the enforcement of the sedition laws. With the judges transformed into little more than political preachers of the Federalist faith, the judiciary earned the cordial hatred of the Jeffersonian party. The Virginia and Kentucky Resolutions of 1798–1799 stood as eloquent testimony of the bitterness of opposition to the tenor of the times and as harbingers of possible future action should the Jeffersonians succeed in gaining power.

Jefferson's View of the Problem

Shortly after Jefferson took office, he revealed his contempt for the Federalist judges and his willingness to use the power of the presidency to combat what he saw as the irresponsible arrogance of the judiciary by pardoning all those convicted under the Sedition Act and halting the prosecution of William Duane, the fiery editor of the Philadelphia *Aurora*. Republican demands for a judicial housecleaning soon took on a more insistent tone as the courts, rather than temper their partisanship, continued to "mount their cannon *en barbette* and play upon all the Republicans from the Gibraltar of the Judicial Department."[7]

Two episodes during Jefferson's first year in office focused the attention of the administration upon the courts and strengthened Jefferson and his colleagues in their resolve to cut judicial pretension down to size. The first was an attempt by judges of the district court of Wash-

6. *Ware* v. *Hylton*, 3 Dallas 171 (1796).
7. *National Intelligencer*, November 18, 1801.

ington to force a prosecution of Samuel Harrison Smith, the Jeffersonian editor of the *National Intelligencer*, on a charge of criminal libel. The editor had published a letter attacking the judiciary for "destroying all freedom of opinion, of executing unconstitutional laws" and other like crimes against the nation. The district attorney of Washington, a Jefferson appointee, refused to prosecute, but the incident remained in the minds of the Jeffersonians as additional evidence of the need for speedy reform of the "least dangerous branch."[8]

The second episode was less clearly partisan, but in reality struck closer to the president directly, for it involved the exercise of presidential powers. Proceedings were instituted in the circuit court of Connecticut for condemnation of an armed French merchantman, the *Peggy*, seized during the naval hostilities with France in 1800. Under the provisions of the treaty with France ratified at the close of the Adams Administration, captured ships not definitely condemned were to be returned to their lawful owners. Jefferson thereby ordered the United States attorney to pay over the proceeds of the sale of the *Peggy* to her French owners. The clerk of the court in whose custody the money rested refused, however, and asked the court to require that the money be paid into the U.S. Treasury. The court agreed, declaring the president's order illegal. Jefferson rejected the decision as a violation of his prerogative. Ironically, he was sustained in his view on appeal by Chief Justice John Marshall some months later, but the significance of the case lies in the confirmation by the original decision of the continuing attempt by the courts to embarrass and obstruct the popular branches of government in the performance of their duties.[9]

When the Jeffersonians assumed office in 1801, important Republicans began to press for a thorough reform of the judiciary. The respected Edmund Pendleton was one of many to suggest sweeping constitutional changes to restrict judicial influence, among them amendments to have judges appointed by Congress and removable on joint address of both houses. That pedantic champion of agrarian democracy, John Taylor of Caroline, added his voice to the chorus of radicals who called for total reform. Taylor at this time had the ear of

8. *Ibid.*, June 12, 1801.
9. Charles Warren, *The Supreme Court in United States History* (Boston, 1923), 1:98–100; Jefferson to Madison, July 15, 1801, Ford, 9:278; *United States v. Schooner Peggy*, 1 Cranch 103 (1802). See also Charles G. Haines, *The Role of the Supreme Court in American Government and Politics, 1789–1835* (Berkeley, Calif., 1944), pp. 226–227.

influential party leaders in Congress, notably Nicholas and Breckinridge, and he appealed through them to the president for leadership in
the constitutional battle to come. In Congress, Giles warned that "the
revolution is incomplete, so long as that strong fortress is in possession
of the enemy."[10] Breckinridge, too, newly arrived in Washington and
eager to press the attack, urged strong action against the Federalist
remnants on the bench.

To effect fundamental changes in the courts required no less than
the full commitment of the president, however, and Jefferson was
uncertain at this time of the proper course to pursue with regard to the
judiciary. As with most questions of reform after he became president,
he sided on this issue with the moderate elements of his party. When
presented with the alternatives of joining the radicals in an all-out war
against the Federalists or seeking a middle way to deal with the courts
without jeopardizing basic institutional arrangements, he chose the
latter course.

Both theoretically and practically, Jefferson was sympathetic to demands to curb the influence of the judicial branch. To take on the
Federalists through an assault on the unrepresentative judiciary would
have been consistent with sound republican doctrine and would,
moreover, have helped to cement Jefferson's position among the more
radical elements in his party, particularly those in the Republican
heartland of the South and West. Battling with the courts would have
been a popular activity, particularly as the judges continued to defy
popular opinion and to reinforce popular prejudices against themselves. For policy reasons, therefore, the Federalist courts presented an
apparently easy target of opportunity by which to follow up the "Revolution of 1800."

Jefferson's well-known views concerning the nature of law and his
general attitude toward the judicial branch made a clash with the
courts seem inevitable. Jefferson considered law to be an instrument of
politics in the sense that the laws, to be valid, must conform to the will
of the political community. "It is the will of the nation which makes
laws obligatory; it is their will which creates or annihilates the organ
which is to declare or announce it."[11] Constitutions (fundamental
laws) and statutes alike were simply instruments by which to carry out

10. "The Danger Not Over," in Mays, *Edmund Pendleton*, 2:332–336; Beveridge,
John Marshall, 3:609–610; Giles to Jefferson, June 1, 1801, LC No. 19373.
11. Jefferson to Edmund Randolph, August 18, 1799, Ford, 9:74

the wishes of the people. This did not mean that the law should mirror the expediential whim of transient majorities, but it should reflect the considered judgment of the community. The fiduciary agents of the people—executive, legislative, and judicial alike—must be prepared to modify the laws to conform to changing reality. Laws, to be valid, must be answerable ultimately to popular will and the lawmakers subject to popular sanctions. From this view developed many of Jefferson's attitudes toward the judiciary: his opposition to judge-made common law; his belief in the necessary mutability of constitutions as well as statute law; his belief in the right and duty of the legitimately "responsible" branches, that is, the elected president and Congress, to decide questions of constitutionality.

Much of Jefferson's recorded hostility to the Supreme Court appears in his private writings after he left the presidency. With the passage of time, his views on the separation of powers and checks and balances shifted, coming in his last years closer to a support for a more rigid separation and a more complete control over governmental institutions by the people.[12] On the question of judicial review, however, his position was well developed during his presidency, and was to remain constant. As early as December, 1801, he had included his opinion in a paragraph of his first annual message to Congress, deleted from the final draft, in which he sought to justify his actions in dismissing the pending prosecutions under the Sedition Act:

Applications from different persons suffering prosecution under the act usually called the Sedition Act, claimed my early attention to that instrument. Our country has thought proper to distribute the powers of its government among 3 equal and independent authorities, constituting each a check on one or both of the others, in all attempts to impair its constitution. To make each an effectual check, it must have a right in cases which arise within the line of its proper functions, where, equally with the others, it acts in the last resort and without appeal, to decide on the validity of an act according to its judgment, and uncontrolled by the opinions of any other department. We have, accordingly, in more than one instance, seen the opinions of different departments in opposition to each other, and no ill ensue.

Having considered the Sedition Act carefully, Jefferson went on to "declare that I hold that act to be in palpable and unqualified contradiction to the Constitution. Considering it then as a nullity, I have relieved from oppression under it those of my fellow-citizens who were

12. On this concept, see Vile, *Constitutionalism*, pp. 163–166.

within the reach of the functions confined to me." As Jefferson inter-preted the Constitution, therefore, "each department is truly indepen-dent of the others and has an equal right to decide for itself what is the meaning of the Constitution in the cases submitted to its action, and especially when it is to act ultimately and without appeal."[13]

Jefferson never explicitly rejected the doctrine that the Supreme Court could decide on the constitutionality of a law as it applied to the Court's own functions. Each branch of government had the right to decide the validity of a law dealing with the performance of its own duties. In a letter to Abigail Adams, Jefferson denied that the Court had a right to decide the validity of the Sedition Act "for the execu-tive," any more than the executive had a right to decide for the judiciary:

The judges, believing the law constitutional, had a duty to pass a sentence of fine and imprisonment; because the power was placed in their hands by the Constitution. But the executive, believing the law to be unconstitutional, was bound to remit the execution of it, because that power has been confided to it by the Constitution. That instrument meant that its co-ordinate branches should be checks on each other. But the opinion which gives to the judges the right to decide what laws are constitutional, and what not, not only for them-selves in their own sphere of action, but for the legislative and executive also, in their spheres, would make the judiciary a despotic branch.[14]

The emphasis on the right of each branch to determine the constitu-tionality of a law in its own sphere of action may explain Jefferson's failure to attack Chief Justice Marshall's assertion of judicial review in *Marbury* v. *Madison.* Jefferson never actually denied the right of the Court to declare an act of Congress unconstitutional; he denied their sole right to do so, and he denied their right to do so in an area outside of the judicial function. In the *Marbury* case, a judicial determination of the unconstitutionality of a provision of the Judiciary Act of 1789 giving the Supreme Court certain mandamus powers would seem to be within the rights of the Court, under Jefferson's theory, because it involved a function of the Court.[15]

Jefferson's concern for the principles of representativeness and ac-

13. Quoted in full in Haines, pp. 207–208. The passage was deleted at the urging of Madison and Gallatin so as not to furnish "something to the opposition to make a handle of" (Jefferson to Spencer Roane, September 6, 1819, Ford, 7:136).

14. Jefferson to Abigail Adams, September 11, 1804, Lipscomb, 11:50–51.

15. See Haines, pp. 244–245. Jefferson's objection to the *Marbury* case was on other grounds: he disputed Marshall's *obiter dictum* concerning Marbury's rights in the case.

countability in government made him inherently suspicious of the judiciary as a haven for men who owed no loyalty to the will of the majority. Life tenure added to the danger. Years later he complained, "The insufficiency of the means provided for their removal gave them a freehold and irresponsibility in office." Judges were no more honest than other men and were given to the "same passions for party, for power, and the privilege of their corps."[16] How his views might have developed had the courts been in the hands of Republicans we will never know. The only experience he knew was with Federalist judges appointed by his predecessors, and the frequent partisanship of these tribunals reinforced his philosophical fears concerning the appointed branch.

Long after he left public office, as he brooded over developments from the relative quiet of his mountaintop, Jefferson allowed free rein to his hostility to the Court and its hated chief. It poured from his pen in a number of sharply critical private letters reflecting on the significance of the long contest. The Republican ascendancy of 1800 was "as real a revolution in the principles of our government as that of 1776 was in its form," albeit a revolution effected by the suffrage rather than the sword. The people dismissed the Federalists from two branches, but alas, "over the judicial department the Constitution has deprived them of their control. The repudiated party took refuge in the courts and from there continued the reprobated system." Marshall and his cohorts had succeeded, furthermore, in coopting to their persuasion the new blood that had been injected into the old. Bitterly, the former president denounced his hated rival for his influence over this "subtle corps of sappers and miners." "An opinion is huddled up in conclave, perhaps by a majority of one, delivered as if unanimous, and with the silent acquiescence of lazy or timid associates, by a crafty chief judge who sophisticates the law to his mind by the turn of his own reason."[17] From the perspective of twenty years, with the evidence for his view having accumulated in a series of court decisions (*Marbury*, *Fletcher* v. *Peck*, *Cohen* v. *Virginia*, *McCulloch* v. *Maryland*), Jefferson's suspicion of the federal judiciary had ripened into a wholesale detestation.

16. Jefferson to Thomas Ritchie, December 25, 1820, Lipscomb, 15:295–299; to W. C. Jarvis, September 28, 1820, 276–279.

17. Jefferson to Spencer Roane, September 6, 1819, *ibid.*, pp. 135–136, and to Ritchie, cited in note 16; see also Jefferson to William Johnson, June 12, 1823, in Padover, *Complete Jefferson*, pp. 320–332.

This maturation, however, was the result of a long evolutionary process that in 1801–1802 had only begun. What to do about the Court was only one of many questions to be considered in the process of reforming the nation's political institutions. Jefferson's response to the question, much like his view of the problem of patronage, was to evolve slowly under the stimulus of events and often in response to the actions of his opponents. Rather than conducting a carefully planned campaign against the judiciary, the president, as Malone has noted, "took one step without being sure of or necessarily committed to the next one."[18]

The Evolution of a Strategy against the Courts

Despite the president's growing hostility toward the courts, he was intent in the summer and autumn of 1801 on finding ways to curb the excesses of the federal judges without altering the Constitution or jeopardizing the essential independence of the judiciary. We have noted his effort to detach the more "sensible" Federalists from their leaders through a policy of conciliation. Throughout these months his hopes were high of consolidating all true republicans into one camp, thereby eliminating the Federalist remnant as a serious threat. Furthermore, Jefferson and his closest advisers were satisfied with the institutional arrangements under the existing Constitution and were not eager to tamper with them unduly. For these reasons Jefferson wished to avoid a major clash with the Federalists over the court question.[19]

He had other reasons as well for his hesitancy. We have demonstrated that in terms of exercising leadership over Congress and within his own executive branch, Jefferson's behavior corresponds clearly to the Neustadtian bargaining model of presidential power. He was a master of the art of political persuasion. The tactics of bargaining, so much in conformity with the character of his political style, were used to great effect in mobilizing legislative majorities and in forging a unified administration. His conception of his presidential role, furthermore, found a reasonable "fit" with the role expectations of his executive and legislative environments. In those instances where a fit was perhaps less than complete initially, Jefferson's record of success

18. *First Term*, pp. 115–116.
19. I am in substantial agreement with Ellis on this point, although the evidence on which to base a judgment is scanty. See Ellis, chap. 2.

and the growing demonstration of public support for his leadership worked mightily to change existing role expectations to conform with the president's conception.

The conditions essential for successful bargaining were absent, however, when it came to dealing with the courts. The relationship between the Republican president and the Federalist Supreme Court was characterized by wide and persistent role incongruence. Furthermore, the president had few resources of power with which to alter existing attitudes in his favor. It takes two to bargain. Both sides must have a vested interest in reaching an agreement. Each side must have something to gain from a *modus vivendi* and something to lose by a failure to attain accommodation. None of these conditions existed to an appreciable degree. The constitutional gulf separating president and Court was widened by unbridgeable political and ideological differences. The tactics of conciliation and persuasion that worked so well in other role-sets were inoperable. And, as we shall see, the extent to which confrontation overrode negotiation and the frontal assault replaced the flanking movement marked the degree to which failure replaced success in Jefferson's efforts to impose his will upon the judiciary.

In the spring and summer of 1801 there was virtual unanimity among Republicans that something must be done about the judiciary, but little firm agreement beyond that. Increasingly, however, opinion was forming behind the necessity to repeal the Judiciary Act of 1801 as a minimum step. If the various elements of the party could not agree on a long-term strategy, they were at least united in their conviction that this measure, passed in the dying days of the Adams administration, was a blatant partisan attempt by the repudiated Federalists to save something from the wreckage of their party at the polls.

The Judiciary Act of 1801 had been signed into law on February 13, 1801, only three weeks before Jefferson's inauguration. The act eliminated the necessity for Supreme Court justices to ride circuit by creating six new federal circuit courts with sixteen judges, Adams's "midnight appointments." As if this were not enough to provoke the Jeffersonians, the measure struck directly at the new president by reducing the number of Supreme Court seats from six to five with the next vacancy, thereby preventing Jefferson from making an appointment. The "midnight appointments" hurt the new president personally, but the reduction of the size of the Court alerted him even more to the larger public threat posed by the Federalist hold over the judiciary. He had predicted a year earlier that "appointments in the nature of freehold render it difficult to undo what is done." But, of course, rendering it difficult was precisely what the Federalist leaders had in mind. Gouverneur Morris, employing an imagery popular in the day, frankly if perhaps unwisely admitted that the Federalists "are about to experience a heavy gale of adverse wind; can they be blamed for casting many anchors to hold their ship through the storm?"[20]

The Republican leadership was determined to thwart the Federalists if it could be done. The lines of battle were drawn, and neither side seemed prepared to surrender its position even a little in an effort to find an accommodation. The precise plans for repeal of the Judiciary Act of 1801 were probably not completed before Congress convened in December, 1801, but the decision for a frontal attack through repeal of the odious measure had been arrived at much earlier. Speaker Macon was writing in the late spring of the probability of repeal, and Elbridge Gerry so informed the president in early May.[21] Richard Ellis in his fine study of the Jeffersonians and the judiciary asserts that the Republicans were so divided and Jefferson so reluctant to commit himself to judicial reform that possibly no action for repeal would have been begun had it not been for the impact made on Republican opinion by the December, 1801, decision of Marshall and his Court to hear argument in the *Marbury* case. The little evidence available, however, seems to point to the conclusion that while the *Marbury* "show cause" order did galvanize Republicans into demands for immediate action and may well have convinced Jefferson to agree to put repeal first on the Senate's agenda at the December session of Congress, the president's basic commitment for repeal had already been made.[22] He had earlier nullified as many of the "midnight" appointments as he could, and his views on the evils of the act were

20. For evidence of the personal insult of the midnight appointments, see Jefferson to Abigail Adams, June 13, 1804, in Lester J. Cappon, ed., *The Adams-Jefferson Letters* (New York, 1959), pp. 269–271. For his reaction to the reduction in the size of the Court, see Jefferson to Joel Barlow, March 14, 1801, Lipscomb, 10:222–223, and to Giles, March 23, 1801, Ford, 9:222. See also William S. Carpenter, "Repeal of the Judiciary Act of 1801," in *American Political Science Review*, 9 (1915), 520; Gouverneur Morris to Robert Livingston, February 20, 1801, cited in Ellis, p. 15.

21. McPherson, "Letters from North Carolinians," p. 271; Elbridge Gerry to Jefferson, May 4, 1801, in Claude G. Bowers, Jr., ed., *The Diary of Elbridge Gerry* (New York, 1927).

22. Ellis, pp. 40–45; also Warren, 1:204; Malone, *First Term*, p. 117.

known to his supporters. In April, Jefferson had confessed that, despised as these "midnight" judges were, their appointment would have to stand "till the law shall be repealed, which we trust will be at the next Congress." The pressure to repeal the act seems to have convinced him by late August, if he needed convincing at that point, for it was then in the course of some remarks on the business being prepared for Congress that he informed his attorney general that "the removal of excrescences from the judiciary is the universal demand."[23] It would be unwise to assume, because Jefferson did not explicitly recommend repeal in his annual message to Congress, that he had not made a decision on the matter. It is true that he simply informed Congress that "the Judicial system of the United States, and especially that portion of it recently erected, will of course present itself to the contemplation of Congress." Jefferson rarely recommended measures directly, however, preferring indirection for the sake of deference to the legislators. The direct reference to the "recently erected" portion of the judiciary and the phrase, "will *of course* present itself" are sufficient evidence of the president's commitment. Gallatin, Jefferson's closest adviser on the preparation of this annual message, was certainly assuming repeal, at least of the provision that had created the new circuit courts, for he was basing his estimates of expenditures for the new year in part on the savings he expected from the civil list by the abolition of the new judgeships.

When a bill for repeal was introduced into the Senate it was done "in pursuance of the *recommendation* of the President's message of December 8." The president, furthermore, aided the forces of repeal by submitting a document purporting to prove by a "careful" marshaling of statistics that there was no need for additional federal courts, since the docket of the courts before 1801 had never been full. That the data for "Document No. 8" had been hastily and carelessly compiled, thus giving the Federalists justifiable grounds for attacking the president, does not detract from the document's pertinence as additional evidence of the president's commitment to repeal prior to the *Marbury* show cause order.[24]

Jefferson was determined to see the "parasitical plant engrafted at

23. Jefferson to Archibald Stuart, April 8, 1801, Ford, 9:247; to Levi Lincoln, August 26, 1801, Lipscomb, 10:276.
24. Gallatin to Jefferson, November 16, 1801, Ford, 9:325n; *Annals of Congress*, 7:1, pp. 24–30. The document was submitted with the annual message on December 8, 1801, Ford, 9:340.

the last session on the judiciary body" removed with all deliberate speed. It was well that he was behind the repeal effort, for the party in Congress needed his leadership. Its majority in the Senate was slim, only 18–14, and two Republican senators were not yet in attendance. Furthermore, some members of the party were not committed to repeal of the entire act. A few had been convinced by the Federalists that repeal was unconstitutional. In the House some members looked with favor at a petition signed by members of the Philadelphia bar (among them such Republicans as A. J. Dallas and Thomas McKean, Jr., son of the Pennsylvania governor) praising the new circuit courts as a valuable improvement over the older inefficient system.[25] The president's commitment to repeal was to prove valuable, therefore, as a rallying point for party spirit and was indeed to be used as an argument in itself for support of repeal.

John C. Breckinridge introduced a resolution in the Senate on January 8, 1802, to repeal the Judiciary Act of 1801. He opened the debate by summarizing the Republican case and stressing the constitutionality of repeal. (The president capped the day's events by hosting one of his "nonpartisan" teas that evening at the Executive Mansion, with members of both parties in attendance.[26]) The debate in Congress lasted two months. The Federalists were determined to publicize the move for repeal as an attempt of the "democrats" to destroy the independence of the judges. The Republicans had not expected an attack of such cohesion and ferocity, and it was soon clear that there would be an all-out, no-holds-barred party fight.

The debate centered on three questions: the constitutionality of repeal, the requirement of the judges to ride circuit, and the need for additional courts. The Republicans made much use of Jefferson's statistics to show that the volume of court business did not warrant additional judges. John Randolph charged the judges with conspiring to the exercise of "an inquisitorial authority over the Cabinet of the Executive, " this a reference to the *Marbury* case.[27] The Federalists countered by raising the specter, if repeal were to succeed, of an

25. Jefferson to Benjamin Rush, December 20, 1801, Ford, 9:345. Unfortunately for the petitioners, their document did not reach Washington until after repeal had passed the Senate.

26. Anne Cary Morris, ed., *Diary of Gouverneur Morris* (London, 1889), January 8, 1802, 2:417.

27. Quoted in Warren, 1:207.

omnipotent legislature subject to no law but its own and bent upon an unrestrained assertion of majority tyranny.

In the course of the battle the congressional Republicans employed a tactic that they were to develop in subsequent legislative contests with some effect: they presented the repeal bill as the *president's* measure. By wrapping the legislation in the presidential mantle, they sought to enhance its appeal by giving it the color of Jefferson's popularity and prestige. As the debate progressed toward an uncertain end, many Republicans took to defending the constitutionality of repeal simply by presenting evidence of the president's support, "an evidence of its constitutionality of so high an authority," as one member put it, "that if it stood singly on that, it would require a federalist host to shake it."[28] Thus, in his first legislative battle as president, Jefferson's imprimatur on legislation was used to forge the unity needed to pass it. The Federalists, too, sought initially to pin the label of "Jefferson" on the repeal legislation with a view to presenting him as a usurper. They soon came to realize, however, that such tactics simply played into the hands of their opponents whose reliance on the presidential embrace of legislation became a tactic for insuring legislative success.

The final vote for repeal in the Senate on February 3 was along party lines, 16 to 15. The Republicans showed remarkable unity on the bill, voting together on all test votes. The outcome in the House was never in doubt, although the sizable Republican majority did not attempt to cut off debate. The bill passed the House in March.

The Republicans quickly followed up their victory with a controversial law reducing the number of Supreme Court terms from two to one per year by abolishing the June and December terms and restoring the old February term. The effect of this was to postpone the next session of the Court fourteen months, to February, 1803. Their purpose was to deny an opportunity for the Court to consider the constitutionality of the Repeal Act before it came into effect and could be given a chance to work. The law appeared to the Federalists and some Republicans, however, to show that the administration was afraid of a confrontation with the Supreme Court.[29] No evidence of Jefferson's

28. *Annals of Congress,* 7:1, p. 113.

29. Monroe, for example, wanted a confrontation with the Court, provided the onus for the battle could be placed on the judiciary and the Federalists and not on the legislative branch and the Republicans. Monroe to Jefferson, April 25, 1802, in Ellis, p. 60.

position on this exists; he did sign it, but since he never vetoed anything, that is no indication of his feeling. There is little doubt, however, that if he had disliked the bill he could have quashed it early in
the debate in Congress.

The Repeal Act threw the Federalist leaders on the defensive. To
the more imaginative it bespoke the end of an independent judiciary
and the beginning of a reign of "licentiousness, tyranny, and anarchy"
leading to the consolidation of government under the hated Jefferson.
Justices Chase and Marshall were asked by a Federalist caucus to void
the Repeal Act by simply refusing to resume riding circuit. Chase was
eager to help, but as usual Marshall was more politically sensible,
pointing out the gravity of such a refusal by the justices to carry out
the law. Federalist acceptance of the situation was ratified at the next
term of Court (February, 1803) when it affirmed the constitutionality
of the Repeal Act.[30]

Marbury v. *Madison*, or Marshall v. Jefferson

Unfortunately for those who wished to see an end to the judicial
controversy, Jefferson and his supporters did not credit Marshall with
his efforts to moderate the situation. At the same session of Court that
upheld the Repeal Act, Marshall convinced Jefferson once more of the
unscrupulousness of the Federalist judges by his decision in the case of
Marbury v. *Madison*.[31] The details of the case, so important to future
constitutional development, will not be repeated here. Its significance
for us, and indeed for its own time, lies in its importance as a Federalist
response to the Republican ascendancy, and in more personal terms as
a key episode in the process of bitter estrangement between Jefferson
and Marshall.

The struggle that began as a contest for the future of popular institutions, the power of the "people" vs. the power of an "unrepresentative" elite, soon developed as well into a contest of authority and will
between the two principal antagonists, Jefferson and Marshall. The
precise origins of their personal animosity are veiled in mystery. The
two Virginians had much in common. They were blood cousins, both

30. Gouverneur Morris to Livingston, March 20, 1802, Morris, *Diary*, 2:423–
424; Malone, *First Term*, pp. 133–134; Ellis, pp. 62–63; *Stuart* v. *Laird*, 1 Cranch
299; see Warren, 1:231.
31. 1 Cranch 137. The case was decided six days before *Stuart* was announced,
thus obscuring the moderating impact of the latter decision.

from frontier counties, both had studied law, both entered politics and took part in the Revolution, Jefferson in Congress and as governor of Virginia, Marshall in the army. Marshall's faithful biographer, Albert Beveridge, finds the seeds of his hero's dislike of Jefferson to lie in these revolutionary years, with Jefferson safely in Virginia while the soldiers (Marshall among them) were enduring the hard winter at Valley Forge. Marshall's suspicions were further aroused by the incidents and rumors surrounding Jefferson's conduct as governor during the British invasion of Virginia in 1780–1781.[32]

Jefferson's distrust of Marshall seems to have emerged early in the 1790's when Marshall's early nationalism, his membership in the Society of the Cincinnati, and his speculations in land seemed to tie him with the Federalists. Marshall led the nationalist forces in the Virginia legislature, blocking the Republican attempt to memorialize Congress on the unconstitutionality of Hamilton's assumption and funding plan. At the time of Jay's Treaty in 1795 Jefferson was confiding to Madison that at long last Marshall had thrown off the mask of republicanism and "come forth in the plenitude of his English principles." There is an element of the turncoat, the traitor to his region and class, in Jefferson's picture of Marshall. By 1798 with Marshall's triumphal return to America in the wake of the "XYZ" affair, Jefferson was writing in an uncharacteristically personal way of his cousin's "lazy, lounging manners" and his "profound hypocrisy." Marshall's support of Burr in the election of the president in the House of Representatives in 1800, and his appointment as chief justice in the closing hours of Adams's tenure further widened the breach between the two Virginians.[33]

Ironically, the choice of Marshall as chief justice was greeted with some hostility in Federalist circles at the time. Oliver Wolcott alerted Fisher Ames to the danger that Marshall would "think too much of the State of Virginia." (!) Theodore Sedgwick deplored Marshall's

32. Beveridge, 1:126, 145; see Julian Boyd, "The Chasm that Separated Thomas Jefferson and John Marshall," in Gottfried Dietze, ed., *Essays on American Constitutionalism* (Englewood Cliffs, N.J., 1964), pp. 3–20.

33. Dumas Malone, *Thomas Jefferson and the Ordeal of Liberty* (Boston, 1962), p. 251; Jefferson to Madison, November 20, 1798, in Warren, 1:182. It was widely rumored at the time, as Beveridge admits (2:540–543), that Marshall wrote an opinion as the newly appointed chief justice that should a deadlock in the House persist, Congress on joint ballot should appoint the chief justice as the president pending a new election; see also Warren, 1:182–183.

hedonism and conviviality, his indolence and indecisiveness in the task of governing. Sedgwick nevertheless put his finger on a key characteristic of the new chief justice: "This gentleman, when aroused, has strong reasoning powers; they are indeed almost unequaled." The core of his genius as a jurist was underscored by a colleague: "His most surprising talent of placing his case in that point of view suited to the purpose he aims at. . . . He speaks like a man of plain common sense."

One man's common sense was another man's sophistry. Justice Story once recalled some comments of Jefferson on the skills of the chief justice: "When conversing with Marshall, I never admit anything. So sure as you admit any position to be good, no matter how remote from the conclusion he seeks to establish, you are gone. So great is his sophistry you must never give him an affirmative answer or you will be forced to grant his conclusion. Why, if he were to ask me if it were daylight or not, I'd reply, 'Sir, I don't know, I can't tell.'"[34]

When the chief justice announced the unanimous opinion of the Supreme Court in the *Marbury* case, he achieved one of those *tours de force* that demonstrate his great fitness to occupy the sensitive office he held. In the course of his lengthy opinion he succeeded in inflicting the maximum of damage upon the president while at the same time carving an impregnable position from which the Court could exercise a final authority within the federal system. As Malone puts it, Marshall managed "to have his cake and eat it" by first affirming in forthright terms poor Marbury's right to redress and then denying the Supreme Court's power to grant it.[35]

It is significant that at the time of the *Marbury* decision virtually no one objected very loudly to the Court's claim to exercise judicial review. Marshall's inclusion of the arguments for its assertion only at the end of a long opinion seemed to focus attention on the earlier portion of the document, which scored the president for illegally withholding Marbury's commission. Such was clearly Marshall's intention, for in his opinion he pointedly reversed the order of the questions put before the Court for decision by Marbury's counsel.

Marshall appears to have stolen a march, in particular, on Jefferson, whose sole concern seemed to be with the studied insult to the executive contained in the chief justice's *obiter dictum*. Jefferson's reaction to the Court's earlier decision simply to hear the case revealed his princi-

34. Warren, 1:179–180, 181–182.
35. *First Term*, p. 149.

pal concern in the matter: the defense of the independent authority of the president over appointments in the face of a judicial attempt at encroachment of that power. During oral arguments in the case, Jefferson refused to permit Madison to testify, to reply to written interrogatories, or even to submit facts in the case. He had determined to ignore a writ of mandamus should one be issued. For the same reason the president took great pains after the *Marbury* decision to deny that Marshall's dictum had any force in law. It stood in his mind as a bald assertion of illegal power by an arrogant judge, and he referred to it often in the following years as an example of Federalist subversion of the Constitution.[36] Jefferson pointed out that in their written opinion, the judges had "disclaimed all cognizance of the case," issuing instead what was confessedly "an extrajudicial opinion, and as such, of no authority." It seems not to have occurred to the president that the chief justice, in taking the care he did to issue such an admitted legal "aside," may have had other purposes in mind.

Jefferson was not alone in missing the larger purpose of the *Marbury* decision. Reaction to it, contrary to Beveridge's assertion, was widespread.[37] Many Republican editors discussed its implications, but attention was almost exclusively devoted to the chief justice's criticism of the chief executive. The genius of Marshall's assertion of judicial review by *denying* the Court a power granted to it by Congress served to mask the significance of his larger intention under a veil of impotence.

While Marshall had succeeded in legitimating an important function of the judiciary, the existing balance between the elected and the appointed branches was in fact little affected by the *Marbury* case. President and Congress continued their efforts to defang the judges, reinforced now by the evidence in Marshall's dictum of the Court's continuing apostasy. "Judicial supremacy may be made to bow before the strong arm of legislative authority," wrote Caesar Rodney at this time. "We shall discover who is master of the ship."[38] In the months following *Marbury*, the Jeffersonians resumed the offensive as

36. See particularly Jefferson to George Hay, June 2, 1807, Lipscomb, 11: 213–215.

37. Beveridge, 3:153. Warren (1:251–253) refutes Beveridge, noting that the *Marbury* opinion was printed in full in the *National Intelligencer* (March 16, 26, 1803), the *New York Spectator* (March 30, April 2, 1803), and the Philadelphia *Aurora* (March 23, 24, 1803), and other newspapers discussed it extensively.

38. Rodney to Joseph H. Nicholson, February 16, 1803, in Warren, 1:228.

the contest with the Court moved once again into the legislative arena.

The Weapon of Impeachment

Alexander Addison was a state judge of the western judicial district of Pennsylvania, whose partisan decisions and political harangues from the bench had earned him notoriety among local Republicans as "the transmontane Goliath of Federalism." Judge Addison's improprieties earned him, as well, the distinction of being the first casualty in the Jeffersonians' campaign to effect by impeachment what was being denied them by death or resignation—the removal of partisan judges. Addison could have been removed simply by a joint address of both houses of the Pennsylvania legislature, but Governor McKean and legislative leaders determined to make an example of him by adopting the political tactic of impeachment. In January, 1803, therefore, he was convicted and removed from office.[39] Flushed with the ease of their victory, Republicans in the following months shifted the scene of battle from the state to the federal arena.

In the first week of February, 1803, Jefferson sent to the House of Representatives a message calling the House's attention to certain charges lately placed before him: "The enclosed letter and affidavits exhibiting matter of complaint against John Pickering, district judge of New Hampshire, which is not within Executive cognizance, I transmit them to the House of Representatives to whom the Constitution has confided a power of instituting proceedings of redress, if they shall be of the opinion that the case calls for them."[40] John Pickering had served his state long and well, but at the time of these charges he was hopelessly insane and unable to carry out his judicial duties. His conduct on the bench was clearly aberrant, given increasingly to wild raving, verbal abuse of opposing counsel, and of late, intoxication. Direct attempts to persuade the judge to resign had proved fruitless, as had efforts to have his friends intercede with him.[41]

The case of Pickering presented a constitutional dilemma to the

39. For an account of this episode, see Sanford W. Higginbotham, *The Keystone of the Democratic Arch: Pennsylvania Politics, 1800–1816* (Philadelphia, 1952), pp. 53–55.

40. Message of February 3, 1802 (received February 4), *Annals of Congress*, 7:2, p. 460.

41. Gallatin tried unsuccessfully to enlist the aid of William Plumer in this effort. See Lynn W. Turner, "The Impeachment of John Pickering," in *American Historical Review*, 54 (April, 1949), 490. See also Ellis, p. 71.

president and his advisers. Article II, Section 4 of the Constitution provides that impeachment should be for "treason, bribery, or other high crimes and misdemeanors," and no other means existed for the removal of federal judges. Impeachment was an awkward, lengthy political process at any time, and the constitutional grounds were not clearly applicable in the case of a judge disabled by insanity or in any other way simply incompetent. The cruelty of removing by impeachment a judge who should not have been held legally responsible for his actions does not seem to have greatly deterred the president and his legislative colleagues, however. Jefferson may not have realized initially the extent of Pickering's mental incapacity (the documents and charges against him had been prepared by local Republican partisans and were undoubtedly one-sided); but he was made aware of it in the course of events and does not seem to have relented from his determination to remove the judge by whatever means were available. He observed to Plumer that "this business of removing judges by impeachment is a bungling way," but since it was apparently the only way, given the judge's intransigence, then it had to be pursued. "If the facts of his denying an appeal and his intoxication, as stated in the impeachment are proven, that will be sufficient cause for removal without further inquiry."[42]

One month after Jefferson's initial communication to Congress, the House impeached Judge Pickering. Formal charges were delayed, however, until the following session of Congress, so that the trial did not begin until March, 1804. Its proceedings were decidedly political in character, with the Republican leadership charting its progress "out of court," as Adams sourly observed:

In the House of Representatives speeches are making every day to dictate to the Senate how they must proceed; and the next morning they proceed accordingly. This day after the Senate adjourned, I saw a cluster of Senators and managers of the House of Representatives collected together around the fireplace; the managers consulted the senators about their opinions on the evidence, and Mr. Randolph contemptously sneering at the idea of insanity being alleged to arrest the judgment against the man.[43]

Many moderate Republicans found their role in convicting an insane man of "high crimes and misdemeanors" highly distasteful. During the trial their uneasiness took the form of voting to permit Pickering's

42. Plumer, *Memorandum*, January 5, 1804, p. 100.
43. Adams, *Memoirs*, March 9, 1804, 1:301–302.

attorneys to introduce evidence of his insanity. The final wording of the votes to convict, "guilty as charged," rather than "guilty of high crimes and misdemeanors," gave many senators an opportunity to avoid what seemed to them a moral dilemma.

Jefferson's role in the proceedings after his initial communication remains unclear, but it is evident that in the Senate the whips were on; it was to be a partisan undertaking and party loyalty was demanded by Senate Republican leaders. The final vote for conviction showed the strength of party pressure, as all nineteen "guilty" votes were Republican, while all seven votes for acquittal were cast by Federalists. Seven senators who sat through the entire proceedings refused to vote, however, and five of these were Republicans. As if to underscore the partisan nature of the conviction, the president rewarded three of the principal prosecution witnesses with lucrative posts. The most insulting of these to New Hampshire Federalists was the appointment of the Republican district attorney who had begun the action against Pickering to replace the ousted judge on the federal bench in that state.[44]

The ease with which their efforts had succeeded in removing Judge Pickering prompted House Republican leaders to press on with their campaign to eliminate recalcitrant Federalist judges through the creaky machinery of impeachment. Raising their sights from the lower federal bench, the Republicans undertook to bring down the formidable figure of Supreme Court Justice Samuel Chase. Here was no demented relic of former glories, but a man of great intellectual as well as political stature, a veteran of the Revolution whose colorful if erratic career had placed him in the front rank of Federalist leaders. The success of impeachment proceedings against Chase would strike directly at the security of the Supreme Court, and might point the way to a wholesale removal of its members and their replacement by men of Jeffersonian principles. Such a development would result either in the long-awaited unity of the tripartite federal system under the principles of popular sovereignty, or the long-dreaded consolidation of the general government under a tyranny of the unchecked majority. How one perceived developments depended upon one's political perspective, but no one doubted that if the Chase impeachment were success-

44. Ellis, p. 75; Beveridge, 3:181; Plumer, *Memorandum*, February 4, 1805, p. 274. Two others were made federal marshal and clerk of the court respectively, and a fourth, John Steele, declined the district attorneyship, expecting to have been named a judge.

ful, great changes would occur in the structure and direction of constitutional government.

The first demand for Chase's removal occurred even before the outcome of Pickering's impeachment trial was known. Chase was a very "visible" jurist, and his intemperate conduct had often attracted the sharp criticism of radical and moderate Republicans alike. He had been hated ever since his strenuous support of the Sedition Act, a hatred abetted by his "indecent and tyrannical" conduct in the Richmond trial of James Thomson Callender. His arbitrariness in the 1798 treason trial of John Fries and his intemperate browbeating of attorneys as well as juries in recent cases had alarmed even some Federalists.[45]

In May, 1803, in a charge to a grand jury in Baltimore, Chase provided the specific ammunition for the impeachment proceedings that followed. The justice attacked the repeal of the Judiciary Act of 1801 and the recent liberalization of the Maryland constitution granting universal white manhood suffrage as attempts to sink the United States Constitution into a "mobocracy." He decried the effects of a political philosophy that attempted to guarantee to all men "equal liberty and equal rights." As to the present administration, they were "weak, relaxed," and incompetent, and "their acts flowed not from a wish for the happiness of the people but for a continuance in unfairly acquired power."[46] The attacks on Jeffersonian policies were surely indiscreet. But the condemnation of the Repeal Act, an act of Congress the constitutionality of which had already been sustained by Chase's own court, was an impropriety for which Republicans were prepared to hold the justice officially responsible.

Contrary to his behavior in the case of Pickering, Jefferson took no public notice of Chase's misconduct. The movement to include the justice in the list of those eligible for the Republican axe, however, may well have begin in a private letter which the president sent to Joseph H. Nicholson, a Maryland congressman and Jefferson lieutenant in the House: "You must have heard of the extraordinary charge of Chase to the Grand Jury of Baltimore. Ought this seditious and official attack on the principles of our Constitution and on the proceedings of a State, to go unpunished? And to whom so pointedly as yourself will the public look for the necessary measures? I ask these

45. Plumer, *Memorandum*, January 10, 1804, 103–104; Warren, 1:281.
46. *Annals of Congress*, 8:2, pp. 675–6; *National Intelligencer*, May 20, 1803.

questions for your consideration, for myself it is better that I should not interfere."[47] Here again is Jefferson planting the seed for future action by others, preferring to influence the course of events from behind the scenes rather than appear to be exercising undue pressure from the executive mansion. He wished to make the attack on the judiciary as broadly based as possible. Better to rely on the impeachment machinery, unwieldy as it might be, and better to have it initiated by a congressman from the very state in which the impeachable offense took place. Impeachment proceedings were already underway against Pickering when the president wrote to Nicholson. Furthermore, the distasteful aspects of the trial had not yet soured Jefferson on the usefulness of the procedures.

His letter to Nicholson is the only evidence of Jefferson's role in the impeachment of Justice Chase. He seems to have left the proceedings entirely in congressional hands, although there is some evidence that his renewed attentions to Vice President Burr in the weeks before the trial were directed to insuring Burr's cooperation.[48] The president's enthusiasm for impeachment was materially weakened by the strongly partisan aspects of the Pickering trial. The conduct of the Chase trial, particularly the violent and erratic incompetence of John Randolph as chief manager for the House, may have provided additional support to the president's decision to adopt a hands-off policy toward the case. At any rate there is no evidence that, as the outcome became increasingly in doubt, he tried to influence wavering Republican senators to vote for conviction. Neither did he appear to sabotage the trial in any way so as to undercut Randolph's position. He seems genuinely to have desired conviction and was disillusioned with Randolph when it eluded his grasp. He followed the trial closely and displayed a keen interest in the votes of the senators on the final charges.[49]

The House did not get around to Chase until January, 1804, when a committee was appointed to investigate the justice's conduct with respect to ascertaining grounds for impeachment. Activity in the House was accompanied by a chorus of voices in the Republican press calling for Chase's expulsion. Nicholson, although named as one of the

47. Jefferson to Joseph H. Nicholson, May 13, 1803, Lipscomb, 10:390.
48. "Burr is flattered and feared by the Administration," wrote Plumer, and Beveridge notes that the vice president's stepson, his brother-in-law, and a close friend received offices in Louisiana during these weeks (3:182).
49. There exists in the Jefferson papers in the Library of Congress a tabulation in his own hand of the votes on eight counts with a column summary of those senators who voted for conviction seven times, six times, five times, and so on.

managers, deferred to Randolph's leadership throughout. The Marylander had become convinced that it would somehow appear unseemly for one who aspired to the seat that would be vacated by the justice if convicted to be in the forefront of his accusers. Opposing Randolph, Nicholson, and Caesar Rodney, the House managers, was an imposing array of counsel for the accused, led by that inebriated genius, Luther Martin (to be heard from again in the Burr trial), Robert Goodloe Harper, and Charles Lee (who had recently gained valuable experience in defending Judge Pickering).[50]

The trial began in February, 1805, having been delayed by the Pickering trial and the first stirrings of the Yazoo controversy. The proceedings closely resembled the earlier affair in their partisanship. Of the charges produced by Randolph, only the seventh dealt at all with Chase's charge to the Baltimore grand jury (the charge that was to prove the most damaging). The others involved the earlier trials and other, even more marginal improprieties. Randolph was ill prepared and his ill-considered histrionics compared unfavorably with the careful and judiciously marshaled arguments of defense counsel. W. B. Giles returned to the Senate from illness to sit in judgment on Chase, but he did not consider it improper to plan daily strategy with Randolph, the chief accuser. To Giles, as to other radical Republicans, there was no difficulty in viewing the trial openly as a *political* proceeding:

He treated with utmost contempt the idea of an *independent* judiciary . . . their pretensions to it were nothing more nor less than an attempt to establish an aristocratic despotism in themselves. . . . If the judges of the Supreme Court should dare, AS THEY HAD DONE, to declare an act of Congress unconstitutional, or to send a mandamus to the Secretary of State, AS THEY HAD DONE, it was the undoubted right of the House of Representatives to impeach them and of the Senate to remove them for giving such opinions. . . . Impeachment was not a criminal prosecution; it was no prosecution at all. The Senate . . . was not a court and ought to discard and reject all process of analogy to a court of justice . . . a removal by impeachment was nothing more than a declaration by Congress to this effect: You hold dangerous opinions, and if you suffer to carry them into effect you will work the destruction of the nation. *We want your offices* for the purpose of giving them to men who will fill them better.[51]

50. See *Aurora*, March 22, 1804; Dodd, *Nathaniel Macon*, pp. 187–188; Warren, 1:289.
51. J. Q. Adams, *Memoirs*, November 29, 1804, 1:318; December 21, 1804, pp. 322–323, emphasis in the original.

If Jefferson did not pressure the faithful to stay that way, Giles and the other leaders in Congress worked to insure the maximum of party loyalty, as in the Pickering case. Yet it was a difficult undertaking, for a number of Giles's colleagues could not agree with him on the nakedly political nature of the trial. The Senate adopted rules of procedure more congenial to a judicial than a legislative proceeding, and permitted Chase a month to prepare his defense. Trial strategy and tactics continued to be discussed "out of doors," but party loyalty was strained by the weakness of the charges and the increasing evidence that the chief manager for the House was acting out of his depth. Randolph's invective, his dramatic but often irrelevant harangues, grated on the sensibilities of senators who were more receptive to sober judicial argument.

The effort to make the trial a political inquest failed early in the proceedings. When the moment came to vote on the charges, each senator was asked if the accused was guilty of "high crimes and misdemeanors" on each charge, a rejection of the irregular form adopted in the Pickering trial. When the results of the voting were announced on March 1, the necessary two-thirds for conviction was attained on no article, although a majority voted to convict on three articles. Not even Giles could bring himself to vote for conviction on every charge.

The acquittal of Justice Chase brought in its train serious political recriminations among the disappointed Republicans. Randolph bore the brunt of the criticism, his stinging remarks about the Senate immediately after the trial contributing to the ease which which his colleagues laid the blame squarely on his shoulders. Jefferson seems to have suffered little adverse effect. His failure to become personally involved in the proceedings may have been prompted by his doubts concerning impeachment, or may have been the result of an intimation of defeat (he was never one for the grand but futile gesture), or simply of a distaste for controversy. Whatever the reason, his detachment worked to his advantage. His Federalist enemies could find no ready opening through which to attack him directly, and he seems to have suffered little if any loss in professional reputation.

His party, however, suffered a major setback. The schism that was soon to open within the party was given a significant impetus by the discreditable performance of Randolph and the evidence of fallibility exhibited by the failure at impeachment. The force of the party's assault on the judiciary was blunted by Chase's acquittal. Although the justice himself did not escape public opprobrium (most senators agreed on the impropriety of his actions), the Court seemingly had weathered the storm of impeachment. To Jefferson, the procedure was now "a mere scarecrow," and the efficacy of its use as a weapon was thoroughly discredited.[52]

The Weapon of Appointment

The Republicans had still not found an effective means of curbing the partisanship and irresponsibility of judges, or so it seemed to them from the perspective of their impeachment defeat. Actually the legislative attacks on the courts accomplished more than the Jeffersonians knew, for although their direct assault failed to carry its immediate objective, the narrow brush with disaster seems to have moderated the conduct of the more partisan jurists, if it did not alter their philosophies. Marshall and his associates, while relieved that the constitutional balance had not been irrevocably altered, were aware nonetheless of the closeness of their reprieve. Their behavior on the bench was already assuming a less narrowly partisan air.

As Jefferson entered his second term as president, he might have reflected that, despite the occasional setbacks received in his efforts to curb the power of the courts, he could point to a number of clear advances in his campaign to effect the "Revolution of 1800." The first two branches of government were firmly in Republican hands, and if the judiciary still sheltered his enemies, they had been properly chastened and their influence somewhat circumscribed. As president he had steadfastly asserted the independence of his office against assaults from the judiciary, most notably in the case of the *Peggy* and in his rejection of the *Marbury* dictum. Congress had responded to his leadership in repealing the Judiciary Act of 1801.[53] If impeachment had proved to be an unwieldy and ultimately unworkable mechanism for judicial reform, its partial success had intimidated the judges and curtailed at least their overt partisanship. For the future, if he could

52. Jefferson to Ritchie, December 25, 1820, Ford, 10:170. Ritchie took the usual consolation in the *Enquirer*: "To impartial persons who resort to a much higher authority . . . he must stand condemned, if not of the highest crimes and misdemeanors, at least of judicial tyranny of no ordinary standard" (*Richmond Enquirer*, March 12, 1805).

53. As part of the effort to curtail the power of the judges, Congress had removed the power of appointment of commissioners of bankruptcy from the courts and lodged it with the president. See Jefferson to Abigail Adams, September 11, 1804, Ford, 10:88–89.

not remove sitting judges by impeachment, he could at least fill vacancies with jurists of solid republican principles.

Unfortunately for the president, his appointees had little effect in altering the complexion of the Supreme Court. The key to this failure seems to have been the chief justice himself. Marshall exerted an enormous influence over his colleagues on the bench. Whether it was through his force of will, his undoubted strength of character, or his prodigious energy, whether it resulted from his great common sense, the lure of his logic, or the insidiousness of his sophistry (as Jefferson would have preferred), the chief justice succeeded in collecting under his ample wing most of his judicial brethren and producing a Court that reflected to an uncommon degree the philosophy of its chief. Those he could not influence he isolated. He preferred, however, much in the manner of his hated cousin, to gain influence by more subtle means. He was a congenial colleague, and presided over his Court with tact, deference, and good humor, winning allegiance more often than not through the charm and force of his personality than through any exercise in jurisprudential brilliance. With one exception, neither Jefferson nor Madison, his successor, was able to "find a character of firmness enough to preserve his independence on the same bench with Marshall."[54]

The exception was Jefferson's first appointee, William Johnson, who, while he managed to oppose Marshall vigorously and with consistency, nevertheless was unable to exert much of an influence over his other colleagues. Jefferson had to wait over three years to make his first appointment to the Supreme Court. Early in 1804 Associate Justice Alfred Moore became ill, and "from a full conviction of a speedy removal by a writ of habeas corpus returnable to Heaven's Chancery," resigned from the Court.[55] Jefferson sought a replacement in New York and South Carolina, finally choosing Johnson, a southerner, at thirty-two the youngest man ever appointed to the Court. He served until 1834 and has earned a reputation as the first in a long line of lonely dissenters.

Jefferson's second appointment had to wait for another two years. In the autumn of 1806, Justice Paterson died, and Jefferson pleased the party leaders in New York by naming to the Court a scion of the

54. Jefferson to Madison, 1811, quoted in Leo Pfeffer, *This Honorable Court* (Boston, 1965), p. 93.

55. William Plumer to Dr. John Parton, February 14, 1804, in Warren, 1:286n.

powerful Livingston clan, New York Supreme Court Judge Brockholst Livingston. Livingston proved a disappointment, however, as he quickly and quietly succumbed to Marshall's charms and disappeared as an independent force on the Court.

In the spring of 1807, with the addition of an extra justice by an act of 1803, Jefferson made his third and final appointment, not without a great deal of difficulty. He wanted to name a westerner and solicited the names of eligible candidates from the congressional delegations of Kentucky, Tennessee, and Ohio. Their first choice was Jefferson's congressional floor leader, George Washington Campbell of Tennessee. Campbell was not a good lawyer, however, and his appointment would have violated the ban on naming a member of Congress who was serving at the time the office was created. So Jefferson named the second choice of nearly everyone, Thomas Todd of Kentucky, who was that state's chief justice.[56] Todd, too, failed to measure up to Republican expectations and pursued an undistinguished career in the shadow of John Marshall.

The Battle Rejoined: The Burr Conspiracy

Brockholst Livingston's elevation to the Supreme Court came as rumors of a great conspiracy in the West began to press for the president's attention. The nomination of Todd occurred as the conspiracy itself lay in ruins and the machinery of law and politics was being geared for another of the great "show trials" of the Jefferson era, the Richmond trial of Aaron Burr and his co-conspirators. While Jefferson sought to influence the Court from within by the appointments process, he resumed his assault from without as well. The Burr conspiracy provided the opportunity once more to flay his principal adversaries, the Federalists and their Court, this time through the medium of his quondam rival, the discredited "Cataline," Aaron Burr.

Relations between Jefferson and Burr had never been anything more than correct, despite sporadic efforts by both men to maintain at least a political cordiality. From the beginning of their personal acquaintance, the Virginian had distrusted the New Yorker, perhaps sensing in him that combination of overweening ambition and unbridled opportunism that was to prove his ultimate undoing. Jefferson recalled his habitual suspicion of Burr in a diary entry of January,

56. *Ibid.*, p. 289.

1804, remembering that he had warned Madison against placing too much trust in the man. What association there had been between the two had been purely political in nature, and stemmed in particular from Jefferson's gratitude for Burr's "extraordinary exertions and successes in the New York election of 1800." But, as the president was quick to point out, "there never had been an intimacy between us, and but little association."[57]

Jefferson's suspicions were increased during the tense weeks of deadlock in the House of Representatives over the presidential election of 1800, when Burr had seemed perfectly prepared to take the presidency by forming an alliance with the Federalists. Shortly after he took office, Jefferson received reports that Burr was seeking legal depositions to prove Jefferson had won the presidency by corrupt bargaining. The clearest evidence of the president's lack of confidence in his vice president was Jefferson's decision to freeze out the Burrites from their share of the patronage in New York. This overt support of the Livingston-Clinton faction marks an exception to Jefferson's normal avoidance of taking sides in factional disputes. (For details, see Chapter 7 below.)

It was common knowledge in Washington that Burr was trying to build a following loyal to him alone, and his rulings from the chair favorable to the defense in the Pickering trial gave further evidence of his lack of scruples in making overtures to the enemy for support. Jefferson moved further to reveal his displeasure by implicitly supporting George Clinton over Burr for governor of New York in 1804. When in this contest, Federalist irreconcilables approached the ever-receptive Burr as their best hope of defeating the Clintonians, Alexander Hamilton took alarm. His hatred of Burr emerged in a series of letters characterized by studied verbal abuse. When Burr took the expected offense and shot Hamilton in the resultant duel at Weehawken, the bullet that ended Hamilton's life also ruined Burr's political career. Burr did return to the Senate chair after the duel, and though the reaction of many was chilly, it was said by Federalists that the "democrats" welcomed him back with open arms.[58] There is little evidence, however, that the president and his colleagues did anything but maintain the necessary courtesies expediency dictated. It was decided to deny Burr renomination as vice president (not a difficult

57. *Anas*, January 26, 1804, p. 227.
58. Plumer, *Memorandum*, November 7, 1804, p. 185.

decision under the circumstances), and his influence in national party circles, low for some time, was exhausted.

Everyone knew it, it seems, except Burr. In late 1804, Plumer wrote an entry in his diary that proved prophetic of the New Yorker's future course: "He can never I think rise again. But surely he is a very extraordinary man and is an exception to all rules. No man is better fitted to browbeat or cajole public opinion. And . . . considering how little restraint laws human or divine have on his mind, [it] is impossible to say what he will attempt—or what he may obtain."[59] What he attempted was a coup d'etat designed to separate the western states from the Union; what he obtained was the complete ruin of his career; but the uproar and controversy that accompanied the process must have given him no little consolation.

Burr's conspiracy was not the first such threat to the integrity of the young republic. It was merely another, if more serious, in a series of combinations, plots, or rumblings that threatened the security of the nation through interposition, secession, or alliance with foreign powers. Jefferson had long been aware of separatist tendencies in New England and the West. Following the acquisition of Louisiana, stirrings of disunion had erupted among the High Federalists of Massachusetts and Connecticut. During the winter of 1805–1806, rumors of disaffection in New England and overtures from private citizens to the British government were rife in Washington.[60]

Burr's own grand scheme was hatched in the spring of 1804, when Burr, General James Wilkinson, then commanding general in the West, and Charles Williamson, an Englishman, agreed upon a plan to separate the western states from the Union and set up an independent state on the Gulf of Mexico, under the rule of Colonel Burr. Eyeing the rich spoils of Mexico, Burr and Wilkinson determined to pry it loose from Spain by provoking a war, if possible, and make it part of the new state. Wilkinson was an ideal member of such a conspiracy, for in addition to holding high posts of confidence under the government of the United States, the good general had been in the pay of the

59. *Ibid.*, December 9, 1804, p. 213.
60. See Plumer's note of May 11, 1829, in Henry Adams, *Documents*, p. 106. For evidence of such a plan of disunion, see letters of Timothy Pickering to Richard Peters, December 24, 1803, to George Cabot, January 29, 1804, to Rufus King, March 4, 1804, and to Theodore Lyman, February 11, 1804, in *ibid.* The plan was to separate New England, New York, and New Jersey from, as Pickering charmingly put it, "negro Presidents and negro Congresses."

Spanish since 1788. The plan for the conspiracy was greatly enhanced, or so it seemed, by the appointment (at Burr's instigation) of Wilkinson to be governor of Louisiana Territory. Charles Williamson was made responsible for overtures to the British for military and financial assistance, and Burr himself assiduously cultivated certain of the leading French and Creole citizens of New Orleans, the possession of whose loyalty was essential for the successful seizure of the city, the key to the whole enterprise.[61]

From the beginning the scheme was characterized by a series of misadventures as Burr and his co-conspirators wove their tenuous web of intrigue. At one time no less a personage than General Andrew Jackson was convinced to offer his support for what he considered to be a grand design on Spanish Mexico. Seeking foreign assistance, Burr was rebuffed first by the British and then (not surprisingly) by the Spanish themselves. When the newspapers began to publish suspicions of a plot, Wilkinson began to get cold feet. He spread a smokescreen of correspondence designed to cover his tracks and insulate him from any link with the domestic side of the conspiracy. The enterprise rested on very shifting sands, indeed.

The details of the conspiracy need not occupy us. We are concerned rather with President Jefferson's response to the plan and, most specifically, to its aftermath, the trial of the chief conspirator. For the significance of the Burr conspiracy lies in the use Jefferson made of it to further his struggle against the Federalists and their judiciary, whom he was convinced were "championing treason" and condoning disunion.

The first inkling of the conspiracy reached the president's desk six months after the scheme was hatched, in the form of an anonymous letter warning of "Col. Burr's intrigues" against the state and cautioning Jefferson to watch Burr's connections with the British minister. No evidence of any kind accompanied the letter, and it appears to have

61. The most satisfying account of the Burr conspiracy is Thomas P. Abernethy, *The Burr Conspiracy* (New York, 1954). I have also drawn upon W. F. McCaleb, *The Aaron Burr Conspiracy* (New York, 1936), as well as primary material from the written records of the period, particularly B. J. Coombs, ed., *Documents of the Trial of Aaron Burr* (Washington, 1864), and V. B. Reed and J. D. Williams, eds., *The Case of Aaron Burr* (Boston, 1960). See also Dumas Malone's detailed account from Jefferson's perspective, in *Jefferson the President: Second Term, 1805–1809* (Boston, 1973), pp. 215–346. Of the memoirs of the period, the most amazing and entertaining, though wildly unreliable, are James Wilkinson, *Memoirs of My Own Times* (Philadel-

been ignored. More significant but still unsubstantiated alarms began to arrive in January, 1806, from an official source, Joseph Hamilton Daveiss, the United States district attorney for Kentucky. Daveiss spoke in his initial letter of "spanish intrigues" for separation of the western states from the Union, and named Wilkinson as in the pay of the Spanish government. He could offer as evidence, however, only hearsay and suspicion.[62]

Additional letters from Daveiss commented on Burr's trip through the West the preceding year and submitted a list of suspected allies of the colonel, most of whom were Republicans—among them Breckinridge, William Henry Harrison, and "Clay, the lawyer." Jefferson replied on February 15, urging full communication of everything heard about the conspiracy. Daveiss continued to supply his suspicions through the summer, but Jefferson began to suspect his informer, a Federalist, of partisan intentions in laying suspicion on nearly the entire Republican leadership in the West. His reply of September 12 was abrupt, merely acknowledging receipt of Daveiss's letters. He seems to have taken no action based on them.[63]

By the summer of 1806, with foreign assistance unlikely and Wilkinson wavering, prospects for the conspiracy's success were dimming. Nevertheless, Burr began active operations. In August he started west with his ultimate destination New Orleans. The staging ground for the descent upon New Orleans was an island in the Ohio River owned by an Irish emigré, Harman Blennerhassett; there Burr assembled the necessary troops and material. The president received warning of the new activity in September from two respectable sources in the West. He was prompted to action by receipt of a letter on October 16 from Gideon Granger, reporting specific communications of a conspiracy and implicating General Wilkinson. Jefferson called a cabinet on the 22d, when for the first time specific action was taken to combat the emerging conspiracy, albeit action limited to

phia, 1816). Abernethy calls Wilkinson "the most skillful and unscrupulous plotter this country has ever produced."

62. Anonymous letter from "Your friend" to Jefferson (received December 1, 1805), in Reed and Williams, p. 23; Daveiss to Jefferson, January 10, 1806. The complete correspondence between Daveiss and the president is printed in Joseph Hamilton Daveiss, "View of the President's Conduct Concerning the Conspiracy of 1806," in *Historical and Philosophical Society of Ohio Quarterly*, 12 (1917).

63. Daveiss to Jefferson, February 10, March 5, April, May, July 14, 1806; Jefferson to Daveiss, September 12, 1806, in Daveiss, "View."

alerting western governors and ordering Burr's arrest at the first sign of overt action.[64]

Three days later the cabinet met again and rescinded the orders to intercept Burr's movements. Jefferson decided not to write to the governors, but merely to send an intermediary to advise them to be on their guard. Why action to stop the rebellion was called off at this meeting is not clear. Abernethy conjectures that Dearborn may have been acting as Burr's man at court, but there is no evidence of this. Malone reasons that an insufficiency of funds to dispatch gunboats was combined with the feeling among the cabinet members that it would be unwise to raise a premature alarm, given the paucity of hard evidence to prove a treasonable combination.[65] This initial administration uncertainty resulted largely from the slowness of communication and the consequent lack of information as to conditions in the West. Jefferson was not convinced that the conspiracy posed a really serious threat to the security of the nation; he still maintained a faith that the good sense of the citizens of the affected region would cause them to see through such a bald and desperate design. But he could not be sure. If Burr were in fact leading a rebellion against the government of the United States, then the most effective tactic for the president to adopt would be to guard against the rebellion's success without unduly alarming the nation or the conspirators. Burr must not be arrested *before* any overt action had been taken, for that would destroy any chance of convicting him on a charge of treason.

Jefferson was also aware of the crucial importance of General Wilkinson, either to the success of the conspiracy or its suppression. If the general were indeed flirting with the conspirators, as rumor had it, then to precipitate action against him might drive him into open opposition to the government. If that were to happen the conspiracy might well succeed, for Jefferson was aware of the weakness of the government's position on the scene. It was essential, therefore, to insure the general's loyalty before taking any action that might force his hand.[66]

64. Commodore Truxtun to Jefferson, August 10, 1806, LC No. 28169; Colonel George Morgan to Jefferson, September 15, 18, 1806; Gideon Granger to Jefferson, October 16, 1806; Cabinet memorandum, October 22, 1806, Ford, 1:318. See also Jefferson to Granger, March 9, 1814, *ibid.*, 11:383–390, for a summary of this correspondence and the president's action during the period. Also, see Abernethy, *Burr*, pp. 58–61.

65. Abernethy, *Burr*, p. 87; Malone, *Second Term*, pp. 244–245.

66. For suspicions of just this sort, see *Aurora*, November 5, 1806, and John

It must have been a great relief when a letter from General Wilkinson arrived on November 25 (dated October 20), in which that worthy reflected a decision made earlier to desert his co-conspirators and cast his lot with the nation he so nearly betrayed. He informed the president of a conspiracy against Mexico, coolly denying any knowledge not only of its leadership but of its plan of action and ultimate purpose.[67]

Whether or not Jefferson believed Wilkinson's professions of innocence, he knew that with the general's loyalty assured for the future the position of the government in the region was immeasurably strengthened. Furthermore, a letter from the commanding general meant that the conspiracy could no longer be publicly ignored. Consequently on November 27, the president issued a proclamation announcing the conspiracy against the dominions of Spain and warning all "faithful" citizens who might have been led into participation in the adventure to cease at once. The proclamation also directed all federal and state officers to search out and punish the leaders of the conspiracy. Jefferson did not mention the domestic side of the plot, for while filibustering expeditions against foreign powers had been outlawed by statute, there was no law against conspiracy to internal rebellion. Burr's name was not mentioned, presumably because the president still hoped to catch the former vice president in an overt act that would make him liable to a charge of treason.[68]

The president referred to the conspiracy only briefly in his annual message to Congress on December 2, again without mentioning Burr by name or the domestic side of the scheme. Through December he waited for news. The post was maddeningly slow, the eastern press was now full of rumors and alarms, and Jefferson was receiving a growing volume of correspondence concerning the machinations in the West, most of it still very circumstantial and vague.[69] While he

Randolph to George Hay, January 3, 1807, in Abernethy, *Burr*, pp. 186–187.

67. Wilkinson to Jefferson, October 20, 1806, Abernethy, *Burr*, pp. 151–152. The president had received independent corroboration of Wilkinson's soundness from a Quaker agriculturist, Isaiah Briggs, just returned from New Orleans (Brant, *Madison*, pp. 349–350).

68. Proclamation of November 27, 1806, Ford, 10:301–302. The president had asked Madison to research the laws which might be applicable. See Madison to Jefferson, received October 30, 1806, LC No. 28383.

69. *Richmond Enquirer*, December 11, 1806; *Norfolk Gazette and Publick Ledger*, December 29, 1806, *National Intelligencer*, January 7, 1807, cited in Reed and Williams, pp. 45–53. See also William Duane to Jefferson, November 16, December 8, 26, 1806, in Ford, "Duane Letters," pp. 286–298.

waited, events were proceeding apace in the West. Having made his decision to be a patriot, General Wilkinson moved with dispatch to crush the "rebellion." Rebuffed by the territorial governor in an attempt to impose martial law in New Orleans, Wilkinson ordered the arrest of two of Burr's chief collaborators in the city, Eric Bollman and John Swartwout. Avoiding a writ of habeas corpus, the general ordered the two prisoners removed from the jurisdiction of the territorial courts and delivered to Washington under a charge of treason. He then initiated a minor reign of terror, arresting everyone in sight (including the judge who had signed the writ), omitting from his dragnet only the most powerful of the local conspirators, men who might be expected to know of the general's own role in the scheme.[70]

The president now informed the governors of the states involved of the nature of the plot, including for the first time the domestic side. The outcome remained uncertain through December, but Jefferson preferred to let the authorities in the states control the conspiracy themselves without the necessity for "a great national armament for it." He did take steps to prepare a contingency force to sail for New Orleans. Replying on December 23 to an urgent appeal by his secretary of the navy to lay evidence of the conspiracy before Congress and to ask for suspension of the writ of habeas corpus, Jefferson promised that if Burr were still unopposed twelve days hence he would present the entire matter to Congress. The secretary was told to prepare transport ships to carry 20,000 militia to New Orleans. There was no reply to the request to suspend habeas corpus.[71]

Information received in Washington in January had convinced Jefferson that the danger of a serious rebellion was far less than had been supposed. There was evidently a good bit of the absurd in Burr's adventure, which the president was now calling "the most extraordinary since the days of Don Quixot."[72] Still, the alarums and excursions exercised over the conspiracy throughout the country, but particularly in the western states, had in Jefferson's opinion served a useful purpose in cementing the national loyalties of those distant citizens. One of the principal elements of Burr's support had come from eastern

70. Abernethy, *Burr*, pp. 179–181.

71. Jefferson to Gov. John Langdon of New Hampshire, December 22, 1806, LC No. 28617; Robert Smith to Jefferson, December 22, 1806, LC No. 28620; Jefferson to Smith, December 23, 1806, Ford, 10:330–331.

72. Jefferson to Charles Clay, January 11, 1807, LC No. 38772.

High Federalists and others who had opposed the expansion of the United States into the new lands of Louisiana and were eager now to sow dissension in the West. If the *potential* gravity of the Burr conspiracy could be stressed and the success of the government and the local citizenry in quashing it made evident, then the confidence of the people in the strength of their enlarged Union would be increased. Such were the motivations behind Jefferson's growing zeal in first running Burr and his cohorts to ground and then bringing them to trial. This heightened interest in prosecuting the conspirators led Jefferson, however, into some of the more regrettable excesses of his public life and exposed him with some justification to charges of violating the legal and civil liberties of the individuals accused as he pursued what he felt to be larger game.

He committed the first of his indiscretions by branding Burr "guilty as charged" not only before he had been tried but before he had been finally apprehended. In his special message to Congress on the conspiracy, the president announced the suppression of the scheme and detailed its development as it was known to him at the time. He revealed publicly for the first time the twin dimensions of Burr's design. He reported that Bollman and Swartwout were on their way under guard to Washington—even though he must have known that they should have been tried in the jurisdiction where they were arrested, he made no criticism of this action—and he repeated his confidence in the honor and fidelity of General Wilkinson. As to Burr, the guilt of "the principal actor," said the president, is "placed beyond question." Most informed persons probably believed this to be true, but as John Adams observed, "if his guilt is as clear as the noonday sun, the first magistrate of the nation ought not to have pronounced it so before a jury had tried him."[73]

The following day the Senate passed a bill to suspend the writ of habeas corpus for three months. The bill was introduced by Giles at the urging of, among others, Navy Secretary Smith, but there is no

73. Special message to Congress, January 22, 1807, Ford, 10:346–356. Jefferson actually condoned Wilkinson's action in a letter of February 3: "Your sending Bollman and Swartwout and adding to them Burr, Blennerhassett, and Tyler, should they fall into your hands, will be supported by public opinion. . . . I hope, however, you will not extend this deportation to persons against whom there is only suspicion—be assured that you will be cordially supported in the line of your duties" (Lipscomb, 11:149–150), For John Adams's remarks, see Peterson, *Thomas Jefferson*, p. 853.

evidence that Jefferson initiated the move or even approved it. Cooler heads prevailed in the House at any event, and the bill was overwhelmingly rejected three days later.[74]

Any faint hope of success lingering in the mind of the conspirators was removed in mid-February when Burr surrendered to civil authorities in the Territory of Mississippi. The grand jury there refused to indict him, saying he had committed no overt act on Mississippi soil, but for some reason Burr jumped bail and fled to West Florida, where he was rearrested and sent off under guard to Richmond.[75]

Before he knew of Burr's seizure but after he had become convinced of the inevitable failure of the colonel's enterprise, Jefferson dispatched a revealing letter to Governor Claiborne of New Orleans. In it, the president first assured the young governor of the support of the administration and of the people of the United States for actions taken beyond "the strict line of the law," drawing again upon his Lockean escape clause. "On great occasions every good officer must be ready to risk himself . . . when the public preservation requires it." He then revealed his own view concerning the significance of the whole affair:

On the whole, this squall, by shewing with what ease our government suppresses movements which in other countries requires armies, has greatly increased its strength by increasing the public confidence in it. It has been a wholesome lesson, too, to our citizens, of the necessary obedience to their government. The Federalists, and the little band of Quids in opposition, will try to make something of the infringement of liberty by the military arrest and deportation of citizens, but if it does not go beyond such offenders as Swartwout, Bollman, Burr, Blennerhassett, Tyler, etc., they will be supported by the public approbation.[76]

The conspiracy and its suppression would serve as an object lesson of the inner strength of republican institutions in withstanding the force of the winds of unrest that from time to time blow across the political landscape. The president's willingness to consider civil liberties as subject to majority opinion is disturbing. To Jefferson, however, the few legal irregularities committed in the course of its sup-

74. McCaleb, p. 246. Warren and Smelser say Jefferson did ask for the suspension, Peterson says he did not, but none cite evidence to prove their contentions. Malone, *Second Term*, discusses the persistence of this charge, p. 272n.

75. See Abernethy, *Burr*, chap. 6. The "overt act" necessary to a charge of treason was deemed to have been committed on Blennerhassett's island in the Ohio River. Since this site lay within the jurisdiction of the federal district court of Virginia, the trial was held at Richmond.

76. Jefferson to Claiborne, February 7, 1807, Ford, 10:346–347.

pression were far outweighed by the avoidance of a deployment of large troop contingents to the region of the conspiracy, with all of the abuses of civil liberties that normally follow in the wake of such military concentrations. To underscore the significance of the conspiracy as Jefferson perceived it, to drive home the object lesson he sought to teach, it was of course necessary for the machinery of the State, acting for an aroused and indignant citizenry, to follow its suppression with the punishment of the plotters. The courts were the proper organs to accomplish this final task, and the chief justice himself was to be the principal instrument for the administration of justice. Thus the stage was set once again for a test of strength between the elected and the appointed branches. It became impossible to conduct the trial of Burr and his friends in an atmosphere free of partisan rivalries and political considerations. The stakes of the battle were much higher than the fate of the accused, and both sides at the Richmond trial represented societal forces that far transcended the interests represented in the little country courtroom.

The Trial at Richmond

Marshall's first brush with Jefferson over the Burr conspiracy occurred in late February, 1807, when the Supreme Court released Burr's two accomplices, Bollman and Swartwout, for lack of evidence of treason. In the hearing, the Chief Justice sought to effect a more precise definition of the crime of treason, and his interpretation ironically was to form the basis of the government's later case against Burr. "Treason," said the Court, involves an "actual *assembling* of men, for the treasonable purpose, to constitute a levying of war." There must be an actual assemblage of men for the purpose; the mere enlisting of men, i.e., *conspiracy* to commit treason, did not constitute treason. Anyone who participated in bringing such a group together, however, was not merely an accessory but a principal to the act of treason.[77]

Republican reaction to the release of Bollman and Swartwout was sharply critical. Giles threatened to seek a "declaratory amendment" to the Constitution, stripping the Court of all jurisdiction in criminal cases. Jefferson's suspicions were instantly aroused and one can date from this point, even if earlier times are arguable, the shift in the target of his opposition from Burr and the conspirators themselves to the

77. *Ex Parte Bollman*, 4 Cranch 75 (1807), emphasis in the original.

courts as the instrument of reactionary Federalism. The president sent for Bollman and by a subtle and somewhat disingenuous use of the carrot and the stick extracted from him a written statement on the conspiracy. A circular questionnaire was dispatched throughout the region of Burr's travels asking for detailed information on the plot, particularly any written correspondence with Burr or his associates, to be sent posthaste to the president in Washington.[78]

Increasingly, Jefferson's view of the real enemy emerged as his suspicions grew that Burr would be set free by a Court set "rigidly against the Government." Less than a week before the March 31 habeas corpus hearing on Burr in Richmond, Jefferson was warning that "the Federalists appear to make Burr's cause their own, and to spare no efforts to screen his adherents. . . . Had a little success dawned on him, their openly joining him might have produced some danger." Elsewhere he wrote, "It is unfortunate that federalism is still predominant in our judicial department, which is consequently in opposition to the legislative and executive branches and is able to battle their measures often."[79]

He could not have been greatly surprised when the chief justice, presiding over the habeas corpus hearing a few days later, bound Burr over on a misdemeanor charge of organizing and preparing a filibustering expedition against Mexico, but dismissed the felony charge of treason brought against him by the government. The treason charge, noted Marshall pointedly, was the one charge "most capable of being employed as the instrument of those malignant and vindictive passions which may rage in the bosoms of contending parties struggling for power." For this reason it was essential to define the charge with the utmost care and precision. Following his rule in the *Bollman* case, Marshall stressed that the mere intention to commit treason was dis-

78. J. Q. Adams, *Memoirs*, February 21, 1807, 1:459. Jefferson had promised never to use Bollman's statement against him and to keep it in his possession. He promptly sent it to George Hay, the prosecutor in Richmond, however, with instructions to conceal it from all save his associate counsel. He also sent the pardon for Bollman to Hay to be used if Bollman would agree to testify. He refused. At this time, Jefferson could write that the conspirators' crimes "are defeated, and whether they shall be punished or not belongs to another department, and is not the subject of even a wish on my part" (Jefferson to Joseph H. Nicholson, February 20, 1807, Lipscomb, 11:157–158.

79. Plumer, *Memorandum*, March 4, 1807, p. 641; Jefferson to Col. George Morgan, March 26, 1807, Lipscomb, 11:173–174; to James Bowdoin, April 2, 1807, pp. 186–187.

tinct "from the actual commission of the crime. . . . Troops must be embodied, men must be actually assembled." Where was the evidence for this? "The assembling of forces to levy war is a visible transaction, and numbers must witness it. It is therefore capable of proof; and when time to collect this proof has been given it ought to be adduced, or suspicion becomes ground too weak to stand on. Several months have elapsed since this fact did occur, if it ever occurred. . . . Why is it not proved?" Finding no evidence of troops having been actually assembled, and ruling that mere suspicion was insufficient, Marshall dismissed the charge.[80]

The tone and thrust of the opinion and the thinly veiled charge of vindictive partisan politics as the motive for Burr's "persecution" could not have failed to ruffle presidential sensibilities. Jefferson, now fully aroused, congratulated the Court for its "new-born zeal for the liberty of those whom we would not permit to overthrow the liberties of their country." Specifically he complained of the "tricks of judges to force trials before it is possible to collect the evidence, dispersed through a line of 2,000 miles from Maine to Orleans." It was not known in Washington until March 26 that Burr was being brought east for trial. Marshall's unfair requirement of "proof" to bind over the prisoner for trial on the treason charge gave clear evidence to the president of the folly of expecting justice from Federalist judges. "We had always before understood that where there was reasonable ground to believe guilt, the offender must be put on his trial. That guilty intentions were probable, the judge believed." Instead, Marshall had demanded proof at a preliminary hearing. Gazing into the future, however, the president predicted a "higher" justice of Burr's guilt: "The nation will judge both the offender and judges for themselves. If a member of the Executive or Legislature does wrong, the day is never far distant when the people will remove him. They will see and amend the error in our Constitution which makes any branch independent of the nation. . . . If their [the judges'] protection of Burr produces this amendment, it will do more good than his condemnation would have done."[81]

The principal reason for Jefferson's awakening zeal in the Burr case is evident in these remarks. The target of his activity was primarily the Federalists and their Court. If Burr were convicted, all well and good;

80. The testimony relating to this hearing as well as the subsequent trial is in Coombs, pp. 1–11 and following.
81. Jefferson to Giles, April 20, 1807, Ford, 10:383–388.

the nation would be saved from the colonel and his schism, which could have done it grave harm. But if, as seemed increasingly more likely, Burr was acquitted by the Court, then Jefferson would secure an even greater "conviction" by his collection and presentation of the evidence, that of the Court and its chief justice at the bar of public opinion. The president's actions prior to the opening of legal proceedings in February and March, 1807, reinforce this interpretation. His early action to crush the conspiracy had been tentative in character, reflecting the caution born of little concrete information. Jefferson knew Burr, knew his flamboyant and quixotic nature, and had faith in the sense of the majority of westerners in withstanding his blandishments. After Marshall had given indications of leniency, however, Jefferson's activity took on a new and different tone, reflecting the nature of the new threat. He actively, though privately, assumed direction of the investigation, solicited evidence, took depositions, questioned witnesses. If his efforts and those of his agents were repudiated by the Court, as he suspected they would be, then the trial of Burr would stand as evidence of "the original error of establishing a judiciary independent of the nation, and which, from the citadel of the law can turn its guns on those they were meant to defend."[82] Jefferson never accepted the view that the acquittal of Burr and his associates represented merely the result of a careful evaluation of the evidence. There is much independent evidence, furthermore, to reinforce the view that Marshall's rulings were based on considerations other than the unbiased administration of blind justice.

In his zeal to pursue the prosecution of Burr, Jefferson overstepped the normal and proper bounds of executive conduct in virtually assuming the role of chief prosecutor. His letters to George Hay, the U.S. attorney for Virginia and prosecutor on the scene at Richmond, are replete with suggestions for strategy and tactics at the trial, hints of possible sources for new evidence, and demands that he be furnished with all the testimony in written form so that the full case might be laid before Congress and the American people in the event of failure to convict.[83]

As the case for the prosecution was being slowly amassed in Richmond and Washington, the temperature of the proceedings was

---

82. Jefferson to John W. Eppes, May 28, 1807, *ibid.*, pp. 412–413.

83. See letters of Jefferson to George Hay, conveniently assembled in *ibid.*, pp. 394–409.

suddenly raised by a seemingly innocuous request from the defendant. Acting on his own behalf, Burr stated that certain papers in the possession of the president, including the colonel's correspondence with General Wilkinson, were essential to his defense. He asked Marshall to issue a subpoena *duces tecum* to the chief executive, requiring him to appear personally with the papers before the Court in Richmond. The request seems to have taken all concerned by surprise. Prosecutor Hay mumbled that he would obtain the papers if he could. Over the weekend Hay recovered sufficiently to suggest the impropriety of calling upon the president to disclose correspondence of a private and possibly confidential nature.

Marshall considered carefully and issued his opinion on June 13.[84] He found no exception in the Constitution or statutes that give to an accused the right to the compulsory process of the Court in obtaining witnesses. While under English common law the king was excused from giving testimony, no such exemption existed for an American president. Marshall likened presidential dignity to that of a chief magistrate of a state, and it had never been doubted that a governor might be subpoenaed. The chief justice dismissed the idea that the press of time should rule out the *issuance* of a subpoena, although it might well be pleaded as grounds for disobeying it. "The court can perceive no legal objection to issuing a subpoena *duces tecum* to any person whatever, provided the case be such as to justify the process."

The ever-prudent Marshall sought to avoid a direct clash with the president, however. In the language of the subpoena as issued were these words: "The transmission to the Clerk of this Court of the original letter of General Wilkinson and of copies duly authenticated of the other papers and documents . . . will be admitted as sufficient observance of the process, without the personal attendance of any or either of the persons therein named."[85] The direct challenge that Jefferson is supposed to have defied was never in fact issued. Nevertheless, the legality and propriety of issuing such a challenge had been asserted, and it was to be answered by the president in the fashion he considered it to deserve, that of silence. He never publicly or officially acknowledged the subpoena, not even to dignify it by

---

84. Coombs, pp. 41–54. The transcript of the subpoena hearing is printed in full here, pp. 37–54.

85. This language is included in the form of an endorsement signed by Burr himself.

denouncing it. Rather, his letters to George Hay constitute his sole response.

On June 12, before the subpoena had been issued but after the request for the papers had been made, Jefferson notified Hay that he was willing to cooperate by furnishing "whatever the purposes of justice may require." He cautioned, however, that as president he reserved the right to decide what papers should be communicated, independent of any court edict. When the subpoena arrived in Washington, Jefferson restrained his anger and wrote again to Hay to the effect that his submission of certain papers of the war and navy secretaries "substantially fulfilled the object" of the subpoena. As to the demand for personal attendance (Jefferson chose to ignore the loophole inserted into the language of the document), "to comply with such calls would leave the nation without an executive branch . . . the sole branch which the Constitution requires to be always in function." A few days later, the president reminded Hay that "the Constitution enjoins the Executive's constant agency in the concerns of 6 millions of people—Is the law paramount to this, which calls on him on behalf of one? . . . Would the Executive be independent of the judiciary if he were subject to the *commands* of the latter, and to imprisonment for disobedience?" In closing, he told Hay (to tell Marshall) that the constitutional independence of each branch "is further manifested by the means it has furnished to each to protect itself from enterprises of force attempted on them by the other, and to none has it given more effectual or diversified means than to the executive."[86] Elsewhere the president took steps to insure that should the Court move to enforce the subpoena, the federal marshals should take no action to assist.

On June 24, the grand jury of Richmond indicted Burr on treason and misdemeanor charges. The actual trial began on August 3. As Abernethy observes, the trial had a ritualistic quality to it, as though all the participants were actors walking through their assigned roles. Burr's counsel, abetted on occasion by Marshall who presided, sought to brand the entire proceedings as a form of personal vendetta by the government against Burr.[87] The prosecution called 140 witnesses, but

86. Jefferson to Hay, June 12, 1807, Ford, 10:398–399; and June 17, 20, 1807, pp. 400–405, emphasis in the original.

87. At one point Marshall openly asserted that the prosecution seemed more intent upon obtaining a conviction than a fair trial. He retracted his remark when called to account by Hay (Peterson, *Thomas Jefferson*, p. 869).

in the end only 11 were permitted to testify, since Marshall ruled that any collateral testimony about events outside the Court's jurisdiction was impermissible. The prosecution relied upon the Court's earlier ruling in the *Bollman* case in its attempt to prove a treasonable assemblage of men on Blennerhassett's island. Marshall cut the ground from under them, however, by substantially revising his *Bollman* definition of treason. An assemblage, to be treasonable, now had to be in considerable force and "in condition to make war." The ruling on the witnesses and this new interpretation of the charge effectively destroyed the government's case. On September 1, after only twenty-five minutes of debate, the jury found Burr not guilty. The cases of the other conspirators were subsequently dropped.

Jefferson had anticipated acquittal and after the verdict took steps to amass a record of the conspiracy and trial to present to Congress for the "proper remedies" to be taken. In his covering letter to Congress on September 20, the president urged either a constitutional amendment or other measures to prevent future encouragement of "the highest order of crimes" by this example of impunity. Newspapers of Republican opinion were violent in their condemnation of Burr, his counsel, and especially the Court for countenancing treason and releasing traitors; they demanded legislative action to curb the power of the judiciary. Two months after the conclusion of the trial, the Republicans introduced a constitutional amendment limiting the terms of federal judges and providing for their removal by the president on address of two-thirds of each House. At Jefferson's request, Giles also introduced a bill to amend the law of treason. Nothing came of either of these proposals. But a sign of the congressional mood is indicated by a move in the Senate to expel Senator John Smith of Ohio, a newly elected member tainted with Burrite sympathies. Smith was saved by the margin of one vote.[88]

What were the consequences of the Burr conspiracy? Burr went free, although he was forced by circumstance to leave the country and his career was ruined. Neither Jefferson nor Marshall, the principal antagonists, behaved at their best in the struggle. Marshall's conduct

88. Jefferson to Hay, September 20, 1807, LC No. 30084; Report to the House of Representatives, September 20, 1807, No. 30083; Jefferson to Wilkinson, same date, Ford, 10:499–500; to William Thompson, September 26, 1807, pp. 501–502; see also *Aurora*, September 11, 1807; *Annals of Congress*, 10:1, November 5, 1807. See J. Q. Adams, *Writings*, 3:173–184, for details of the expulsion proceedings in which Adams was closely involved.

of the pretrial hearings and the trial itself was hardly a model of fairness, and his obvious suspicion of the government (not necessarily support of Burr) contributed little to his judicial reputation. His acerbity about the malignant hand of government at Burr's throat, his attendance at a dinner given for Burr during the trial, his murky and confused rulings from the bench which could only seem to the prosecution as motivated by partisan considerations—all permit one to agree with Marshall Smelser that Marshall "let the trial become a party contest, a hint that he was grasping at judicial supremacy."[89]

Jefferson too displayed partisanship, a certain vindictiveness that was quite out of character, and a somewhat careless disregard for legal and ethical niceties. He publicly prejudged Burr's guilt, acted on occasion as his own prosecutor, surrendered to inferential leaps of judgment on the basis of scanty and circumstantial evidence, condoned certain abuses of civil liberties, dealt in a dubious way with witnesses, and paid too little heed to the dangers of guilt by implication and association. His questionable conduct seems derived, in part at least, from laudable motives, a determination as chief executive to defend the public safety against what he deemed to be a threat from two directions. As Peterson writes, "in cases where the nation itself was attacked, as he believed it was in this case, the judiciary ought not to conjure with the law to cover traitors."[90] In such a case, the judiciary itself posed a threat to national security. Still, Jefferson appears to have paid too little attention to the threat to individual liberties arising from such reasoning, a failure doubly surprising in a man of his libertarian sensibilities. It is clear, furthermore, that his prosecutory zeal was in direct proportion to his frustration in bringing the courts under the force of his will.

Jefferson's rejection of Marshall's subpoena had lasting significance for the development of the presidency. His refusal to recognize the subpoena was never formally acknowledged as legitimate by the Court, although Marshall in issuing the subpoena all but confessed his impotence in enforcing it; but Jefferson's refusal was never challenged either, perhaps because the president manifested substantial com-

89. *The Democratic Republic: 1801–1816* (New York, 1968), p. 122. See also Warren, 1:315, and A. C. McLaughlin, "The Life of John Marshall," in *American Bar Association Journal*, 7 (1921), 233.

90. *Thomas Jefferson*, p. 873.

pliance by sending or having sent the documents called for. It is true, nevertheless, that presidents since Jefferson have rested their refusal to comply with subpoenas on his action in the Burr case, often with only a tentative grasp of what he actually did and did not do. Until recently, furthermore, they met with success.

The Burr trial and the controversy surrounding it had additional implications. The outcome of the trial and the subsequent publication of the facts in Congress and the newspapers (a publication that would not have been possible without the president's care in compiling a record of events) further contributed to weakening public confidence in the authority of Federalist-dominated courts. The Burr conspiracy thus contributed to the larger effort that Jefferson and his supporters had been making throughout his administration to curb the power of appointed judges and bring their behavior into accord with the will of the people, as expressed through their agents in the elected branches of government.

Jefferson and the Court: Success or Failure?

In terms of structural reform the campaign in these years against the judiciary had little effect. Except for the repeal of the Judiciary Act of 1801 and the removal of Judge Pickering, "the national judiciary remained much as it had been under twelve years of Federalist rule; judges held their positions for life tenure during good behavior, the federal courts were organized in much the same way as they had been under the Judiciary Act of 1789, and the Supreme Court remained staffed almost exclusively by Federalists" or their fellow-travelers.[91]

Jefferson had achieved something of an intangible but nonetheless effective nature. He had employed the resources of his party and its domination of Congress as a weapon against the courts, albeit within limits, for he would not go so far as to alter fundamentally the existing constitutional arrangements. The efficacy of these resources operating within these limits was, of course, itself limited. He had also used what little powers were available in the presidency itself, largely the power of appointment in an effort to reform the Court by altering the political complexion of its membership. As many presidents since Jefferson have experienced, however, this tactic proved less than overwhelm-

91. Ellis, p. 235.

ingly successful, as the Jeffersonian judges found themselves falling under the beguiling influence of the Federalist chief justice. Jefferson tried to bring his influence to bear in other ways upon the problem of curbing the unrepresentative courts. He committed his prestige and reputation as the people's agent in appealing to public opinion after the Burr trial to repudiate the actions of judges who would violate the public confidence.

Separately each of these techniques was limited in its effectiveness. The president and his associates lacked the political leverage in dealing with the judiciary that they possessed in exerting influence in other spheres. Together, however, the techniques had some modest success. The assaults on the judges, through legislation, impeachment, appointment, trial, and public opinion, had a salutary effect in curbing judicial pretension and muting the judges' overt partisanship. Marshall's sensitive political antennae were attuned to the vibrations around him, and he succeeded by and large in lowering the stridency and moderating the thrust of judicial activity even as he succeeded in carving a suitable, long-lasting position of influence for the Court to occupy. The Supreme Court did not become Jeffersonian, in either output or outlook. In the years to follow, furthermore, the legal and constitutional philosophy of the Marshall Court was to have at least as much significance on the long-term development of America's social and economic structure as was that of the Jeffersonians. The judiciary did cease, however, to be narrowly Federalist, choosing instead under the guiding hand of its great Chief Justice and prodded by the constant pressure of popular leaders, to become the defender of a more efficacious nationalism, a posture that not only acquired for the Court a new and more respectable constituency, but served the country well.

Jefferson's inconclusive battles with the judges were merely one manifestation of a larger effort to remold the nation's political institutions in a popular cast. That he failed in his effort to produce substantial reform in the philosophy and policy of the judicial branch stands as an illustration of the essential resources necessary for the cultivation of presidential influence. In the absence of those resources, the process of persuasion must yield to the politics of confrontation, and such a politics, given the nature of the American system of divided powers, is almost a guarantee of frustration, stalemate, or drift.

The president's struggles were not entirely in vain, of course. His efforts served to strengthen his presidency through enhancing his popular prestige as a leader ever willing to "do battle" for the people's interests. If he could not appreciably alter the relationship between president and Court, he could use that failure to improve the relationship between president and people.

∽

CHAPTER 7

The Cultivation of Political Support: The Party and the Party Press

The development of the political party in the 1790's, sparked by the partisan battles in Congress after 1792 and abetted by the contest for the presidency in 1796, had provided Jefferson and his colleagues with a useful, if somewhat erratic, instrument not only for the election of a new government but the accomplishment of the tasks of that government. After the Republican triumph in the election of 1800, men of the Jeffersonian persuasion came to dominate the elective branches of government, and the party with the president at its head became a major implement for the creation of a government of design and not of chance.

The permanent success of the Republican "revolution" depended, of course, upon the Jeffersonians' ability to muster broad public support for their ideals and policies. As the party became the engine for modest policy innovation in Washington, it was essential that its strength in Congress be undergirded by strong partisan identification in the states as well, particularly in those states where competition from the opposition remained strong. These state parties would, the leaders hoped, serve a variety of purposes, some of purely local importance but others of significance to the party at the national level. They would perform the electoral functions of recruiting and nominating candidates for office. In addition, state organizations, however rudimentary, could be expected to serve a "proselytizing function," spreading the word about national party leaders and policies. By fulfilling these programmatic functions they would aid in the essential purpose of building a broad consensus of loyal partisans behind Jefferson and the national Republican movement. Such support was vital to the preservation of unity within the party in Washington and thus to the legislative success of the party program.

In this chapter we will consider the ways in which Jefferson acted to aid the cause of party unity in the states as a device to strengthen his own and his party's influence on the larger scene. We will examine the extent to which he employed another important resource of political mobilization, the partisan press, and the nature of that employment in enhancing political communication between the people's government and the people. The chapter is not intended as an exploration of Republican party development in the Jefferson years. Such a task is beyond the scope of this work and has been done effectively by others.[1] Nor is it designed to be a study of the Jeffersonian press as such; that, too, has been well accomplished.[2] Rather the focus will be, as always, upon Jefferson. We are concerned to indicate the extent to which he employed the resources of political mobilization available to him. What role did he conceive for himself as head of the party and what influence did he exert upon party affairs and party loyalists below the national level? How involved did he become in internal state party politics, and to what purpose? What limits were placed upon him in exercising his party leadership role by an environment of state factionalism? How sensitive was Jefferson to the potential of publicity and the use of the medium of the party press to expand his public support? What were his views on the role of the press in a republic, and what were the methods he adopted to make use of the press as an organ for political communication? These are some of the questions with which this chapter is concerned.

The Pattern of Party Development

Students of American party development agree that the first stirrings of party activity in the United States began in Congress and arose in response to national issues.[3] Party divisions developed during the debates over Hamilton's economic system and emerged more fully during the conflict over Jay's Treaty and the French question. By 1795 rudimentary but recognizable party groupings existed in Con-

---

1. See, for example, Wilfred Binkley, *American Political Parties: Their Natural History* (New York, 1962); Noble S. Cunningham, *The Jeffersonian Republicans: The Formation of Party Organization, 1789–1801* (Chapel Hill, N.C., 1957), and his *Jeffersonian Republicans in Power*; and Chambers, *Political Parties*.

2. Frank Luther Mott, *Jefferson and the Press*, and his *American Journalism* (New York, 1941); also Worthington C. Ford, "Jefferson and the Newspaper," in *Records* of the Columbia Historical Society, 8 (1905).

3. See, for example, Cunningham, *Formation*, and Chambers.

gress. The presidential election of 1796 served to dramatize the party cleavages and helped to create, in Jefferson, a rallying symbol for partisan orientation.

Despite their national origins, however, the pattern of decentralization that has come to characterize modern American parties appeared quite early. As parties emerged in the states, local conditions, local personalities, and local organizational imperatives took hold. The major problem Jefferson faced in trying to use the party to lubricate the wheels of government was its unstable and tentative nature. The Republican party of Jefferson was the prototype of future American parties, a "holding company for complex and interlacing clusters of local groups revolving around men holding or contending for innumerable state and local offices."[4] In the nation's capital, this party existed as a substantially stable and persistent elite grouping, but in the nation as a whole party consciousness emerged only slowly, in fits and starts, and with a decided irregularity from state to state. While men in the states did at times perceive a need to form national political alliances as national or international issues impinged upon local and regional interests, such coordination as was achieved was crude and approximate, limited not only on occasion by the priority of local concerns, but also by the slowness of communication and the rudimentary methods of producing and disseminating information. As Paul Goodman has observed, "the first parties did not have deep institutional roots. Even in their heyday they had been loose collections of provincial interests. Moreover, they lacked well-established forms of political organization and procedures which might have promoted survival. Highly local, evolving from rivalries within the towns and cities, counties and states, they appealed to an electorate without firmly anchored hereditary loyalties."[5]

Jefferson served as a unifying force over what was at times a bewildering array of heterogeneous ideological and political groupings. In some states "party" was the major reference group for the voters; in

4. James MacGregor Burns, *Roosevelt: The Lion and the Fox* (New York, 1956), p. 378.

5. *Democratic Republicans in Massachusetts* (Cambridge, Mass., 1964), pp. 65–66. For discussion of this phenomenon which is critical of the idea of a "first party system," see Formisano, "Deferential-Participant Politics," pp. 481–487, and Michael Wallace, "Changing Concepts of Party in the U.S.: New York, 1815–1828," in *American Historical Review*, 74 (December, 1968), 453–491.

others there was little or no organized identification of candidates with a party label. Voter cohesion in partisan groupings was uneven even within a given state, varying with the level of office being sought. Men might feel a loose sense of "party" identification in terms of national politics, with Jefferson and the ideology of Republicanism providing the unifying focus, while at the state or local level the motivation to vote persistently in terms of partisan identification might be weak or entirely absent.

The development of a national party followed the growth of democracy and national feeling as well as the development of techniques of party organization that could be used to coordinate diverse elements and transcend regional differences and parochial priorities. In the Jeffersonian party there was little or no central control, often not even any central *state* control over nominations to Congress. Men often stood as Republicans or as Federalists or Independents solely on their own vouchers.[6] Party machinery for presidential elections was crude, at times almost invisible; the national party hardly operated as such, except every four years, and then only as a clearinghouse for party propaganda and a collection post for the gathering of political intelligence on the developing state campaigns. There was no national committee—or any other organization existing on a continuing basis at the national level. The growth of the national party depended on informal alliances between and among state party groups, coalitions based on a common view of national and international problems and, in the early years, a common desire to dethrone the establishment, for as Murray Edelman has observed, "Political forms [not only] symbolize what large masses of men need to believe about the State to reassure themselves . . . but political forms also convey goods, services, and power to specific groups of men."[7]

The "New York-Virginia Axis" was the coalition that formed the backbone of national party development. It emerged from a series of personal affiliations dating in some respects from the Revolution, and it was established by 1796 when Jefferson became the agreed-upon

6. Gallatin wrote Jefferson of the results of the Pennsylvania congressional elections of 1804: "It is generally believed that this state will return 15 Republican members and only 2 Federalists. . . . All the returns are not, however, complete, and as there are 10 new members, the politics of some may not be fully understood" (May 11, 1804, Gallatin, *Writings*, 1:191–193).

7. *Symbolic Uses of Politics*, p. 2.

candidate of the New York and Virginia Republicans for president.[8] The Axis represented a marriage of convenience between North and South, and the future success of the Republican party rested on the health of that marriage. The coalition of interests that elected Jefferson in 1800 reflected the broad appeal the party leaders had succeeded in cultivating: farmers and planters who feared the commercial exploitation of the agrarian states by Federalist merchants and financiers; southerners, westerners, and veterans who hated the tariff and the internal taxes that the Federalist regime used to pay off eastern bondholders; "mechanics" and artisans in eastern cities and towns who wished to seize the political and economic power promised them by the democratic ideals of the Revolution; advocates of state rights who were struggling against the consolidating tendencies of the Hamiltonians; civil libertarians appalled by the Sedition Act; men of varying descriptions who simply opposed the establishment in their localities; new men of the rising middle and lower classes who saw their best hope for advancement in the success of the Republican party.

The name of "Jefferson" was employed by all these men to trigger in the public mind a complex of related responses that they hoped would culminate in electoral success. His position in the pantheon of the Founding Fathers (and the skill with which Republican propagandists succeeded in keeping him there) insured his preeminence at the head of the movement and provided the party activists in every state with a unifying point around which to rally the faithful. The Republican leadership gained many instrumental advantages with the election of Jefferson in 1800, as well: a strengthened congressional caucus to act as an arena for national party activity; federal patronage to expand party influence in the states; the powers and prerogatives of the executive establishment. The unity of the party, however, continued to depend on informal alliances and the lure of mutual advantage. The maintenance of a cohesive interest and its continuance as a force for political reform rested upon the success of the leaders in controlling the impact of internal state party tensions. Factionalism within the broad coalition of the party was a constant threat to such purposes and had to be contained.

Increasingly the central factor in the preservation of unity was the presence of Jefferson himself. Despite the existence of factional differ-

8. Alfred F. Young, *The Democratic Republicans of New York: The Origins, 1763–1797* (Chapel Hill, N.C., 1967), pp. 546–547.

ences and the ever-present danger of schism within a number of state parties, virtually all Republicans acknowledged Jefferson as leader. As the leader, he aimed not at arbitrating disputes but rather at providing his good offices to prevent internal squabbles from threatening the power of the party in Washington. To illustrate the dimensions of his task it will be instructive to examine the conditions of party organization and leadership in four states—Massachusetts, Virginia, New York, and Pennsylvania—selected as representative of the several sections of the country and as indicative of the spectrum of considerations with which Jefferson had to contend.

Massachusetts and New England

Party rivalry in the New England states represented, more than in other regions of the country, a struggle between an established political, economic, and social elite and a rising body of diverse individuals and groups distinguished by their dissatisfaction with existing power relationships. "Successful merchants and rising local worthies, fearful of war with France and anxious for the preferments of power, joined with religious dissenters and landless squatters to reorder life and broaden opportunities." It would be a vast oversimplification (and in some cases misleading) to see the struggle as a battle between economic classes. Some of the wealthiest men in New England were Republicans, while Federalist strength in some areas rested on the rocky foundation of yeoman farmers. Religion was an important factor dividing New Englanders across social class lines. Orthodox Congregationalist leadership dominated the political life of Connecticut, while the separation of church and state became an especially strong issue for Republicans in Massachusetts, as dissent grew apace after the Revolution.[9]

This caveat having been entered, however, it is nonetheless true that the great feature of the Republican movement throughout New England was the increase it provided in political interest and participation among social groups that had been excluded from the establishment, particularly the "yeomen and mechanics." The Republicans offered the exciting proposition that ordinary men could exercise responsibility for governing themselves. This new political awareness

9. Goodman, p. 127, 92. See also Richard J. Purcell, *Connecticut in Transition: 1775–1818* (Middletown, Conn., 1918, reissued, 1963), and William A. Robinson, *Jeffersonian Democracy in New England* (New Haven, 1916), pp. 118–119.

most often manifested itself as an assault upon the established powers. Federalist strength lay particularly in the propertied and professional classes, and the Federalists' contempt for the Republicans was that of the "educated, prosperous, conservative possessors of political power who see the encroachments of a different order of people which they have regarded as not entitled to a share in such privileges."[10] The Republicans cordially returned this contempt as they attacked the financial, commercial, religious, and political interests that sought to keep them in their place.

The key to the success of the Republicans in spreading their strength throughout the New England region was their achievements in Massachusetts, the most populous and wealthiest state in the region and the bearer, with Virginia, of the reputation of having been the "cradle of liberty" in the late Revolution. Party organization had begun to develop early in Massachusetts, and Jefferson and the national Republican party benefited in 1800 and after from the organizational groundwork already accomplished. By 1795–1796, party leaders were already nominating candidates, planning elections, and raising money, and the task of spreading the concept of "party" into the far reaches of the state was largely accomplished.[11]

Republicans in Massachusetts were not wholly united behind Jefferson for president in 1799–1800. A strong faction felt that President Adams would be better able to destroy Hamiltonianism than would Jefferson, who was not overly popular in New England. Nevertheless, after the nomination was made, Massachusetts Republicans quickly fell into line as champions of Jefferson. As the minority party in a competitive state, they felt the need to cultivate their ties to national party leaders in order to gain luster from the president's rising star and patronage from the party's largesse. The loyalty of state party men to the national party and its leader was reinforced as well by the fact that Jefferson, in an effort to forge a tighter organizational link to the state's Republicans, had taken two of their most influential leaders into his cabinet. Levi Lincoln was highly respected for his political sagacity and connections, and Henry Dearborn was influential in transforming the Maine District of Massachusetts into a bastion of Republican strength.

Jefferson, through Lincoln and Dearborn, relied on a network of

10. Robinson, p. 108.
11. *Ibid.*, pp. 53–56, 62.

personal and political friendships and social connections among elites to spread party influence. In Massachusetts the party benefited from the allegiance of some of the best families; when a Gerry married a Townsend, or a Eustis wed a Langdon, political as well as conjugal alliances were cemented.

Important among Jeffersonian leaders in Massachusetts, in addition to those already mentioned, were veterans of the Revolution such as Thompson Skinner, probably the most influential Republican in the Berkshires, and General William Hull, who later became Jefferson's territorial governor of Michigan. Also notable were members of the social aristocracy such as James Bowdoin, son of a governor and later Jefferson's minister to France; the Crowninshield family, especially Jacob, the leading Republican spokesman on maritime affairs, and Benjamin, who became Monroe's secretary of the navy; and the Cutts family and William King, merchants and "gentlemen of talents and prosperity," who were always welcome in Republican ranks.[12]

The work of these men and others in spreading the name of Jefferson and expanding party influence contributed greatly to the steady progress that the Jeffersonians enjoyed in Massachusetts. The expansion of the franchise during the Jefferson years and the diligence of party activists in getting out the vote stimulated the pace of this progress, as did the success of administration policies in lowering or removing taxes, reforming the judiciary, and presiding over a mounting economic prosperity during Jefferson's first term. In late 1802, John Quincy Adams charted the growth of Republicanism in his native state during these years, observing the precipitous decline of Federalism; two years later he "congratulated" the president on the completion of his "popular" revolution in the state. By the summer of 1807, Jefferson could agree that the state had indeed "returned to the fold." At that time eleven of seventeen congressmen from Massachusetts were Republican.[13]

Republican success in New England was strongest in Vermont and Rhode Island, where the party profited from a deep antiestablishment strain. New Hampshire was a bit more resistant to Republican charms, but the party's successes in the elections of 1804 caused the

12. *Ibid.*, p. 62.
13. John Quincy Adams to Rufus King, October 8, 1802; to John Adams, November, 1804, in J. Q. Adams, *Writings*, 3:9, 81; Jefferson to Gov.-elect James Sullivan of Massachusetts, June 19, 1807, Ford, 10:420–423.

state's maverick Federalist senator, William Plumer, to deplore conditions there. "A mania has seized the public mind" in succumbing to the "wiles and subtleties" of the "democrats." Republicans won the governorship in 1805 and dominated the congressional delegation for the next three years.[14]

The toughest nut for the Jeffersonians to crack in New England was the Federalist stronghold in Connecticut. The Connecticut oligarchy, unlike the establishment in Massachusetts, was narrowly provincial in its views, stressing the preservation of its rule above any concern for national issues. Republicanism in Connecticut was late in blooming, and its health was always delicate. The ruling coalition of economic and religious conservatives had managed successfully to brand pro-French elements in the 1790's as "jacobinical," and the Congregationalist farmers were loath to break with clerical leadership. The "freemen" of Connecticut freely supported the "benevolent paternalism" of the established order long after their counterparts in other states had joined the Republican ranks.[15]

Patronage was the major instrument of influence that Jefferson possessed in the struggle to "republicanize" New England. His desire to broaden his appeal in the region had resulted, as we have noted, in a policy of conciliation whereby the patronage power was to be used selectively and with moderation, not in a wholesale and ruthless fashion, to weed out unsatisfactory Federalist partisans. Such a policy, he hoped, would wean the body of citizens from old allegiances, but its success depended on its being carried out with tact and discretion. As Granger reminded the president, "the people of New England must be conciliated and persuaded." Their sectional pride and independence must not be offended by hasty or vindictive acts.[16] In those New England states where the Republicans did not control the state political machinery, Washington was almost the only source of government jobs. A radical replacement policy was the only way to care for the party faithful, but Jefferson refused to be rushed. Only in Connecticut, which he had written off as fertile ground for conciliation, did he feel himself free to reward the beleaguered party loyalists to the limit of his ability.[17]

14. Plumer, *Memorandum*, November 17, 1804, pp. 197–198; Robinson, p. 48.
15. Purcell, pp. 139, 147–148. The Federalist legislature passed a Standup Law, abolishing secret balloting and requiring voters to stand, thus pinpointing dissenters.
16. Granger to Jefferson, July 6, 1801, LC No. 27997.
17. Goodman, pp. 146–147.

Internal schism never constituted the threat in New England that it did in New York or Pennsylvania (see below), but Jefferson nonetheless sought to distribute the patronage and seek political advice from the widest possible spectrum of party opinion. In Massachusetts, he successfully overcame the incipient patronage rivalry between the Dearborn-Lincoln faction on the one hand and the Crowninshields on the other by encouraging a geographical demarcation of the spoils. In 1804, after running Elbridge Gerry four times unsuccessfully for governor, Massachusetts Republicans chose James Sullivan to run. An anti-Sullivan faction appealed to Jefferson to help them by removing Sullivan from contention, naming him to the vacant U.S. attorney generalship. Jefferson, however, partly on the advice of Lincoln, chose not to intervene, preferring to let local Republicans settle a dispute between groups both of which were composed of loyal Jeffersonians.[18]

Virginia and the South

Whereas party life for the Republicans of New England began and functioned under the pressure of a strong and often dominant oppositon, the party in the South arose amid an environment vastly different. While some areas of the South exhibited Federalist sympathies after 1801, over most of the region the Republican interest won an easy and permanent ascendancy. Federalist strength remained a factor in the Chesapeake Bay area, in Tidewater and Shenandoah Valley, Virginia, in the Wilmington coastal region of North Carolina, and in Charleston. Elsewhere, usual conditions were aptly characterized by Delbert Gilpatrick's phrase—"rampant Republicanism."[19]

The basis of Republican voting strength in the South as elsewhere consisted of artisans, farmers, "mechanics," and small manufacturers. In the South, however, this base was topped by a solid social, cultural, and political elite of planters, small-town lawyers, and rural opinion leaders which gave the Republican movement a respectability missing in the New England states. "Overwhelmingly rural, predominantly agricultural, more or less dependent on slave labor, and largely immune to the economic and demographic changes that influenced the northern states," southern politics were characterized by a pater-

---

18. *Ibid.*, pp. 130–131.
19. *Jeffersonian Democracy in North Carolina: 1789–1816* (New York, 1931), p. 127.

nalism, personalism, and localism that obviated the need for more than a skeletal party organization.[20] Furthermore, since the political machinery of the states in the South was in Republican hands throughout the Jefferson years, there was less need for federal patronage to fuel the fires of party spirit and keep alive the party's prospects for the future.

Virginia, although atypical in certain respects, was far and away the most important state in the region measured from any socio-politico-economic perspective. The political and governmental structure of Virginia during this period, however, was simplicity itself. The eighteenth-century politics of deference in which political affairs were seen as the prerogative of the landed gentry continued to exist in Virginia well into the nineteenth century. There was little incentive for elaborate party machinery, and party management was accomplished through informal arrangements among elites. What differences existed among the state's elites developed as a result of national issues, and the parties divided along those lines. In the formative years, 1791–1801, says Harry Ammon, not a single local or state issue divided Republicans from Federalists. Republican leaders from Virginia, secure in their local control, could thus devote time to national politics.[21] Popular pressures from below, from people seeking to control their own affairs and obtain a voice in politics, failed to develop in the Virginia party. Its affairs were in the control of a small group.

Jefferson's early success in Virginia was due in large measure to his membership in the state's governing aristocracy. The Jeffersonian Republicans in Virginia had emerged in the 1790's as an amalgam of "federalists and anti-federalists," i.e., supporters and opponents of the constitutional arrangements of 1787, and by the late 1790's Jefferson and Madison, and to a lesser extent Monroe and Giles, had become the acknowledged leaders of the party. They did not direct state party affairs, however, except through their substantial influence over the state leaders with whom they corresponded. In the state itself after 1800, political affairs came to be controlled by a small group of some twenty men, known in later years as the Richmond Junto.[22] The

20. Richard P. McCormick, *The Second American Party System* (Chapel Hill, N.C., 1966), pp. 177–178.

21. Harry Ammon, "The Jeffersonian Republicans in Virginia: An Interpretation," in *Virginia Magazine of History and Biography*, 71 (1963).

22. The best description of the Junto is contained in Ammon, "Richmond Junto," pp. 395–418.

group held no regular meetings, was not even formally organized, and its activities and precise membership remain somewhat obscure (the Junto was so secret that Ammon could find only one mention of it in the press between 1800 and 1816). The strength of the Junto rested on family connections, and most of the members were related to one another by blood or marriage.

Its two most influential members were Wilson Cary Nicholas and Spencer Roane. Nicholas has been described as a "cloakroom politician," with little forensic ability but much skill in the subtler arts of political influence. He was one of the few members of the Junto to serve often in national office, being a congressman and a senator and one of Jefferson's legislative leiutenants in Washington for a time (see Chapter 5 above). Spencer Roane was an eminent lawyer and legal scholar, "distinguished by his intellectual vigor, profound legal knowledge, strong passions, and morose manners." He was a good organizer, vain, ambitious, "in his acts a despot, but in profession a democratic republican."[23]

Nicholas's brother, Philip, was a Junto member, as was Roane's son-in-law, William Selden. Dr. William Foushee, the postmaster of Richmond, was an important member and the father-in-law of Thomas Ritchie, publisher and editor of the *Richmond Enquirer*, which after 1804 became the Junto organ. Other members included George Hay, district attorney of Richmond, prosecutor of Aaron Burr and son-in-law of James Monroe, and William Wirt, a rising young legal wizard and co-prosecutor of Burr.

The Richmond Junto sought to proceed on the aristocratic principle of disinterested public service, and there was thus little effort to create a patronage system to reward the party faithful.[24] Jefferson's popularity and prestige, however, bound the state party leaders to him, and the Junto supported the president regularly, except for the Yazoo settlement; even then they did not break with him (although some, like Ritchie, wavered a bit). As long as Jefferson's hand was on the tiller, the Virginia party gave him its loyalty and support. (The strength of Jefferson's unifying presence is revealed by the fact that no sooner did he determine to leave office than the Junto split between the supporters of Madison and those of Monroe).

23. *Ibid.*, p. 397, 400.
24. What little patronage existed was dispensed in the main by Madison, Giles, and Nicholas.

The other states of the South, less consciously aristocratic, more primitive socially and economically, were more open to political pressures from below. In North Carolina, as in Virginia, elected offices were few; hence there was little incentive to party organization. Internal tension, however, was greater in North Carolina than in Virginia between the conservative, mainly tidewater planters and merchants and the backcountry farmers and frontiersmen who were dissatisfied with a severely malapportioned legislature that failed to represent their interests. The successful results of the elections in 1800 ended a brief Federalist revival in North Carolina and, under the leadership of Nathaniel Macon, the loyalty of North Carolina Republicans on national questions was unswerving during the Jefferson administration.

Party organization was weak throughout the southern region, but nowhere more so than in Georgia and Tennessee. Both states were little more than frontier regions in the years of Jefferson's presidency. In such an environment, politics was a personal and local phenomenon that put a premium on elections as boisterous, sometimes violent theater. Political allegiances were built around those individuals who best exhibited the virtues of a frontier culture. "Politics was a combination of sport and drama, played before a crude, semi-literate audience that preferred action to dull prose."[25] Conventional party machinery was unknown; rather, these frontier states were governed by an oligarchy of frontier aristocrats whose political alignments in state politics bore little or no relationship to the national parties; in Tennessee in particular, all politicians, were at least nominally Republican and all claimed Jefferson as their patron saint.

What small amount of patronage was available to Jefferson in these frontier states, with little of the activity of commerce and sea trade requiring federal regulation and supervision, was dispensed through the members of the congressional delegations. In Tennessee, Jefferson relied for recommendations upon G. W. Campbell, his House floor leader, and also upon members of the Blount faction, notably Andrew Jackson and Archibald Roane. The factional disputes that enlivened (and rendered dangerous) the politics of these backcountry regions, for example, the bitter rivalry between William Blount and John Sevier in Tennessee, had no effect on their loyalty to the national Republican party, and Jefferson never had cause to concern himself with them.

25. McCormick, p. 238.

Party Development in New York and Pennsylvania

Two characteristics set the middle states apart from their sisters in New England and to the South and caused them to be prominent influences on the thought and behavior of Jefferson and his colleagues in Washington. There was, first, the closely competitive nature of the two party groupings in most of the middle states, and second, the importance of patronage and the spoils of office to the ordering of political life in the region. These features gave to the conduct of politics a complexity which not only confused participants and observers alike, but which, for Jefferson's purposes, threatened the unity and effectiveness of the party at the national level. It was one thing for Jefferson to ignore the factional disputes of Georgia or Tennessee, where the outcome would have no effect on party strength in Congress or at presidential election time. It was quite another to be indifferent to intrastate party disputes that in their schismatic tendencies might throw the state into the arms of the Federalists at the next elections. Jefferson's concern with factionalism and the threat of party schism in the middle states, particularly in New York and Pennsylvania, was a constant feature of his relations with party leaders in these states and played the major role in determining the use of federal patronage, again the primary instrumental resource for presidential influence in state party fortunes.

Early in his presidency, Jefferson had recognized the dangers to the party that might accompany the successful outcome of the struggle against Federalism. In the summer of his first year in office, he confided to colleagues his fears of the effects of internal Republican squabbling on the larger task at hand. Federalism appeared to be a discredited philosophy, but it represented a tendency that could easily reappear in new guises and under new leadership. It was essential to preserve the unity and the militancy of the Republican ranks to guard against such a Federalist resurgence. The dilemma was presented, however, by the fact that the vanquishing of Federalism as an active opposition meant a removal of the one force capable of binding the disparate elements of the Republican coalition into a cohesive whole. "The divisions among the republicans which you speak of are distressing," the president wrote to Nicholas, "but they are not unexpected to me. From the moment I foresaw the entire prostration of federalism, I knew that at that epoch more distressing divisions would take its place. The opinions of men are as various as their faces, and they will always find some rallying principle or point at which those nearest to it will unite, reducing themselves to two stations, under a common name for each." Again he observed, "I had always expected that when the republicans should have put down all things under their feet, they would schismatize among themselves. I always expected, too, that whatever names the parties might bear, the real division would be into moderate and ardent republicanism."[26]

Jefferson determined, if at all possible, "never to take part in any schism of republicans, nor in distributing the public trusts ever to ask of which section a party was." He realized that his prestige in all camps and with all factions was a central factor in the maintenance of overall party cohesion, and to support one group over another would be to weaken the force of his authority as party leader. It must be remembered that to Jefferson his party did not represent merely one of a number of legitimate political persuasions vying for the spoils of office. As he put it, "the republicans are the *nation*."[27] A schism "on either men or measures" would be a threat to the integrity of the nation itself. Thus in his view there was more at stake in the breakup of Republican unity than the possibility of temporary electoral defeat. A strong party was essential to preclude the return to power of an "illegitimate faction" whose claim to govern a republic, as he argued in another context, was as absurd as admitting atheists to the priesthood.

If the national Republican party was not a monolithic movement but a heterogeneous collection of groupings whose loyalties were determined by expediency and mutual advantage, no state better illustrated the nature of that heterogeneity than did New York. New York politics throughout the Jeffersonian period was characterized by a whirl of shifting alliances among the great landowning families and their satellites who had controlled affairs in the state since early colonial days. The De Lanceys and Van Cortlandts had given way to the Clintons and the Livingstons, but the undemocratic dominance of a landed aristocracy continued with only minor modifications until the Jacksonian era. The political interests of these New York families were supported by a conservative constitution and a patronage system

26. Jefferson to W. C. Nicholas, March 26, 1805, Ford, 10:137–138; to Thomas Cooper, July 9, 1807, pp. 450–451; see also Jefferson to John Dickinson, July 23, 1801, 9:280–282.

27. Jefferson to Andrew Ellicott, November 1, 1806, *ibid.*, 10:299–300; to William Duane, March 8, 1811, 11:194, emphasis in the original.

that would have made the "Court Party" of Georgian England green with envy. The spoils system was an integral part of New York political life from an early date and was to give a distinctive cast to parties and factional politics in the Jefferson years.[28]

Partisan organization began earlier in New York than in any other state; some say as early as 1789. The New York Republican faction existed independently of Jefferson, Madison, and the Virginians, and the alliance that was first created for the election of 1796 was a coalition of equals. The New Yorkers backed Jefferson for president because of the strength of his opposition to Federalism, not because of his independent influence among state party leaders, and it was not until after 1801 that New York Republicans could correctly be called "Jeffersonians."[29] The New Yorkers had been an essential component of national Republican success in 1800, and the continuance of party hegemony in the state remained of primary importance to the success of the party in Washington.

The Republican party in New York was never a unified cohesive group, however. The Livingstons and the Clintons were sometimes in alliance but more often in opposition to each other and to every other faction within the party. The constant attention needed to placate these family groupings, to minister to their sensitivities and heal their rifts, tried the patience of all concerned, Jefferson not the least. As other leaders not associated with the two powerful families appeared, additional problems of coordination developed. Aaron Burr, Morgan Lewis, and Daniel D. Tompkins at one time or another commanded the allegiance of important segments of party opinion. Indeed for a time after 1800 Burr constituted a third force all his own in the state. Party politics was thus a kaleidoscope, constantly changing shape and coloration, with the Federalists waiting in the wings to support that faction whose victory at any moment would most severely compromise the Jeffersonian cause.

The dominant political force in New York in the 1790's had been

28. The best accounts of New York politics in these years are Jabez D. Hammond, *The History of Political Parties in the State of New York* (Albany, 1842), and Dixon Ryan Fox, "The Decline of Aristocracy in the Politics of New York," in Columbia University Studies in History, Economics, and Public Law, vol. 86. A more recent account is Young, *New York*, but it does not extend into the Jefferson years. For party developments after 1815, see Wallace, "Changing Concepts of Party," and McCormick, pp. 106–107.

29. Young, *New York*, p. 578.

George Clinton. As governor for many years, he had claims, or thought he had, to the leadership of the national Republican movement. When his star was eclipsed by Jefferson in the Republican galaxy, Clinton cooled toward the Virginian. His coolness was no doubt instrumental in Jefferson's decision as president to placate the Clintonians with the weight of federal patronage in New York. This move entailed a conscious attempt to eliminate the Burr faction from a voice in patronage considerations, but as we have seen, Jefferson had ample grounds for making this decision after Burr's behavior in the disputed election of 1800 and after. Burr had been instrumental in engineering the Republican electoral victories in New York in 1800, but in so doing he had threatened the power base of the Clinton-Livingston group.[30]

The elimination of Burr from leadership in New York had begun quite independently of Jefferson and was not accomplished at the direction of those in Washington. Nevertheless, the process of isolation was aided by the administration's patronage decisions, which began to fall against Burr shortly after inauguration day. This was the only case in which Jefferson took such an unequivocal position in favor of one side of a state factional dispute.[31] The party press in New York broke with Burr early in 1802, charging him with inconstancy and instability of a sort impossible to condone or tolerate.

By 1803 Burr had been isolated in Washington as well. Jefferson, as was his habit, wished to avoid an open break with the colonel, but let it be known privately that the vice president was persona non grata in inner administration circles. An example of his technique can be found in a reply to a request from De Witt Clinton for the president's opposition to Burr as a candidate for governor in 1804. Jefferson informed Clinton that while he would regret any change in the administration of New York's government, the delicacy of the situation, "considering who may be competitors, forbids my intermeddling even so far as to write the letter you suggest. I can therefore only brood in silence over my secret wishes."[32] No doubt Clinton showed that letter around in important circles, as Jefferson knew he would.

During Jefferson's second term another intraparty dispute broke

30. Hammond, pp. 125, 172–173.
31. See Ernest Wilder Spaulding, *His Excellency George Clinton* (New York, 1938), chap. 21, for a description of this battle in detail.
32. Hammond, pp. 190–192; Jefferson to Clinton, December 2, 1803, Ford, 10:54–55.

out in New York, threatening the unity of the national party because it occurred amid the jockeying for position for the presidential race in 1808. De Witt Clinton had been punished by Governor Morgan Lewis for his interference in the Council of Appointment by being removed as mayor of New York City. The bitterness between the Livingston and Clinton connections over this incident foretold dangerous days ahead, particularly after the aged and by now incompetent vice president, George Clinton, let it be known that he would not be averse to a draft for the presidency in 1808. When this trial balloon collapsed, the Clintonians made a halfhearted attempt at an alliance with the Virginia Quids to nominate Monroe over Madison for president. Madison's hold over the congressional caucus succeeded in stifling this opposition to his nomination, but the evidence of increasing intraparty factionalism spilling over from the state to the national level was there for all to see and deplore.[33]

Pennsylvania, like New York, was a large and heterogeneous state with a complex political physiognomy, but unlike her northern neighbor, the Commonwealth lacked an aristocratic political heritage, and her politics reflected sectional cleavages. Pennsylvania politics displayed an egalitarian temper that gave to its affairs a loose, unruly, often indistinct character. The Pennsylvania Republicans, furthermore, were much more Jeffersonian than were the aristocratic families of New York. They considered their state to be the "Keystone of the Democratic Arch" and resented what they felt to be an inadequate influence in national party councils. The overwhelming majority of Pennsylvanians were rural, but the state also had commercial enterprises sufficient to rank it third in trade, behind New York and Massachusetts. Philadelphia had not yet been outstripped by New York City as the financial center of the nation, and the Philadelphia area led the nation in manufacturing.[34]

The Republicans came to power in Pennsylvania in 1799 as the result of a combination of good organization and the attractive issues of high taxation and sedition. With the election of Jefferson in 1800, the eclipse of Federalism in the state accelerated. After the fall elec-

33. Hammond, p. 217; Spaulding; New York Clintonian newspapers complained of the arrogance of Virginians who cherished the view that no non-Virginian was fit for the first office in the land. Madison's position in the party was thus politically weak independently of issues such as the embargo or institutional factors such as the independence of the House of Representatives. See Chapter 8 below.

34. The phrase, "Keystone of the Democratic Arch," is Duane's in the *Aurora*, October 8, 1803; see Higginbotham, *Keystone*, pp. 1, 13.

tions of 1802, national Federalist leaders deplored the "palsied" state of their fortunes in Pennsylvania. By the end of Jefferson's first term, the party had become so discredited as to win only one state senate seat and five of the eighty-six seats in the lower house.[35] Republican politics in Pennsylvania after 1800 came to represent a classic illustration of the dangers Jefferson had warned might result from the absence of a strong opposition party. Local divisions began almost immediately among Republicans and the threat of statewide schism haunted the president throughout his tenure in Washington.

Gallatin and William Duane both attested to the absence of great party leaders in Pennsylvania. Furthermore, from the earliest days of the Republican ascendancy, the party was divided into two major warring factions. The moderates followed the nominal leadership of the governor, Thomas McKean, a veteran of the Revolution, signer of the Declaration of Independence, and president of the Continental Congress. McKean was the type of leader who generally spawns schism, imperious and autocratic, dogmatic in his views and intolerant of opposition. He was, furthermore, a keen student of the spoils system and used his authority over patronage to great effect in punishing his enemies. He alienated many legislators by his free use of the veto to kill measures of which he disapproved, a practice not yet generally accepted as legitimate. McKean as governor was the titular head of the party, but he had little deep influence statewide beyond his control of the patronage.[36]

The most influential leader of the moderate or conservative faction was the secretary of the Commonwealth, Alexander James Dallas. Dallas was perhaps Pennsylvania's greatest lawyer and an excellent behind-the-scenes political organizer. He was instrumental in earning for his faction the cloak of legitimacy as the articulator of Jeffersonian principles and programs. He was a force for moderation in distributing patronage and was helpful to Jefferson and Gallatin in reining in the spirited spoilsmanship of McKean. Jefferson was to reward Dallas for his services by appointing him district attorney of Pennsylvania.[37]

The radical faction in Pennsylvania was led by two of the state's most colorful firebrands, William Duane and Michael Leib. Duane,

35. J. Q. Adams to Rufus King, October 8, 1802, Adams, *Writings*, 3:8; Higginbotham, pp. 26–27, 65.
36. Higginbotham, p. 15.
37. *Ibid.*, pp. 15–16.

the successor to Benjamin Franklin Bache as editor of the influential Republican newspaper, the Philadelphia *Aurora*, was intemperate in speech and print, dogmatic, stubborn, and opinionated, a man best suited to the tasks of opposition. In the course of his flamboyant editorial career (which included an indictment under the Sedition Act, quashed by Jefferson), he had become the most hated Republican in the state to the Federalists. Duane was sorely disappointed when Jefferson favored Samuel Harrison Smith's *National Intelligencer* in Washington as the chief administration organ of opinion. He continued to give the president frequent information and advice on national and state affairs, but his conduct in state factional disputes became increasingly violent and divisive. Jefferson continued to praise the *Aurora* for its "comfort in the gloomiest days" and its service as a "watchful sentinel" against the Federalists, but Duane's influence declined after 1801–1802 in national party circles.[38]

Dr. Michael Leib was a physician and a congressman from Philadelphia. He was militantly ambitious for power and possessed a streak of vindictive cruelty and ruthlessness that endeared him to few men. Leib was an avid spoilsman, and his suspicion of Jefferson and Gallatin was reinforced most markedly, despite their protestations of neutrality, by their apparent efforts to distribute patronage away from his faction.[39] Joining Duane and Leib on the radical wing of the party were Peter Muhlenberg, the German who had gained the distinction of being the first Speaker of the U.S. House of Representatives, Thomas Leiper, another leader in the German community, and Simon Snyder, whose candidacy for governor against McKean in 1805 brought the schism into the open.

The first signs of trouble within the ranks occurred early in 1801, when a few dissident Republicans allied temporarily with the Federalists in the legislature to elect Muhlenberg to the United States Senate over McKean's (and Jefferson's) close friend, George Logan. Jefferson, about to be inaugurated, was eager to keep peace in Pennsylvania. He was persuaded by McKean to name Muhlenberg supervisor of revenue so that the governor could appoint Logan to the new Senate vacancy. A year later Jefferson again came to McKean's

38. Allan C. Clark, "William Duane," in *Records* of the Columbia Historical Society, 9 (1906), 25; Ford, "Jefferson and the Newspaper," pp. 89–91; Higginbotham, p. 16. In one year alone, Duane received sixty suits for libel.

39. Higginbotham, p. 15.

aid by removing Muhlenberg as a gubernatorial rival with the lucrative post of collector of the port of Philadelphia.[40]

Major internal divisions soon appeared in Pennsylvania over national issues. Duane and his friends pushed hard in support for the repeal of the Judiciary Act of 1801, and felt stabbed in the back by the letter from the Philadelphia bar, over Dallas's signature, urging retention of the act's provisions for circuit court judges. Dallas and Duane broke also over the question of federal patronage. Duane was true to his radical persuasion in urging a clean sweep of Federalist officeholders, while Dallas endorsed Jefferson's policy of gradualism. The quarrel over patronage almost reached an open break during the election of 1803 when an attempt by Leib to complain formally to the president about the slowness of removals was countered by allies of Dallas in the House who informed Jefferson that dissatisfaction with him was felt by only a "small minority" of interested "individuals."[41]

Jefferson was occasionally amused, more often bemused and irritated with his schismatic supporters in Pennsylvania. He tried to be philosophical about it all, but its implications plainly worried him. "I have," he wrote, "for some time been satisfied a schism was taking place in Pennsylvania between the moderates and high flyers. The same will take place in Congress whenever a proper head for the latter shall start up, and we must expect divisions of the same kind in other states as soon as the Republicans shall be so strong as to fear no other enemy." To his correspondents in Pennsylvania he urged "a mutual indulgence and candor among brethren" to overcome the divisiveness which could destroy the party: "Although I shall learn it with concern whenever it does happen, and think it possibly may happen that we shall divide among ourselves whenever federalism is completely eradicated, yet I think it the duty of every republican to make great sacrifices of opinion to put off the evil day."[42]

Jefferson was by no means confident that the menace of Federalism had been eradicated. With the presidential election of 1804 approaching it was essential that the party's health and effectiveness be preserved as an electoral machine in all the states, but Pennsylvania was

40. Thomas McKean to Jefferson, February 20, 1801, LC No. 18758; Higginbotham, p. 41.

41. Higginbotham, p. 42, 58–59; also see Gallatin to Jefferson, August 17, 1801, Gallatin, *Writings*, 1:39.

42. Jefferson to Gallatin, March 28, 1803, Ford, 9:456; to Joseph Scott, March 9, 1804; to Thomas Leiper, June 11, 1804, 10:82–84.

crucial. As the intraparty battles grew more intense, Jefferson became concerned about their effects on that state's loyalty to the national cause. Thinly veiled attacks began appearing in the Duane-Leib press against Gallatin and the Treasury influence in state elections. As it developed, the local squabble did not interfere with the presidential election. Jefferson and Clinton were endorsed by a legislative caucus in March, and in the election Jefferson's Pennsylvania electors out-polled the Federalists, 22 to 1. Still, the president saw storm clouds on the horizon. "Pennsylvania seems to have in its bowels a good deal of volcanic matter, and some explosion may be expected." When it occurred in the summer of 1805 over the gubernatorial rivalry of McKean and the Duane-Leib faction, Jefferson resolutely refused to lend his support to either side. McKean's narrow victory was viewed as pyrrhic, since it required Federalist support to achieve it.[43]

In 1806 at the time of the Randolph schism, a segment of the Duane-Leib group flirted with the idea of supporting the Virginia Quids. Momentary reunion of all factions was effected, however, by mutual support for Jefferson's foreign policy against British commercial aggressions. In 1807 tensions again broke the surface as Duane and Leib tried unsuccessfully to impeach Governor McKean. Jefferson again pleaded for unity in the light of their fundamental differences with the Federalists, and as the only means of preserving the revolutionary principles for which the party had fought so long.[44]

Such pleas were not successful in healing the wounds of schism in Pennsylvania, but they did serve to preserve the "undivided approbation and esteem" of all factions for the president as the leader of all Republicans. Jefferson's authority operated as a deterrent to any open attacks on him, and criticism of the national administration by dissident Republicans was rarely directed against the president himself, but rather against one or more of his associates. The Quids in Virginia chose Madison as the target of their dissatisfaction, while in Pennsylvania the brunt of dissident attack was borne by Gallatin. As in other states, both groups of Republicans in Pennsylvania spoke as the "legitimate" representatives of Jeffersonian principles and both

43. Jefferson to Robert Smith, August 28, 1804, *ibid.*, 10:99; to George Logan, May 11, 1805, Lipscomb, 11:71–72; to Michael Leib, August 12, 1805, Ford, 10:143–144; Higginbotham, p. 100.

44. Higginbotham, pp. 103, 107–108; Jefferson to Timothy Matlack, March 12, 1807, LC No. 29156.

claimed Jefferson as their leader and looked to him as the embodiment of their political aspirations.

We have noted how Jefferson tended throughout the course of his administration to align himself on most issues with the moderates of his party rather than with the "high flyers." This did not mean, however, that he was prepared to write off the support of his party's more militant adherents. Richard Ellis has criticized Jefferson's maintenance of party unity for the price it paid in the lack of clarity in defining party objectives and the inconsistency of the party in pursuing them: "Many of the moderates were experienced politicians who realized that the party was composed of groups with irreconcilable ideas, and they waited only for the proper moment to disassociate themselves from the radical and other militant members of their party. This same *realism* cannot be attributed to Jefferson, who never shared the distaste and fear that most moderates held for the extremists in their party, and who never was prepared to purge them."[45] Jefferson, of course, did purge radical elements when in his view their conduct had placed them beyond the embrace of the party's ideals and purposes; witness his repudiation of Randolph and his followers. More important, however, this criticism fails to perceive what many Republican moderates failed to grasp. The party from its inception was a coalition of interests and attitudes. Its strength as a political movement depended upon the preservation of that coalition, or as much of it as possible, and the greatest danger to the party would come from the centrifugal forces applied to it by ideological purists. Jefferson saw that to purge the radicals and militants from the ranks would not only deprive the party of much of its drive, its zeal, and its idealism, but would endanger its electoral security by making it subject to internal dissolution as well as external assault by Federalists. It was the essence of Jefferson's own political realism to perceive the dangers inherent in too great attention to programmatic clarity and doctrinal purity. His concern for the preservation of a strong party unity reflected the actual character of American politics with its decentralized and delimited institutions and its sectional as well as class interests. He was, therefore, instrumental in establishing the character of American political parties as broad-based electoral coalitions with a programmatic content rather than ideological movements of narrow membership and narrower appeal.

45. *Jeffersonian Crisis*, pp. 29–30, emphasis added.

Resources for Political Mobilization

In our discussion of Jefferson's concept of executive power we noted that he viewed his office as a popularly based institution and pioneered many of the techniques and resources that facilitated the gradual transformation of the presidency into a popular office. As with most pioneering efforts, of course, while many resources were thoroughly exploited others were not used or were used only tentatively. We have noted the equivocal nature of Jefferson's approach to patronage, his recognition of its constructive function as a means of insuring sympathy with administration purposes, but his hesitation to employ it directly as "carrot and stick" to bargain for votes or favors. He lacked the instinctive inclination of the true spoilsman and was unwilling to exploit what still seemed to him to be an illegitimate tool of political persuasion. Even had he wished to use patronage in this fashion, the resources available to him in terms of the nature of the "rewards," the attractiveness of these rewards to those he would have needed to influence, and the willingness of those being rewarded to respond favorably—all essential to the bargaining process, as the Neustadtian model illustrates—were less developed than they were to become in a later age.

The same considerations apply to the mobilization of political support among the people. The techniques of electioneering, the use of direct appeals to the public, the development of the techniques of publicity and propaganda—in none of these acceptable tools of popular political mobilization for the modern political actor did Jefferson employ all the resources potentially available to him; with none did he feel completely at ease. Yet in each area he and his supporters made certain advances of a pioneering nature.

In the presidential election campaigns of 1800 and 1804, Jefferson adopted the mode of behavior that the opinion of the age deemed appropriate for candidates for high office. To seek high office by campaigning for it openly was a practice forbidden by the conventions of the day, and ruled out as well by his own political style. Jefferson in company with the majority of his contemporaries remained convinced of the unseemliness of political leaders appearing to court the favor of the electorate. The proper posture for a candidate was to let the office seek him; if he was worthy of it, his friends and supporters, those who thought him worthy, would become actively engaged in his behalf. It was considered improper to make campaign speeches. For Jefferson, "respect for myself as well as for the public requires that I should be the silent and passive subject of their consideration."[46]

In the campaigns for the presidency, therefore, Jefferson took no public role in his own behalf. He did take a very active role behind the scenes, personally supervising the distribution of political literature, soliciting funds from friends and allies, and writing numerous letters to Republican leaders in key states. He also participated in the formulation of electoral strategy and kept himself informed of all developments in the various state campaigns for presidential electors. The active prosecution of the campaign in other ways, however, he left to others.[47]

Under the leadership of Madison, Gallatin, and tireless managers such as John Beckley, a command post and clearinghouse was established for the control of the voluminous correspondence with state leaders, and Republicans developed and used techniques of electioneering that many older politicians found to be distasteful and subversive of good order and free elections. State, county, village, and precinct organizations in some states, in addition to their obligations to local and state candidates, aided the national ticket by disseminating campaign literature, spreading election information, getting voters to the polls, and performing a myriad of other services. Campaigns for a time developed that air of boisterous exuberance which was to characterize elections of a later period. Under the stimulus of local party enthusiasts, electioneering increasingly began to feature fireworks, the firing of salutes, parades, highly charged stump orations, and public dinners.[48]

Jefferson's own attitude toward the new campaign techniques was equivocal. His leadership marked a period of transition in the practices of politics from an age of aristocratic deference to a more egalitarian era characterized by wide suffrage and mass participation. Jefferson himself embodied the tensions and contradictions of that transition. While his political philosophy and his policies pointed to the more

46. Jefferson to Thomas McKean, January 17, 1804, Ford, 10:68–69.
47. For accounts of the election campaign of 1800 and Jefferson's role in it, see Chambers, pp. 152–157; Noble S. Cunningham, "John Beckley: An Early American Party Manager," in *William and Mary Quarterly*, 13, 3d series (1956), 40–54; Philip M. Marsh, "John Beckley: Mystery Man of the Early Jeffersonians," in *Pennsylvania Magazine of History and Biography*, 72 (1948), 54–69; and Charles O. Lerche, "Jefferson and the Election of 1800: A Case Study in the Political Smear," in *William and Mary Quarterly*, 5, new series, (1948), pp. 467–491.
48. Robinson, pp. 65–66.

egalitarian age ahead, his political style had been formed at an earlier time; Jefferson remained the prisoner of certain of the behavioral assumptions of that bygone age.

He lacked a developed sense of the political efficacy of a president actively encouraging public adulation of himself. While he encouraged the cultivation of public opinion in favor of the policies of his administration, he did not feel it proper to seek personal publicity. (Fortunately, his supporters were less reluctant to exploit the political effectiveness of the symbolic Jefferson). Though he was the first president to perceive his role as that of a popular leader, he resorted to only a few of the devices potentially available to him to enhance his *personal* image. He made few public speeches. He declined even to adopt a technique that Washington had used to great effect to enhance presidential prestige: the undertaking of a Grand Tour of the nation. To Massachusetts Governor James Sullivan's suggestion for such a State visit to New England, Jefferson replied: "I confess that I am not reconciled to the idea of a chief magistrate parading himself through the several states as an object of public gaze, and in quest of applause which, to be valuable, should be purely voluntary. I had rather acquire silent good will by a faithful discharge of my duties, than owe expressions of it to my putting myself in the way of receiving them."[49]

This leader of the people, then, possessed few of the traits of the archetypal mass politician of the future. His reluctance to undertake the "swing around the circle" was motivated by a natural diffidence and distaste for public display, but it also reflected his determination to underline the virtues of republican simplicity and popular *self-government.* He had no wish to cultivate an undue sense of majesty in the executive office by the adoption of a practice so clearly tinged with the vestiges of monarchy. In his concern to shun the monarchical pretensions of his predecessors, of course, Jefferson was hindered from clearly recognizing the efficacy of such tactics for popular purposes.

Even had the climate of opinion and Jefferson's own inclinations permitted it, other factors inhibited a president from employing many direct avenues of personal appeal to voters. The facilities for such an appeal were poor. The media of mass communications were inadequate for the attainment of quick results. Transportation was agonizingly slow. The mails were transported either by sea or overland on horseback or stage over roads that, except in a few populated

---

49. Jefferson to Sullivan, June 19, 1807, Ford, 10:320–323.

areas along the eastern seaboard north of Baltimore, were few in number and dreadful in condition. Mail service from Washington to Baltimore took an entire day, to New York three days, to Boston five if the weather was good. News of events in Washington reached New Orleans only three or four weeks later and took even longer to arrive in the frontier communities of Ohio, Michigan, Kentucky, and Tennessee. It was therefore in keeping with the state of technological development to tailor popular appeals for generalized responses and to depend on other means for cultivating support.

Jefferson relied essentially upon three methods for the flow of political intelligence and the dissemination of information and propaganda: correspondence through private letter; public replies to formal addresses and memorials; and most important, the party press.

A crucial requisite for effective leadership in any context is the possession of reliable information. Jefferson was always eager for accurate and timely political intelligence from all parts of the country, and his papers reveal the pains he took to insure a continuous flow of information on a broad range of subjects from a wide variety of correspondents. Few men had as extensive a correspondence as Jefferson; if one considers the time it took him to compose the thousands of letters that fill his files, most of them written in his own hand, the quantity of this correspondence becomes truly awesome. He exhorted friends to write regularly to him about their thoughts on the state of affairs in their region or locality, and to call upon him in the capital or at Monticello for a more detailed and wider ranging exchange of views. Distant acquaintances and men of differing shades of opinion were encouraged to do the same.[50]

Jefferson's practice of gauging public opinion from private correspondence had its obvious pitfalls, including the dangers of sycophancy or one-sidedness, as party leaders might give the president only news that would enhance their own reputations or positions. But it remained the most readily available source of information, and a reading of such correspondence impresses one with the candor of many of these men. The politically sophisticated among them, leaders

50. To Charles Pinckney, for example, the president observed that "the most valuable source of information we have is that of the members of the legislature," and while that avenue would be resorted to with "great freedom," conversation with visitors to Washington were of great value as well. He invited Pinckney to dine "with our mess tomorrow . . . and if you could come half an hour before dinner, I would be alone that we might have some conversation" (March 6, 1801, *ibid.*, 9:200–201).

in their own right, had the ability to feel the public pulse in their parts of the country, and they proved useful to the president in describing and often anticipating the state of public opinion and the tenor of public needs. He was, in addition, kept informed of conditions in state politics, particularly as to local intraparty rivalries and factional disputes.[51]

In the dark days of the late 1790's, when a cloud of conspiracy hung in the political air, Jefferson had been reluctant to confide detailed or sensitive political intelligence by letter, lest it be intercepted and read by Federalist spies in the post offices (as had happened). Since the unauthorized publication of his notorious letter to Philip Mazzei in 1796, he had entrusted his letters when possible, to friends to deliver in person.[52] This practice he continued as president, even after the postal services were in the hands of his own supporters. During his presidency his political correspondence increased. At least the number of letters to him increased; his ability to reply was restricted by the press of public business. Much correspondence was handled indirectly, however, in a fanlike fashion, as Madison, Gallatin, Lincoln, Granger, and others wrote to their own political confidants in the states who in turn disseminated intelligence from and transmitted news to Jefferson's colleagues in Washington.

As president, Jefferson continued his earlier practice of writing to colleagues and allies urging them to "take up pen" in the party's cause to answer some political attack or to introduce some proposal into the public debates. This proved to be a shrewd and effective way of spreading his principles, encouraging the expansion of the party, and protecting him from being the sole target of Federalist abuse. By diverting the attack of his enemies onto a broad front, he could guard his presidential prestige by appearing as chief of state to be above the mire of political controversy. The attackers were made to appear mean, vindictive, ungentlemanly, while the president could appear the very image of the calm, benevolent statesman.

51. See, for example, Nathaniel Macon to Jefferson, June 17, 1802, in Dodd, *Nathaniel Macon*, pp. 177–178; Granger to Jefferson, June 4, 1800, LC No. 18298; Hugh H. Brackinridge to Jefferson, January 19, 1801, No. 18645; Stephens T. Mason to Jefferson, September 5, 1800, No. 18256.

52. See the note of Thomas Mendenhall to Jefferson, January 21, 1801, LC No. 18666, offering his services as a courier. Jefferson was not the only one who suspected the mails. Monroe felt it was unsafe to rely on the "fidelity of the post office." See Monroe to Jefferson, April 23, 1800, No. 18268.

His correspondence was by no means limited to political leaders. He received many letters from ordinary citizens who seemed to see in him what he hoped to portray, a leader with a unique relationship to the people he led. The correspondence from people of diverse backgrounds and stations stands as testimony to the power of "Jefferson" as a public symbol. Many of the letters were of a trivial nature, praising his conduct as president, asking for jobs, favors, even money. Some were from pests who plagued the president and his cabinet colleagues with pleas for patronage or influence. A few letters were candidly issue-oriented, a number were from would-be journalists asking for presidential support to start a Jeffersonian newspaper. There were, as well, a few letters of personal abuse, almost invariably anonymous.[53]

Jefferson replied to many of these letters personally, was never (or rarely) condescending, and often quite helpful in directing the writers to a source that could help them. He was gracious in his replies to letters of praise and frank in his answers to thoughtful letters of criticism. The personal replies in their own small way must have contributed to the cultivation of his popularity when they were proudly displayed to friends in the hometowns of the recipients and framed in an honored place on the wall of many a home as a prized relic of a moment of intimacy with a president.

In a similar vein Jefferson's response to the numerous formal addresses, testimonials, and memorials that he received from organized groups contributed to the dissemination of his views and the promotion of his image. The memorial address was a widely popular device for party supporters and interested citizens to display their approval of the president and his administration. In addition, it served local purposes in focusing popular attention upon the program of the party and giving a sense of participation in political life to numbers of ordinary people. The Jefferson papers include dozens of these addresses, mostly from Republican organizations around the country.[54] They generally took the form of expressing the "approbation" of the citizenry of "x" township or "y" Republican committee, and would include some gen-

53. See, for example, an anonymous letter from "A.B.," January 25, 1801, *ibid.*, No. 18306; also Samuel Morse to Jefferson, June 26, 1800, No. 18307.

54. The use of the memorial address quickly became a popular device among party activists. The presence in Jefferson's papers of a number of these memorials from New York State Republican organizations, all within a two-week period, suggests a coordinated campaign by state party groups. See *ibid.*, Nos. 28714, 28721, 28723, 28736, 28762, 28764, 28788, 28807.

eral policy "guidance" (never very far from known administration positions) for the president's consideration. Each memorial was composed by the local "Shakespeare" or "Tom Paine" and exemplified the highest flowering of the poet's eloquence. Jefferson wisely sensed the political significance of these memorials and sought to exploit their value as instruments for the mobilization of support. As he observed to Lincoln: "I have generally endeavored to turn them to some account, by making them the occasion, by way of answer, of sowing useful truths and principles among the people, which might germinate and become rooted among their political tenets."[55]

Jefferson and the Press

The most useful and widely employed medium for the transmission of political intelligence and the mobilization of popular support in Jefferson's day was the partisan press. The American reading public consumed newspapers with their daily bread, and much of the adult population probably read little else. Tocqueville wrote of the power of the American press in impelling "the circulation of political life through all the districts of that vast territory. . . . In America there is scarcely a hamlet which has not its newspaper." He was describing conditions in the early 1830's, but the remarkable spread of newspapers to the far reaches of the American backwoods was already underway during the Jefferson years. An English traveler of the period marveled that "the influence and circulation of newspapers is great beyond anything ever known in Europe. . . . Every village, nay almost every hamlet, has its press. . . . Newspapers penetrate to every crevice of the nation."[56]

The expansion of newspapers in the first thirty years of the century was dramatic in its extent. Frank Luther Mott, perhaps the leading student of the history of American journalism, has calculated that the number of newspapers of all descriptions rose from 200 in 1801 to about 1200 by 1833; the number of dailies rose less rapidly, from 20 to 65 in the same period. The United States had a larger number of newspapers with a larger aggregate circulation than any other country in the world at the time. Mott sees this expansion of the press as occurring under the impetus of Jefferson's advent to power as well as

55. Jefferson to Levi Lincoln, January 1, 1802, Lipscomb, 10:305.

56. Alexis de Tocqueville, *Democracy in America* (New York, 1966), pp. 94–95; Thomas Hamilton, *Men and Manners in America* (Philadelphia, 1833), 2:168.

the shift of the national capital to Washington. In 1803 the Louisiana Purchase opened up vast new territories for the spread of population and newspapers to accompany them. Of greater significance to the easy delivery and exchange of newspapers was the rapid development of the postal system and the construction of post roads under Jefferson and his busy postmaster general, Gideon Granger. The pages of the *National Intelligencer* during these years contain ever-lengthening lists of the postal routes opening to new traffic.

The political beneficiaries of the rapid growth of newspapers were Jefferson and the Republican party. Few were the newspapers started after 1801 that did not embrace the Republican cause in one fashion or another. Even new periodicals in New England tended to be Republican. An early student of the subject found that whereas as late as 1804, two-thirds of the press was Federalist in sympathies, by 1810 one-half was Republican.[57]

A survey of the content of the press in the Jeffersonian period substantiates Mott's conclusion that national politics was "the one great continuous news story of the period."[58] No provincial newspaper established its own resident correspondent in Washington until the 1820's, but there is no doubt that events in the national capital were of primary importance to most editors. Indeed, if the mail bringing the newspapers from Washington failed to arrive in time for the press deadline, many editors were hard pressed to fill their columns; some simply did not bother to print that issue. Local or even state events were rarely considered important enough to feature. Rather the news columns of the *Arkansas Gazette*, the Vincennes *Western Sun*, the *Kentucky Gazette*, and other distant papers were taken up with the debates in Congress, addresses and messages of the president, official reports from the Treasury, and editorials on national topics reprinted (usually with acknowledgments) from the *National Intelligencer*, the *Aurora*, the *Maryland Gazette*, the New York *American Citizen*, and the *Richmond Enquirer*.

The biggest news story of the period, after the Napoleonic Wars, was Jefferson's embargo. The recurrent presidential elections and every utterance of the president were always news. The Burr conspiracy and trial received extensive coverage, as did the Louisiana Pur-

57. Mott, *American Journalism*, p. 167; Isaiah Thomas, *The History of Printing in America* (Worcester, Mass., 1810), 2:515–524.
58. *American Journalism*, p. 55.

chase. Indeed, the detailed coverage of national politics by the provincial press would seem to contradict James S. Young's contention that the Washington community operated "out of sight and out of mind." The political intelligence network of the period, crude and slow as it was, served well to inform the voters back home of affairs at the capital. The nationally distributed newspapers, particularly the Washington *National Intelligencer*, served as a rudimentary national "news service," as local editors borrowed news items and editorials from these arbiters of national partisan opinion.

To say that newspapers expanded rapidly and that their content emphasized national news is not to say, however, that the quality of that content was high. Mott asserts that the years 1790–1815 constitute "the Dark Ages of partisan journalism" in America. The press emphasized politics, and nearly every editor expressed opinions on the issues and personalities of the day. But the ideals of journalism were quite low, and the most extreme partisanship became a way of life for many newspaper proprietors. Most periodicals were poorly edited; many reflected the low standards of taste and boisterous respect for violence of a rough society. Personalities were attacked with little restraint; no subject pertaining to a political figure, however personal, was off limits. To Mott, the period exceeded all others in "scurrility and vulgar attack on personal character." An earlier student of the Jeffersonian press described most of these newspapers as consisting of little more than "a plentiful supply of billingsgate" and characterized by "intense partisanship, a trace or suspicion of intelligence, and a bigoted assurance that the opposing party was entirely in the wrong."[59]

No political figure was immune from the virulent pen of some Cobbett, Bache, Fenno, Duane, or Callender. It is safe to assume that Jefferson, as the leader of a movement that purported to reorder the political and social life of the nation, had to endure as much as or more than most. With his desire for harmony, sensitivity to criticism, and distaste for cant, he must have suffered much from the attacks of his enemies and from the special pleadings of his more exuberant friends. There is no doubt, however, that he and his administration profited from the "favorable" press they received as the decade lengthened and more Republican newspapers sprang up to promote the Jeffersonian

59. *Ibid.*, pp. 167–169; Ford, "Jefferson and the Newspaper," pp. 79–80.

cause. Partisan Republican sheets did their best to cultivate the Jefferson image and their role in the propagation of the Republican faith must be granted.

Jefferson has long been considered a champion of the freedom of the press. Some of the most eloquent portions of his writings are addressed to the subject of the essential relation of a free press to a free society. From his observation post in Paris in 1787, he observed in a famous passage: "The basis of our governments being the opinion of the people, the first object should be to keep that right, and were it left to me to decide whether we should have a government without newspapers or newspapers without a government, I should not hesitate a moment to prefer the latter."[60] He spoke of the role of the press in providing full information to the people about their affairs. This remained for him the essential function of the press; if truthful, it fulfilled the role of educator and molder of a "sound" public opinion. Belief in a free press was an integral part of his larger belief in the capacity of men effectively to govern their affairs, provided they were educated, enlightened, and well informed. "Where the press is free and every man able to read, all is safe."[61]

His exalted (Leonard Levy says "idealistic and unrealizable") vision of the proper function of a free press was sorely tested at the hands of his editorial enemies, and while it is fair to say that his vision never left him, its very exaltedness meant that his expectations of press performance must have been sharply disappointed. His belief in the existence of an objective "truth," the ability of newspaper editors to find it, its publication somehow to educate the people and enable them to govern themselves with wisdom—all led him inexorably to a disillusionment with the press of his day. As we have seen, the bitter attacks during the 1790's forced him to guard his pen and keep his letters secret from prying eyes. After he became president, the attacks seemed, if anything, to intensify in their fury. Little was sacred against the diatribes of partisanship. As only one of many examples, the editor of the Federalist *Port Folio* of Philadelphia fired both barrels in an issue of October, 1802, denouncing the Declaration of Independence as a "false, and flatulent, and foolish paper," and smearing its author with the dark brush of the Sally Hemmings affair:

60. Jefferson to Edward Carrington, January 16, 1787, Ford, 5:253.
61. Jefferson to Charles Yancey, January 6, 1816, Lipscomb, 14:384.

Dear Thomas, deem it no disgrace
With slaves to mend thy breed,
Nor let the wench's smutty face
Deter thee from thy deed.

One can little wonder at Jefferson's increasing bitterness against the "brutal hackings and hewings of these heroes of billingsgate."[62] Indeed, as these assaults by the opposition press continued, the president's repeated assurances that the soundness and wisdom of the people would see through these attacks came more and more to resemble the automatic invocation, "God's will be done," by the habitually religious.

As a political leader, however, Jefferson never lost sight of the political uses to which a partisan press can be put. He was what Mott calls a "practical idealist" where the press was concerned. He understood, if he could not bring himself to condone, the imperatives that governed the conduct of editors. "A coalition of sentiments is not for the interest of printers," he wrote. "They, like the clergy, live by the zeal they can kindle and the schisms they can create. It is contest of opinion in politics as well as religion which makes us take great interest in them, and bestow our money liberally on those who furnish aliment to our appetite. . . .So the printers can never leave us in a state of perfect rest and union of opinion."[63]

Jefferson's idealistic view of the role of the press, his code of proper conduct, his hatred of controversy, his shyness of demeanor—all prevented him from catering personally to the needs of the "printers" and exploiting the organs of public opinion to the fullest extent. He did manage, however, to mobilize more of the resources of popular journalism than other presidents of his era to disseminate his policies and philosophy among the people. As to the significance of the "artillery of the press" leveled against the president and his administration, Jefferson could wax philosophic, at least in public, as he did in his second inaugural address:

These abuses of an institution so important to freedom and science, are deeply to be regretted, inasmuch as they tend to lessen its usefulness, and to sap its safety; they might, indeed, have been corrected by the wholesome punish-

62. Philadelphia *Port Folio*, October 30, 1802; Jefferson to James Sullivan, May 21, 1805, Ford, 10:144–145.
63. Jefferson to Gerry, March 29, 1801, Ford, 9:243.

ments reserved and provided by the laws of the several States against false-hood and defamation; but public duties more urgent press on the time of public servants, and the offenders have therefore been left to find their punishments in the public indignation.

Nor was it uninteresting to the world, that an experiment should be fairly and fully made, whether freedom of discussion unaided by power, is not sufficient for the propagation and protection of truth. . . . The experiment has been tried; you have witnessed the scene; our fellow citizens have looked on, cool and collected; they gathered around their public functionaries, and when the constitution called them to the decision by suffrage, they pronounced their verdict, honorable to those who had served them, and consolatory to the friend of man, who believes he may be trusted with his own affairs.[64]

Jefferson concluded his inaugural remarks on the press with the warning, however, that *state* laws penalizing newspapers for "false and defamatory" statements should be enforced. He was consistent in his support for state libel laws; as he confided to Plumer, "Individuals who are injured should be secured in their right to prosecute printers for the injury they suffer from libels." His position on the justice of such procedures for redress was expressed as early as 1776 in his draft constitution for Virginia. He repeated it in the draft amendment he suggested to the United States Constitution in 1789: "The people shall not be deprived of their right to speak, to write, or otherwise to publish anything but false facts affecting injuriously the life, liberty, or reputation of others, or affecting the peace of the confederacy with other nations."[65] His support of libel trials by the states was not necessarily inconsistent with his advocacy of the Bill of Rights because his major purpose in supporting the Bill of Rights was to provide a safeguard for majority rule against the potential tyranny of the general government, not to create a shield against a possible tyranny of the majority over individuals. He saw little serious danger of tyranny arising from individual state governments, particularly as they could

64. Second inaugural address, March 4, 1805, *ibid.*, 10:133–134. After his presidency, the conscious restraints he had imposed upon himself in his response to press abuses were lifted, and his private letters attest to his profound disgust with the quality of the newspapers. See particularly Jefferson to Walter Jones, January 2, 1814, 11:373–374. Even before he left office he discouraged a young man who had sought advice on starting a newspaper: "Nothing can now be believed which is seen in a newspaper. . . . Defamation is becoming a necessary of life" (to John Norvell, June 14, 1807, 10:415–419).

65. Plumer, *Memorandum*, December 27, 1806, pp. 545–546; Jefferson to Madison, August 28, 1789, Lipscomb, 7:450.

be controlled by a federal government limited by a bill of rights. Most of his statements on the subject before 1803 urged patience and restraint and "right example" rather than punishment for the evils of the press. It is true, however, that after 1803 his views hardened and his advocacy of state libel prosecutions increased.[66]

Leonard Levy in his justly famous study of Jefferson and civil liberties makes much of the fact that Jefferson as president was not in the vanguard of civil libertarian opinion in his day. He did not believe, as a few did, that freedom of the press was an absolute. Despite a reputation based upon his "habitual repetition of inspired reveries about freedom," says Levy, Jefferson had a "darker" side to his political life that permitted him to advocate cracking down on political dissenters through libel suits. Levy's criticisms of Jefferson provide a useful corrective to the conventional wisdom that pictures him as the patron saint of libertarians everywhere. In many ways, however, the case is overdrawn. The fundamental problem with Levy's argument is that it depicts Jefferson again primarily as a philosopher in politics rather than as a public man with an informed philosophical view. As Levy himself admits, Jefferson was even more devoted to popular government, and the preservation of the republican experiment sometimes took precedence even over the libertarian ideal. Jefferson's responsibility to the people as president was, as Malone has observed, "to guard their security as well as their freedom, and in organized society hardly any freedom can be safely regarded as absolute."[67] Rather than dwell upon his libertarian lapses, and there were some, perhaps it would be well to credit his capacity as a public man amid the crosswinds of public life to exercise the restraint he managed to maintain. His lapses were few; he made a conscientious effort to approximate his actions to his ideals, and his performance, if not reflective of the most advanced thinking of the day, was more libertarian than that dictated by the conventional wisdom. He confessed to a Parisian friend the difficulty

66. Jefferson to Levi Lincoln, March 24, 1802, Ford, 9:356–358. But see his famous letter to Gov. McKean of Pennsylvania, February 19, 1803, pp. 451–452, where he hinted that "a few prosecutions of the most prominent offenders would have a wholesome effect in restoring the integrity of the presses." He suggested a subject for such a prosecution, which was readily accepted. See also Jefferson to Thomas Seymour, February 11, 1807, 10:366–369.

67. Levy, *Jefferson and Civil Liberties: The Darker Side* (Cambridge, Mass., 1963), pp. 19, 21. Malone, "Presidential Leadership," p. 12.

in drawing "a clear line of separation between the abuse and the wholesome use of the press."[68] A philosopher could perhaps maintain that no line need be drawn; as a public man, Jefferson was constrained to make the attempt.

The Uses of a Partisan Press

Jefferson was far more effective in cultivating the positive uses of a party press than in curtailing its evil effects. He had long been aware of the necessity for a vehicle to circulate party intelligence and combat the propaganda of the opposition. While serving as secretary of state he had encouraged and actively aided Philip Freneau in establishing his *National Gazette* in Philadelphia. Although he denied to Washington having anything to do with it, he in fact tried to get subscribers for the paper, gave it official State Department notices and acts of Congress to print, and even offered Freneau a sinecure in his department. Later in the decade when Freneau's newspaper was succeeded by Benjamin Franklin Bache's *Aurora*, Jefferson again sought subscribers to it, mailed copies to friends, and made a small financial contribution to the editor.[69]

When the Republicans took power in 1801, the new president continued his efforts, albeit more indirectly, to encourage a Republican press. The task of first importance was to decide upon a newspaper to bear the burdens and reap the rewards as principal administration mouthpiece. Duane's *Aurora* seemed a likely choice, at least to Duane, and he was somewhat embittered when the selection went to Samuel Harrison Smith, who was persuaded by the president to move to Washington and create a new journal to serve as the official publisher of government documents. Smith was a man of fine social qualities and good political sense, and his wife was a great hostess and ardent admirer of Jefferson. Smith's editorial talents and his moderate Republicanism served to make the *National Intelligencer* a relatively reliable (at least to Republicans) newspaper.

Early in the first session of the Seventh Congress (Jefferson's first as

---

68. Jefferson to M. Pictet, February 15, 1803, Lipscomb, 10:357.

69. Jefferson to Philip Freneau, February 28, 1791, *ibid.*, 8:133; to Washington, September 9, 1792, pp. 403–406; to T. M. Randolph, November 2, 1793, Ford, 6:428; see also *Anas*, May 23, 1793, pp. 124–125; Jefferson to Madison, April 26, 1798, Lipscomb, 10:32; to Monroe, January 23, 1799, Ford, 9:12; and to Tench Coxe, May 21, 1799, Lipscomb, 7:378–379.

president), Smith was selected to sit on the floor of the House of Representatives and record the debates in shorthand. It was his status as semi-official House reporter that gave to the *National Intelligencer* a prominence in American journalism it retained for decades. It came to serve, as was noted earlier, as a kind of national news service, as the provincial newspapers clipped and quoted liberally from its informed pages. There is little evidence that Jefferson sought to intervene in the daily operations of the *Intelligencer* or try to control its editorial policy. Even if he entertained the idea, he had no need. The two men, Jefferson and Smith, thought very much alike; besides, Smith knew quite well the sources of his own influence and was content to function as the semi-official barometer of administration thinking.[70]

Jefferson was directly influential in the creation of only a few party newspapers, but he seemed to have a knack for picking the right men to edit them. He could make mistakes in judgment, as in the case of Callender and perhaps Duane. But he scored a success with Smith, as he had earlier with Freneau and Bache, and would later with Thomas Ritchie, a sober, reasonable, articulate, and altogether able man whom Jefferson asked to start a Republican organ in Richmond to counter the heavy concentration of Federalist newspapers in eastern Virginia. Ritchie became a leader of the ruling Junto in Virginia, and his *Richmond Enquirer* was for forty years the major newspaper in the state.[71]

Other administration officials and party leaders contributed their talents to the task of creating a party press. Granger and Elbridge Gerry were helpful in the inauguration of a number of party sheets in New England. Nathaniel Macon was concerned to found a reliable newspaper in his home state of North Carolina. He became the mentor of Joseph Gales, who established the *Raleigh Register*, which quickly took its place beside Ritchie's *Enquirer* as a leading disseminator of party views in the South.[72]

70. Mott, *American Journalism*, pp. 66–67; Smith, *First Forty Years*, pp. 9–10. Jefferson felt free to call to editor Smith's attention errors of fact found in his paper. See Plumer, *Memorandum*, February 4, 1807, pp. 600–601.

71. Charles H. Ambler, *Thomas Ritchie: A Study in Virginia Politics* (Richmond, Va., 1913).

72. For a discussion of the activities of Granger and Gerry in setting up newspapers, among them the Worcester (Mass.) *National Aegis*, and the *Eastern Argus* in Maine, see Robinson, pp. 68–69; Granger to Jefferson, September 5, 1802, Gerry to Jefferson, May 4, 1801, LC Nos. 19247–19251.

Madison had an important role to play in the spread of party newspapers through his control over the issuance of contracts for the public printing. These licenses to print laws and notices, stationery contracts, and other awards were eagerly sought by editors (they could often make or break a provincial newspaper), and conferral was tantamount to receiving official imprimatur as party spokesman in a particular town. Congress also had public printing to confer, and the Republicans' control of this patronage because of their majorities in the House and Senate gave congressional leaders additional influence in molding public opinion.[73]

As well as benefiting from the favorable press coverage they received as a matter of course from the Republican press, Jefferson and his colleagues made use of these newspapers in more direct ways when it was to their advantage. Jefferson was less than candid when he assured Thomas Paine that he had no more connection with administration newspapers such as the *Aurora* or the *National Intelligencer* "than our antipodes have; nor know what is to be in them until I see it in them, except proclamations and other documents sent for publication." These "proclamations and other documents," of course, gave Smith's newspaper a great importance as the official outlet for communications from the government. But the relationship was more than a merely official one.[74] There is no evidence that Jefferson or his aides ever did as rumor had it Amos Kendall did for President Andrew Jackson—write letters that were sent from Washington to remote newspapers, where they were collected, forwarded back to Washington and published in Jackson's party organ, the *Washington Globe*, as "demonstrations of public opinion." But they did send material to the *National Intelligencer*, provided Smith with what we would refer to today as "background briefings," and took care that friendly editors were kept generally informed of administration thinking.[75]

Jefferson knew the importance of having his public messages

73. See, for example, Gallatin to Jefferson, December 15, 1801, in Ford, "Duane Letters," where Gallatin criticizes the clerk of the House for failing to give Duane a share of the public printing.

74. Jefferson to Thomas Paine, June 5, 1805, Ford, 10:150–152; Madison to Jefferson, August 13, 1803, in Brant, *Madison*, p. 151.

75. Marquis James, *Andrew Jackson: Portrait of a President* (New York, 1937), p. 279. See Jefferson to Madison, May 5, 1807, Ford, 10:392–393: "Could S. H. Smith put better matter into his paper than the 12 pages above mentioned, and will you suggest it to him?"

broadcast to the people as an aid in spreading administration views. He sent an advance copy of his first annual message to Congress to Smith, who printed copies to distribute to all congressmen soon after the message was read. One astonished Federalist marveled "with what expedition these Democrats do business! It was in the press and probably numbers struck off, before it was communicated to Congress, that numerous copies might be forwarded by this day's mail to every part of the country."[76] Thus began a regular practice of dispatching presidential messages quickly and widely throughout the nation, with the *National Intelligencer* acting as the vehicle for dissemination. Jefferson also caused to be printed in Smith's paper many of the favorable addresses and memorials he received from groups, as well as his own replies. In this way statements of his were frequently before the public, despite his failure to make public speeches.

Jefferson rarely found it expedient or necessary, even had it been possible, to discipline partisan Republican editors who opposed him on particular administration measures, but he could make his displeasure known upon occasion. His irritation with James Cheetham of the New York *American Citizen* for his intimacy with Burr and his constant entreaties on behalf of friends for office led the president to withdraw his favor in 1804. During the Randolph schism the administration apparently let it be known through intermediaries that the flirtations of Duane and Ritchie with the Quids might mean the withdrawal of a variety of official favors. In both cases the corrective seems to have worked. Ritchie's relations with Randolph were short-lived, and Duane used his earnest support for Jefferson's foreign policy to work his way back into the president's good graces.[77]

The Jeffersonian Image

The absence of modern mass media of communication made Jefferson as a living, breathing person virtually unknown to most Americans. Most people never saw their president, never heard his voice, never had an opportunity to receive firsthand impressions of him. This

76. Manasseh Cutler to Dr. Torrey, December 8, 1801, in Lacy, "Jefferson and Congress," p. 49. Plumer commented on the usefulness of this innovation, *Memorandum*, December 5, 1805, p. 342.

77. The Cheetham incidents are discussed in Ford, "Jefferson and the Newspapers," pp. 97–98; for Duane's Quiddist flirtations, see Higginbotham, pp. 111–116, 136; for the moves against Ritchie, see Plumer, *Memorandum*, January 5, 1807, p. 558.

remoteness was reinforced by the political restraints imposed upon most political figures by the expectations of the day, and by Jefferson's own style.

Somewhat ironically, the very remoteness of the president from the people was of benefit in fashioning the Jefferson image in the public imagination. Physical remoteness served to heighten his symbolic intimacy. For most Americans the check of reality was missing. Their freedom to equate the symbolic "Jefferson" with all the positive values in their lives was unchecked by any direct awareness of Jefferson the partisan, the wielder of power, the compromiser of his principles. To borrow Edelman's phrase, Jefferson became for many people a "condensation symbol." In the name of Jefferson, men could condense "patriotic pride, anxieties, remembrance of past glories or humilities, promises of future greatness."[78]

The remoteness, furthermore, enabled Jefferson and the Jeffersonians more easily to tailor his and their image, to create a symbol to represent the values of their own choosing. The press served as the vehicle for transmitting that symbolic representation and the set of values it embodied to millions of Americans who would never have occasion to meet a president or to form their judgments of him firsthand. For the age and within the limitations referred to, Jefferson and his party colleagues made what might be considered optimum use of the press as they sought to disseminate political intelligence and mobilize partisan loyalties. As a test of their success one might consider the extent to which Jefferson's public prestige and his popularity with the masses sustained him during the dark days at the close of his administration when his search for a viable alternative to war led him to adopt a policy which strained that popularity to the utmost. It is to the embargo of 1808–1809 that we must now turn.

78. Edelman, p. 6.

PART THREE

❧

THE LIMITS
OF LEADERSHIP

Leadership does not take place in a vacuum; it is situational and interactional. Political leaders "behave with reference to expectations."[1] The leader possesses a concept of himself as acting *in terms of others* in a continuum of events or situations, each of which calls for a pattern of responses in keeping with the expectations of those to be affected. Earlier we examined the variety of responses called forth, for Jefferson, by the differing expectations of cabinet, Congress, and Court. The fact that a political leader performs in a highly complex environment and cannot control all the factors that affect situational outcomes, however, means that he is likely at some time or other to violate the expectations of one or more elements in the environment. As men and institutions adjust to new demands, strains result. They occur when the political leader's existing role perception becomes unsuitable to newly emerging role demands, or when his attempt to evolve a new role in response to changing reality comes into conflict with the expectations of key subelements in his environment.[2]

Such strains on a political leader can be caused by a number of factors, among them the leader's own conflicting role norms, the ambiguity of the situation confronting him, the diffusion of responsibility for effecting and administering policy decisions, and the intractability of events.[3] In the case of the embargo, the concluding subject of this

1. Gross, et al., *Exploration*, p. 17.
2. On role conflict, see *ibid.*; McFarland, "Role and Role Conflict"; Robert K. Merton, "The Role–Set: Problems in Sociological Theory," in *British Journal of Sociology*, 8 (June, 1957); and Jackson W. Toby, "Some Variables in Role Conflict Analysis," in *Social Forces*, 30 (March, 1952).
3. William C. Mitchell, "Occupational Role Strains: The American Elective Official," in *Administrative Science Quarterly* (September, 1958), reprinted in John H. Kessel, George F. Cole, and Robert G. Seddig, eds., *Micropolitics* (New York, 1970), pp. 177–189.

book, each of these factors may be said to be partially responsible for the dilemma that Jefferson confronted, and each to varying degrees may be considered to have contributed to his failure to effect his policy goals.

In devising an embargo policy, Jefferson began within prevailing political expectations. The issue to be resolved—how to deal with British and French threats to American political and commercial interests—was a question of foreign policy, and thus was primarily a presidential responsibility. Congress and the American people were prepared to give wide latitude to the president in formulating relations with foreign governments. Jefferson, as we have noted, accepted such responsibility as his right and was prepared to act accordingly.

From the inception of the embargo policy, however, strains developed in this leader-led relationship. The carrying out of the embargo required actions that came into conflict with Jefferson's conception of his presidential role, worked to undermine his system of political values, and did violence to his accustomed leadership style. The previously untried nature of the embargo policy and the faultiness of the assumptions underlying such a massive effort at economic coercion produced persistent uncertainties in the administration of the law and rising severity in the punishment of its violators. The intransigence of British and French reaction to the embargo and the resistance of large segments of the American people to its strictures underline for us the crucial significance of events beyond a leader's control in determining his success or failure.

As an alternative to the evils of war in settling disagreements among states and peoples, the embargo was a noble experiment, but its failure as a viable policy had important consequences for the exercise of presidential leadership in the years following Jefferson's retirement. The causes of that failure stemmed from the embargo's inability to force Britain and France to change their restrictive interference with American trade and the unwillingness of important parts of the American population to submit to the economic and personal hardships engendered by the policy.

The fact of the embargo's failure contributed greatly to the decline of presidential prestige and the shift of effective power from the executive to the legislative branch following Jefferson's departure from office. The failure of the embargo damaged the credibility of executive policy leadership at a time when that leadership was passing into the hands of one whose skills were weaker to begin with. Madison inherited a discredited policy and his identification with it combined with defects in his personal qualities of leadership to reduce his influence. Jefferson in his pursuit of the embargo had distended the legitimate limits of presidential power in peacetime. When that policy failed, the image of presidential infallibility that had seemed to surround the office and its holder during Jefferson's tenure was damaged. The failure further weakened the strained unity of the Republican party coalition and provided the motive force for the transfer of effective power to congressional leaders in the void that followed.

Jefferson thus contributed to weakening presidential influence not by an improper deference to Congress, not even alone by an "illegitimate" use of executive authority (in the sense of violating environmental expectations), but by his hardened commitment to a policy the failure of which served to discredit for a time the persons and the institution responsible for it.

❧

CHAPTER 8

The Embargo: A Case Study in the Limits of Presidential Leadership

Foreign affairs occupied a relatively minor portion of Jefferson's time during his first administration, a fact that greatly aided the Republicans in the pursuit of their program of domestic reform. The European world was at war as Jefferson took office, and certain of the problems that were later to cloud Anglo-American and Franco-American relations were already evident in 1801. Changes in the British cabinet and peace overtures in Europe in the winter of 1801–1802, however, eased the burden of impressments, and American trade with the West Indies was permitted to proceed for a time unhindered. In March, 1802, the Treaty of Amiens brought a momentary peace of sorts between England and France. While Napoleon continued to harass the English on the seas and in the colonies, Jefferson sought to preserve a careful neutrality between the two major powers, believing that by favoring neither side the United States could profit from both through the acquisition of the carrying trade of their colonies.[1]

When hostilities between Britain and France resumed, Jefferson resolved to continue his policy of neutrality, but with a careful attention to the preservation of American independence from encroachments by either Power. The shifting uncertainties of European alliances during 1804 prevented the Powers from paying much attention to the fledgling nation across the Atlantic. Peace abroad and increased prosperity at home enabled the administration to devote its energies to reducing taxes, cutting expenditures, and paying off the public debt.

1. See, for example, Jefferson's instructions to Minister Robert Livingston in Paris, October 10, 1802, Ford, 9:396–398.

The reemergence of foreign affairs to center stage coincided with the beginning of Jefferson's second term. Napoleon's coronation as emperor in January, 1805, followed by the creation of the Third Coalition and the active resumption of full-scale military and naval operations necessitated a reassessment of American policy as the activities of the belligerents once again threatened American rights as a neutral nation.

The common charge by the Federalists that Jefferson and his friends were the "French" party, and that presidential policy sought to favor the French cause had long ceased to be accurate by 1805. Jefferson's enthusiasm for the Revolution for the rights of man had long been dimmed by Napoleon's "betrayal" of it and the threats posed by French pretensions to world domination. Jefferson sought conscientiously to maintain a strict neutrality, and the record of American policy in these years is dotted with numerous overtures, now to one side and now to the other, as the balance of power shifted in the theater of war or as violations of American neutrality by one belligerent drove Jefferson and Madison in the direction of the other. The most serious threat in 1802–1803 had come from the French, and the president did not hesitate to consider the possibility, however distasteful, of a naval alliance with England to combat French influence in the Gulf of Mexico. Any need for a British alliance was obviated by the purchase of Louisiana, however, and the resumption of active British belligerency at sea in 1804–1805 was eloquent testimony to the unlikelihood of any productive arrangement with the erstwhile mother country in the foreseeable future.

An additional effort at rapprochement with the British was nonetheless made following Napoleon's assertion of hegemony over Spain, but was thwarted by a change in British maritime policy in July, 1805, toward a harsher position with regard to the neutral carrying trade. The admiralty court in the *Essex* decision ordered a return to the old Rule of 1756 whereby a trade closed in time of peace could not be opened in time of war; American ships carrying produce from the French or Spanish West Indies to Europe were henceforth subject to seizure by British warships. The *Essex* decision, furthermore, rejected the practice of the "broken voyage," whereby American carriers could temporarily offload West Indies cargos in U.S. ports, pay duties on them (which would be reimbursed), and then re-export the cargos to the Continent.

The *Essex* decision and the renewed naval belligerency it presaged posed a serious interference with the American view of neutral rights at sea. The neutral carrying trade was vital to America's continued prosperity, and thus the new British action was a direct threat to her economic independence. If such a policy were not effectively resisted, Americans would remain "colonists" of Britain in every meaningful sense save one.

Non-importation

Developments in the continental war did nothing to relieve the pressure of British commercial interference and impressment of American seamen. Napoleon's victory at Austerlitz wrecked the Third Coalition and gave the French hegemony on the continent, but the British after Trafalgar ruled the seas and harassment of American ships increased. Jefferson believed in the winter of 1805–1806 that by far the greater threat came from the British, whose assaults on American rights were systematic and persevering.[2] In December the president's annual message to Congress reflected the altered state of foreign relations, as he told of the *Essex* decision and its implications, and of mounting depredations on American commerce. In recommending increased naval armaments and improved fortifications as well as a larger army along the Spanish frontier, Jefferson urged moderation and wisdom in meeting these foreign threats. He warned, however, that some threats "are of a nature to be met by force only and all of them may lead to it." The speech was more warlike in tone than any of the president's previous messages and was greeted with general praise from friend and foe alike in Congress. A secret message that accompanied it, however, was much less belligerent than the address designed for domestic and foreign public consumption; it sought an appropriation to purchase Florida and ease the tensions with Spain.[3]

The firmness of Jefferson's public posture was belied by the uncertainty and caution in his mind. It was his hope to play for time and permit events to alter circumstances for the better. He was not to be allowed such luxury, however, for Congress for the first time grasped

2. Plumer, *Memorandum*, November 29, 1805, p. 335.

3. Fifth annual message, December 3, 1805, Ford, 10:181–198. See Plumer, *Memorandum*, December 3–5, 1805, pp. 339–342, for reaction to the speech. The secret message was the spark that prompted John Randolph's open revolt against the administration.

the momentary initiative in foreign affairs and forced an unwanted policy upon him. As British seizures of American shipping threatened mercantile interests (impressed seamen were more easily replaced than confiscated vessels and cargoes), representatives of these interests in Congress began to agitate for firmer action. Led by Senator Samuel Smith, whose own commercial holdings in Maryland were threatened, Congress passed a selective Non-Importation Act against Great Britain to take effect nine months later. The bill also directed the president to appoint a special mission to aid Minister Monroe in London in negotiating a settlement of the outstanding questions.

This policy was not conceived in the executive branch as a clever tactic to involve Congress in negotiations and thereby strengthen the president's hand. Smith and his friends forced it upon Jefferson, fearing that without it he "would prove too timid to negotiate with effect."[4] Jefferson indeed appeared to many during the first weeks of 1806 to be hesitant and indecisive. It is often true that a leader's "leadership" appears shakiest in the lull before the storm of crisis breaks. In that difficult time before action has been decided upon, when tensions are high and rumors of disaster are rife, discontent is often at its highest, and the leader is charged with irresolution and weakness. Sometimes the charges are justified. The winter of 1805–1806 marked one of the low points of Jefferson's presidency: the Randolph schism was at its peak, dissension among Republicans in Congress was high, and Jefferson's leadership was undergoing its first serious attack. These domestic intraparty troubles were reflected in the resolution of foreign policy as well. Jefferson confessed that he was yielding to a Congress that forced his hand on non-importation. The president's own opinion favored economic coercion as a tactic, to be sure, but he saw it as his "ace in the hole" to be used only when the time was ripe. He felt it to be premature at that point. Furthermore, he did not wish to send a special mission to London. Such a mission would be viewed by Monroe as an insult to his abilities; it would also make necessary a formal treaty which, to be acceptable, would have to settle the major differences. Unless it did so, it would be worse than no agreement at all, and Jefferson did not wish to repeat the experience of John Jay's unfortunate treaty.[5]

4. This was Plumer's assumption. See *Memorandum*, November 29, 1805, p. 335; also February 13, 1806, p. 429.

5. Monroe was in fact offended and other Republicans dissatisfied with the choice

Events soon after the passage of the Non-Importation Act seemed to obviate the need to invoke it. In March, 1806, news reached Washington of the fall of the belligerent Pitt government and its replacement by a more "reasonable" ministry under Charles James Fox. The *Leander* affair in April, in which cannon fire from a British man-of-war in New York harbor killed an American citizen, was resolved by an attitude of restraint on Jefferson's part and an apology from the British government. The administration was unable to take advantage of the conciliatory mood of the Fox ministry, however. Monroe decided to wait for the arrival of his co-minister, William Pinkney, before beginning negotiations, and in September Fox died. The attention of official Washington, meanwhile, was riveted upon the Burr conspiracy, and there was an apparent lull in foreign developments. (On November 21, 1806, Napoleon issued his Berlin Decree imposing a paper blockade around the British Isles and prohibiting any vessel whose voyage originated in Britain or her colonies from trading with any ports controlled by France, but this decree was not known in Washington for a number of weeks.

On the last day of 1806, Monroe and Pinkney signed a treaty in London. Rumors of an agreement ignoring the question of impressment circulated in Washington in February, prompting a cabinet meeting at which a decision was taken to reject any treaty that did not contain a British stipulation to end the odious practice. The treaty itself reached the capital in early March, and the president's worse fears were realized. It contained nothing about impressment; even more distressing, Monroe had agreed to a British reservation that would in effect have obligated the Americans to a war with France on British terms.[6] Jefferson was angry. He had not wanted a formal treaty in the first place, and the one on his desk was completely unacceptable. It might prove embarrassing to the administration, and especially to Monroe, to refuse to send it to the Senate for approval, but to do otherwise would be to submit to a series of clearly intolerable British demands. Jefferson tried to let Monroe down easily by writing him a

---

of former Federalist, William Pinkney, as special envoy and successor to Monroe as minister.

6. In fact, the British acted unilaterally on January 7, 1807 (only a week after the treaty was signed and without giving the United States an opportunity to respond) by Orders in Council declaring a paper blockade of Europe (Peterson, *Thomas Jefferson*, p. 862).

gentle letter explaining the deficiencies of the treaty and urging a resumption of negotiations with a view to settling the question of impressment. But this maneuver was clearly intended only as a means of gaining time, for Jefferson held no hopes for a successful treaty. He was determined never to "tie up our hands by treaty from the right of passing a non-importation or non-intercourse act" as the British desired.[7]

The *Chesapeake* Affair

Hard upon the heels of the abortive treaty, relations with Britain were severely jolted by a naval action off Hampton Roads. On July 2, 1807, the American warship *Chesapeake*, standing out from Norfolk en route to the Mediterranean station and not cleared for action, was stopped at sea by H.M.S. *Leopard*. Refusing to heave to, *Chesapeake* received a broadside from *Leopard* that killed three and wounded eighteen. The defenseless *Chesapeake* struck her colors and was boarded. Four "deserters" were forcibly removed, and the ship was allowed to return to port.

Popular reaction to the *Chesapeake* incident was instantaneous and sharp. British sailors were attacked in American ports, and mass meetings pressured Congress and the chief Executive in Washington for firm retaliation, not excluding war. Even the Federalists joined in the war fever sweeping the country. "Never since the Battle of Lexington have I seen this country in such a state of exasperation as at present," Jefferson wrote, "and even that did not produce such unanimity."[8]

The president decided to use the force of public anger to demand a final redress of grievances from the British government. He issued a proclamation banning all British warships from American waters and demanding not only an apology for the outrage but a settlement of outstanding differences between the two countries. The Mediterranean squadron was recalled and other military preparations were quietly undertaken. To the vice president, Jefferson confided that he wished to give time for American merchant shipping to reach home ports before the outbreak of war. In addition he observed that the

---

7. Jefferson to Monroe, March 21, 1807, Ford, 10:374–377; see also Jefferson to Livingston, March 24, 1807, p. 377, to Levi Lincoln, March 25, 1807, p. 378, and to James Bowdoin, April 2, 1807, pp. 379–383.

8. Jefferson to Dupont de Nemours, July 14, 1807, *ibid.*, pp. 460–462.

executive should let Congress exercise the final authority of determining on war.[9]

In fact Jefferson intended to use the opportunity afforded by the *Chesapeake* incident for peace, not war, but he was fully prepared to accept war if it came through British refusal to atone for the outrage. He displayed a fine sense of timing throughout the months following the crisis as he sought to maintain the unanimity of public opinion behind firm measures while giving a chance for cooler heads to prevail both in London and at home. Congress was called to meet earlier than the normal December sitting, on October 26, but that date, more than three months after the incident, would provide time for passions to subside and for the several possible courses of action to be weighed with care.

War with Britain was not a prospect devoutly to be wished. War and the preparation for it would retard and perhaps destroy the possibilities for growth of the American experiment in self-government. The United States required a breathing spell from international involvements in which to develop its economic and political independence. Jefferson's confidence in the ultimate outcome of such a war never flagged; if thirteen disunited colonies could defeat the might of the British Lion in the revolutionary struggles of the 1770–1780's, then certainly a united republic of sixteen states could do the same against a Great Britain beset by the continental threat of Napoleon's armies. Yet the administration was not ignorant of the difficulties in waging such a struggle, nor of the evil consequences it would produce, win or lose. As Gallatin reflected, "We will be poorer, both as a nation and as a government, our debt and taxes will increase, and our progress in every respect be interrupted." Gallatin also perceived that the exigencies of fighting such a war would pose grave dangers to the delicate balance of republican institutions achieved by the Republican reformation, by requiring "a necessary increase of executive power and influence . . . and the introduction of permanent military and naval establishments."[10] The activities of Jefferson and his principal advisers in the months following the *Chesapeake* incident were directed toward discovering a policy that would avoid the costly horrors of war *and* the intolerable humiliation of submission.

9. Proclamation of July 2, 1807, *ibid.*, pp. 434–447; Jefferson to George Clinton, July 6, 1807, pp. 448–449.

10. Gallatin to J. H. Nicholson, July 17, 1807, Gallatin, *Writings*, 1:338.

The Evolution of an Embargo Policy

A leading student of the embargo has ascribed Jefferson's search for an alternative to war to his "pacifism,"[11] but such a conclusion seems dubious when one examines the corpus of evidence concerning Jefferson's attitudes and behavior on questions of war and peace. There can be little doubt that he was a peace-loving man. He was surely no pacifist, however, if one defines pacifism as a philosophical and moral objection to all war. Jefferson did not oppose the Revolutionary War; as war governor of Virginia he was vigorous within the limits of his powers in its prosecution. He found the posturings of Great Powers distasteful, but he was determined to guard the national honor of the United States. He carefully calculated the merits of using force in each situation as it arose. He clearly preferred war to negotiation with the Barbary pirates, even for a time as minister to France working for a European league against them. Later as president he sent a naval squadron to the Mediterranean to deal summarily with the Barbary States.[12]

Neutrality for Jefferson was never an end in itself, but a means to a larger purpose. During the discussions in Washington's cabinet over the Proclamation of Neutrality in 1793, Jefferson had opposed its issuance not primarily because the executive would be exceeding his authority vis-à-vis Congress, but because such a proclamation would reduce American diplomatic leverage. He had spoken in cabinet for a more flexible approach so that foreign nations would not be assured in advance of American neutrality, but rather be kept doubtful of it. As president he voiced the same opinion in the spring of 1803 as the cabinet was debating whether to issue a neutrality proclamation upon the resumption of the Anglo-French war. Jefferson said no, because "as to foreign nations it will be assuring them of our neutrality without price, whereas France may be willing to give New Orleans for it, and England to engage a just and respectful conduct."[13]

His attitude toward war, rather than being dictated by a philosophical aversion to war itself, was determined by expediency and the

11. Sears, *Jefferson and the Embargo*.

12. His skepticism toward pacifists when they interfered with important obligations to the nation is revealed by a circular letter to the county lieutenants of Virginia during the Revolution urging all those whose consciences forbade them to take up arms to take refuge behind the British lines (Ford, 3:145; Peterson, *Thomas Jefferson*, pp. 312–314).

13. *Anas*, November 8, 1793, p. 176; May 7, 1803, p. 219.

calculation of advantage. His reluctance to engage in war with Britain or France or both was based upon a weighing of the costs to American independence and to the prospects for American growth and prosperity. It cannot be denied, furthermore, that the enticing prospect of material gain for the nation's commerce from the lucrative neutral carrying trade entered into these calculations. As Jefferson once remarked of the European Powers, "our object is to feed and theirs to fight. If we are not forced by England, we shall have a gainful time of it."[14]

Economic coercion had for some time seemed to Jefferson a workable alternative to war as a means of exerting influence over the conduct of European nations. He had long believed that American commerce was so valuable to the Powers "that they will be glad to purchase it when the only price we ask is to do justice." As early as 1774 after the Boston Port Bill, he had urged a non-importation policy against British goods; in 1793 he had proposed a retaliatory embargo against the British blockade of France. In September, 1803, he included in the first draft of his annual message to Congress a warning of the possible severance of commercial intercourse with any belligerent who should violate American rights at sea.[15]

The president was by no means alone in his conviction of the efficacy of such a policy. Even before Jefferson's inauguration, John Beckley was encouraging him to look upon embargo as "the most sure, safe, cheap, and effectual" means of defending American commercial interests. Madison echoed his chief's enthusiasm for economic coercion. He had suggested retaliatory tariffs on British goods to combat her navigation laws in 1789 and 1791. Early in 1805 the secretary of state had written of the efficacy of commercial weapons "to force all the nations having colonies in this quarter of the globe to respect our rights." That summer Madison and Jefferson talked seriously of embargo against Spain to pressure her for a settlement of the Florida question. Madison was convinced that the unemployment and misery in the proscribed countries would quickly force their governments to moderate their policies. He seems not to have anticipated the unemployment and misery in his own country from the cessation of trade; rather he saw positive advantages in a total embargo. "Our own manu-

14. Jefferson to Monroe, July 11, 1790, Ford, 6:89.

15. Jefferson to George Logan, March 21, 1801, *ibid.*, 9:220; see Brant, *Madison*, p. 155. Madison advised against the passage as premature and it was deleted.

factures would be efficiently fostered. . . . No event can be more desirable," since it would increase the country's independence from the British, create new channels of trade, and develop the resources of Louisiana.[16]

Outside the official family other influential Republicans favored an embargo. Jacob Crowninshield spoke for his merchant friends in Massachusetts in supporting the 1806 non-importation bill. Jefferson's friend John Page saw an embargo as "of more consequence than any naval and military preparations we can ever make" in bringing George III and his minions to heel. Judge Joseph Barnes of Massachusetts was confident that under the pressure of an embargo the manufacturers and industrial workers of England would "rise in Mass and *compel* the Minister to open our ports at any price or they would Massacre him."[17] The rosy assumptions of the effectiveness of such measures were in fact shared by a sizable cross-section of Republican opinion. Non-importation, non-intercourse, and embargo were in the air, a legitimate part of the body of policy alternatives available to the administration as they attempted to deal with the growing problems of Great Power belligerency.

The Decision Is Made

Amid the darkening atmosphere of the *Chesapeake* denouement Congress convened. The Tenth Congress that assembled early at Jefferson's call had been elected a year earlier when administration popularity was at a peak with the closing of ranks following the Randolph schism. It was a Jefferson Congress. Joseph B. Varnum was Speaker in place of Macon, tarnished momentarily by his Quiddist flirtation. Jefferson's lieutenant, G. W. Campbell, was chairman of the Committee on Ways and Means, replacing Randolph. The mood of the members was one of firmness and in some cases belligerency. They were more receptive to measures for improving the nation's defenses than at any other time in Jefferson's administration.

In his annual message submitted the day after Congress met, Jefferson sought to match their mood. The final message was toned down from the warlike phrases of the first draft at the urging of Gallatin,

16. John Beckley to Jefferson, February 27, 1801, LC No. 18801; Brant, pp. 285, 399, 401.

17. Goodman, *Democratic Republicans*, p. 43; John Page to Jefferson, July 12, 1807, LC; Sears, p. 55.

who feared a premature incitement to war while the country was so ill prepared against attack. The president was content to sketch the background of the present troubles, including the abortive Monroe mission, the British Orders in Council interdicting neutral trade, and the *Chesapeake* incident and aftermath. As constructive measures for congressional attention, he recommended additional appropriations to build harbor fortifications and gunboats.[18] Bills for implementing these requests were promptly sent to the appropriate committees, and Jefferson men easily controlled the course of their expeditious passage into law.

Beyond preparing defenses, the administration had not decided what policy to pursue in the worsening situation. The dilemma for Jefferson was to select a policy from alternatives no one of which was intrinsically desirable. There were, as he saw it, four options from which to choose should the belligerents fail to alter their courses. The choice of war was fraught with the obvious perils of waste, destruction, and possible defeat, but the real problem with the option of war was in deciding which country to fight, Britain or France, or—horror of horrors—both at once. To wage a successful war simultaneously against the greatest land power and the greatest sea power in the world was out of the question; a choice was essential. Whichever of the two should be chosen, however, internal dissension and disunity could be expected. The Francophilic-Anglophilic divisions of the 1790's had not vanished from American politics.

The second and third alternatives were related and equally risky: the use of warships to protect American commerce or the arming of merchant vessels to the same purpose. The warship option would be more effective militarily but would require a great expansion of the fleet at enormous cost and would anyway run a considerable risk of provoking a war. Armed merchantmen would entail the same risk of war and would be less effective against British men-of-war. The fourth option, then, an embargo on all commercial intercourse with the offending nation or nations, appeared increasingly to be the most feasible solution.

Throughout November, Jefferson and Madison played for time, hoping that a favorable response from the British over the *Chesapeake* affair would ease current tensions. Jefferson, meanwhile, sounded out

18. Seventh annual message, October 27, 1807, Ford, 10:503–526.

certain of his associates on the idea of an embargo. Doubts of the effectiveness of such a plan reached him from New England, Governor James Sullivan warning that while war was unacceptable to the citizens of Massachusetts, an embargo would be almost unenforceable in an area where the state and federal courts, militia officers, and even the federal attorneys were on the side of Great Britain. Gallatin, too, expressed doubts about an embargo and urged instead the replacing of the existing selective non-importation law, now suspended, with a more general one. Madison objected to this, and Jefferson suggested the possibility of simply continuing the suspension of the present law in hopes that it might induce the British to cooperate.[19] Clearly at this stage the options were still under debate, although it appeared that some form of economic coercion was the policy most likely to be adopted.

At the end of November, Madison and Jefferson learned of Britain's uncompromising position on the *Chesapeake* affair. Rumors (later confirmed) also reached Washington of an extension by Napoleon of the French paper blockade to the United States, as well as reports of new British Orders in Council strengthening the blockade of Europe. The United States appeared to be caught in an ever-tightening vise, the only way out of which seemed to be through embargo on trade with both powers.

Cabinet discussions in late November and again in mid-December narrowed the options and prepared the way for a resolution of the dilemma. The secretiveness of these discussions and the seeming lack of action by the president led some observers to misread Jefferson's intentions. John Quincy Adams, for one, suspected procrastination to be the sum total of administration designs.[20] He later came to understand and accept the need for secrecy in determining upon an embargo in order to prevent a wholesale dispatch of ships from U.S. ports by merchants eager to gain the last bit of advantage.

In early December, the suspended Non-Importation Act against Britain was permitted to go into effect. After further brief consulta-

19. Jefferson to T. M. Randolph, October 26, 1807, in William H. Gaines, *Thomas Mann Randolph* (Baton Rouge, La., 1966), p. 182; Gov. James Sullivan to Jefferson, December 4, 1807, January 4, 1808, LC Nos. 30560–30562, 30725–30726; Gallatin to Jefferson, December 2, 1807, Jefferson to Gallatin, December 3, 1807, Gallatin, *Writings*, 1:367.

20. J. Q. Adams to John Adams, November 30, 1807, in J. Q. Adams, *Writings*, 3:164.

tions, the president determined upon a total embargo as the necessary next step. While it is true that little consideration was given to the long-range implications of the embargo policy, Henry Adams's assertion that the embargo was Jefferson's measure alone, taken without warning or discussion merely on his own recommendation is inaccurate. Not only was embargo a concept considered by many men as a likely alternative to war, but the actual decision to recommend it had emerged slowly over a number of weeks as Jefferson and his advisers discussed and narrowed their options. The cabinet considered the final recommendation only briefly, but Jefferson had discussed the matter often with his closest advisers. Madison was thoroughly convinced of the appropriateness of an embargo, worked closely with the president on the measure, and in fact wrote the final lines of the message to Congress recommending it.[21]

Gallatin, though skeptical of the feasibility of a full embargo, was not unsympathetic to the adoption of some form of economic coercion. He wished to avoid war, which would disrupt his hopes of reducing taxes and paying off the public debt. His objections to the final embargo proposal were directed toward limiting its scope and duration, anticipating as he did the uncertainties ahead and sensing the difficulties that would follow from an attempt to enforce such a policy over a substantial period of time.

I prefer war to a permanent embargo. Government prohibitions do always more mischief than had been calculated; and it is not without much hesitation that a statesman should hazard to regulate the concerns of individuals as if he could do it better than themselves. The measure being of a doubtful policy and hastily adopted on the first view of our foreign intelligence, I think that we had better recommend it with modifications, and, at first, for such a limited time as will afford time for reconsideration, and if we think proper, for an alteration in our course without appearing to retract.[22]

Jefferson was opposed to a stated time limit, believing it would only serve as a signal to the proscribed nations simply to wait out the embargo until the allotted time had elapsed. In this he was probably correct, but it would have been better for the future success of his policy had he possessed more of his Treasury secretary's cautious sensitivity to the implications of enforcement difficulties. Gallatin, far more accurately than Jefferson with his more trusting nature, per-

21. Henry Adams, *History of the United States*, 4:176; Brant, p. 395.
22. Gallatin to Jefferson, December 18, 1807, Gallatin, *Writings*, 1:368.

ceived the contradictions inherent in an attempt by a responsible popular government to enforce a set of increasingly unpopular and oppressive laws upon a people large numbers of whom are determined to resist.

While only a few men foresaw the rocky road ahead, it is inaccurate to suppose that the embargo came as a total surprise to the political community in Washington. Advance publicity had to be ruled out lest the initial effect be weakened and its impact delayed by merchants dispatching all their available ships in advance of passage. The congressional leadership was not surprised by the proposal, however. One of the motives for invoking the suspended Non-Importation Act had been to get as much of American shipping as possible into home ports before an embargo was enacted.

On December 18, the president sent a special message to Congress on the subject of commercial depredations, recommending a full embargo. The message was brief, and the recommendations were couched in more direct language than was customary for Jefferson.[23] In accompanying papers the president informed Congress that Napoleon had put his Berlin Decree into effect and that King George had explicitly authorized impressment of seamen.

Samuel Smith (he of the Non-Importation Act) was the floor leader for the bill in the Senate. He also chaired the special committee to which the request was immediately submitted. The committee reported a bill that very afternoon. Adams had initially argued for delay because he doubted the propriety of an embargo. He was persuaded of the wisdom of the measure, however, and his remarks to the Senate later that day reveal at this early time the emerging pattern of deference to the president in foreign affairs based on his greater command of information and the need for speed during a crisis. Adams referred years later to the fears that drove the leadership to hurry the bill's enactment: "Every hour of debate tended to defeat the object of the message. For the instant it should be known in the commercial cities that an embargo was impending, the spirit of desperate adventure would have rushed to sea, with every plank that could have been made to float."[24]

With the rules suspended the Senate passed the Embargo Act the

23. Special message on commercial depredations, December 18, 1807, Ford, 10:530–531.
24. J. Q. Adams to *New England Palladium*, undated, *Writings*, 3:228, 225.

same day by a lopsided vote of 22 to 6. Some delay developed in the House consideration of the bill, but the lower body passed the measure with minor amendments on December 21. The Senate quickly agreed to the House version, and the bill was signed into law the following day.[25]

Once again a Republican Congress had responded favorably and quickly to a Jeffersonian recommendation. The national legislature had yielded to the superior "knowledge" and "expertise" of the chief executive, had deferred to the presidential prerogative in the conduct of the nation's foreign relations. They acted largely on faith, in the belief that Jefferson and his advisers must have had good and sufficient reasons for advocating that particular policy at that particular time. No one, not even Gallatin, foresaw the magnitude of the experiment the government had launched so effortlessly, however. The members of Congress were not even aware of all the reasons for the embargo. It had been presented largely as a measure to protect the commerce of the United States against the marauding guns of British warships and the preying talons of French customs officials. To Adams and other senators, the telling evidence in its favor had been the accounts from abroad that proved that the commerce and seamen of the United States were threatened with the utmost dangers.[26] Few people expected that the embargo would last more than ninety days, the same time required for most of the American merchant fleet to reach home ports. After that, it was thought, the policy would be reassessed and fresh alternatives decided upon.

To Jefferson, however, the embargo was conceived as an alternative to war, not merely as a temporary expedient preparatory to war. It had long been his view that American commerce was too attractive to European nations for them to permit its cessation or interruption for long. Cessation of trade could be expected in time to force Britain and France to their knees. For the president such a coercive use of the Embargo was the central reason for its adoption, a reason, however, which had not been made clear to Congress, the mercantile community, or the public. Most seriously for his hopes of success, it had not been made clear to the belligerents. Jefferson must be held responsible for this failure to communicate his intentions. To make such a policy of coercion work, it was imperative that all talk of a short-term, tempo-

25. J. Q. Adams, *Memoirs*, December 18, 22, 1807, 1:490–492.
26. Adams to *New England Palladium*, cited in note 24.

rary embargo be scotched. Otherwise the countries for which it was intended would simply wait it out. Congress, the members of his party, and the public should have been informed forcefully and immediately of the nature and extent of the sacrifices they were being called upon to make. It is, of course, conceivable that public opinion would have rejected his call for sacrifice and repudiated his intentions, but that outcome would have been most unlikely. Be that as it may, his only hope for success lay in convincing the American people of the necessity to endure, and thereby convincing the British and French governments of American determination to do so. By initially concealing the coercive aspects of the embargo, the president lessened the impact that the policy could make upon the ruling circles of the belligerent Powers.

Enforcement of the Law

The implications of this failure were scarcely perceived in the first weeks following enactment of the law, however. Administration confidence was high. Initial reaction to the embargo was cautiously favorable, although the Federalists predictably denounced the measure as but a thinly veiled attack on Britain alone, since France required little commerce with America to exist, while without trade the British islands could not survive. They also viewed the embargo as a direct assault upon one section of the economy—the commercial interests—and one section of the country—New England—by a party dominated by southern agrarians. The Reverend Samuel Taggart predicted that the revenue would be destroyed, credit ruined, agriculture rotting, and that unemployment, starvation, and economic ruin lay ahead. To Taggart the embargo as a mode of warfare was like the circumstance when "a man humps my toe and hurts a corn; to be revenged, I knock my own brains out." Similar objections were registered from New Orleans, still smarting from the turmoil of the Burr conspiracy. One editor denounced the government for declaring war against its own citizens.[27]

Among Republicans the initial reaction was more favorable, although party leaders in New England expressed fears that the embargo would damage Republican expansion and stimulate "the British party" in that region. Vice President Clinton never approved of the

27. Taggart to Taylor, December 22, 1807, A.A.S. *Proceedings*, p. 224; Thomas P. Abernethy, *The South in the New Nation* (Baton Rouge, La., 1961), p. 322.

measure, and Monroe felt it was hazardous to the Republican cause. Most Republicans, however, reacted with the guarded optimism expressed by John Quincy Adams, who considered it as a "measure eminently calculated for the preservation of peace" by reducing the temptation of the enemy to plunder and to war and by preparing the American people for possibly sterner measures ahead. "I have always considered that the true and only alternative was this—embargo or war; and I remain unshaken in that belief." In preferring embargo to war, he was preferring "the bite of a flea to the bite of a rattlesnake."[28]

Although Jefferson failed adequately to inform the public by proclamation or public message of the real purposes of the embargo, the attempt was made indirectly in the pages of the party organ, the *National Intelligencer*. A series of articles, later attributed to Madison, appeared shortly after the passage of the act, explaining in approving tones the rationale behind the policy. The coercive purpose was referred to as a "collateral effect" of forcing other nations under threat of severe economic injury to "change the system which has driven our commerce from the ocean." In addition, however, the embargo could be expected to produce positive effects domestically, with the growth of manufactures, the conversion by the home market to domestic consumption, and the liberation of Americans from the bondage of foreign fashion and luxuries. The conscious embrace of the alternative of peace over war, furthermore, would go far to develop a national character of virtue, firmness, and moderation, as well as of sacrifice.[29]

The president, while failing to issue a public defense of the embargo, did defend it privately to a wide circle of political correspondents. He used many of the arguments found in the *Intelligencer* articles, including a newfound fondness for manufacturing. His principal defense still rested, however, on the argument that the embargo had averted war and saved American ships from the depredations of the enemy. The coercive intent of the act was implied only in his stated resolve to "discontinue all intercourse with these nations till they should return again to some sense of moral right."[30]

Jefferson had determined to enforce the embargo personally, with Gallatin, and in the early days of the law he was feeling his way with

28. James Sullivan to J. Q. Adams, January 4, 1808, in J. Q. Adams, *Memoirs*, 1:502; White, *Jeffersonians*, pp. 425–426.

29. Peterson, *Thomas Jefferson*, pp. 885–886.

30. Jefferson to Gideon Granger, January 22, 1808, LC No. 30814.

regard to the limits of his power under the act to regulate commerce. Clearly he had little idea in the beginning of the size of the administrative task before him. Nevertheless, both men worked diligently to decide the myriad of details in enforcement procedure and to provide guidance for the customs collectors who would bear the brunt of enforcement in the field.

The initial Embargo Act of December 22[31] had been couched in general language, and problems of interpretation soon emerged as customs officials in different localities placed different meanings on it. Jefferson and Gallatin found themselves exercising the functions of an administrative court of final appeal. The original act had required owners or masters to post bond totaling twice the value of ship and cargo to land in a U.S. port. Foreign vessels in port at the time of passage of the act were permitted to leave, but collectors could not clear any American ship to a foreign country without permission of the president.

Almost immediately Gallatin discovered two major deficiencies in the law. Officials were granted no power of detention or of levying penalties against vessels in violation of the law; and the act applied only to American vessels engaged in foreign trade. Coastal shipping was exempt from the bonds imposed on ocean-going vessels. Acting upon the Treasury secretary's recommendations, Congress passed a second Embargo Act on January 9, 1808, which substantially tightened the original act. It placed coastal shipping under bond not to visit foreign ports. Heavy penalties were provided for ships that left port without clearance—forfeiture of the entire ship and cargo if they were seized; if not, the owner was required to forfeit twice the value of ship and goods. In addition, masters could be fined up to twenty thousand dollars.

Initially it was felt that this second law would be sufficient to insure an adequate enforcement of the embargo. Three lines of enforcement agencies were available to the government: the normal agencies of the Treasury and the courts (collectors, revenue cutters, federal attorneys and marshals, and federal judges); the regular navy; and the militia and regular army. It was assumed in the early days that the first line would be sufficient. On the whole they did creditable work. Enforcement rested ultimately on the allegiance and zeal of the collectors in

---

31. Statues-at-Large, 2 Stat. 451 (December 22, 1807).

the field, and most were consistently loyal and energetic under the most trying of circumstances. A few, accused of collaboration with violators, were removed. Others, though loyal enough, proved incompetent or were simply overwhelmed by the sheer volume of illegal traffic they were supposed to interdict. Most collectors responded adequately, however, and the general record of federal enforcement was satisfactory. Standards and guidelines for collectors were provided through a series of circular letters from the secretary of the Treasury. Gallatin urged them to apply the embargo provisions energetically and to exercise their discretionary powers on the side of detention and investigation in doubtful cases. Local pressures often made it difficult to achieve consistency in administration, however, and partisanship sometimes determined a collector's decision to recommend or oppose the granting of a clearance. "Warm friends of the government" could receive more favorable consideration from officials, although there is no evidence that Jefferson or Gallatin ever used his own authority in narrowly partisan ways.

As the net of the law swept American shipping from the seas, criticism of the embargo mounted. Letters from outraged merchants, ruined seamen, and frightened shopkeepers soon reached the president's desk. Some of these early letters must have touched his sympathy before the monotony of their litany and the partisanship of many hardened him against their pleas. One that must have warmed his heart was a scribble from a Revolutionary War veteran and the father of seven children who, despite the evident hardship caused by the embargo, was "ready to lift my musquit [*sic*] again should there be any invation [*sic*]" by the hated British.[32]

Where the embargo was felt most severely, as in parts of New England, there were partisan opponents of the administration to sustain the violators; Federalist strength showed signs of revival north of New York. Jefferson admitted that "our embargo has worked hard. It has in fact federalized three of the New England states." The High Federalists launched a campaign to cause the legislature of Massachusetts to interpose its opposition to the embargo, and the Pickerings, Cabots, and Parsons began openly to defend the British right of impressment. When the Massachusetts lawmakers passed resolutions condemning the embargo, Senator John Quincy Adams, who had

32. James Lewis to Jefferson, February 16, 1808, LC No. 30979.

fought the growing disunionist sentiment in his native state, resigned his seat in protest.[33]

The virulence of these attacks from New England convinced the president of the partisan nature of opposition to his embargo. This development was unfortunate because it tended to harden his mind against more objective evidence of hardship and discontent. The majority of the letters he received during the spring of 1808, however, supported his intentions and strengthened his resolve to pursue the embargo wholeheartedly.[34]

Jefferson received encouraging dispatches as well from his envoys in Europe, and these carried considerable weight in his mind. James Bowdoin cheered the president with news that the British public was beginning to chafe under the shortages inflicted by the embargo and to stir against the hardliners in the cabinet. Continued economic pressure was all that was wanted to force a reassessment of British policy. Thus heartened, the president ordered Madison to advise the British government (similar advice went to the French) that war would soon be preferable to a continuance of embargo, and that the first nation to repeal her discriminatory decrees against the United States would find an American declaration of war against her enemy.[35] As preparation against such an eventuality, Congress approved the president's request for enlargement of the regular army.[36]

Both the executive and Congress soon felt the need for further improvement in the embargo laws. A bill was introduced to extend the embargo to imports and exports by land as well as by sea in order to curtail the enlarged flow of traffic across the Canadian border. This proved the last straw for some of the Federalists. A New York Con-

33. J. Q. Adams to Harrison Gray Otis, March 31, 1808, Adams, *Writings*, 3:189; Adams, *Memoirs*, May 10, 1808, 1:534–535. Adams's resignation from the Senate removed a valuable supporter of the embargo, one whom Jefferson had sought to use to neutralize some of the opposition to his policies in New England.

34. William Tatham to Jefferson, February 10, 1808, in McPherson, "Letters from North Carolinians," pp. 359–360. The opinion as to the tenor of the majority of letters to Jefferson in this period was formed after a perusal of his correspondence in the Library of Congress collection.

35. James Bowdoin to Jefferson, February 17, 1808, LC 30982; Jefferson to Madison, March 11, 1808, Ford, 11:12–18.

36. Dodd, *Nathaniel Macon*, pp. 226–227. Leonard Levy asserts that Jefferson wanted these additional troops to suppress insurrections against the embargo. There is no reason to doubt Jefferson here, however, in light of his letter to Madison cited above. Besides, no major acts of defiance had by this time (early March) occurred to necessitate such a use of regular forces.

gressman, Barent Gardinier, flayed the House with a violent denunciation of the embargo. The coercive function of the law was now revealed, he argued, since the ban on commerce by land had nothing to do with the protection of shipping. Over calls for order, Gardinier accused the administration of being guided in its policies by the "unseen hand" of Napoleon: "Darkness and mystery overshadow this House and this whole nation. We know nothing, we are permitted to know nothing. We sit here as mere automata; we legislate without knowing, nay Sir, without wishing to know why or wherefore. . . . We are to have faith and find out our own reasons for it."[37] Despite the eloquence of the congressman's plea, the bill passed on March 12.[38] It extended the embargo to land traffic and provided further penalties for violations.

In the spring and early summer, support for the embargo continued to be expressed widely from Pennsylvania south, while the opposition in New England became more strident. Jefferson's conviction that the opposition was Federalist in origin deepened, and his determination to persevere was reinforced. "My principle," he wrote, "is that the convenience of our citizens shall yield reasonably, and their taste generally to the importance of giving the present experiment so fair a trial that on future occasions our legislators may know with certainty how far they may count on it as an engine for national purposes."[39]

Professions of affection for the embargo did not prevent Southerners from violating it. Smuggling in flour, rum, sugar, rice, and other goods into the coves and inlets of North and South Carolina and Georgia flourished. More and more administrative time was taken up by the need to deal with violators. Growing evasions along the Canadian border demanded ever harsher enforcement procedures. Jefferson was driven by events to a more severe advocacy of strict measures. He wanted to give collectors the power to seize goods under *suspicion* of being in violation of the law. Gallatin, opposing this idea as unworkable and "very oppressive," sensed the tragic irony of such a course by a Republican administration.[40] Nevertheless the logic of events seemed to point inexorably to such an expansion of executive power,

37. February 20, 1808, cited in Walter W. Jennings, *The American Embargo: 1807–1809* (Iowa City, Iowa, 1921), pp. 64–65.

38. 2 Stat. 433 (March 12, 1808).

39. Quoted in Levy, *Jefferson and Civil Liberties*, p. 215.

40. Gallatin to Jefferson, April 1, 1808, Gallatin, *Writings*, 1:381.

despite the violence that its exercise inflicted upon Republican doctrine and upon Jefferson's own political style and system of values.

Shortly before it adjourned for the summer, Congress passed a measure that, in Leonard Levy's words, "carried the Administration to the precipice of unlimited and arbitrary power as measured by any American standard then known." The Enforcement Act of April 25, 1808,[41] ended certain relaxations provided for coastal shipping under the previous law. All ships were now required to secure clearance and furnish a certificate to that effect upon landing. To depart even for an American port if it was adjacent to a foreign harbor now required the special permission of the president. For the first time, the president was expressly empowered to employ ships and gunboats of the regular navy to stop ships on mere suspicion. Despite Gallatin's reservations, collectors were authorized to detain coastal shipping on suspicion, pending a decision by the president. The president was empowered to suspend the embargo on his own authority if changes in the foreign situation warranted it. This last provision, a remarkable grant of executive discretion by a Republican Congress, was inserted apparently at the behest of the secretary of state.[42]

Never before in the short history of the republic had a chief executive exercised such a concentration of powers over such a wide range of functions, and none would again for half a century. By its employment of the navy against American citizens, and by its disregard of the constitutional protections against unreasonable search and seizure, the first Enforcement Act certainly rocked the foundations of republicanism. Congress adjourned at the end of April, not to reconvene until October. During the intervening months, Jefferson and Gallatin administered the embargo—in effect controlled every major aspect of the commercial life of the country—without any legislative supervision. Jefferson's great political skills and the sizable administrative talents of his secretary of the Treasury were "pitted against forces which might baffle a superman." The president was determined to use the vast powers granted to him by Congress, "that we may, by a fair experiment, know the power of this great weapon, the embargo." All else increasingly took second place to the embargo; "agriculture, commerce, navigation," all is nothing "when it carries with it the danger of defeating the objects of the Embargo." Ironically, as he

---

41. 2 Stat. 499 (April 25, 1808).
42. J. Q. Adams, *Memoirs*, April 6, 1808, 1:526.

tested the effectiveness of the embargo, Jefferson demonstrated to himself and to those who observed his performance the limits of presidential power, as the maximum use of near dictatorial powers failed to achieve the success he sought. Violations of the embargo continued through the summer, in some locales reaching the point of open rebellion. In response, the president's resolve only stiffened as he applied virtually every means at his disposal to force compliance. Yet success eluded him as the sheer intractability of the problem became ever more evident.[43]

The Opposition Grows

Jefferson continued to hope that the strangulation of European trade by the Embargo would force one or the other of the belligerents to yield. Reports from Europe in the early summer, however, dampened his optimism. Hopes for repeal of the Berlin and Milan Decrees were dashed in late July by reports of Napoleon's resolve to stand firm and his denunciation of American trade as simply a conduit for the transfer of continental money into British coffers. Initial anxiety in Britain gave way in the summer to optimism that the loss of American trade could be neutralized by Wellington's victories in Spain and the consequent opening up of Spain's South American colonies to British traders. This hope was to prove chimerical, but it existed at a time when evidence of British submission was sorely needed in Washington. Jefferson was bitter in his denunciation of the "puffed up" British nation and its government of "no faith," for he knew that only favorable news from Europe could prevent Congress from modifying the embargo when it returned in October, with the very real possibility of a declaration of war.[44]

Students of the embargo agree that it did have some deleterious effects on the economies of France and Britain, especially the latter nation. Prices rose in England, particularly on rice, tobacco, and cotton. The greatest hardship, as in the American Civil War a half century later, was the limitation on the cotton supply. Textile workers suffered the most severely; alas, for Jefferson, they had almost no influence, nor did their employers at this time, upon the British government. The British cabinet, armed with plenary war powers, was

43. Sears, p. 73; Jefferson to Gallatin, May 6, 27, 1808, Lipscomb, 12:52–53, 66.

44. John Armstrong to Jefferson, July 18, 1808, LC Nos. 31781–31785; Jefferson to Thomas Diggs, August 10, 1808, *ibid.*, No. 31853.

not about to yield, especially as the skills of British seamen made smuggling such a prosperous pastime.[45]

Jefferson still received letters of encouragement almost daily from friends of the administration. Many echoed William A. Burwell's assurances that the people would support the embargo with patience as long as it seemed to be the only honorable alternative to war, although it would be hopeless to continue it beyond the autumn, for unless success seemed imminent then, the people would demand a new direction for their energies. Jefferson took comfort from these somewhat lukewarm assurances and sought to bolster his policy through private correspondence. He sensed that the body of American citizens heartily approved and supported the embargo. He denounced the Federalists for fomenting trouble, and warned his correspondents that should the embargo fail the alternative must surely be war.[46]

Cracks were beginning to appear once again in the surface of Republican party unity. As the embargo dragged on without signs of success, party behavior throughout New England showed definite signs of strain. Disaffection surfaced elsewhere as well. The pressure of events began to exact its toll on Jefferson's celebrated magnanimity. He seems to have lost some of his innate courtesy and deference in dealing with members of Congress. The political style that had proved so effective in earlier situations was suffering a severe jolt. Leaders who had quietly supported the embargo despite evidence of its ill effects in their states were little consulted; grumbled Macon, "we feel as much out of fashion as our grandmother's ruffle cuffs."[47]

The embargo enabled partisan editors to outdo themselves in political invective. Republican editors defended it as a noble alternative to war, while the Federalists denounced it as a tool of French foreign policy. The Republican *Washington Monitor*, Madison's organ, printed a widely quoted comparison between the "temporary inconvenience" and minor economic loss caused by the embargo and the "loss of millions of dollars, burning and sacking of towns and cities, rape, theft, murders, streams of blood, weeping widows, helpless orphans, the beggary of thousands" which would result from war. A Federalist

45. Jennings, pp. 72–73, 79; see also Sears, chaps. 9–10, and White, *Jeffersonians*, p. 471.
46. William A. Burwell to Jefferson, May 21, 1808, LC 31461; Jefferson to Gen. Benjamin Smith, 20 May, 1808, Ford, 11:31–32, and to Thomas Leib, June 23, 1808, pp. 33–35.
47. Ammon, "Richmond Junto," p. 404n; Chambers, *Political Parties*, p. 187.

editor meanwhile resorted to the sarcasm of riddle to underscore his contempt for Jeffersonian policies:

> Why is the Embargo like good strong coffee?
> Because Bonaparte is remarkably fond of it. . . .
> Why is the Embargo like red wine when we have no white?
> Because it makes us stick to *Port*.[48]

Tracking down violators absorbed more and more time during these months. The obscure inlets of Georgia and South Carolina continued to conceal an active smuggling trade in goods from the West Indies. But it was along the Canadian border that the most serious violations occurred. After the Embargo Act of March 12 had sealed off land as well as seaborne traffic, evasions mounted. Jefferson, who had opposed the legitimate use of governmental coercion against the Pennsylvania farmers in the Whiskey Rebellion a decade earlier, was forced by the logic of his present position to use all the coercive powers at his disposal to control the behavior of the farmers of New York, Vermont, and Maine. Smuggling in these border regions along the St. Lawrence River became so systematic that collectors were resigning rather than trying to enforce the law in the teeth of neighborhood hostility.[49]

Jefferson decided to meet force with force. He told Gallatin to inform the collectors that *every* shipment of provisions should be considered "as sufficiently suspicious for detention and reference here." As Treasury cutters proved unable to handle the problem, Jefferson ordered the navy to cooperate. There is a tragic irony in this reliance upon the navy, which the president had worked to reduce, to wage war on his own people; but the embargo's success now outweighed almost all other considerations in his mind. As he observed to Secretary Smith, "I do consider the severe enforcement of the embargo to be of an importance not to be measured by money for our future government as well as present objects." The navy, long out of favor, responded admirably and was of major assistance in aiding the beleaguered revenue cutters of the Treasury.[50]

48. *Northampton* (Massachusetts) *Republican Spy*, July 20, 1808; *Massachusetts Spy* or *Worcester Gazette*, September 21, 1808, in Jennings, p. 44.

49. See Ford, "Duane Letters," pp. 310–311; Gallatin to Jefferson, May 16, 1808, Gallatin, *Writings*, 1:387–389, May 23, 1808, pp. 390–391. Gallatin reported that revenue boats had been fired upon and open violations continued.

50. Jefferson to Gallatin, May 6, 1808, Gallatin, *Writings*, 1:385–386; to Robert Smith, July 16, 1808, Lipscomb, 12:93.

Flour was a commodity tailor-made for the smuggler and many of the violations in coastal traffic involved its illegal movement. To ease the problem for collectors in deciding when to detain a shipment, Jefferson created the "Governor's Certificate of Necessity," whereby a governor could grant permission for a specified shipper to import a specified amount of flour to meet the domestic needs of a stated locality. Jefferson hoped in this manner to insure a sufficient supply of necessities while preventing need from serving as a cover for violations. He also hoped to decentralize the administration of the embargo in accordance with his general view of administration and to broaden the responsibility (and divert some of the criticism) away from Washington and on to the shoulders of the governors.[51]

Gallatin objected to this grant of discretion as unnecessary and less efficient than the uniform control by the Treasury. Decentralization was a noble objective, but the administration would thereby lose control to men "who were afraid of clamor and of popularity." He cautioned, "Knowing Governors Sullivan and Charles Pinckney as we do, we can have no confidence in the last, and must rest assured that the other will refuse no certificates." Pinckney and most of the other governors actually caused no problem, but Gallatin's fears of Sullivan's timidity proved well founded. He could refuse practically no one and the violations of the spirit of the regulation under his lax authority became little short of scandalous. Jefferson called Sullivan to heel, but the governor, dreading the cost to his popularity that enforcement would exact, continued to look the other way when known smugglers requested and received his certificates. The leak was not finally stemmed until Sullivan's death in December and his replacement by the loyal Levi Lincoln.[52]

Jefferson's rapidly expanding view of executive discretion in enforcement met resistance from an unexpected source, one of his own appointees to the Supreme Court. Customs officials had been granted authority by Congress in the Enforcement Act of April 25 to detain vessels on suspicion of intent to violate the embargo. Jefferson in a circular letter forwarded by Gallatin to the collectors had interpreted

51. Jefferson to the governors of Georgia, South Carolina, Massachusetts, New Hampshire, and New Orleans Territory, May 6, 1808, Lipscomb, 12:51–52.

52. Gallatin to Jefferson, May 23, 1808, Gallatin, *Writings*, 1:391; also May 28, 1808, pp. 393–394, and July 15, 1808, p. 394; Sullivan to Jefferson, July 23, 1808, LC Nos. 31751–31753; Jefferson to Dearborn, August 9, 1808, Ford, 11:40–41; Gallatin to Jefferson, September 16, 1808, Gallatin, *Writings*, 1:418.

the statute as if it vested the power in the president himself. He gave the collectors detailed guidance which limited their own discretion. In a case in the circuit court of South Carolina involving a Charleston merchant denied a clearance on the basis of the president's letter, Justice William Johnson ruled that the president had exceeded his statutory authority with regard to detention. In a studied rebuke of the president who appointed him, Johnson cautioned that "the officers of the government, from highest to lowest, are equally subject to legal restraint," and all should avoid any "unsanctioned encroachment upon individual liberty."[53] Such a choice of words must have particularly rankled Jefferson, whose reputation rested in part on his avowed concern for individual liberties. The opinion reflects the extent to which Jefferson's conduct of his office was beginning to conflict with the public expectations even of those who might be expected to sympathize with him. The decision served to confuse the administration of the embargo in the field and provided added ammunition to those who were chipping away at presidential prestige.

As the summer drew to a close and the time for Congress to meet neared, Gallatin's growing pessimism with regard to the embargo caused him to consider the reasons for its failure to date and the hard choices that faced the administration in the near future. His letter to Jefferson underscores the general malaise that afflicted administration policy-makers and the evils the embargo's enforcement was doing to traditional American values. Reflecting first upon the continued violations in New York and New England, the secretary ascribed their cause to the early inefficiencies in the law itself, to the want of energy in enforcing it of federal officials in the field, "together with avarice and the open encouragement by Federalists." A greater cause, however, could be found in the lack of a "single object which might rouse their patriotism and unite their passions and affections; selfishness has assumed the reins in several quarters." These remarks reveal Gallatin's awareness of the true problem that policies such as an embargo pose for policy-makers: the enervating effect upon the public spirit of a policy that demands not action but inaction, not instantaneous gratification through physical exertion but a deferred reward earned by patience and long-suffering endurance. Such a policy in fact demands

---

53. *Gilchrist, et al.* v. *Collector of Port of Charleston* (10 Fed. Cases 355, C.C. District of South Carolina, 5420), May 28, 1808.

more of human nature than a war policy demands, for a "just" war has precisely the tendency to rouse a people's patriotism and "unite their passions and affections" in such a way as to galvanize and mobilize the popular will to sacrifice. The embargo, furthermore, provided no timetable for success, no guideposts by which the people could gauge progress. Jefferson and his advisers were calling upon the people, in Sear's words, to sacrifice "not their lives but only their moneybags,"[54] and the ironical truth is that often people can be more readily persuaded to surrender the former than the latter.

Despite the growing recognition by Jefferson and Gallatin of the full dimensions of their difficulty, they revealed in their summer exchanges the bankruptcy of administration thinking on the prospects for solving it. Gallatin saw only two alternatives to pursue: either the president must be given the "most arbitrary powers and sufficient force to carry the Embargo into effect or give it up altogether."[55] He recommended two courses of action: first, not a single vessel be permitted to move without direct permission of the president; and second, collectors be given power to seize property anywhere and if necessary to disable a vessel to prevent its departure from harbor.

Jefferson in reply confessed his own bewilderment at the course of events. "This embargo law is certainly the most embarrassing one we have had to execute. I did not expect a crop of so sudden and rank growth of fraud and open opposition by force could have grown up in the United States." Yet he could bring himself to consider no alternative to a draconian enforcement of the embargo, save war, which he seems to have ruled out. "I am satisfied with you that if orders and decrees are not repealed, and a continuation of the embargo is preferred to war (which sentiment is universal here), Congress must legalize all *means* which may be necessary to obtain its end."[56] Both leaders seemed to consider only the two extremes; they seem to have given no thought to a revival of one of the more moderate alternatives of action considered and rejected earlier. The monetary costs of the embargo to date and the likely costs of war should it come were alike greater than the expense of the construction of a fleet of warships to convoy American merchant vessels would have been.

54. Gallatin to Jefferson, July 29, 1808, Gallatin, *Writings*, 1:396–399; Sears, p. 74.
55. Gallatin to Jefferson, July 29, 1808, cited in note 54.
56. Jefferson to Gallatin, August 11, 1808, Ford, 11:41, emphasis in the original.

Fears of the political effects of a continuation of the embargo also pressed upon the minds of the president and his advisers. In August Gallatin was dreading the loss of the presidential election unless a successful outcome of the embargo was achieved by October. Madison could still assure the Treasury head that the public mind in Virginia "appears to be unshaken," but Gallatin felt he could rely only on the states of the West and Virginia, South Carolina, and perhaps Georgia as sound.[57]

Despite charges by the Federalists that the embargo was a southern agrarian plot against the commercial interests of New England, it was the southern agrarians who suffered most deeply under the restrictions of trade. Planters and farmers had not enjoyed the enormous profits gained by their northern brethren in the years before the embargo. Prices of domestic produce fell markedly in 1808, while the price of imported products soared. The economy of the southern states was insufficiently diversified to permit the shift of resources to manufacturing which occurred in the middle Atlantic and New England regions.

With a few notable exceptions, however, it was the people of the South who most readily accepted the hardships and restrictions of Jefferson's embargo. In some quarters men seemed to wear their losses as badges of distinction, as a mark of greater sacrifice for their country. The economic "irrationality" of this southern acceptance in the face of economic disaster must be attributed to the political persuasion of the people of the region. Viewing the southern experience, one can understand Jefferson's contention that the fierce resistance of New England was fostered not so much by economic hardship per se as by political opposition. Support for the embargo in the South became a measure of faith for all loyal Republicans, and while loyalty was not uniform and pockets of opposition certainly existed, support for Jefferson and the Virginia dynasty was the determining factor in southern adherence to the embargo.[58]

Republican fortunes suffered their most serious setbacks in New England, where the embargo had, in Jefferson's words, succeeded in "federalizing three states" and weakening the party in the other two. Initially, there was substantial support for the measure among New England merchants and financiers, particularly those who were Re-

57. Gallatin to Jefferson, August 6, 1808, LC No. 31827; Madison to Gallatin, August 31, 1808, in Gallatin, *Writings*, 1:41–42.

58. On this point, see Sears, pp. 230–231.

publicans. Many in the merchant class preferred an embargo to war or continual seizures by the British navy, and they were unwilling to sacrifice continental trade to appease the British. But as the embargo ate deeply into the economic structure of the region, attitudes began to change. At the height of the embargo 30,000 seamen were out of work, and the industries associated with seaborne trade were idle. The merchant community, which voiced the loudest opposition, was not so severely damaged as the working classes, however. Boston suffered less than New York. Nevertheless, the aggressive political opposition of the Federalists who sought a return to power on the strength of the embargo's failure set the tone for the reaction that steadily set in. Talk of disunion was fairly common, and pro-British sentiment was high. The Republicans throughout the region were forced on the defensive. They charged the Federalists with disrupting the integrity of the Union, of an active smear campaign against the embargo, of pro-British sympathies, but they had to admit the harshness of the policy even while stressing its patriotic necessity and urging the people to put aside selfish interests in favor of honor and national pride.[59]

The political losses suffered by the Republicans in New England were serious but, as it turned, out not permanent. Even more troublesome for the hopes of a continuation of the embargo was the transformation in attitude experienced by the New England Republicans themselves. Many who had supported the measure in its early months came to Washington in November, 1808, prepared to modify or repeal it. Orchard Cook, a pro-embargo congressman from the District of Maine, for example, was forced under pressure from the lumber exporters in his region to join with Joseph Story, Ezekiel Bacon, and others in working for repeal. The changing attitude of Levi Lincoln exemplifies the altered view of many New Englanders. Lincoln, who had written in April of the unabated confidence and support of the people in their government's policies, was by September favoring the most flexible interpretation of the law possible.[60]

Presidential Leadership Falters

Such was the mood of the people and the political prospects for the

---

59. Goodman, p. 192–197; Peterson, *Thomas Jefferson*, pp. 892–893; John Quincy Adams to Plumer, October 6, 1810, in Goodman, p. 198; Purcell, *Connecticut in Transition*, pp 176–177; *Boston Independent Chronicle*, December 13, 1808.
60. Goodman, p. 197; Lincoln to Jefferson, September 10, 1808, LC. 32051.

Republican party as Jefferson faced the coming congressional session and the likely changes that the embargo would undergo unless some material progress could be reported from Europe. He continued to receive encouragement from Pinkney in London, but he doubted that minister's judgment of the good faith of George Canning and the British government. From France, John Armstrong reported the continuing obstinacy of Napoleon as he preserved a satisfied silence in the face of American overtures.[61]

As the instances of violations of the embargo grew into a pattern of systematic evasion, Jefferson grew more severe in his attitude toward enforcement. He spoke of the possible condemnation of whole communities rather than the punishment of individual violators. He seemed to embrace guilt by association and the implication that men are guilty until proven innocent as he urged that "we may fairly require proof that the individual of a town tainted with a general spirit of disobedience has never said or done anything himself to countenance that spirit." The president even approved one attempt to indict a group of embargo violators on a charge of treason, but the case was indignantly thrown out of court by another Jefferson appointee, Brockholst Livingston.[62]

Jefferson's sole victory in the federal courts on the embargo was tinged with gall, for it came at the hands of a staunch Federalist in Massachusetts. Judge John Davis sustained the constitutionality of the Embargo Acts, basing his decision upon a broad construction of the "commerce" clause and the inherent sovereignty of the United States under the "necessary and proper" clause. Elsewhere, as in Johnson's *Gilchrist* decision and a later case voiding criminal indictments under the Embargo Acts, the courts tended to weaken enforcement and thereby further to convince the beleaguered president of the partisan malice of the judges.[63]

61. Jefferson to John W. Eppes, September 20, 1808, LC 32100; Armstrong to Jefferson, October 27, 1808, No. 32121.

62. Jefferson to Gallatin, November 13, 1808, Lipscomb, 12:194. On the treason charge, see Jefferson to Gallatin, September 9, 1808, p. 160. The case was *United States* v. *Hoxie*, 26 Fed. Cases 15, 407 (C.C. District of Vermont). Jefferson also considered having all the boats and canoes on the American side of the St. Lawrence River destroyed with compensation, but Gallatin quashed the idea (Jefferson to Gallatin, December 28, 1808, p. 221).

63. *United States* v. *Brigantine William*, 28 Fed. Cases 614, (October 3, 1808), C.C. District of Massachusetts; *United States* v. *William Smith*, in Warren, *Supreme Court*, 1:355–356.

By November, 1808, when Congress met, the lifespan of the embargo was rapidly approaching its limit. During the crucial summer months when Jefferson and Gallatin had exercised a free hand in enforcement, the legislators had been at home in their districts where discussions with their constituents had informed them of the impact the laws had made directly on the people. They returned to Washington with their confidence shaken and their thoughts reflecting different conclusions about the efficacy of continuing the embargo.

Wide room for executive leadership still remained, however, in determining upon a new policy or a modification of the old. Congressional Republicans were of at least three minds: some for war, others for a stronger embargo, still others for peace without embargo. "By the little conversation I have had with members," wrote Jefferson, "I perceive there will be some divisions on this among the Republicans, but what will be its extent cannot be known till they shall have . . . had some days to confer and make up their opinions."[64]

The cabinet had discussed alternatives during October, but no agreement had been reached. The need for some change in policy was evident to all, but whether the embargo should be repealed or modified or replaced by a selective non-intercourse measure and when such action should be taken remained questions without answers. Jefferson did instruct Gallatin to prepare a bill to correct additional defects in the existing legislation, but agreed that this would in no way commit Congress to a continuance beyond the spring.[65]

The president greeted Congress with a confession of failure, a promise of perseverance, and little else. In his annual message on November 8, he spoke of the rejections by Britain and France of American proposals for settlement of the differences between them. Despite these setbacks, he listed the achievements of the embargo in saving shipping, providing time to prepare defenses, and demonstrating to the world the moderation and firmness of the American nation in the face of repeated provocations. The message included no recommendations for congressional consideration, however; "it will rest with the wisdom of Congress to decide on the course best adapted to such a state of things," to "weigh and compare the painful alternatives out of which a choice is to be made."[66] The president had publicly deferred in such a

64. Jefferson to Gallatin, November 8, 1808, LC No. 32347.
65. Jefferson to Gallatin, October 25, 1808, Gallatin, *Writings*, 1:419–420.
66. Annual message, November 8, 1808, Ford, 11:56–72.

way to Congress before, but always in the past he had followed it up with drafts of proposed legislation and private efforts to mobilize support for their passage. This time, however, the follow-up did not occur. He included at the close of his address remarks instead of a valedictory nature, alluding to his "retiring from the charge" of affairs, remarks that hardly seemed appropriate at the start of such a crucial session.

Gallatin sensed the drift in executive leadership and sought to avoid the chaos of a leaderless Congress cut loose to find for itself a way out of the situation. Unable to find a solution himself, Gallatin urged Jefferson to convene a cabinet and decide some "precise and distinct course" for Congress to pursue. "I think that we must, or rather *you* must, decide the question absolutely, so that we may point out a decisive course either way to our friends."[67]

The president, however, chose this time virtually to abdicate his leadership and withdraw from responsibility for the formulation of new policy. He had announced his intention to retire as early as March, 1806, an announcement that Plumer foresaw as "letting down his importance—Most men shun the setting, but all seek the rising sun." Now with the election of his successor imminent and with the identity of that successor all but a certainty, Jefferson decided to leave the major decisions of policy to Madison. As he confided to Lincoln early in the congressional session: "On this occasion, I think it is fair to leave to those who are to act on them, the decisions they prefer, being to be myself but a spectator. I should not feel justified in directing measures which those who are to execute them would disapprove."[68]

The precise reasons for Jefferson's abdication of leadership four months before his surrender of the responsibility of office remain wrapped in enigma. He said he wished to give Madison a free hand unfettered by his own lame-duck decisions. Perhaps the bitter legacy bequeathed to him by his predecessor, Adams—the midnight appointments, and so on—made him sensitive to the need to avoid such a mistake with his successor. Madison, however, was his own colleague. Their philosophies and policies were almost as one, with Madison being one of the more vocal champions of the embargo.

67. Gallatin to Jefferson, November 15, 1808, Gallatin, *Writings*, 1:428, emphasis added.

68. Plumer, *Memorandum*, March 16, 1806, p. 453; Jefferson to Levi Lincoln, November 13, 1808, Ford, 11:73–75.

Madison's victory by an electoral vote of 122 to 47, while not of Jeffersonian magnitude, could be interpreted, nonetheless, as a general vindication of Jeffersonian policies and a wish for their continuance. If consideration for Madison was indeed the only motive for withdrawal from leadership, Jefferson's behavior here conflicts sharply with the keen sensitivity to power resources that he expressed and displayed on most other occasions during his presidency. He knew the importance of executive direction in keeping Congress on track; indeed, it was central to his view of executive leadership. To fail to perceive the void that his abdicating (without relinquishing the responsibility) would create was, considering past behavior, a remarkable lapse.

Leonard White sees his withdrawal as resulting from a massive loss of self-confidence amid the defeat of the embargo. This may be a partial explanation, although his withdrawal began in mid-November, well before the fate of his embargo was known and at a time when the available evidence points to his conviction of its ultimate success. Still, a psychological explanation may be the most satisfactory under the circumstances. His surrender of policy initiative at this time may have been related in a larger sense to his desire to escape from conflict. One of the recognized methods among political actors for the resolution of conflict is illness or resignation. One form of "resignation" might well be a psychological abdication of power.[69] Jefferson was heartily tired of public office by this time, and anticipated with great relief his impending retirement. As a sensitive man, always loathe to engage in the brawl of political life and weary with the fatigue of a hundred battles, he may well have chosen this means to resolve the conflicts that grew out of his embargo policy. Then, too, his pride may have prevented him from submitting to the petty defeats and snubs that he could expect as a lame-duck president whose power was draining away to others. He had a foretaste of this in the rejection of a minor nomination to office which he had taken "every private occasion" to promote and the outcome of which he learned "with much mortification."[70]

69. White, *Jeffersonians*, p. 7. For discussions of this phenomenon, see Toby, "Some Variables in Role Conflict Analysis," p. 326, and McFarland, "Role and Role Conflict," pp. 9–15. It was about this time that Jefferson wrote his letter to his grandson advising politeness and the avoidance of argument as the hallmarks of a proper public as well as private character.

70. Jefferson to St. George Tucker, December 8, 1808, LC No. 32512.

Whatever the reasons for his withdrawal from active policy leadership, he pursued his new role as "unmeddling listener to what others say" with discouraging consistency. He did not withdraw completely, of course; he still talked privately with congressmen and private citizens, shared his general views with them and sought their specific views in turn. He kept informed of developments as they occurred and continued his correspondence. He maintained a keen interest in seeing the embargo through to success. He made no effort, however, to guide Congress or indeed his own cabinet colleagues, Madison and Gallatin, in the formulation of policy. As he confided to Monroe: "I am now so near the moment of retiring that I take no part in affairs beyond the expression of an opinion. I think it is fair that my successor should now originate those measures of which he will be charged with the execution and responsibility and that it is my duty to clothe them with the forms of authority."[71]

Such a solution was doomed to failure. Without the final responsibility Madison could not act with final authority. Jefferson still possessed not only the "forms" but the substance of authority, his was still the regnant star, and without his prestige, lacking his position as the architect of the Republican program and the leader of all factions in the party, Madison could not hope to create and guide through Congress a program that would be acceptable to the party and the country as authoritative and legitimate.

Madison and Gallatin did try to guide Congress's deliberations, but they never really had control. Having in the past acted only as agents of the president, they could not now on their own behalf but within the shadow of the still serving Jefferson expect to end the confusion that beset the members of Congress. Word soon spread of the president's withdrawal. Samuel Taggart reported "considerable fluttering among the troops of the palace." Macon confessed to the confusion in Congress in the absence of executive direction: "The war men in the House of Representatives are, I conceive, gaining strength, and I should not be surprised if we should not be at war with both Great Britain and France before the 4th of March. Gallatin is most decidedly for war, and I think the V.P. and W. C. Nicholas are of the same opinion. It is said that the President gives no opinion as to the measure that ought to be adopted; it is not known whether he be for war or for

71. Jefferson to George Logan, December 27, 1808, *ibid.*, No. 32634; to Monroe, January 28, 1809, Ford, 11:93–96.

peace."[72] Such was the situation as Congress set about deliberating the proper course to take in the crucial months ahead.

The Congress Tries its Hand

In the absence of any new policy decisions, Madison and Gallatin determined to proceed as if a condition of status quo existed. At the president's suggestion, Gallatin sent a list of ideas for revisions in the existing embargo laws to Giles, advocating increased bonding requirements on coastal shipping and more centralized power of detention for the president to exercise personally. He also corresponded with Campbell, the Republican leader in the House, and in fact wrote the report issued by Campbell's Committee on the Embargo in November, reaffirming the expediency of resisting the belligerents by means of the embargo.[73] This initial activity succeeded momentarily in stiffening the resolve of both Houses to defeat attempts to repeal it.

Already, however, control of the situation was slipping from the hands of the administration as Jefferson declined to provide the needed direction. He revealed the perplexity and waywardness of members of Congress in a letter to his son-in-law in late November, informing him of action contemplated by congressional leaders to forestall any final decision between embargo or war until near the close of the session. By mid-December, the confusion was even more apparent.

There is a sincere wish to take off the embargo before Congress rises prevailing with everybody but the Federalists who (notwithstanding their clamors) it is perfectly known would deprecate it as their greatest calamity. The difficulty is how to separate the belligerents so as to have trade with one while we have war with the other; because a war with both continues the embargo in effect with war added to it. Perhaps time may be taken early in summer to get a repeal of edicts by one party, and Congress meet in May or June to declare war against the other. But this is conjectural.[74]

While Congress was moving with its left hand toward some major policy demarche, with its right it was working to stiffen the existing embargo laws. A Senate committee under Giles completed work on

72. Taggart to Taylor, December 30, 1808, A.A.S. *Proceedings*, pp. 328–329; Macon to Joseph H. Nicholson, December 4, 1808, in Dodd, p. 239.

73. Gallatin to Giles, November 24, 1808, Gallatin, *Writings*, 1:428–435; see the copy of the committee report in *ibid.*, pp. 435–446.

74. Jefferson to T. M. Randolph, November 22, 1808, LC No. 32402, and December 13, 1808, No. 32550.

the fifth and most stringent of the acts to toughen enforcement procedures. The bill followed closely upon Gallatin's recommendations. It forbade the act of *loading* a ship or land vehicle without express permission of a customs collector, and the collectors were explicitly placed under the policy guidance of the president (to circumvent the *Gilchrist* decision). Capture, distress, or accident were no longer accepted as excuses for coastal vessels touching at foreign ports. The most extraordinary provision of this act was the grant of power to collectors to call out the regular army, navy, or state militia to enforce the embargo.[75]

The bill passed the Senate on December 21 by a partisan vote. It met rougher going in the House, however, where New England Republicans faced a dilemma of conflicting loyalties. They wished to support the administration as party loyalty and past history dictated; yet the pressures of constituency discontent and their own growing doubt of the embargo's utility made the decision a difficult one. Friends of the government sought to stiffen their resolve. John Quincy Adams, by now an avowed administration supporter (though no longer in the Senate), urged his New England friends in Congress not "to weaken the government's position further in the face of the inveteracy of its opponents."[76]

Despite the hesitations of many members, the act passed the House on January 6, 1809, by a vote of 71 to 32. Significantly, 19 of the "nay" votes came from New England. Three days later the President signed it into law. This lopsided approval might be interpreted as a decisive vindication of the embargo by the people's representatives, but the victory was pyrrhic indeed. The harshness of the act represented to many the emptiness of administration thinking. As Merrill Peterson has written, "the measure mocked every principle Jefferson held except the one principle, that of the Embargo itself, which he believed the crisis of affairs had made a national imperative." Leonard Levy calls the fifth Embargo Act "the most oppressive and unconstitutional legislation ever enacted by Congress in time of peace."[77]

75. 2 Stat. 506 (January 9, 1809); Jefferson to Charles Simms, January 22, 1809, Lipscomb, 12:239.
76. J. Q. Adams to Nahum Parker, December 5, 1808, also to Orchard Cook, December 8, 1808, J. Q. Adams, *Writings*, 3:259–260; the *Portsmouth Oracle* of January 21, 1809, reported the uneasiness of a New Hampshire member in voting for the Enforcement Act.
77. Peterson, *Thomas Jefferson*, p. 913; Levy, p. 139.

The legislation marked the final insult to New England. Federalist editors denounced the measure as despotic. William Coleman informed his *New York Evening Post* readers that the bill "places the country under the arbitrary and absolute will of the President;—his mere instructions—are rendered paramount over the laws of the land . . . and the constitution itself." Other critics saw the act as evidence of the impending repeal of the embargo. One Federalist congressman assured a constituent that "though it becomes a law, it never can nor never will be carried into effect, and I hardly think it is really believed that it will." A Baltimore writer had it on good authority that the "drill sergeants of the palatine troops" passed the bill only after they were assured that it was preparatory to a removal of the embargo. Republican papers attempted to counterattack with praise for the government's firmness, but the uproar in New England reached such proportions as to alarm the administration with fears of nullification or even secession. Town meetings demanding repeal of the embargo were followed by a threatened noncompliance with the law by the legislature of Massachusetts.[78] The New England Republicans in Congress were now fully alarmed by the violence of the opposition in their home districts. They were not prepared to risk their seats and their careers for a policy that not even the president was willing any longer to defend in public. Efforts at military repression of resisters, they feared, might lead to open civil war in New England. The young Massachusetts congressman Joseph Story feared attempts by the Essex Junto to effect a separation of the eastern states from the Union.[79]

Under mounting pressure the House passed a resolution on January 30 calling for a special session of the new Congress elected in the preceding fall to meet on May 22. Jefferson tried to interpret this new development: "This substantially decides the course they mean to pursue; that is, to let the embargo continue until then, when it will

78. *New York Evening Post*, January 3, 1809; see also *United States Gazette* of Philadelphia, January 12, 1809; Taggart to Taylor, January 7, 1809, A.A.S. *Proceedings*, p. 330; (Baltimore) *Federal Republican*, January 16, 1809. For Republican opinion, see, for example, Ritchie's *Richmond Enquirer*, January 12, 1809; (Hartford) *American Mercury*, January 19, 1809; and (Portsmouth) *New Hampshire Gazette*, January 17, 24, 1809. On the legislature's actions, see Timothy Pickering to S. P. Gardner, no date (presumably January, 1809) in Henry Adams, *Documents*, p. 380.

79. J. Q. Adams to Ezekiel Bacon, November 17, 1808, J. Q. Adams, *Writings*, 3:250–251; William W. Story, ed., *Life and Letters of Joseph Story* (Boston, 1851), 1:174.

cease, and letters of marque and reprisal be issued against such nations as shall not then have repealed their obnoxious edicts."[80] He was reduced to hoping that something of his policy would be salvaged in the weeks ahead, but matters were now rushing to an unpredictable conclusion.

A revulsion from the embargo continued to spread through New England. Republican editors, anticipating the desire of many congressmen to flee from it as from a plague, sought to drum up war fever among the people to pressure Congress into voting a war as a replacement. Ritchie saw no alternative but to "fly to arms" against Great Britain. Madison's Washington organ, the *Monitor*, was calling its readers to the colors "in a righteous cause; on the side of Heaven." Other Republican papers were less certain of American ability to wage a successful war to defend commercial rights. Said one, it would be the most "foolhardy bravery or the deepest insanity, to *Put our heads out*, when we all know so well that they would be taken off."[81]

In Congress a collection of Republican dissidents—mostly Quids and anti-Madison supporters of Clinton—joined temporarily with the uneasy New Englanders in a revolt against the party leadership who, without help from the executive, was powerless to stem it. On January 30, Nicholas introduced a resolution for repeal of the embargo beyond a certain date left blank, and its replacement by letters of marque and reprisal. He suggested filling in the blank with "June 1." John Randolph suggested "immediately." This was defeated, but a few days later in a revolt the House voted to insert "March 4," the date (not coincidentally) for the inauguration of a new president.

The administration, without Jefferson's leadership, was no longer in control of the situation and could do nothing. Jefferson's own conviction of the rightness of his policy blinded him to the drift of public opinion, which he had always prided himself on sensing. So unaware had he become of changing moods in the congressional majority that he could write to his son-in-law the day after the crucial vote in the House:

I thought Congress had taken their ground firmly for continuing their embargo till June, and then war. But a sudden and unaccountable revolution of

80. Jefferson to Thomas Leiper, January 21, 1809, Lipscomb, 12:237; see also Jefferson to T. M. Randolph, January 2, 1809, LC No. 32735.

81. *Connecticut Courant*, February 3, 1809; *Richmond Enquirer*, January 7, 1809; *Washington Monitor*, January 10, 1809; *Virginia Argus*, January 17, 1809, emphasis in the original.

opinion took place the last week, chiefly among the New England and New York members, and in a kind of panic they voted the 4th of March for removing the embargo, and by such a majority as gave all reason to believe they would not agree either to war or non-intercourse. . . . The majority of Congress, however, has now rallied to the removing of the embargo on the 4th of March, non-intercourse with France and Great Britain, trade everywhere else, and continuing war preparations.

Not even the non-intercourse alternative was a certainty at this point; administration leaders had to work hard in late February to salvage even this much of the president's policy, and in a final snub the House removed the clause for issuance of letters of marque and reprisal.[82]

The precise combination of persons and pressures that engineered the repeal is not known. Certainly the public pressures from the people of New England and New York upon their delegations were of great importance, and the conviction that the embargo no longer represented a workable policy was fairly general among congressional Republicans. There can be little doubt that the removal at this crucial stage of Jefferson's guiding hand was of major significance in determining the nature and the timing of repeal. In his bitterness the president attributed the downfall of his policy to the "ascendancy which Great Britain exercises over us" and her ability to force the legislative and executive authorities "from the measures which their judgment would have approved." He saw the majority in Congress, *his* majority, "driven from the ground they had taken by a minority availing themselves of transient delusions." He focused his wrath upon one man in particular, Massachusetts congressman Joseph Story, a "pseudo-republican" who "came on . . . and staid [*sic*] only a few days, long enough, however, to get complete control of Bacon, who giving in . . . became panick struck, and communicated his panick to his colleagues, and they to a majority of the sound members of Congress."[83]

Story saw it differently. The Enforcement Act of January 9, by its very severity, seemed to mark the end of the embargo's effectiveness. He recorded the heavy pressures brought upon him by Giles, Nicholas, and Campbell, among others, to yield his opinion to that of the administration.

82. Jefferson to T. M. Randolph, January 31, 1809, LC No. 32919, and February 7, 28, 1809, Lipscomb, 12:248, 257–258.
83. Jefferson to Alexander Macrae, February 8, 1809, LC No. 32990; to Henry Dearborn, July 16, 1810, Ford, 11:143–144.

I knew at the time, that Mr. Jefferson had no ulterior motive in view, and was determined on protecting the embargo for an indefinite period, even for years. I was well satisfied that such a course would not and could not be borne by New England and would bring on a direct rebellion. It would be the ruin of the whole country. Yet Mr. Jefferson with his usual visionary obstinacy, was determined to maintain it, and the New England Republicans were to be made the instruments. Mr. Bacon and myself resisted, and measures were concerted by us, with the aid of Pennsylvania, to compel him to abandon his mad scheme.[84]

Final repeal of the embargo occurred on February 28, and on March 1, three days before its effective date and three days before his final retirement from public life, Jefferson was constrained to sign the repeal bill into law. It is little wonder that he looked upon his impending retirement with eager anticipation. Confiding to an old friend the joy he felt in returning to family, books, and farm, he confessed: "Never did a prisoner, released from his chains, feel such relief as I shall on shaking off the shackles of power. Nature intended me for the tranquil pursuits of science. . . . But the enormities of the times in which I have lived, have forced me to take part in resisting them, and to commit myself on the boisterous ocean of political passions. I thank God for the opportunity of retiring from them without censure, and carrying with me the most consoling proofs of public approbation."[85]

This last statement reflects one of the most remarkable facts of these months. Despite the damage to his programs and the tarnish to his professional reputation, Jefferson left office with his general popularity little impaired by the course of recent events. The symbolic Jefferson maintained for the most part a high luster. He did not carry with him into retirement the contempt and repudiation that can be and often is inflicted upon a retiring president whose greatest policy has been discredited. There is no accurate way of measuring the complexion of public opinion concerning Jefferson as he left office, but the nature and volume of adulatory letters, addresses, and memorials which poured into the executive mansion in these weeks and the unanimity of the party press in its praise for Jefferson's accomplishments and performance would seem to indicate at least among the party faithful a popularity uniquely resistant to erosion from policy reverses. Few encomiums were received from New England, where the newspapers,

84. Joseph Story to Edward Everett, in Story, 1:187.
85. 2 Stat. 528 (March 1, 1809); Jefferson to Dupont de Nemours, March 2, 1809, Lipscomb, 12:259–260.

except for the Republican sheets, either barely acknowledged his retirement or wrote scathingly of his tenure. But the expressions of approval from the middle states, the West, and especially the South reveal that the fundamental strength of his popular prestige was largely unshaken.[86]

Neustadt has observed that people tend to transfer the blame for their frustrations and physical hardships onto their political leaders. Public events and policies that increase popular frustration can weaken presidential prestige quickly (Hoover's depression, Lyndon Johnson's war). Often a president is not free to control events, so he must do his best with people's hopes. "If he can make them think the hardship necessary, and can make them want to bear it with good grace, his prestige may not suffer when they feel it."[87] This precisely describes Jefferson's situation at the time of the embargo.

But if his popularity with the general public suffered little apparent decline, what effect did the embargo, its failure, and Jefferson's intimate association with that failure have upon his professional reputation as a leader and upon the institution of the presidency? In considering the significance of the embargo period in a study of Jefferson's presidential leadership, we must first consider why the embargo failed, and second, what effect its failure was to have upon the capacity of future presidents to emulate his leadership.

The Reasons for Failure

The failure of the embargo can be traced to a fundamental flaw in the assumptions possessed by the proponents of economic coercion: that a policy of attrition would "starve a great and powerful nation into terms" before it exhausted the American people's patience and capacity for endurance. The failure, then, is attributable to an error in the policy itself, and only secondarily to the manner of its execution. Students of the embargo are agreed that it failed because of the injury it inflicted upon too many people during a time of "peace." Its success, as Levy has observed, "depended ultimately on the willingness of a free people to suffer acute economic privation for a great national

---

86. This conclusion is based upon a careful examination of press sentiment at the time of his retirement, using the newspaper collection of the Library of Congress and the Cornell University Library microfilm collection, as well as a perusal of his private correspondence during the period.

87. Neustadt, *Presidential Power*, p. 99.

goal."[88] Their ultimate unwillingness to do so, however, was manifested only after it had become plain that the embargo would not achieve its intended impact abroad. Thus a satisfactory explanation of the policy's collapse must stress the inextricable linkage between domestic economic privation and foreign diplomatic intransigence.

The success of economic coercion was absolutely dependent upon the vagaries of European politics. Any hope of success was tied to the willingness of either Power or both to agree to terms. Their refusal to do so was the most prominent and visible cause of the policy's collapse, and the factor that not incidentally was least susceptible to presidential action. Once again, we see the practical limitations on Jefferson's influence revealed by a bargaining model of presidential power. Once the embargo was begun and a commitment to its powers of attrition made, nothing remained to be done, aside from diplomatic proddings and pleadings, but to wait patiently for the pressure of trade cessation to work its magic.

Although Jefferson never surrendered his belief in the moral rightness of the embargo, nor indeed in its ultimate success had the American people been prepared to endure a bit longer, he was aware of the difficulties presented by the international situation.

At any other period, the even-handed justice we have observed towards all nations, the efforts we have made to merit their esteem by every act which candor or liberality could exercise, would have preserved our peace, and secured the unqualified confidence of all other nations in our faith and probity. But the hurricane which is now blasting the world, physical and moral, has prostrated all the mounds of reason as well as right. All those calculations which, at any other period, would have been deemed honorable, of the existence of a moral sense in man, individually or associated, of the connection which the laws of nature have established between his duties and his interests, of a regard for honest fame and the esteem of our fellow men, have been a matter of reproach to us, as evidences of imbecility. As if it could be a folly for an honest man to suppose that others could be honest also, when it is their interest to be so.[89]

Jefferson felt a great moral indignation that the defeat of his embargo represented the defeat as well of the rule of law and reason as an alternative to violence and war. He attributed in his bitterness only the basest of motives to the British government, which had thwarted his

88. *Portsmouth Oracle*, January 28, 1809; Levy, p. 93; see also Stuart G. Brown, *The American Presidency* (New York, 1966), pp. 206–208.

89. Jefferson to Caesar Rodney, February 10, 1810, Ford, 11:135.

hopes for mankind. Keenly jealous of slights inflicted upon the honor of his own country, he was unable to attribute to his age-old enemy any considerations of a similar nature, never understanding the imperatives that governed Britain's conduct in her war to the death with Napoleon. Whatever her motives, however, he knew only too well that the nature of her response would determine the success or failure of his entire enterprise.

If Jefferson's calculation concerning the behavior of foreign governments was wishful, his faith in the selfless morality of his own citizens was equally too trusting. He expected too much of human nature. Others had cautioned him of the difficulties to be expected in regulating the economic lives of the people while the slow attrition of the embargo worked its coercive effect. He underestimated the extent to which his own people would seek to evade what seemed to him so clearly the only policy worth pursuing. When evasions occurred, he directed his disillusionment upon his old enemies, the Federalists, attributing to them the sole responsibility for fomenting and directing the resistance to his policies. This tendency to attribute partisan origins and traitorous motives to the embargo's critics served to conceal from him the extent of hardship and the depths of discontent that it generated among the people. As these hardships increased and the belligerents showed no signs of yielding, others became convinced that the policy could bring few rewards to outweigh the lengthening list of damages it brought to the economic health of the nation and the political health of the Republican party.

Jefferson failed fully to appreciate in advance the impact of his foreign policy upon domestic tranquility. The conduct of foreign affairs was peculiarly the president's preserve. Feeling the welfare of the nation *qua* nation to be at stake, he too little appreciated the average citizen's difficulty in placing things in the same perspective. The irony of the embargo for Jefferson lies in the fact that while it was conceived as a device to coerce the European Powers into a just respect for American independence, it resulted in the coercion of his own people to a degree that threatened the very principles that independence was intended to secure.

If the overriding causes of the embargo's failure can be found in the American people's reluctance to endure economic hardship and political repression in the face of continued European intransigence, the methods by which the policy was executed contributed to the difficulties and must bear examination. Leonard Levy maintains that Jefferson could have succeeded in the embargo with "careful planning and democratic, but firm, presidential leadership, taking the people into confidence rather than taking them for granted."[90] Careful planning would indeed have been helpful in legislating the embargo and in administering and enforcing its provisions. Despite the need for secrecy noted above, more careful attention to possible contingencies would have helped in the drafting of workable legislation; advance planning could have eased the administrative burden by codifying regulation criteria and coordinating enforcement procedures. To say this, however, is in some ways to underestimate the difficulties of advance planning. The embargoing of the trade of an entire nation in peacetime had never before been attempted. No policy of such enormous dimensions had ever been undertaken by an American government in time of peace. There were no precedents to follow, no past experience upon which to draw in planning it. Many contingencies were unforeseen even by Gallatin, who can be credited with a substantial prescience in many aspects of the problem. Not even he predicted the systematic evasion that developed, nor did he anticipate the extent to which the enforcement agencies would have to be augmented and centralized. The enforcement machinery of the Treasury, though sizable for an executive department of the period, was strained to the utmost and occasionally broke down under the weight of its new and unanticipated responsibilities. Still, despite the troubles of evasion and the complication of the law, embargo enforcement agencies succeeded surprisingly well in accomplishing their task.

Under Levy's other criterion for success in the embargo, "democratic, but firm, presidential leadership," there was more room for improvement. This study of Jefferson's leadership has stressed the skillful use of many of the resources of power available to him and his development of new ones to enhance his power and extend his influence through the government. It is a curious but unavoidable fact that in the most controversial policy initiative of his administration, the embargo, he failed adequately to utilize some of these resources which he had successfully employed in earlier political initiatives. The man who charted the course for future presidents in dealing effectively with Congress lost control of that body in the final months of his term because he virtually abdicated any responsibility for creative policy-

90. Levy, p. 94.

making and guidance of the legislative branch, a responsibility that had formed a fundamental element of his approach to executive leadership. Even earlier, he had failed to take Congress into his confidence in his usual careful way. The embargo had been planned in the executive, with Congress brought in merely to pass the needed legislation, then allowed to adjourn and leave the execution of the laws to the executive alone. Jefferson's own legislative lieutenants smarted under the yoke of presidential indifference, as he failed to take them fully into his confidence or to seek their advice over the course of events. A president noted for his openness and willingness to consider the advice of others now closed himself off somewhat from useful exposure to differing opinions. This comparative isolation from congressional opinion ill-served the president when he most needed an accurate picture of public reaction to his policy. It led directly to the condition in the final months when Jefferson seemed, as never before, to be out of touch with congressional opinion and unable to contribute that guidance and leadership to which the party in Congress had become accustomed.

Levy is also critical of Jefferson for his failure to explain the embargo to the American people by public message and thus neutralize the opposition to it. Jefferson, of course, can be faulted for his failure to make a detailed defense of the embargo publicly and directly, as he can be faulted for failure to sympathize fully with the real hardships suffered by large numbers of people. It would perhaps have been better had he more fully exploited the possibilities of public appeals. Yet, as we saw in Chapter 7 above, such appeals were never Jefferson's way; he had never appealed to the people directly over the heads of their representatives, and neither his popularity nor the people's sensitivity to his aims and policies seems to have suffered for it. The available evidence tends to show, furthermore, that despite his public silence the people managed to get the idea about the embargo. An examination of the correspondence Jefferson received concerning the policy causes one to agree with Sears that Jefferson was probably justified in thinking from his mail that, while the embargo was producing hardships, by and large the people understood the reasons for its enactment and were willing to give it a try. This conclusion is reinforced by an examination of the content of contemporary newspapers, which took pains to explain the purposes of the measure and, in the case of partisan Republican papers, to cultivate support for it.

While he was silent publicly, it is important to recall that privately he was active in promoting his policy until the final months answering questions about it to correspondents and visitors, and using the press to sell it as he had other policies in the past. A letter to editor Smith of the *National Intelligencer* is revealing of his method: "I troubled you by the last post with an answer to the petitions against the embargo. I now enclose the copy of an answer to the counter-addresses which being not likely to be so numerous, I will pray you to print me 50-60 copies, and to send them by the post which will leave Washington on Monday, the 19th inst."[91] This not only reveals Jefferson's awareness of a sizable anti-embargo sentiment, but indicates his method of answering his critics by the mass distribution of his views to influential persons. So Jefferson was not completely idle in the vital task of molding public opinion behind his embargo.

As to the question of "democratic, but firm" leadership, the tragedy of Jefferson's experience with the embargo lies in his assumption of near dictatorial powers over a major aspect of the life of his countrymen. He was not blind to the threat this represented to the integrity of his political values. He and Gallatin were reluctant to assume many of the powers available to them. The pressure of events forced them to assert ever tighter control in order to assure adequate obedience to the law. The president worried a good deal about keeping enforcement decentralized and democratic. There came a time, however, when firmness took precedence, and he did not hesitate long in taking whatever action he felt was required to stem the rising tide of lawlessness.

There can be no doubt that under the pressure of administering the law, Jefferson's qualities of leadership were distorted and his principles suffered. His leadership came to lack that sense of mastery that others had grown to expect of him as President. It is possible that he could have achieved a short-term success of sorts had he taken pains to cultivate Congress in his usual manner and to mobilize public support more directly. Had he exercised leadership in the final months, for instance, he probably could have prevented an early repeal of the embargo; almost certainly he could have avoided signing the repeal of his own policy to take effect the day of his retirement. He could thus have prevented any major policy reversal from marring his last days in office. He would have succeeded, however, only in postponing the

91. Jefferson to Samuel Harrison Smith, September 13, 1808, LC No. 32065.

inevitable, perhaps at much greater cost to Madison, who would have inherited the policy and been forced to preside over its demise after more months of economic hardship and political decay. Despite certain lapses in Jefferson's methods of leadership, even including his virtual withdrawal in the final months, the embargo did not fail primarily because of any failure in execution. As Peterson notes, "to have contained the rising discontents in 1809 would have required more force and energy than the American government could command and more obedience than a free and enterprising people could give."[92] Government policy was made to yield, as Jefferson had always wanted, to the force of popular will, and as many lost heart and others turned on the administration with increasing fury, that will could no longer be depended upon to support the insupportable.

The Embargo and Presidential Leadership

We have still to consider the second of our questions concerning the significance of the embargo for presidential leadership: what effect did its failure have upon the institution of the presidency and upon the future exercise of presidential power?

We must begin with the frank admission that presidential leadership between Jefferson and Jackson was not a conspicuous success. Madison, Monroe, and the second Adams in no way exercised the influence over policy that Jefferson exercised and Jackson was to resume. The leadership of the government shifted during this twenty-year period to Congress. In order to explain why this occurred, why Congress took the initiative in leadership from the president after Jefferson left office, it is necessary to consider certain explanations which have been offered by students of the problem. Four interrelated reasons have been advanced to explain this shift in power. All possess some validity, and all are useful in gaining an understanding of the problem.

(1) The John Marshall charge, echoed by later scholars, that Jefferson weakened the office of president by too great a deference to Congress, specifically, that he "embodied himself in the House of Representatives."[93]

(2) The fundamental weakness of the presidential office in leading

92. *Thomas Jefferson*, p. 918.
93. See Wilfred Binkley, *President and Congress* (New York, 1962), and Clinton Rossiter, *The American Presidency* (New York, 1960), pp. 94–96.

Congress, particularly the weakness of the resources of bargaining and persuasion, in the Jeffersonian period.

(3) Institutional changes within Congress, such as the development of standing committees and the rise of the party caucus, which gave additional resources of power to the congressional leadership.

(4) The lack of political skills and leadership capacity among Jefferson's successors in the presidency.

To this list of explanations, all but the first of which possess significant validity, must be added a fifth:

(5) The political damage to the executive office, the Republican party, and to President Madison in particular caused by the collapse of the embargo and the removal of Jefferson's unifying leadership.

Of these five explanations, the first three refer to structural or institutional variables that contributed to the decline of presidential influence, while the last two are more directly concerned with personal, situational, environmental, and political variables. The latter category seems to offer a more satisfactory, though by no means exclusive, explanation.

The first explanation, that Jefferson somehow weakened the office of president by "embodying himself" in the House, can best be answered if one considers more fully the second explanation, the crucial weakness of the office and the bargaining resources available to its occupant in terms of leading Congress. As noted in Chapter 1, Marshall's famous warning misses one significant point: far from Jefferson's weakening any of the formal authority of the president, the office in terms of leading Congress was weak to begin with, and designedly so. The formal constitutional powers of the president would have proved inadequate at whatever point leadership of Congress became accepted as a legitimate presidential function, because a majority at the Constitutional Convention had designed the system in such a way as to stress the separation of the executive from the legislative power. Jefferson saw that for the government to function effectively the president would have to develop and employ extra-constitutional resources of power by which to influence Congress and would have to expend his political skills to the utmost to make them effective. As reflection upon the bargaining model recalls, it is the need for the exercise of statecraft over the legislative branch that makes presidential leadership such a personalized phenomenon, dependent upon the clever employment of personal skills and varying with the talents of the incumbent. Jefferson did not weaken the constitutional presidency; it was weak to begin with. Rather, by stressing the importance of extra-constitutional power resources as prerequisites for presidential leadership and by demonstrating their effectiveness in practice, he pioneered a successful method for strengthening the office as the motive force of government.[94]

Institutional changes within Congress, the growth of specialized committees, and the rise to prominence of the party caucus provided machinery that proved quite useful for the later assertion of congressional initiative. By giving to Congress alternative sources of information and expertise, the committee system served to enhance Congress's potential for influence. The rise of committees had begun in the late 1790's, however, and developed apace during the years of Jefferson's presidency. The congressional party caucus, though functioning during Jefferson's tenure, did not achieve real prominence until after 1810. If we are to assign importance to such internal institutional developments, we must still explain why Congress failed to employ its developing structures to assert its influence during Jefferson's administration. Constitutional and structural explanations for the decline of presidential influence after Jefferson would seem to leave too much unexplained; the answer may better be found through attention to the political and environmental factors at work in the years during which this shift of power occurred.

Leonard White has observed, "The Republican doctrine of legislative supremacy replaced the Federalist theory of executive leadership because after 1809, presidents were weak or frustrated by factional opposition beyond their control, not because presidents avowed as a guiding principle their subordination to Congress."[95] White may be guilty of discounting other factors, as he tacitly admits later by referring to the "heavy hand of past commitments to doctrine" that limited the field of action available to later presidents. His statement points, however, to a central truth; the importance of the shifting pattern of events, personalities, and political relationships, in understanding the great weakness of Madison's position as Jefferson's successor. The most significant of these factors are (1) the evident differences in leadership capacity between the two men, (2) related to those differences, the relative positions of authority over the Republican party

94. On this point, see Young, *Washington Community*, pp. 189–191, 206.
95. *Jeffersonians*, pp. 42–43.

enjoyed by the two, and (3) the damage to the credibility of executive leadership from the failure of a major policy bearing the stamp of executive design and responsibility, namely, the embargo.

Even without the burden of inheriting a discredited policy, Madison would have had difficulty in charting a successful course as president. Jefferson, in modern parlance, was a tough act to follow. Madison lacked the personal qualities of leadership that Jefferson so clearly possessed. He was small in stature and tended to melt into the background in a crowd. His shyness, unlike Jefferson's, was manifested less in a quiet amiability than in a frosty reserve. He did not possess his predecessor's talents for conciliation and persuasion. He had once been a successful legislator, but his years as secretary of state had removed him from frequent contact with most members of Congress, and he seems to have lost his taste for the informalities of legislative bargaining. He had not cultivated the tools of executive power that Jefferson had developed and used, nor did he relish their use in mastering Congress. In addition, he lacked the mystique that surrounded Jefferson as a popular leader. Timothy Pickering was not alone in his conviction that Madison would "never acquire [Jefferson's] ascendancy over the mind of the people." Madison differed from Jefferson as well in his expectations of government. He wanted less government and was less willing to be a spur to governmental action. Jefferson was more willing, in James MacGregor Burns's words, "to forsake his old preferences for checks and balances in order to do what must be done."[96]

Of equal significance with the purely personal differences between the two men were their differences in political standing within their party. Jefferson had been for well over eight years the undisputed leader of the party, and had exerted for at least seven of those eight years a unifying influence that had kept the divisive forces within the party coalition under control. Madison had never enjoyed a comparable stature within the party as a whole. Having labored for so many years, in effect, as Jefferson's second-in-command, Madison would have found it difficult under any circumstances to assert a new authority as sole party leader after Jefferson's retirement. But he had been at best a factional leader throughout the Jefferson years. He was associated with the moderate wing of the party, had alienated at one

96. Pickering to George Rose, March 13, 1808, in Henry Adams, *Documents*, p. 367; Burns, *Deadlock of Democracy*, p. 44.

time or another a number of party leaders (Clinton, Randolph, for a time even Monroe), and was anathema to many orthodox Republicans of the old school. He had a number of strong enemies and rivals, and while he could inherit the presidential office, he could not inherit undisputed control of the party.

These personal and political disadvantages which Madison possessed as he succeeded to the presidency were exacerbated by the wounds inflicted by the embargo debacle. Jefferson's successful experiment with party government ended abruptly in 1808–1809, and Madison never regained the initiative because of the collapse of the embargo and the exaggerated effect of that collapse upon the existing problems of transition. Jefferson in his single-minded effort to win success for his policy had exceeded the legitimate limits of presidential power in peacetime. It was not the expanded exercise of presidential authority per se, however, that damaged the prestige of the office, but rather the *failure* of the policy for which it was exercised. He had extended the limits of presidential power before, even in the case of Louisiana exceeding his narrow statutory authority (something he did *not* do in connection with the embargo), and had been rewarded with widespread praise when his innovations were crowned with success. In role terms, he had succeeded in altering the expectations of his environment in the direction of his own role interpretation. But the embargo was a failure, and in its failure it left, as one editor complained, "a nation divided, a commerce destroyed, a treasury emptied, and all the certain symptoms of political dissolution."[97]

Its effects upon the political institutions of government were equally momentous. The embargo failure struck at the political system in two ways: it damaged the credibility of executive leadership, and it weakened further the already strained unity of the Republican party. As a result it provided the motive force for the dispersal of effective political power within the general government. Loss of faith in Jefferson's embargo policy led quickly and naturally to a loss of faith in what had almost seemed the infallibility of the presidency. Executive prestige suffered a serious blow as awareness was revived of the damage that could be wrought by executive energy and initiative. Jefferson's failure in the final months to assert his leadership in finding an alternative to the discredited embargo contributed to the decline of executive

97. *Providence American*, March 3, 1809.

influence as the president-elect and his reputed choice for secretary of state, Gallatin, floundered about in the period before Jefferson relinquished the responsibilities of office. Party support, both in Congress and in the country (and there was a good deal of it until the very end) could not withstand the effects of a bankrupt, though noble, policy.

Madison inherited the bankruptcy. Any successor would have had a difficult time in salvaging the remnants of leadership in such circumstances. But Madison, who had supported the concept of embargo from the beginning and had labored long and hard in its service, was tainted with the discredited policy before he took office as chief executive. He seemed to have little else in terms of policy to offer, and his relative lack of personal political talents for the job meant that other, fresher voices would be added to the policy-making ensemble. Factional leaders in Congress, potential rivals to Madison for party leadership, began after a few months to assume an initiative that they were not to relinquish for twenty years, until another president, building upon the extra-constitutional and political foundations Jefferson had laid, resumed for a time the leadership that he had so skillfully exercised.

Jefferson may be said to have contributed to weakening presidential influence not by an unseemly deference to Congress, not even alone by the "illegitimate" use of massive executive authority, but by the unswerving commitment to a policy the failure of which was so momentous in its consequences as to discredit for a time the institution that had conceived and executed it. Jefferson himself escaped without any significant loss of popularity, but he lost his grip when his policies failed, and the collapse of those policies contributed to a decline of influence of the presidency and those persons most associated with it. The delicate balance of constitutional authority that Jefferson had labored to produce was thus upset for a time, and the potential for presidential leadership that he had illuminated through his skillful use of the resources of power was obscured for a generation under the weight of the embargo's collapse.

CHAPTER 9

Reflections on Jeffersonian Leadership

Throughout this book we have examined the presidential leadership of Thomas Jefferson by focusing essentially on three variables: political style, role, and environment or setting. The relationship between the individual and his setting is depicted specifically in terms of the use of power "resources." If, as Neustadt has asserted, "presidential power is the power to persuade," then the study of presidential leadership can be illumined by an examination of the resources of power—constitutional, statutory, extra-constitutional, personal—by which a president can achieve, maintain, and exercise his leadership. Since in practice "power" and "influence" become interchangeable terms to describe the same phenomenon,[1] the resources of power that are most significant are more often the informal, extra-constitutional "tools of persuasion," the effective use of which can enable a president to cultivate his influence over the rest of the government.

1. "Power" and "influence" are often separated in analytical discussions of the concept of power. See, for example, Robert Bierstedt, "An Analysis of Social Power," in L. A. Coser and B. Rosenberg, eds., *Sociological Theory: A Book of Readings* (New York, 1957), where the distinction is made between influence, which is persuasive, and power, which is coercive. This distinction tends to break down when one attempts to discuss the "power" of a political leader, and not merely an elected leader in a constitutional system. Central to Neustadt's interpretation of presidential power is the notion of the intricate and inextricable linkage between coercion and persuasion. The coercive element of sanctions underlies and makes more *persuasive* the influence a president can exert; yet, ironically, the application of coercive "power" by a president is often a confession of *failure* of his power, not an example of its effective use. Moreover, real "power" can be possessed by one who possesses few formal powers, simply by the force of one's "influence." The typical relationship between, for example, Woodrow Wilson and Colonel E. M. House points to the possession of genuine power by the personal adviser, even though his capacity to affect policy stems not from formal authority but solely from his influence with the president.

James McGregor Burns has written that the test of great political leadership consists of "first, whether the leader makes the most of existing materials he has to work with, and second, whether he creates new materials to help him meet his goals."[2] What Burns is writing about in this context are "resources," the mark of effective leadership being the skillful use of existing resources and the cultivation of new ones to meet conditions that existing resources seem unable to affect. This study has sought to apply these criteria of leadership to the Jeffersonian presidency.

An attempt to determine why some individuals acquire more influence than others must clearly begin with the point that some have more political resources at their disposal than do others. One significant pattern of resources available to a president, for example, is derived from his constitutional authority as chief executive, a formal source of power that places him at an initial advantage in influencing the behavior of others. Yet within the universe of available resources, some leaders use more of them than do others to gain influence, and some use them more skillfully. It is not, then, simply the number of resources available to an individual, but the number he employs and the skill with which he employs them that determine his actual, not potential, influence.[3] The degree to which available resources are used and new ones created and the skill with which they are used vary widely, of course, and it is at this point where individual personality, style, and role expectations become significant as explanatory variables.

The model of presidential power developed by Richard Neustadt has proved useful as a conceptual tool in the study of Jeffersonian presidential leadership because of its emphasis on power resources and the variability of their exercise. Neustadt's bargaining model causes one to focus attention upon power, the quest for it and the need for it. From the employment of this model one gains a better insight into the pervasive nature of power, its importance, indeed its necessity, even in the Jeffersonian age when the possession of power was seen as dangerous and its use suspect. One of the cardinal assumptions of the model is that a president to be effective must seek to maximize his power. It was conceivable that this maximization-of-power hypothesis,

2. *Roosevelt*, p. 401.

3. For discussion of this point, see Robert Dahl, "Power and Influence," chap. 5 in his *Modern Political Analysis* (Englewood Cliffs, N.J., 1963), pp. 47–49.

while appropriate to our own age, might break down when applied to a political community characterized by a deep suspicion of power in all its guises. A study of Jefferson's presidency, however, reveals that in his day even as in our own the possession and use of power, however suspect, was essential for the effective conduct of public affairs. The exercise of power might, as in Jefferson's case, be concealed under an elaborate antipower rhetoric or dressed in the camouflage of persuasion, conciliation, and reason. Nevertheless, as Jefferson knew, in a government characterized by the "almost unlimited resources of the enormous power of sitting still,"[4] it was incumbent upon the president to develop his political influence, to cultivate and enhance his power prospects in order to energize the motive force of government, in order to make the Madisonian system work.

Neustadt's power model was conceived in order to interpret the modern presidency with its heightened complexities and expanded responsibilities. This study, however, indicates that the model, with its emphasis on the cultivation of extra-constitutional tools of persuasion to insure leadership, is just as useful, and perhaps more so, for the task of understanding the requisites of leadership in Jefferson's day. In the "loose and fragile polity" of Jeffersonian America, the formal powers of a president were weak where they were most needed, in providing legitimate and sustained policy leadership for the national government. This condition placed an added premium upon the acquisition of influence through the skillful use of informal methods of persuasion. The more personal qualities of leadership were intensified by the imperatives of overcoming the rigid separation of powers by which the Framers had sought to encapsulate each branch of government within its own "legitimate" sphere of activity. The experience of several years under this system underscored for Jefferson the formalistic and often unrealistic nature of its division of labor. The instruments of government had somehow to be made to reflect the reality of the policy-making process with its mutuality of interest and coordination of effort.

One of the major resources of statecraft which Jefferson employed was the quality of his own political style and personality. His style, an amalgam of aristocratic predilections and democratic impulses, was congruent with the expectations of a political culture in transition

4. Neustadt, *Presidential Power*, p. 42.

from a pattern of deference to a pattern of participation. His ideals for proper conduct were characterized by good humor, politeness, deference, conciliation, and the avoidance of unnecessary contention. He sought above all, in his private as well as in his public life, the maintenance of harmony in his personal and political relationships. His qualities of temperament coincided with the requirements of political persuasion in dealing with his independent associates in Congress. Jefferson looked upon politics as he did his personal relations, in Henry James's phrase, as "the land of consideration." Political power *was* the power to persuade, to cultivate one's personal influence by ingratiating oneself with others.

Other factors contributing to his standing as a political leader were his record of public service and his symbolic embodiment of the dominant ideals of the American polity. His long and successful career served to enhance his professional reputation, while his symbolic identity contributed greatly to his high public prestige. He possessed a formidable hold over the public imagination. It is no small source of Jefferson's power that he helped mightily to shape the political and philosophical norms of his society. The norms that came to be accepted as "American" were "Jeffersonian" norms. It need hardly be added that such a source of power is uniquely personal and virtually impossible to transfer *in toto* to a successor, although the successor can profit by identifying himself with these norms.

Jefferson's conception of executive power, while generally consonant with accepted expectations, led to a redirection of presidential leadership in ways that set new role expectations for future holders of that office. In his rejection of Washington's conception of the "patriot king" and of Hamilton's notion of ministerial government, Jefferson sensed the added source of legitimate power available to a president who assumed a policy initiative grounded upon a base of popular support. He sought, within the limits of his political culture, to develop and employ informal resources of power that could contribute to the cultivation of his popular influence. He combined his considerable personal talents for bargaining and conciliation with a skillful use of the instrumental tools of persuasion which were his by virtue of his office and his own sense of responsibility in that office. Through the course of this book we have described a number of these resources— patronage and the power of appointment, the party as the bridge to Congress, the use of legislative lieutenants and executive liaison, the application of the president's own persuasive talents through legislative dinners, private negotiation, and the like, the party press—which were employed, in the absence of a more material reward structure, to create, maintain, and extend presidential leadership.

The political program that Jefferson came to embrace as president placed him in the moderate rather than the radical wing of his party. He was criticized not only by the Federalists to his right but by the Republican ideologues to his left, who feared that his efforts to conciliate the opposition and unify the people might jeopardize the opportunity for major political reform along "true" republican lines. In policy, however, Jefferson supported existing constitutional arrangements with small modifications; he favored popular institutions but not legislative supremacy; he proscribed Federalist leaders but not their followers; he opposed judicial hegemony and judicial review but supported an independent judiciary. Jefferson sensed the good fortune that came to him by virtue of his succession to the presidency. He was the leader who effected the first peaceful transfer of power in American history from one political persuasion to another, and he with others was not unmindful of the significance of that "most interesting scene a free people can witness."[5] His tendency to moderation was reinforced by his conviction that as the first president to assume office after the transfer of power he, like Washington before him, was destined to establish precedents that future generations would follow.

Jefferson's accession to the presidency represented as well the triumph of a popular movement that sought to effect a "progressive" return to first principles of popular government and political liberty, principles that all Republicans agreed had been distorted and all but discarded by the monarchist pretentions of the Federalists. As John Quincy Adams recognized: "The power of the [Jefferson] administration rests upon the support of a much stronger majority of the people throughout the Union than the former administrations ever possessed since the first establishment of the Constitution. Whatever the merits or demerits of the former administrations may have been, there never was a system of measures more completely and irrevocably abandoned and rejected by the popular vote."[6] Jefferson would have greeted these observations with deep satisfaction, for it was his principal ambition as president to eliminate the "monarchical" element forever from the

5. Smith, *First Forty Years*, p. 25.
6. J. Q. Adams, *Writings*, 3:9.

political life of the nation. He sought to replace the former system with a government more closely attuned to the deeper interests of the majority of the people, a national government of limited scope and responsive to the popular will.

Jefferson's great contributions to the presidency lay in his dramatization of the linkage that could and should exist between the chief executive and the people, and his pioneering efforts in the creation of resources to effect that linkage. Through his development of the extra-constitutional role of party leader he succeeded in indicating one means consistent with republican principles by which a president can exert the leadership of Congress which is essential in making the power-resistant Madisonian system function. In the conduct of practical affairs, Jefferson reinforced his theoretical assumptions with a political skill of a high order. His talents for gaining influence through the subtle arts of persuasion and bargaining contributed greatly to his sustained and effective policy leadership.

In those areas of the political environment where bargaining leverage was weak, as in his relations with the courts, or almost nonexistent, as in his attempts to influence foreign governments during the embargo, the president's capacity for effecting his will was lessened. These situations required a more direct confrontation of power with power; in some cases presidential power prevailed, in others no amount of executive power could materially affect the course of events. The process of cultivating influence is by definition tenuous and closely subject to changes in personalities and alterations of circumstance. Without an effective head in the Executive Mansion, however, one who possessed personal qualities of leadership as well as the political sensitivity to understand the power implications involved, the locus of power was subject to changes in the direction of those who *were* prepared to exercise leadership.

The experience of Jefferson's presidency reveals foreign affairs as the field most open to the exercise of presidential influence. Both the Louisiana Purchase, Jefferson's crowning success, and the embargo, his one significant failure, were policies conceived and executed by the executive agencies of government with only limited contributions from the legislative branch. On both occasions Jefferson as president asserted his executive prerogative with vigor and imagination. The success of Louisiana revealed the heights of achievement that could be attained through executive initiative when it was sustained by popular approbation. The failure of the embargo exhibited the futility of even the strongest initiative when confronted by popular rejection and frustrated by factors beyond the reach of executive power. Louisiana and the embargo are, furthermore, examples that underscore the importance to a president's power prospects of the decisions he makes along the way. Neustadt was surely correct in observing that the nature of these decisions contributes to a president's generalized influence and their general pattern over time will determine the likelihood of success or failure in the future. Each decision a president makes contributes to the raising or lowering of presidential credibility and the enhancement or damaging of a president's professional reputation.

In the case of Jefferson, over the years of his presidency a pattern of successful decisions reinforced his ability to exercise influence at a future time. In particular, the success of the Louisiana acquisition served to cement his reputation as a successful practitioner of diplomacy and thus to reinforce the likelihood that future policy proposals in that field would be received with favor. The president's success in obtaining legislative approval for his embargo policy reflected the impact of an unbroken record of past successes. His high professional reputation thus contributed to another series of "successes" as he gained approval for the embargo laws.

The ultimate collapse of the embargo and the hardships wrought in the course of its failure, by contrast, broke the string of successes and cracked the awesome edifice of credibility that had come to surround Jefferson's exercise of the presidential office. The result, while not immediately reflected in his popularity with the people, was inevitably to lessen his reputation with the governing elites and to reduce the willingness of those men to accept as readily decisions made by future presidents. Thus the failure of a major presidential policy served to drain away the president's store of accumulated influence and contributed to a decline in his power prospects for the future.

In the long view, however, the positive contributions of Jefferson's tenure to the development of the presidency far outweigh the damage to its leadership prospects inflicted by the embargo. With few of the material resources available to modern presidents, Jefferson's successful performance revealed what could be achieved by identifying the office with the popular aspirations of the people and by applying the personal skills of effective leadership in the quest to transform those aspirations into political reality. By most standards—the extent to which the president got his programs passed into law; how well he represented the prevailing majority interests; the extent to which he risked his prestige to accomplish his perceived tasks—Jefferson's presidency was a success. In matters of policy Jefferson and his administration achieved changes of a substantial nature while preserving and legitimating constitutional arrangements that they inherited from the first two presidents.

Few presidents of the period, it must be said in closing, had the initial advantages that Jefferson enjoyed as the symbol of the aspirations of the majority of his countrymen. As a biographer of Abraham Lincoln once wrote of Jefferson:

He imparted to the very recent historical origin of his country, and his followers imparted to its material conditions, a certain element of poetry, and the felt presence of a wholesome national idea. The patriotism of an older country derives its glory and its pride from influences deep rooted in the past, creating a tradition of public and private action which needs no definite formula. The man who did more than any other to supply this lack in a new country, by imbuing its national consciousness—even its national cant—with high aspiration, did—it may well be—more than any strong administrator or constructive statesman to create a Union which should hereafter seem worth preserving.[7]

Jefferson's influence *as* a constructive statesman was undergirded and extended by his perceived symbolic identity with the national consciousness. Through the skillful application of his personal persuasive talents, the pioneering cultivation of new presidential roles, and the employment of additional resources and techniques of influence, Jefferson helped greatly to make the presidency and indeed the entire machinery of government more reflective of that consciousness. This was the purpose for which he labored as president, and the stamp of his programs and philosophy upon the character of American political arrangements for the balance of the century may serve to mark the extent of its achievement.

7. Lord Charnwood, *Abraham Lincoln* (New York, 1917), pp. 34–35.

Bibliography

NEWSPAPERS

American Mercury (Hartford, Conn.)
Aurora (Philadelphia)
The Balance and New York State Journal (Albany)
Baltimore Whig
Bartgis's Republican Gazette (Frederickstown, Va.)
Charleston (S.C.) *Courier*
Columbian Museum (Savannah)
Columbian Sentinel (Boston)
Connecticut Courant (Hartford)
Connecticut Herald (New Haven)
Connecticut Mirror (Hartford)
Eastern Argus (Portland, Me.)
Farmer's Repository (Charlestown, Va.)
Federal Republican and Commercial Advertiser (Baltimore)
Georgia Gazette (Savannah)
Independent Chronicle (Boston)
Kentucky Gazette (Lexington)
Liberty Hall and Cincinnati Mercury
National Intelligencer (Washington, D.C.)
New England Palladium (Boston)
New Hampshire Gazette (Portsmouth)
New Jersey Journal (Elizabeth Town)
New Orleans Gazette
New York Argus
New York Evening Post
New York Republican Watchtower
New York Spectator
Newport (R.I.) *Mercury*
Norfolk Gazette and Publick Ledger
Norfolk Herald
Northampton (Mass.) *Republican Spy*
Port Folio (Philadelphia)
Portsmouth (N.H.) *Oracle*
Providence American
Providence Gazette
Public Advertiser (New York)

Raleigh (N.C.) *Register*
Richmond Enquirer
Salem (Mass.) *Gazette*
Scioto Gazette (Chillicothe, Ohio)
Tennessee Gazette (Nashville)
Trenton Federalist
United States Gazette (Philadelphia)
Universal Gazette (Georgetown, D.C.)
Vermont Journal
Virginia Argus (Richmond)
Virginia Herald (Fredericksburg)
Washington Federalist
Washington Monitor
Worcester (Mass.) *Gazette*

PRIMARY SOURCES

Adams, Henry, ed. *Documents Relating to New England Federalism.* Boston: Little, Brown, 1877.

Adams, John. *Diary and Autobiography.* Ed. Lyman K. Butterfield. Cambridge, Mass.: Belknap Press, 1961. 4 vols.

——. *The Political Writings of John Adams.* Ed. George A. Peek. Jr.. New York: Liberal Arts Press, 1954.

——. *The Works of John Adams.* Ed. Charles Francis Adams. Boston: Little, Brown, 1850–1856. 10 vols.

——, and Thomas Jefferson. *The Adams-Jefferson Letters.* Ed. Lester J. Cappon. New York: Clarion, 1959.

Adams, John Quincy. *Memoirs of John Quincy Adams.* Ed. Charles Francis Adams. Philadelphia: Lippincott, 1874. 12 vols.

——.*The Writings of John Quincy Adams.* Ed. Worthington C. Ford. New York: Macmillan, 1914. 14 vols.

Annals of Congress, 1801–1809.

Bayard, James A. "Papers of James A. Bayard." Ed. Elizabeth Donnan. *Annual Report* of the American Historical Association, 2 (1913).

Bernard, John. *Retrospectives of America, 1797–1811.* New York: Harper, 1887.

Boorstin, Daniel, ed. *An American Primer.* Chicago: University of Chicago Press, 1966. 2 vols.

Bradbury, John. *Travels in the Interior of America.* Cleveland: A. H. Clark, 1804.

Burwell, William A. "Private Memoir." Manuscript edition, Library of Congress.

Caldwell, John E. *A Tour through Part of Virginia in 1808.* Ed. William M. E. Rachal. Richmond: Dietz, 1951.

Coombs, B. J., ed. *Documents of the Trial of Aaron Burr.* Washington, D.C.: W. H. and O. H. Morrison, 1864.

Daveiss, Joseph Hamilton. "A View of the President's Conduct Concerning the Conspiracy of 1806." *Historical and Philosophical Society of Ohio Quarterly*, 12 (1917).

Dodge, Nehemiah. *Discourse in Honor of the Election of Thomas Jefferson*. Norwich, Conn.: Sterry & Porter, 1805.

Duane, William. "Letters of William Duane." Ed. Worthington C. Ford. Massachusetts Historical Society *Proceedings*, 20, 3d series (1906–7).

The Federalist Papers. Ed. Clinton Rossiter. New York: New American Library, 1961.

Few, Francis. *Diary of Francis Few*. Ed. Noble S. Cunningham. *Journal of Southern History*, 29 (1963).

Gallatin, Albert. *The Writings of Albert Gallatin*. Ed. Henry Adams. Philadelphia: Lippincott, 1879. 3 vols.

Gerry, Elbridge. *The Diary of Elbridge Gerry*. Ed. Claude G. Bowers. New York: Brentano, 1927.

Hamilton, Alexander. *The Papers of Alexander Hamilton*. Ed. Harold C. Syrett. New York: Columbia University Press, 1961–9. 15 vols.

———. *The Works of Alexander Hamilton*. Ed. Henry Cabot Lodge. New York: Scribner's, 1904. 12 vols.

Hamilton, Thomas. *Men and Manners in America*. Philadelphia, 1833.

Hay, George. *An Essay on the Liberty of the Press*. Richmond: Samuel Pleasants, Jr., 1803.

Jefferson, Thomas. *The Anas of Thomas Jefferson*. Ed. Franklin B. Sawvel. New York: Round Table, 1903.

———. *The Complete Jefferson*. Ed. Saul K. Padover. New York: Duell, Sloane, & Pearce, 1943.

———. *Letters of Thomas Jefferson*. Ed. Wilson Whitman. Eau Claire, Wis.: E. M. Hale, 1940.

———. *The Papers of Thomas Jefferson*. Ed. Julian Boyd. Princeton: Princeton University Press, 1950—.

———. *The Papers of Thomas Jefferson*. Microfilm edition, Library of Congress.

———. *The Writings of Thomas Jefferson*. Ed. Paul Leicester Ford. New York: Putnam, 1904–1905. 12 vols.

———. *The Writings of Thomas Jefferson*. Ed. Andrew A. Lipscomb & Albert E. Bergh. Washington, D.C.: Thomas Jefferson Memorial Association, 1903. 20 vols.

Kendall, Edward A. *Travels through the Northern Parts of the United States in 1807–8*. New York: Riley, 1809. 3 vols.

King, Rufus. *Life and Correspondence of Rufus King*. Ed. Charles R. King. New York: Putnam, 1896–1897. 6 vols.

Locke, John. *The Second Treatise on Government*. New York: Mentor, 1965.

Madison, Dolley. *Memoirs and Letters*. Ed. Lucia B. Cutts. Boston: Houghton Mifflin, 1886.

Madison, James. *The Writings of James Madison*. Ed. Gaillard Hunt. New York: Putnam, 1900–1910. 9 vols.

McPherson, Elizabeth Gregory, ed. "Unpublished Letters from North Carolinians to Jefferson." *North Carolina Historical Review*, 12 (1935).

Melish, John. *Travels in the United States of America, 1806–7*. Philadelphia: J. Melish, 1812. 2 vols.

Mitchell, Samuel L. "Letters from Washington: 1801–1813." *Harper's Magazine*, 58 (1879).

Monroe, James. *The Writings of James Monroe*. Ed. S. M. Hamilton. New York: Putnam, 1898–1903. 7 vols.

Morris, Gouverneur. *Diary of Gouverneur Morris*. Ed. Anne Cary Morris London: K. Paul, Trench, 1889. 2 vols.

Nicholas, Wilson Cary. *The Papers of Wilson Cary Nicholas*. Microfilm edition, Library of Congress.

Nicholson, Joseph H. *The Papers of Joseph H. Nicholson*. Microfilm edition, Library of Congress.

Plumer, William. *Memorandum of Proceedings in the United States Senate, 1803–7*. Ed. E. S. Brown. New York: Macmillan, 1923.

Reed, V. B., and J. D. Williams, eds. *The Case of Aaron Burr*. Boston: Houghton Mifflin, 1960.

Richardson, James Daniel, ed. *The Messages and Papers of the Presidents*. New York: Bureau of National Literature, 1917. 20 vols.

Rush, Benjamin. *Letters of Dr. Benjamin Rush*. Ed. Lyman K. Butterfield. Princeton, N.J.: Princeton University Press, 1951. 2 vols.

Smith, Margaret Bayard. *The First Forty Years of Washington Society*. New York: Scribner's, 1906.

Smith, Robert. "Some Papers of Robert Smith." Ed. Bernard C. Steiner. *Maryland Historical Magazine*, 15 (1925).

Smith, Samuel. *The Papers of Samuel Smith*. Microfilm edition, Library of Congress.

(Smith, William Loughton). *The Pretensions of Thomas Jefferson to the Presidency Examined*. Philadelphia: 1796.

Steele, John. *The Papers of John Steele*. Ed. H. M. Wigstaff. Raleigh: North Carolina Historical Society, 1924. 2 vols.

Story, Joseph. *Life and Letters of Joseph Story*. Ed. William W. Story. Boston: Little, Brown, 1851.

Taggart, Samuel. "Letters, 1803–1814." Ed. George Haynes. American Antiquarian Society *Proceedings*, new series, 33 (1923).

Taylor, John. *Letters, 1793–1823*. Ashland, Va.: John P. Branch Historical Papers of Randolph-Macon College, 1908. 2 vols.

Wilkinson, James. *Memoirs of My Own Times*. Philadelphia: 1816. 3 vols.

Young, Allen, defendants, printer. *Defense against the Libel of Thomas Jefferson*. Boston: A. Young, 1805.

SECONDARY SOURCES

Abernethy, Thomas P. *The Burr Conspiracy*. New York: Oxford University Press, 1954.

——. *From Frontier to Plantation in Tennessee*. Chapel Hill, N.C.: University of North Carolina Press, 1932.

——. *The South in the New Nation*. Baton Rouge: Louisiana State University Press, 1961.

Adams, Henry. *The History of the United States during the Administration of Thomas Jefferson*. New York: Albert & Charles Boni, 1930. 2 vols.

——. *The Life of Albert Gallatin*. Philadelphia: Lippincott, 1879.

Agar, Herbert. *The Price of Union*. Boston: Little, Brown, 1950.

Ambler, Charles H. *Thomas Ritchie: A Study in Virginia Politics*. Richmond: Bell, 1913.

Ammon, Harry. *James Monroe: The Quest For National Identity*. New York: McGraw-Hill, 1971.

——. "The Jeffersonian Republicans in Virginia: An Interpretation." *Virginia Magazine of History and Biography*, 71 (1963).

——. "The Richmond Junto: 1800–1828." *Virginia Magazine of History and Biography*, 61 (1953).

Anderson, Dice R. *William Branch Giles*. Menasha, Wis.: George Banta, 1914.

Aronson, Sidney H. *Status and Kinship in the Higher Civil Service*. Cambridge: Harvard University Press, 1964.

Bachrach, Peter. *A Critique of Democratic Elitism*. Boston: Little, Brown, 1967.

Bailyn, Bernard. *The Ideological Origins of the American Revolution*. Cambridge: Harvard University Press, 1967.

Balinky, Alexander. *Albert Gallatin: Fiscal Theories and Policies*. New Brunswick, N.J.: Rutgers University Press, 1958.

Banner, James M., Jr., *To the Hartford Convention: The Federalists and the Origins of Party Politics in Massachusetts, 1789–1815*. New York: Knopf, 1970.

Barber, James David. "Classifying and Predicting Presidential Styles: Two 'Weak' Presidents." *The Presidency*. Ed. Aaron Wildavsky. Boston: Little, Brown, 1969.

——. *The Lawmakers*. New Haven: Yale University Press, 1965.

——. *Presidential Character*. Englewood Cliffs, N.J.: Prentice-Hall, 1972.

Barnhart, John D. *Valley of Democracy: Frontier vs. Plantation in the Ohio Valley, 1775–1818*. Bloomington, Ind.: Indiana University Press, 1953.

Beveridge, Albert. *The Life of John Marshall*. Boston: Houghton Mifflin, 1919. 4 vols.

Bierstedt, Robert. "An Analysis of Social Power." *Sociological Theory: A Book of Readings*. Ed. Lewis A. Coser and B. Rosenberg. New York: Macmillan, 1957.

Binkley, Wilfred. *American Political Parties: Their Natural History*. New York: Knopf, 1962.

——. *President and Congress*. New York: Harper, 1962.

Boulton, James T. *The Language of Politics in the Age of Wilkes and Burke*. London: Routledge & K. Paul, 1963.

Bowers, Claude G. *Jefferson in Power*. Boston: Houghton Mifflin, 1936.

Boyd, Julian P. "The Chasm that Separated Thomas Jefferson and John Marshall." *Essays on American Constitutionalism*. Ed. Gottfried Dietze. Englewood Cliffs, N.J.: Prentice-Hall, 1964.

Brant, Irving. *Madison: Secretary of State, 1801–1809*. Indianapolis: Bobbs-Merrill, 1953.

Brown, Everett J. *Constitutional History of the Louisiana Purchase, 1803–1812*. Berkeley: University of California Press, 1930.

Brown, Glenn. *History of the U. S. Capital*. Washington, D.C.: U. S. Government Printing Office, 1900. 2 vols.

Brown, Stuart G. *The American Presidency*. New York: Macmillan, 1966.

Bruce, William C. *John Randolph of Roanoke*. New York: Putnam, 1922. 2 vols.

Burns, James MacGregor. *The Deadlock of Democracy*. Englewood Cliffs, N.J.: Prentice-Hall, 1963.

——. *Presidential Government*. Boston: Houghton Mifflin, 1966.

——. *Roosevelt: The Lion and the Fox*. New York: Harcourt, Brace, and World, 1956.

Caldwell, Lynton K. *The Administrative Theories of Hamilton and Jefferson*. Chicago: University of Chicago Press, 1944.

Carpenter, William S. "The Repeal of the Judiciary Act of 1801." *American Political Science Review*, 9 (1915).

Chambers, William Nisbet. *Political Parties in the New Nation*. New York: Oxford University Press, 1963.

Champlin, John R.. "On the Study of Power." *Politics and Society*, 1 (1970).

Channing, Edward. *The Jeffersonian System*. New York: Harper, 1906.

Chapman, William P. "Jefferson in his Relations to the Constitution prior to 1801." Unpublished Ph.D. dissertation, Cornell University (1895).

Charnwood, Lord. *Abraham Lincoln*. New York: Henry Holt, 1917.

Clark, Allan C.. "William Duane." *Records* of the Columbia Historical Society, 9 (1906).

Coit, Margaret. *John C. Calhoun: An American Portrait*. Boston: Houghton Mifflin, 1950.

Coleman, Peter J. *The Transformation of Rhode Island*. Providence: Brown University Press, 1963.

Cooper, Joseph. "Jeffersonian Attitudes toward Executive Leadership and Committee Development in the House of Representatives, 1789–1829." *Western Political Quarterly*, 18 (1965).

Cornwell, Elmer E., Jr. *Presidential Leadership of Public Opinion*. Bloomington, Ind.: Indiana University Press, 1965.

Corwin, Edward S. *John Marshall and the Constitution*. New Haven: Yale University Press, 1919.

Crick, Bernard. *The American Science of Politics*. Berkeley: University of California Press, 1967.

Cunningham, Noble S. *The Jeffersonian Republicans: The Formation of Party Organization, 1789–1801*. Chapel Hill: University of North Carolina Press, 1957.

——. *The Jeffersonian Republicans in Power: Party Operations, 1801–1809*. Chapel Hill: University of North Carolina Press, 1963.

——. "John Beckley: An Early American Party Manager." *William and Mary Quarterly*. 13, 3d series (1956).

Dahl, Robert. *Modern Political Analysis*. Englewood Cliffs, N.J.: Prentice-Hall, 1963.

Dauer, Manning J. *The Adams Federalists.* Baltimore: Johns Hopkins University Press, 1953.

Dodd, William E. *The Life of Nathaniel Macon.* Raleigh, N.C., Edwards & Broughton, 1903.

Edelman, Murray. *The Symbolic Uses of Politics.* Urbana, Ill.: University of Illinois Press, 1964.

Edinger, Lewis J. *Kurt Schumacher: A Study in Personality and Political Behavior.* Stanford: Stanford University Press, 1965.

———. "Political Science and Political Biography: Reflections on the Study of Leadership." *Journal of Politics,* 26 (1964).

Ellis, Richard E. *The Jeffersonian Crisis: Courts and Politics in the Young Republic.* New York: Oxford University Press, 1971.

Eriksson, Erik M. "The Federal Civil Service under President Jackson." *Mississippi Valley Historical Review,* 13 (1927).

Eulau, Heinz. *The Behavioral Persuasion in Politics.* New York: Dutton, 1963.

Faulkner, Robert K. "John Marshall and the Burr Trial." *Journal of American History,* 53 (1966).

Fischer, David H. *The Revolution of American Conservatism: The Federalist Party in the Era of Jeffersonian Democracy.* New York: Harper & Row, 1965.

Fish, Carl Russell. *The Civil Service and the Patronage.* New York: Longmans, Green, 1905.

Flexner, James Thomas. *George Washington and the New Nation.* Boston: Little, Brown, 1970.

Ford, Worthington C. "Jefferson and the Newspaper." *Records* of the Columbia Historical Society, 8 (1905).

Formisano, Ronald P. "Deferential-Participant Politics: The Early Republic's Political Culture, 1789–1840." *American Political Science Review,* 68 (June, 1974).

Fox, Dixon Ryan. "The Decline of Aristocracy in the Politics of New York." Columbia University *Studies* in History, Economics, and Public Law, 86.

French, John R. P., and Bertram Raven. "The Bases of Social Power." *Group Dynamics.* ed. Dorwin Cartwright and Alvin Zander. Evanston, Ill.: Row, Peterson, 1960.

Gaines, Edwin M. "Governor Cabell and the Republican Schism in Virginia, 1805–8." *Essays in History,* 2 (1955).

Gaines, William H. *Thomas Mann Randolph.* Baton Rouge: Louisiana State University Press, 1966.

Galpin, W. Freeman. "The American Grain Trade under the Embargo of 1808." *Journal of Economic and Business History,* 2 (1929–1930).

George, Alexander L., and Juliette L. George. *Woodrow Wilson and Colonel House: A Personality Study.* New York, John Day, 1956.

Gilpatrick, Delbert H. *Jeffersonian Democracy in North Carolina: 1789–1816* New York: Columbia University Press, 1931.

Goodman, Paul. *Democratic Republicans in Massachusetts.* Cambridge: Harvard University Press, 1964.

Green, Constance. *Washington: Village and Capital, 1800–1828*. Princeton, N.J.: Princeton University Press, 1962.

Gross, Neal R., Ward S. Mason, and Alexander W. McEachern. *Explorations in Role Analysis*. New York: Wiley, 1958.

Haines, Charles G. *The Role of the Supreme Court in American Government and Politics, 1789–1835*. Berkeley: University of California Press, 1944.

Hammond, Bray. *Banks and Politics in America*. Princeton, N.J.: Princeton University Press, 1951.

Hammond, Jabez D. *The History of Political Parties in the State of New York*. Albany: C. Van Benthuysen, 1842.

Hargrove, Erwin C. *Presidential Leadership*. New York: Macmillan, 1966.

Harlow, Ralph V. *A History of Legislative Methods before 1825*. New Haven: Yale University Press, 1917.

Higginbotham, Sanford W. *The Keystone of the Democratic Arch: Pennsylvania Politics, 1800–1816*. Philadelphia: Pennsylvania Historical and Museum Commission, 1952.

Hoffmann, Stanley, and Inge Hoffmann. "De Gaulle as Political Artist." *Daedalus*, 97 (1968).

Hofstadter, Richard. *The American Political Tradition*. New York: Vintage Books, 1954.

———. *The Idea of a Party System*. Berkeley: University of California Press, 1969.

Hunt, Gaillard. "Office-seeking during Jefferson's Administration." *American Historical Review*. 3 (1898).

Hutcheson, Harold. *Tench Coxe*. Baltimore: Johns Hopkins University Press, 1938.

Irwin, Ray W. *Diplomatic Relations of the United States with the Barbary Powers, 1776–1816*. Chapel Hill: University of North Carolina Press, 1931.

Jacob, Charles E. "The Limits of Presidential Leadership." *South Atlantic Quarterly*, 62 (1963).

Jaffa, Harry. *The Crisis of the House Divided*. New York: Doubleday, 1959.

James, Marquis. *Andrew Jackson: Portrait of a President*. New York: Bobbs-Merrill, 1937.

Janda, Kenneth F. "Toward the Explication of the Concept of Leadership in Terms of the Concept of Power." *Human Relations*, 13 (1960).

Jennings, Walter W. *The American Embargo: 1807–1809*. Iowa City: University of Iowa Press, 1921.

Johnson, Allen. *Jefferson and his Colleagues, 1801–1809*. New Haven: Yale University Press, 1921.

Kaplan, Lawrence S. *Jefferson and France: An Essay*. New Haven: Yale University Press, 1961.

Kennedy, John P. *Memoirs of the Life of William Wirt*. Philadelphia: Lea and Blanchard, 1849.

Kessel, John H., George F. Cole, and Robert G. Seddig, eds. *Micropolitics*. New York: Holt, Rinehart and Winston, 1970.

Koch, Adrienne. *Jefferson and Madison: The Great Collaboration.* New York: Oxford University Press, 1964.

Krislov, Samuel. "Jefferson and Judicial Review: Refereeing Cahn, Commager, and Mendelson." *Journal of Public Law,* 9 (1960).

Lacy, Alexander B. "Jefferson and Congress." Unpublished Ph.D. dissertation, University of Virginia (1964).

Lasswell, Harold D. *Power and Personality.* New York: Norton, 1948.

——. *Psychopathology and Politics.* Chicago: University of Chicago Press, 1930.

Lerche, Charles O. "Jefferson and the Election of 1800: A Case Study in the Political Smear." *William and Mary Quarterly,* 5, new series (1948).

Levy, Leonard. *Jefferson and Civil Liberties: The Darker Side.* Cambridge: Harvard University Press, 1963.

Lindzey, Gardner, ed. *Handbook of Social Psychology.* Cambridge, Mass.: Addison Wesley, 1952.

Lipset, Seymour Martin. *The First New Nation.* New York: Doubleday, 1967.

Lodge, Henry Cabot. *Studies in History.* Boston: Houghton Mifflin, 1892.

Longaker, Richard P. *The President and Civil Liberties.* Ithaca, N.Y.: Cornell University Press, 1961.

McBain, Howard L. *De Witt Clinton and the Origins of the Spoils System in New York.* New York: Columbia University Press, 1907.

McCaleb, Walter F. *The Aaron Burr Conspiracy.* New York: Wilson-Erickson, reprint, 1936.

McCormick, Richard P. *The Second American Party System.* Chapel Hill: University of North Carolina Press, 1966.

McFarland, Andrew S. "Role and Role Conflict." *The Presidency.* Ed. Aaron Wildavsky. Boston: Little, Brown, 1969.

McLaughlin, A. C. "The Life of John Marshall." *American Bar Association Journal,* 7 (1921).

Macleod, Julia H. "Jefferson and the Navy: A Defense." *Huntington Library Quarterly,* 8 (1945).

Macmillan, Margaret B. *The War Governors in the American Revolution.* New York: Columbia University Press, 1943.

Magrath, C. Peter. *Yazoo: Law and Politics in the New Republic.* Providence: Brown University Press, 1966.

Malone, Dumas. *Jefferson the President: First Term, 1801–1805.* Boston: Little, Brown, 1970.

——. *Jefferson the President: Second Term, 1805–1809.* Boston: Little, Brown, 1973.

——. "Presidential Leadership and National Unity: The Jeffersonian Example." *Journal of Southern History,* 35 (1969).

——. *Thomas Jefferson and the Ordeal of Liberty.* Boston: Little, Brown, 1962.

——. *Thomas Jefferson as Political Leader.* Berkeley: University of California Press, 1965.

Marsh, Philip M. "John Beckley: Mystery Man of the Early Jeffersonians." *Pennsylvania Magazine of History and Biography,* 72 (1948).

Mays, David John. *Edmund Pendleton.* Cambridge: Harvard University Press, 1952.

Merriam, Charles H., and Frank P. Bourgin. "Jefferson as a Planner of National Resources." *Ethics*, 53 (July, 1943).

Merton, Robert K. "The Role-Set: Problems in Sociological Theory." *British Journal of Sociology*, 8 (1957).

Miller, John C. *Alexander Hamilton and the Growth of the New Nation.* New York: Harper, 1959.

Mitchell, Broadus. *Alexander Hamilton.* New York: Macmillan, 1957–1962. 2 vols.

Mott, Frank Luther. *American Journalism.* New York: Macmillan, 1941.

———. *Jefferson and the Press.* Baton Rouge: Louisiana State University Press, 1943.

Mumford, Lewis. *The Pentagon of Power: The Myth of the Machine.* New York: Harcourt, Brace, Jovanovich, 1970.

Munroe, John A. *Federalist Delaware, 1775–1815.* New Brunswick, N.J.: Rutgers University Press, 1954.

Neustadt, Richard E. *Presidential Power.* New York: New American Library, 1964.

Niebuhr, Reinhold. "The Social Myths of the Cold War." *Faith and Politics.* New York: Braziller, 1968.

Ostrogorski, M. I. *Democracy and the Organization of Political Parties.* New York: Macmillan, 1902.

———. "The Rise and Fall of the Nominating Caucus, Legislative and Congressional." *American Historical Review*, 5 (December, 1899).

Paige, Glenn D., ed. *Political Leadership: Readings For an Emerging Field.* New York: Free Press, 1972.

Perkins, Bradford. *The First Rapprochement: England and the United States, 1795–1805.* Philadelphia: University of Pennsylvania Press, 1955.

———. *Prologue to War: England and the United States, 1805–1812.* Berkeley: University of California Press, 1961.

Peterson, Merrill D. *The Jeffersonian Image in the American Mind.* New York: Oxford University Press, 1960.

———. *Thomas Jefferson and the New Nation.* New York: Oxford University Press, 1970.

Pfeffer, Leo. *This Honorable Court.* Boston: Beacon, 1965.

Prince, Carl. *New Jersey's Jeffersonian Republicans.* Chapel Hill: University of North Carolina Press, 1967.

Purcell, Richard J. *Connecticut in Transition, 1775–1818.* Middletown, Conn.: Wesleyan University Press, 1918, reissued 1963.

Risjord, Norman K. *The Old Republicans: Southern Conservatives in the Age of Jefferson.* New York: Columbia University Press, 1965.

Robinson, William A. *Jeffersonian Democracy in New England.* New Haven: Yale University Press, 1916.

Ross, E. A. *Social Control.* New York: Harpers, 1916.

Rossiter, Clinton. *Alexander Hamilton and the Constitution*. New York: Harcourt, Brace, 1964.

——. *The American Presidency*. New York: Harcourt, Brace, 1960.

Rustow, Dankwart A. Introduction to "Philosophers and Kings: Studies in Leadership." *Daedalus*, 97 (1968).

Ryan, Mary P. "Party Formation in the U.S. Congress, 1789–1796: A Quantitative Analysis." *William and Mary Quarterly*, 28 (October, 1971).

Scanlon, James E. "A Sudden Conceit: Jefferson and the Louisiana Government Bill of 1804." *Louisiana History*, 9 (1968).

Schachner, Nathan. *Aaron Burr*. New York: F. A. Stokes, 1937.

Scharf, J. Thomas, and Thompson Westcott. *History of Philadelphia, 1609–1884*. Philadelphia: L. H. Everts, 1884. 3 vols.

Schlesinger, Arthur M., Jr. *The Imperial Presidency*. Boston: Houghton Mifflin, 1973.

Searing, Donald D. "Models and Images of Man and Society in Leadership Theory." *Political Leadership*. Ed. Glenn D. Paige. New York: Free Press, 1972.

Sears, Louis. *Jefferson and the Embargo*. Durham, N.C.: Duke University Press, 1927.

Seligman, Lester G. "The Study of Political Leadership." *American Political Science Review*, 44 (December, 1950).

Sherif, Muzafer, ed. *Intergroup Relations and Leadership*. New York: Wiley, 1962.

Skinner, B. F. *Beyond Freedom and Dignity* New York: Knopf, 1971.

Small, Norman J. *Some Presidential Interpretations of the Presidency*. Baltimore: Johns Hopkins University Press, 1932.

Smelser, Marshall. *The Democratic Republic: 1801–1816*. New York: Harper, 1968.

Smith, T. V. "Thomas Jefferson and the Perfectability of Mankind." *Ethics*, 53 (July, 1943).

Spaulding, Ernest Wilder. *His Excellency George Clinton*. New York: Macmillan, 1938.

Sperlich, Peter W. "Bargaining and Overload: An Essay on Presidential Power." *The Presidency*. Ed. Aaron Wildavsky. Boston: Little, Brown, 1969.

Sprout, Harold H., and Margaret Sprout. *The Rise of American Naval Power, 1776–1918*. Princeton: Princeton University Press, 1939.

Stogdill, Ralph M. "Personal Factors Associated with Leadership: A Survey of the Literature." *Journal of Psychology*, 25 (1948).

Sydnor, Charles. *Gentlemen Freeholders: Political Parties in Washington's Virginia*. Chapel Hill: University of North Carolina Press, 1952.

——. "The One-Party Period of American History." *American Historical Review*, 51 (April, 1946).

Thomas, Isaiah. *The History of Printing in America*. Worcester, Mass.: Isaiah Thomas, 1810, 2 vols.

Tinkcom, Harry M. *Republicans and Federalists in Pennsylvania, 1790–1801.* Harrisburg: Historical and Museum Commission of Pennsylvania, 1950.

Toby, Jackson W. "Some Variables in Role Conflict Analysis." *Social Forces*, 30 (1952).

Tocqueville, Alexis de. *Democracy in America.* Ed. Richard D. Heffner. New York: Mentor, 1966.

Tucker, Robert C. "The Theory of Charismatic Leadership." *Daedalus*, 97 (1968).

Turner, Lynn W. "The Impeachment of John Pickering." *American Historical Review*, 54 (1949).

———. *William Plumer.* Chapel Hill: University of North Carolina Press, 1962.

Van Der Linden, Frank. *The Turning Point: Jefferson's Battle for the Presidency.* Washington, D.C.: R. B. Luce, 1962.

Vile, M. J. C. *Constitutionalism and the Separation of Powers.* New York: Oxford University Press, 1967.

Wallace, Michael. "Changing Concepts of Party in the U.S.: New York, 1815–1828." *American Historical Review*, 74 (December, 1968).

Walters, Raymond. *Alexander James Dallas.* Philadelphia: University of Pennsylvania Press, 1943.

Warren, Charles. *The Supreme Court in United States History.* Boston: Little, Brown, 1923. 3 vols.

Weber, Max. *The Theory of Social and Economic Organization.* New York: Oxford University Press, 1947.

White, Leonard D. *The Federalists.* New York: Free Press, 1948.

———. *The Jeffersonians.* New York: Free Press, 1951.

Wills, Garry. *Nixon Agonistes.* Boston: Houghton Mifflin, 1970.

Wilson, Woodrow. *History of the American People.* New York: Harper, 1902.

Wiltse, Charles M. *The Jeffersonian Tradition in American Democracy.* New York: Hill and Wang, 1935.

Wolford, Thorp L. "Democratic Republican Reaction in Massachusetts to the Embargo of 1807." *New England Quarterly*, 15 (1942).

Young, Alfred F. *The Democratic Republicans of New York: The Origins, 1763–1797.* Chapel Hill: University of North Carolina Press, 1967.

Young, James Sterling. *The Washington Community: 1800–1825.* New York: Columbia University Press, 1966.

Index

(Thomas Jefferson is referred to as TJ throughout.)

Library of Congress Cataloging in Publication Data
(For library cataloging purposes only)

Johnstone, Robert M   1939–
    Jefferson and the Presidency.

    Bibliography: p.
    Includes index.
    1. United States—Politics and government—1801–1809. 2. Executive power—
United States—History. 3. Jefferson, Thomas, Pres. U. S., 1743–1826. 4. Presi-
dents—United States—Biography. I. Title.
E331.J69   353.03'13'0924   77–17460
ISBN 0–8014–1150–5